SHAKESPEARE, NATIONAL POET-PLAYWRIGHT

Shakespeare, National Poet-Playwright is an important new book which reassesses Shakespeare as a poet and dramatist. Patrick Cheney contests critical preoccupation with Shakespeare as 'a man of the theatre' by recovering his original standing as an early modern author: he is a working dramatist who composes some of the most extraordinary poems in English. The book accounts for this form of authorship by reconstructing the historical preconditions for its emergence, in England as in Europe, including the building of the commercial theatres and the consolidation of the printing press. Cheney traces the literary origin to Shakespeare's favourite author, Ovid, who wrote the *Amores* and *Metamorphoses* alongside the tragedy *Medea*. Cheney also examines Shakespeare's literary relations with his contemporary authors Edmund Spenser and Christopher Marlowe. The book concentrates on Shakespeare's freestanding poems, but makes frequent reference to the plays, and ranges widely through the work of other Renaissance writers.

PATRICK CHENEY is Professor of English and Comparative Literature at Pennsylvania State University. He is the author of *Marlowe's Counterfeit Profession: Ovid, Spenser, Counter-Nationhood* (1997) and *Spenser's Famous Flight: A Renaissance Idea of a Literary Career* (1993) and editor of *The Cambridge Companion to Marlowe* (2004) and *The Cambridge Companion to Shakespeare's Poetry* (forthcoming).

SHAKESPEARE, NATIONAL POET-PLAYWRIGHT

PATRICK CHENEY

Pennsylvania State University

PUBLISHED BY THE PRESS SYNDICATE OF THE UNIVERSITY OF CAMBRIDGE
The Pitt Building, Trumpington Street, Cambridge, United Kingdom

CAMBRIDGE UNIVERSITY PRESS
The Edinburgh Building, Cambridge, CB2 2RU, UK
40 West 20th Street, New York, NY 10011–4211, USA
477 Williamstown Road, Port Melbourne, VIC 3207, Australia
Ruiz de Alarcón 13, 28014 Madrid, Spain
Dock House, The Waterfront, Cape Town 8001, South Africa

http://www.cambridge.org

© Patrick Cheney 2004

First published 2004

Printed in the United Kingdom at the University Press, Cambridge

Typeface Adobe Garamond 11/12.5 pt.   *System* LaTeX 2ε   [TB]

A catalogue record for this book is available from the British Library

Library of Congress cataloguing in publication data
Cheney Patrick Gerard, 1949–
Shakespeare, national poet-playwright / Patrick Cheney.
p.   cm.
Includes bibliographical references and index.
ISBN 0 521 83923 8 (hardback)
1. Shakespeare, William, 1564–1616 – Poetic works.   2. Shakespeare, William, 1564–1616 – Criticism
and interpretation.   3. Shakespeare, William, 1564–1616 – Knowledge – Literature.   4. Shakespeare,
William, 1564–1616 – Contemporaries.   5. Ovid, 43 B.C. – 17 or 18 A.D. – Influence.
6. Authorship – History – 16th century.   7. English poetry – Roman influences.
8. Renaissance – England.   I. Title.
PR2984.C48   2004
821′.3 – dc22   2004045176

ISBN 0 521 83923 8 hardback

For Evan and Kelton

Contents

Illustrations

Acknowledgements

In researching this book, I have been guided by colleagues, students, friends, and family members. Those who have offered advice, assistance, support, and sometimes materials include Albert Ascoli, Jane Bellamy, Gordon Braden, Georgia Brown, Dympna Callaghan, Helen Cooper, Tony Cousins, Fred de Armas, Margreta de Grazia, Heather Dubrow, Joe Farrell, Elizabeth Fowler, Kenneth Gross, Andrew Hadfield, Park Honan, Carol Kaske, Bill Kennedy, Terry Krier, Roger Kuin, Joe Loewenstein, Laurie Maguire, Claire McManus, David Lee Miller, Robert Miola, Stephen Orgel, Anne Lake Prescott, David Quint, David Riggs, Sasha Roberts, James Schiffer, Shirley Sharon-Zisser, Lauren Silberman, Bruce Smith, Tiffany Stern, Margaret Tudeau-Clayton, Bart van Es, John Watkins, Germaine Warkentin, Stephen Wheeler and Ramona Wray. Those who have generously read portions of the manuscript include a series of very good colleagues indeed: Heather James, Laura Knoppers, Gail Paster, and Mike Schoenfeldt.

During its long term, the project benefited from the expertise of a fine group of Research Assistants, without whom the considerable burden could not have been borne: Elizabeth Gross, Amy Barber, and Colin Fewer. Toward the end, undergraduate interns included Letitia Montgomery and Julie Noblick, who conscientiously helped with the "Works cited" list, tracked down materials, and provided general bookkeeping. Thanks also to my graduate seminar on Shakespeare's poems during spring 2003, including Dustin Stegner, Doc Rissel, Steele Nowlin, and Tim Arner.

During the past several years, I have been grateful for the opportunity to present my work to the following institutions, through the kindness of their hosts: David Galbraith at the University of Toronto; Peter Stallybrass at the University of Pennsylvania; Martin Dzelzainis and Roy Booth at the University of London; Mark Thornton Burnett at Queen's University, Belfast; Nigel Smith and Denis Feeney at Princeton University; William J. Kennedy at Cornell University; Lukas Erne at the University of Geneva and Ewan Fernie at Royal Holloway, University of London. It has been a lot of fun, and I learned a lot. I also appreciate the opportunity provided by Emily Grosholz to lecture in her Philosophy 413 class at Penn State on "*The Tempest* and Philosophy" – the results of which make their way into the book's final paragraph.

Richard A. McCabe kindly served as host to my Visiting Research Fellowship at Merton College, Oxford, during Michaelmas 2001, when a substantial part of the research was undertaken. I am also grateful to the Warden, Dame Jessica Rawson, and to the Fellows for their collegiality, including Stephen Gunn and the Merton Librarian, Julia Walworth.

Thanks, too, to the rare books librarians at the Bodleian Library, Oxford; the University Library and Trinity College Library, Cambridge; and the Huntington Library, San Marino, California, especially Stephen Tabor.

Research grants and fellowships helped fund an expensive project. Robert R. Edwards and the Institute for the Arts and Humanistic Studies at Penn State provided a three-year Term Fellowship; and Raymond Lombra and the Research and Graduate Studies Office offered an Internal Faculty Award. My former English Department Head, Don Bialostosky, was unswerving in his support of my work, and I am pleased to acknowledge the help of my new Department Head, Robert Caserio. As always, Caroline D. Eckhardt, Head of the Comparative Literature Department, offered complementary support.

One part of the manuscript has appeared in slightly different form: chapter 7, in *Shakespeare Quarterly* 52.2 (2001): 222–54. Thanks to the journal editor, Gail Kern Paster, for her professional expertise.

Special thanks go to Sarah Stanton at Cambridge University Press for her commitment to the project, for settling on the final form of the book and even coming up with its title, and for overseeing the project expertly through the publication process. I am grateful to one anonymous reviewer for the Press, who provided confirmation at an important juncture. Thanks also to Jackie Warren for cordially ushering the manuscript through production, and to Maureen Leach for expertly copyediting it.

Friends outside the academy who lent their interest and support include, in State College, Martha Freeman and Loanne Snavely; and, in Oxford, Mick and Karen Foley, Danny Carrick and Anne Varty, Douglas Barrie and Tish Francis, Mark Fricker and Helen Harvey, and Jem Whiteley.

In looking back over the project, I also realize how lucky I have been in benefiting from the expertise of a band of scholars who helped so deeply that they functioned as something like consultants, reading portions of the manuscript, answering emails, and generally providing direction and conversation. The work of Colin Burrow on Shakespeare's poems has been instrumental to my research, and it has been a pleasure to exchange ideas and material over several years on our complementary projects. James Bednarz's work on literary rivalry has also been inspiring, and I am grateful for his willingness to read parts of the text, especially on "The Phoenix and Turtle." Lukas Erne entered the project during its last year, serving as a reader for the Press; he also proved decisive through his groundbreaking book on Shakespeare and finally by reading the entire manuscript. My running partner Garrett Sullivan has generously talked with me for hours on the project (often in motion), and commented deftly on some of the script. Bob Edwards continues into his second decade as my close friend and advisor at Penn State, in things professional, familial, and athletic; Bob read a large portion and made important refinements at a critical time. I also wish to acknowledge the contribution of Robert B. Johnstone, my mentor from the University of Montana since 1972, for talking with me faithfully about Shakespeare and the idea of this book.

Finally, I would like to thank my wife Debora for her care and advice these thirty years. I dedicate this book to our sons, Evan Gerard and Kelton David, ages thirteen and ten. Evan, affable iconoclast and voracious reader, kept wondering why I would "squander [my] life on Shakespeare," when I could be reading that other "William" from the *Just William* stories – those of "ham, bacon, and eggs" fame – or his other preferred line of useful material, which stretches from Tolkien and Lewis to Rowling and Pullman. Kelton, genial sports enthusiast, at an early age developed an uncanny sympathy for Romeo and Juliet and for an aged father who lost his heart in Britain, and he keeps his own father cheerfully headed to the pastoral field of sport.

Note on texts

All quotations from Shakespeare's poems and plays come from *The Riverside Shakespeare*, ed. G. Blakemore Evans, et al. (Boston: Houghton, 1997), unless otherwise indicated.

Quotations from Spenser's poetry come from *The Poetical Works of Edmund Spenser*, ed. J. C. Smith and Ernest De Sélincourt (Oxford: Clarendon, 1909–10).

Quotations from Marlowe's plays come from *Christopher Marlowe: The Complete Plays*, ed. Mark Thornton Burnett, Everyman Library (London: Dent; and Rutland, VT: Tuttle, 1999), while quotations from Marlowe's verse come from *Christopher Marlowe: The Complete Poems and Translations*, ed. Stephen Orgel (Harmondsworth: Penguin, 1971), unless otherwise noted.

Quotations from Ovid come from *Ovid in Six Volumes*, Loeb Classical Library, trans. Grant Showerman, 2nd edn., rev. G. P. Goold, 6 vols. (Cambridge, MA: Harvard University Press; London: Heinemann, 1977–89), with the exception of the *Amores*, where I use Marlowe's translation (*Ovid's Elegies*), unless otherwise noted. The numbering of the *Amores* elegies in the Loeb volume differs from that in Marlowe's translation, because the Loeb prints 3.5 on Ovid's dream vision, which Marlowe does not translate, since it did not appear in the edition he was using. Thus those poems in *Ovid's Elegies* after 3.4 differ in numbering from the Loeb volume. Similarly, the line numbering in the Orgel edition of *Ovid's Elegies*, which begins with the four-line prologue to the work, differs from that in the Loeb, which begins with 1.1.

Unless otherwise noted, quotations and translations from other classical authors – including Virgil – come from the Loeb Classical Library. Major exceptions include Homer's *Iliad* and *Odyssey*, which come from the translations of Richmond Lattimore; Plato's dialogues, from the edition of Edith Hamilton and Huntington Cairns; Aristotle's works, from the edition of Richard McKeon; Lucan, from the translation of Jane Wilson Joyce (except

Book 1, which comes from Marlowe's translation); and the Bible, from the facsimile of the Geneva edition of 1560 published by the University of Wisconsin Press.

Throughout, I modernize the archaic i–j and u–v of Renaissance texts, as well as other obsolete typographical conventions such as the italicizing of names and places.

For citation, I rely on the "works cited" format from *The MLA Style Manual* (1985); this format relies on a system of abbreviation in the text and the notes, and thus it includes full citations only in the list of works cited at the end. The Cambridge University Press has brought certain features of the text into conformity with house style.

Proem
Shakespeare's "Plaies and Poems"

In 1640, the publisher John Benson presents to his English reading public a Shakespeare who is now largely lost to us: the national author of poems and plays. By printing his modest octavo edition of the *Poems: Written By Wil. Shake-speare. Gent.*, Benson curiously aims to complement the 1623 printing venture of Shakespeare's theatre colleagues, John Heminge and Henry Condell, who had presented *Mr. William Shakespeares Comedies, Histories, & Tragedies* in their monumental First Folio. Thus, in his own *Dedicatory Epistle* "To the Reader," Benson remarks that he presents "some excellent and sweetly composed Poems," which "had not the fortune by reason of their Infancie in his death, to have the due accommodation of proportionable glory, with the rest of his everliving Workes" (*2ʳ). Indeed, as recent scholarship demonstrates, Benson boldly prints his octavo *Poems* on the model of Heminge and Condell's Folio Plays.[1]

Not simply does Benson's volume share its printer, Thomas Cotes, with the 1632 Folio, but both editions begin with an identical format: an engraved portrait of the author; a dedicatory epistle "To the Reader"; and a set of commendatory verses, with Leonard Digges contributing an important celebratory poem to both volumes. Benson's engraving by William Marshall even derives from the famous Martin Droeshout engraving in the First Folio, and six of the eight lines beneath Benson's engraving are borrowed from Ben Jonson's famed memorial poem to Shakespeare in that volume. Accordingly, Benson takes his publishing goal from Heminge and Condell. They aim to "keepe the memory of such worthy a Friend, & Fellow alive" (*Dedicatory Epistle* to the earls of Pembroke and Montgomery, reprinted in *Riverside*, 94), while he aims "to be serviceable for the continuance of glory to the deserved Author" ("To the Reader," *2ᵛ). In effect, what Heminge and Condell had done for the plays, Benson does for the poems. But the purpose of his edition is more comprehensive:

---

[1] De Grazia, *Verbatim*, 166–73. The following paragraph is indebted to De Grazia, 166–67.

to preserve William Shakespeare, Gentleman, to posterity as a national poet-playwright.[2]

This book begins with Benson because it argues that he, not Heminge and Condell, most accurately imprints Shakespeare as an early modern author. In fact, while Benson is careful to print the poems within the remembrance of the plays, Heminge and Condell forget the poems altogether. Nowhere is this paradigm of memory and forgetting clearer than in the two commendatory verses by Digges. In Benson's edition, Digges presents Shakespeare as the author of "Plaies and Poems" (*3ᵛ), but in Heminge and Condell's volume he presents Shakespeare as the author from the "Stage" who wrote such plays as *Romeo and Juliet*.[3] By carefully matching his volume with the First Folio, Benson completes the historical preservation of Shakespearean authorship that Heminge and Condell had left incomplete, and that in large part because of their monumental success would become effaced during the ensuing centuries. The story of Shakespeare's original practice as an English and European author of poems and plays in print, and then the gradual erasure of this practice, forms the primary subject of this book.

Paradoxically, Benson had something to do with this erasure, for he badly botches the job. Measured beside the monumental folio of the plays, how could his slender octavo of the poems hold a plea? But his failure is not merely one of textual scale; it includes failures of completion and the editorial principles of printing content. For starters, Benson does not print all of the poems; he excludes Shakespeare's most popular works during the period, *Venus and Adonis* and *The Rape of Lucrece*. But he also disrupts the original publications of the poems he does print. Most infamously, he rearranges the sonnets from the 1609 quarto; he supplies titles to some of the poems in the young-man sequence so that they address a mistress; and he splices in the twenty-nine poems from the 1612 edition of William Jaggard's *The Passionate Pilgrim*, which spuriously includes Shakespeare's name on one version of its title page while including poems by other authors. Thus the *Poems: Written By Wil. Shake-speare. Gent.* is really a volume by more than one gentleman-poet. Not merely in size, but in authenticity the octavo *Poems* cannot compete with the folio *Plays*.

---

[2] As S. Roberts reminds us, "the octavo format Benson chose for the *Poems* ensured their longevity since octavos were more portable, more likely to be bound and thus better preserved than the ephemeral quarto publication" (*Reading Shakespeare's Poems*, 159). On Benson, see also Baker, "Cavalier Shakespeare."

[3] In chapter 2, we shall return to Digges, to learn that his poem in the First Folio *imitates* Shakespeare's Sonnets – the only category of trace the book leaves of the poems.

It is true that "For almost 150 years, the matching formats cou-
pled together the folio and octavo volumes, the drama and the poetry,
to comprise Shakespeare's complete works" (De Grazia, *Verbatim*, 168).
Nonetheless, in the emergent conversation about Shakespeare as the
"national poet," his poems lose their voice by the latter half of the
seventeenth century, as readers, authors, and critics turn to the plays – and
turn the plays into what John Dryden memorably calls "Dramatick Poesie"
(reprinted in B. Vickers, ed. *Critical Heritage*, 1: 136), as if in mourning
over an unnamed loss that Benson for one seems rightly to have discerned.
As *The Shakspere Allusion-Book* makes clear, for the next century-and-a-
half readers leave little record of their interest in Shakespeare's "poems"
as Benson preserves them.[4] Not simply Nicholas Rowe's pioneering edition of Shakespeare's works in 1709, which first includes *Venus and Adonis*
and *The Rape of Lucrece* along with the plays, but up to the end of the
eighteenth century, when Edmund Malone inherits the project, editions
rely on Benson's 1640 version of the poems.[5] In his 1780 supplement to
the Johnson–Steevens edition of 1778, Malone returns to the original 1609
quarto of *Shake-speares Sonnets* for both the Sonnets and *A Lover's Complaint*, and then in his own 1790 *Plays and Poems of William Shakespeare* he
includes the quarto version in his final volume (see Figure 1). Even so, in his
disciplined attempt to print an author he believes authentic, Malone takes
considerable license with *The Passionate Pilgrim* in particular (chapter 5),
and even more importantly, he monumentalizes an editorial practice that
prevails today: the burying of the "Poems" at the back of an edition of the
"Works" (chapter 2). In other words, Benson's attempt to make Shakespeare
a national poet-playwright is paradoxically instrumental in the un-making
of this very author.

Yet by taking the cue of Benson's intent (rather than his execution), the
present book returns to the years when "Shakespeare" was active in print
as both a poet and a playwright, 1593–1612, to discover as accurately as
possible the conditions under which he composes both his poems and his
plays and in which his poems and (some of his) plays are in turn printed by
others. The book concentrates on the poems, but unlike previous studies
of this topic, it discusses all of the poems as a corpus in its own right,
and does so not by severing the poems from the plays, but precisely by
embedding them within Shakespeare's career as a playwright, actor, and

---

[4] Paul D. Cannan is now researching this topic (personal communication, 12 December 2002); see his
"Early Shakespeare Criticism."
[5] In 1709, Bernard Lintott issues an unauthorized supplement to Rowe that prints *Venus* and *Lucrece*,
along with the 1609 Sonnets (see Alexander, "Province of Pirates").

shareholder in a theatre company.[6] The effect, I hope, is to form a more complex, accurate, and complete view of Shakespearean authorship than recent criticism allows.

Such a view does not reduce Shakespeare's production of poetry to an "interlude" in his theatrical career. To the contrary, it counters this model by trying to explain the strange and curious mixture of poems and plays throughout his career, from the early 1590s into the second decade of the seventeenth century. It does so by recalling a neglected historical fact: an author's combination of these two literary forms within a single career is fundamentally a sixteenth-century phenomenon (chapter 1). Shakespeare participates in this phenomenon, and changes the institution of authorship forever.

Furthermore, Shakespeare's intertwined authorship of poems and plays, throughout his career, is not static but dynamic. His authorship of poems (like that of his plays) changes over time, and in three print installments. The first occurs near the beginning of his career, during the early 1590s, when he publishes his first poems, *Venus and Adonis* (1593) and *The Rape of Lucrece* (1594), complete with signed dedicatory epistles from author to patron, the earl of Southampton. The second installment occurs during the mid-point of his career, when others publish volumes of poems in collaboration with poems by Shakespeare: Jaggard's *The Passionate Pilgrim* (1599, 1st and 2nd editions), which includes Shakespeare's name on the title page but which prints only five poems known to be by him, leaving fifteen thought to be by other hands; and Robert Chester's *Love's Martyr*, which prints "The Phoenix and Turtle" as a commissioned poem, along with poems by Jonson, John Marston, George Chapman, the anonymous "Ignoto," and Chester himself. And the third installment occurs toward the end of Shakespeare's career, when the Sonnets and *A Lover's Complaint* appear together in the 1609 quarto – whether authorized by the author or not, we are still debating.

---

[6] Cf. other recent monographs on the poems: Dubrow, *Victors*, and more recently Cousins, *Shakespeare's Sonnets*, who both include chapters only on *Venus*, *Lucrece*, and the Sonnets. To an extent D. Kay's book, *Sonnets and Poems*, in the Twayne series is an exception, although he groups "The Phoenix and Turtle" and *The Passionate Pilgrim* along with other poems under a single chapter titled "Miscellaneous Poems." Countless books concentrate on the Sonnets, e.g., most memorably Fineman, *Perjured*. Most editions of the poems follow this practice (Arden, Cambridge, Penguin, Pelican), but for an exception, see Burrow's Oxford edition of *Sonnets and Poems*, which "stands as a physical encouragement to readers to think about these poems together" (2). After this book was completed, three monographs on the poems appeared. S. Roberts' *Reading Shakespeare's Poems*, however, does not consider all the poems, absenting "The Phoenix and Turtle" (18); Hyland's *Introduction to Shakespeare's Poems* includes only a short section on *A Lover's Complaint* in a chapter on the Sonnets, and relegates "The Phoenix and Turtle" to a short discussion under "Various Poems"; and Schalkwyk's *Speech and Performance in Shakespeare's Sonnets and Plays* examines only the Sonnets. Nonetheless, these books signal a new phase of Shakespearean scholarship.

Date	Editor	Title		Contents
1623	Heminge and Condell	*Mr. William Shakespeares Comedies, Histories, & Tragedies*	Plays	
1640	Benson	*Poems: Written By Wil. Shake-speare. Gent*		Poems: Sonnets rearranged; poems from *Passionate Pilgrim* spliced in; "Phoenix and Turtle" and *A Lover's Complaint*; but not *Venus* or *Lucrece*
1709	Rowe	*The Works of Mr. William Shakespeare*, 6 vols.	Plays	
1709	Lintott	*A Collection of Poems, viz.: I. Venus and Adonis; II. The Rape of Lucrece; III. The Passionate Pilgrim; IV. Sonnets to Sundry Notes of Musick, by Mr. William Shakespeare* [unauthorized supplement to Rowe]		Poems: *Venus*; *Lucrece*; *Passionate Pilgrim*; "Phoenix and Turtle"; *A Lover's Complaint*
1710	Lintott	Same, with Sonnets added. [unauthorized supplement to Rowe]		Poems: *Venus*; *Lucrece*; *Passionate Pilgrim*; "Phoenix and Turtle"; *A Lover's Complaint*; 1609 Sonnets
1710	Curll-Gildon	*The Works of Mr. William Shakespeare, Volume the Seventh, containing Venus and Adonis, Tarquin and Lucrece and His Miscellany Poems* [another unauthorized supplement to Rowe]		Poems: *Venus*; *Lucrece*; *Passionate Pilgrim*; "Phoenix and Turtle"; *A Lover's Complaint*; Benson Sonnets

Figure 1. Benson to Malone. The publication of Shakespeare's poems and plays. The figure shows the complex evolution of the printing of Shakespeare's poems alongside his plays. (For the purpose of economy, the lists of plays are not included.) The right-hand column charts the distinction between the printing of Benson's poems, especially the Sonnets, and the printing of Shakespeare's poems from the earliest editions, especially the 1609 Sonnets. Most importantly, perhaps, the figure charts the way in which the printing solely of Shakespeare's plays recurrently produced a response volume on the poems, with Benson responding to Heminge and Condell, both Lintott and Curll-Gildon to Rowe, Sewell to Pope, and perhaps Evans to Capell, until Steevens, Bell, and Malone individually began to combine plays and poems in a single edition (boldface).

Date	Editor	Title		Contents
1714	Rowe	*The Works of Mr. William Shakespeare,* 2nd edn., expanded	Plays	
1714	Gildon	*The Works of Mr. William Shakespear, Volume the Ninth* [unauthorized supplement to Rowe]		Poems: *Venus; Lucrece; Passionate Pilgrim*; "Phoenix and Turtle"; *A Lover's Complaint*; Benson Sonnets
1725	Pope	*The Works of Mr. William Shakespeare,* 6 vols.	Plays	
1725	Sewell	*The Works of Mr. William Shakespeare, the Seventh Volume, containing Venus and Adonis, Tarquin and Lucrece and Mr. Shakespear's Miscellany Poems* [unauthorized supplement to Pope]		*Venus; Lucrece; Passionate Pilgrim*; "Phoenix and Turtle"; *A Lover's Complaint*; Benson Sonnets
1728	Pope	2nd edn. of 1725 edition	Plays	
1728	Sewell	2nd edn. of 1725 edition		Poems [same as 1st ed.]
1733	Theobald	*The Works of Shakespeare,* 7 vols.	Plays	
1744	Hanmer	*The Works of Shakespeare,* 6 vols.	Plays	
1747	Pope and Warburton	*The Works of Shakespeare,* 8 vols.	Plays	
1765	Johnson	*The Plays of William Shakespeare,* 8 vols.	Plays	
1766	**Steevens**	***Twenty of the Plays of Shakespeare***	**Plays**	**Poems: 1609 Sonnets**
1767–68	Capell	*Mr. William Shakespeare his Comedies, Histories, and Tragedies,* 10 vols.	Plays	
1771	Hanmer	2nd edn. of Hanmer edition	Plays	
1773	Johnson and Steevens	*The Plays of William Shakespeare,* 10 vols.	Plays	

Figure 1. (*cont.*)

Date	Editor	Title		Contents
1773–74	**Bell**	***Bell's Edition of Shakespeare's Plays, 9 vols.***	**Plays**	**Poems:** *Venus; Lucrece; Passionate Pilgrim;* "Phoenix and Turtle"; *A Lover's Complaint;* **Benson Sonnets**
1775	Evans	*Poems Written by Mr. William Shakespeare*		Poems: *Venus; Lucrece; Passionate Pilgrim;* "Phoenix and Turtle"; *A Lover's Complaint;* Benson Sonnets
1780	Bathurst and Malone	*Supplement to the Edition of Shakespeare's Plays Published in 1778,* 2 vols.	Plays [7 new plays ascribed to him]	Poems: *Venus; Lucrece; Passionate Pilgrim;* "Phoenix and Turtle"; *A Lover's Complaint;* 1609 Sonnets
1785	Bathurst and Malone	3rd edn. of Johnson and Steevens	Plays	
1786	Rann	*The Dramatic Works of Shakespeare, in Six volumes,* 6 vols.	Plays	
1790	**Malone**	***The Plays and Poems of William Shakspeare,* 10 vols.**	**Plays**	**Poems:** *Venus; Lucrece; Passionate Pilgrim;* "Phoenix and Turtle"; *A Lover's Complaint;* **1609 Sonnets**

While the first part of the book introduces the historical and critical contexts for viewing Shakespeare as England's great national poet-playwright, the remaining three parts trace the dynamics of this tripartite printing of Shakespeare as an author of poems within his theatrical career. Part two on *Venus* and *Lucrece* shows Shakespeare as a self-conscious print poet presenting himself as such, competing with colleagues like Spenser (and Marlowe) for readership and for national authority. Part three shows a quite different author, as both Jaggard in *The Passionate Pilgrim* and Chester in *Love's Martyr* print Shakespeare in mutually appropriating ways yet for quite different purposes. Part four looks at the Sonnets and *A Lover's Complaint* to show how the 1609 quarto imprints the very divide between the self-conscious print poet and the manuscript poet who is brought into print by others. Shakespeare's poems are thus an anomaly; his career as a poet, a genuine mystery. That makes it hard to capture; yet the effort is necessary, if we are to understand his authorship more fully within the available evidence.

Formalizing this dynamic view of Shakespeare as an author of poems, the book suggests that he himself represents a struggle over authorship throughout his career. Past criticism tends to understand this struggle as one between print and manuscript, but I concentrate on a slightly different opposition, neglected in modern criticism: Shakespeare also labors between a literary career in printed poetry and a professional career in staged theatre.[7] Not merely is Shakespeare originally a national poet-playwright, but his works sustain a deep reflection on the historical predicament of performing such a new role for the English author. He does so both in his poems and in his plays, from the beginning of his career to the end.

A full analysis of this topic requires more than a single monograph, so the present book is the first of two (planned) volumes. The first volume, presented here, introduces the general argument and specifies it primarily through the poems. The second will summarize the argument and specify it primarily through the plays. Even so, the first volume seeks to place the poems within the specific context of Shakespeare's work in the theatre, and it stands as a full argument. Thus, chapters 1 and 2, which aim to outline that argument, foreground the plays, while the "Play Scenes" introducing Parts two, three, and four join the Epilogue in recalling the plays Shakespeare was working on during the phases of his print career as a poet and during the final phase, after 1609 and before he retires. To take just a single example: the play scene to Part two situates *The Rape of Lucrece* within the context of another 1594 publication, Shakespeare's first tragedy, *Titus Andronicus*, which refers several times to the historical (legendary) story of Lucrece and the foundation of the Roman Republic, while also sharing with the poem a fixation on Philomela, the arch-Ovidian myth of the raped woman who is also an author. Moreover, the commentaries on the poems in each of chapters 3–8 formalize this procedure by emphasizing the very compound of poetry and theatre in the discourse of the poems themselves – the first study to do so. Such a strategy allows for a comprehensive examination of the collected corpus of Shakespeare's poems but embeds it securely within Shakespeare's work for the stage.[8]

---

[7] On Shakespeare as a manuscript poet, see, e.g., Marotti, "Literary" and *Manuscript, Print,* and Love, *Scribal Publications*; as a manuscript poet worrying about print publication, see Wall, *Imprint* and Burrow, "Life"; and as a "professional" writer making his living through the stage, rather than as a laureate poet with a literary career, see Helgerson, *Laureates*, 4–5. More recently, see Erne, *Literary Dramatist*, for Shakespeare as a print playwright concerned about the literary future of his plays.

[8] Burrow reminds us that "Each of the poems . . . is distinctly that of a dramatist" (*Sonnets and Poems*, 5). At least since Charles Gildon (see Cannan, "Early Shakespeare Criticism"), scholars have been obsessed with examining the connection between Shakespeare's plays and poems, with Schalkwyk's *Speech and Performance* the most recent manifestation of this project. As yet, however, no one has looked at how the plays and poems each share a discourse of both poetry and theatre.

Shakespeare processes his self-reflection on the problem of being a new English poet-playwright by representing a dialogue between two oppositional aesthetics, which are arguably the two dominant aesthetics of the day. The first I call Spenserian, because it so closely models the aesthetics of the leading Elizabethan print poet, Edmund Spenser, who advertised himself as England's Virgil (and was advertised as such by others). The second I call Marlovian, because it so closely models the aesthetics of England's first major poet-playwright, Christopher Marlowe, who vigorously counters Spenser's Virgilian program of pastoral and epic with his own Ovidian *cursus* of amorous poems, poems in the epic register, and stage tragedy.[9] Long after Marlowe and Spenser are dead (1593 and 1599, respectively), Shakespeare is haunted by their ghostly inventions. Not simply does he carry on a dialogue with the two leading authors of his day, even boldly bringing the mighty opposites face to face: powerfully, he forges his unique version of early modern authorship out of the ashes of their titanic collision.[10] As such, the book attempts to place Shakespeare's poems and plays within a historical literary context. In addition to Marlowe and Spenser, this context foregrounds Ovid and Virgil, Lucan and Petrarch, but it also attempts to lend interest to such authors as Dante and Chaucer, Tasso and Cervantes, Daniel and Jonson.

While Shakespeare's poems and plays both rehearse a professional dialogue between a Spenserian and a Marlovian aesthetics in order to step decisively beyond both, we may note a complicating feature: Shakespeare may have contributed to his own effacement as an early modern poet-playwright. In at least one poem ("The Phoenix and Turtle") and one play (*Titus Andronicus*), he rehearses the historic transition from a culture of print poetry to one of staged theatre. Shakespeare is an English poet-playwright who appears willing, as Jonson does not, to privilege theatre over poetry. In other words, Benson's attempt to preserve the poems conjoined with the plays is both a belated register and a final reversal of Shakespeare's self-conscious version of the conjunction itself.

---

[9] These are the respective topics of my previous monographs, *Spenser's Famous Flight* and *Marlowe's Counterfeit Profession*. In my Introduction to *The Cambridge Companion to Marlowe*, I discuss Marlowe as England's first major poet-playwright and his effect on Shakespeare and Jonson.

[10] This argument in no way implies that other authors do not enter the fray. Recent scholarship argues for the importance of such authors to Shakespeare as Thomas Nashe, Samuel Daniel, and of course Jonson, to name only the mightiest (see chapters 1 and 2). James P. Bednarz is researching "Shakespeare's Beginnings" in such authors as Kyd, Greene, and Marlowe (personal communication, 30 December 2002). On Spenser and Marlowe as "mighty opposites, poised in antagonism," see Greenblatt, *Fashioning* (222), the opening to his chapter on *Othello*, which curiously avoids seeing Shakespeare as processing the opposition between these mighty authors.

There are, however, further complications. Much of the energy of the book forms to show that Shakespeare's works sustain a deep interest not merely in theatre but in poetry. Periodically, the author reveals that he also became concerned to rehearse the absolute dependence of theatre on poetry – and not simply early in a play such as *Love's Labor's Lost* but late in a play such as *The Tempest*.

Throughout, the book focuses on Shakespeare's representation of a figure I call the poet-playwright – the so-called governor figure who so often directs the action in a Shakespearean fiction. While most work on this figure emphasizes his or her theatrical direction, I seek to show that more often than not the governor combines "poetical" with "theatrical" direction – the use of both page and stage, book and theatre, song and play, to bring about the denouement – in comedy, tragedy, history, and "romance" alike, even in the narrative poems, the Sonnets, and a lyric such as "The Phoenix and Turtle."[11] Thus, Shakespeare's poems and plays record a sustained conversation not merely on theatre but also on the art of poetry, and often the works conjoin a discourse of poetry and theatre in engaging and historically important ways. By listening in on this conversation, we can become attuned to a particular Shakespearean language of authorship that we might not have known existed, yet right where we are used to looking.

By titling the study *Shakespeare, National Poet-Playwright*, I wish to alert readers to my primary project: the full, original, and compound form of Shakespearean authorship in a national setting. For such a project, the national setting is manifested by a nascent print culture that allows for individual agency and complicates it. In particular, the word "national" operates in two directions simultaneously: it picks up the major critical term for classifying the construction of Shakespeare as an author in centuries subsequent to his own (he became the "national poet"); and it suggests that he himself self-consciously wrote the nation in both his poems and plays, through a combined discourse of poetry and theatre, and thereby that he participates in his own historical making.

Underlying the enclosed study of Shakespeare's poems as a corpus is another paradox: his are fundamentally "scattered poems." The phrase recalls Petrarch's scattered rhymes and their printing in the *Rime sparse*. In turn, this Petrarchism recalls an Ovidian genealogy of authorship, since for Petrarch, as for Shakespeare and other Elizabethans and Jacobeans,

---

[11] I do not examine *A Funeral Elegy for Master William Peter*, because recent scholarship concludes that Shakespeare did not author this poem; see Abrams and Foster; Monsarrat; and B. Vickers, "*Counterfeiting*," all on this poem.

This Shadowe is renowned Shakespear's? Soule of th'age
The applause? delight? the wonder of the Stage.
Nature her selfe, was proud of his designes
And joy'd to weare the dressing of his lines,
The learned will Confess, his works are such,
As neither man, nor Muse, can prayse to much.
For ever live thy fame, the world to tell,
Thy like, no age, shall ever paralell.

                                        W. M. sculpsit.

Figure 2. Frontispiece to *Poems: Written By Wil. Shake-speare. Gent.*, edited by
John Benson (London, 1640).

Ovid is the great classical author of scattering, dispersal, fluidity, and meta-morphosis, epitomized in Ovid's originary myth of authorship, Apollo's pursuit of Daphne, with her "scattred haire" (line 664).[12] But as mention of this myth implies, the phrase also refers to the unfortunate dismemberment of the Shakespearean poetic corpus in recent criticism, as well as our strange need to detach these worthy limbs from the monumental dramatic corpus. In fact, Petrarch derived his Ovidian title most directly from Dante, who writes at the very end of the *Divine Comedy*, "In its profundity I saw – ingathered / and bound by love into one single volume– / what, in the universe, seems separate, scattered" (*Paradiso*, 33.85–87). If for Dante God's love is scattered unbound throughout the cosmos but finally bound in the volume of the apocalyptic yellow rose of paradise, for Petrarch the term *scattering* (writes Robert M. Durling, ed., *Petrarch's Lyric Poems*) "expresses the intensely self-critical awareness that all integration of selves and texts is relative, temporary, threatened" (26). Finally, *Shakespeare, National Poet-Playwright* hopes for a twenty-first century re-collection of the entire Shakespearean body in its original historic shape. Nowhere, perhaps, is this body illustrated more palpably than in Benson's 1640 rehearsal of the 1623 portrait itself, where Marshall's once handless Droeshout author of the plays now dramatically holds the collected leaves of the laureate poet (Figure 2).

[12] Golding, trans. *"Metamorphoses." Shakespeare's Ovid*. On Apollo and Daphne as "the dominant myth" of the *Rime sparse*, see Braden, "Ovid, Petrarch," 101. On Petrarch in Shakespeare's Sonnets, see Cheney, "Sonnet 106."

PART ONE

The imprint of Shakespearean authorship

Prelude: Shakespeare, Cervantes, Petrarch

"One of the things," said Don Quixote in reply, "which shall give the greatest pleasure to a virtuous and eminent man is to see himself in his lifetime printed and in the press, and with a good name on people's tongues."

"Poetry . . . is fashioned of an alchemy of such power that anyone who knows how to treat her will transmute her into the purest gold of inestimable price. He who possesses her must . . . not let . . . her descend to base lampoons or impious sonnets; she must not be displayed for sale, unless in heroic poems, in mournful tragedies, or in merry and artificial comedies."

(Cervantes, *Don Quixote*, Part 2 [1615]: chapter 3, p. 546 and chapter 16, pp. 635–36)

These two excerpts from Part 2 of *Don Quixote* address two major coordinates of the present book. In the first, during a discussion between the Don and the Bachelor, Sanson Carrasco, Cervantes narrativizes the literal making of the "book" we are reading (544): from its inspiration in other books of chivalry, to the enactment of those books on the myriad roads of La Mancha, to the writing of the book itself by one Cid Hamete Benengeli, to its printing in the nascent medium of print, to the reception of Part 1, and finally to its continuation in Part 2. In the second excerpt, when the Don defends "Poetry" before his new friend, Don Diego de Miranda, Cervantes introduces another one of those great moments when the author pauses to reflect on his medium, including its value for the Spanish "people" or what Cervantes earlier widens to "the universal entertainment of mankind" (545). Cervantes does not divide the literary art into poetic and theatrical forms but rather into those like "base lampoons or impious sonnets" that are impure ethically and those like epic, tragedy, and comedy that are pure. Yet in the process we may discern how naturally Cervantes combines reference to forms associated with the theatre and forms usually called "non-dramatic."

Such a combination takes on resonance when we recall that Cervantes himself was not merely the great inventor of the modern novel but simultaneously an early modern poet-playwright. Born in 1547, in 1566–67 he began to write poetry and published his first sonnet, celebrating the birth of Princess Catalina Michaela, daughter of Phillip II and Isabel of Valois. In 1581, he attempted to establish himself as a dramatist, but only two plays from this period survive: the historical tragedy *La Numancia* (*Numantia: A Tragedy*) and *El trato de Argel* (*The Traffic of Algiers*). In 1585, he published a prose pastoral romance modeled on the Ovidian story of Polyphemus and Galatea, *La Galatea*. Later, between the two installments of *Don Quixote*, he published a long allegorical poem in a satiric mode titled *Viage del Parnaso* (1614; *Voyage To Parnassus*). In 1615, a year before he died, he published a collection of plays titled *Ocho comedias, y ocho entremeses nuevos* (*Eight Plays and Eight New Interludes*). In 1617, a year after he died, a prose work in the heroic vein of Heliodrous' *Aetheopica*, *Los Trabajos de Persiles y Sigismunda* (*The Trials of Persiles and Sigismunda*), was published.[1]

On the surface, the pattern of Cervantes' publications, like Shakespeare's, looks arbitrary, the product simply of exigencies characterizing the author's own often-taxing professional career. Yet the eclectic nature of Cervantes' wide generic practice is also a fundamentally Renaissance practice, indebted most obviously to Petrarch, whose career combined such genres as epic, pastoral, sonnet sequence, triumph, letters, and prose dialogue – in no set order. Nonetheless, embedded deeply in Petrarch's wide formal experimentation is his commitment to Virgil, including practice of the two genres that make up the Renaissance version of the Virgilian progression: pastoral and epic (Fowler, *Kinds* 240; see Coolidge, "Great Things"). Yet Petrarch began composing the *Africa* before he attempted the *Bucolicum carmen*, and only the pastoral appeared during his lifetime – late in his lifetime. Altogether, then, Petrarch's career is notable for its prodigious mixing of two contradictory career models: a haphazard generic eclecticism, which shows his interest in wide formal experimentation; and the Virgilian progression, which shows his interest in presenting himself to Europe as the modern heir to Virgil.[2] The fact is: Petrarch's major heirs in sixteenth- and seventeenth-century Europe reproduce their own versions of such mixing, from Sannazaro and Tasso in Italy, to Ronsard in France, to Spenser and Milton in England. What has escaped notice until recently is that Cervantes' eclectic career also subscribes to a Virgilian pattern (de Armas, "Wheel").

Recently, Harold Bloom has reminded us that the lost play *Cardenio*, coauthored by Shakespeare and John Fletcher, is modeled on an episode in Part 2 of *Don Quixote* – giving Bloom his prompt to match the Spanish with

---

[1] See Cascardi, ed., *Cambridge Companion to Cervantes*, including Cascardi's Introduction; de Armas, "Italian"; McKendrick, "Writings."

[2] For details, see Cheney, *Flight* 59–62; Kennedy, "Career."

the English author in his 100-author "mosaic" of literary genius, for reasons that the present book tries to complicate: "Shakespeare usurps all modern drama, Cervantes the novel" (*Genius* 15).[3] Although Shakespeare wrote some of the most gifted prose in English (most notably, for Falstaff), he is not known to have composed a prose fiction in the manner of Cervantes – or Marguerite de Navarre, or Sir Philip Sidney, even Robert Greene or Thomas Nashe. What Shakespeare does share with Cervantes is certainly what Thomas Carlyle called "superiority of intellect" (quoted in Bloom, *Genius*, 9) but also the early modern mixing of career models. The first is his seemingly haphazard combination of poems and plays within a single literary career – a combination we will characterize in chapter 1 as "Ovidian" and find practiced most prominently in England by Marlowe. The second career model emerges from Shakespeare's interest in Renaissance Virgilianism, especially the genres of pastoral and epic within a national frame. As we will see, Shakespeare tends to attenuate Virgil with his favorite author, Ovid, and to understand this Ovidian project in terms of Marlowe's similar attempt to attenuate the Virgilian Spenser.

This first part to the book divides into two chapters that set up subsequent chapters on individual poems by laying out necessary historical material for contextualizing Shakespeare's Ovidian combination of poems and plays within a nationalist, Virgilian, or Spenserian frame. The first chapter, "The Sixteenth-Century Poet-Playwright," provides a more detailed orientation to the project; it reviews the details of Shakespeare's professional career, inventories critical models on it, and introduces the main features of the argument. The second chapter, "Francis Meres, the Ovidian Poet-Playwright, and Shakespeare Criticism," views five sets of evidence external to Shakespeare's works to support the general argument.

---

[3] For evidence that Thomas Shelton's English translation of *Don Quixote*, though not published in 1612, circulated in manuscript as early as 1607, see Bliss, "Don Quixote." For parallels between the love triangles in *Don Quixote* and Shakespeare's Sonnets, see Erne, "Mark."

CHAPTER I

The sixteenth-century poet-playwright

Shakespeare, National Poet-Playwright offers a new explanation for appro-aching one of the perennial problems in Shakespeare criticism: just how to relate Shakespeare's poems to his plays. While Shakespeare wrote many more plays than poems, he nonetheless combined the two forms during a professional career that spanned nearly twenty-five years. As modern scholarship reveals, Shakespeare wrote or collaborated on forty-two known plays, but he also penned five substantial poems and a number of shorter ones (many of them extant), as well as over one hundred songs written for the plays; he also found himself the author of a printed book of poems that he did not wholly write or authorize.

While Shakespeare's work in the new English theatre most likely stretched from the late 1580s until about 1614, his poems were published between 1593 and 1609 – or 1612, if we include the third edition of *The Passionate Pilgrim* (important to the present argument). In addition to such famous plays produced in the genres of comedy, history, tragedy, and "romance" as *A Midsummer Night's Dream*, *1 Henry IV*, *Hamlet*, and *The Tempest*, he bequeathed to us three major poems of longstanding value and two shorter poems of genuine recent interest. In the very middle of his career, he was so popular a writer, both in poetry and in drama, that he could have a volume of poems pirated under his name. Not simply does he write much of his drama in blank or rhymed verse (as is well known), but habitually he punc-tuates his plays with the recording of original songs, the singing of popular ballads, the composition of original poems, and the quotation of popu-lar verse from his day, including of such contemporaries as Christopher Marlowe and Sir Philip Sidney. At the same time, he relies on the Renais-sance notion of imitation to carry on a dialogue with such poets from antiquity as Virgil and Ovid, and such poets from England as Chaucer and Spenser.

Indeed, from the beginning to the end of his career, Shakespeare stages dramatic characters who turn out to have poetry on their minds – sometimes in places we might not expect, as this from Lorenzo to Jessica under the glistening night sky of Belmont:

> therefore the poet
> Did feign that Orpheus drew trees, stones, and floods;
> Since nought so stock fish, hard, and full of rage,
> But music for the time doth change his nature.
> The man that hath no music in himself,
> Nor is not moved with concord of sweet sounds,
> Is fit for treasons, stratagems, and spoils;
> The motions of his spirit are dull as night,
> And his affections dark as [Erebus]:
> Let no such man be trusted.
>
> (*Merchant of Venice*, 5. 1. 79–88)

Lorenzo is trying to rationalize the mystery of the music he and Jessica are hearing – an "air" (76) that seems as much "in" them as outside them. He expresses at once a romantic form of discourse to his beloved and a penetrating defense of poetry to the theatre audience. And this art he and his creator understand to have psychological, social, religious, and national value: poetry can represent music as creating the very "spirit" of mental balance, interpersonal faith, and patriotic duty. To explain the mystery and outline the defense, Lorenzo turns to an unnamed poet and his verse-feigning of the story of Orpheus, the Renaissance archetype of the poet who used his art for such a civilizing power (Cain, "Orpheus").

For Shakespeare, we should not be surprised to discern here an important energizing idea central to his canon as a whole: the poet is a figure of "trust," his poetry an art of faith, an external artifact that secretly secures the most intimate bonds of life and culture. For his part, the playwright is the keeper of this bond, the play the cultural ceremony responsible for disseminating faith to the public at large.[1] This scene at Belmont is thus not isolated but exemplary, arguing for a more sustained interlock of poetry and theatre than recent classifications of Shakespeare as an early modern author allow. We can witness this interlock both within the representations of his fictions (as here) and in the actual forms of his professional production. Together, the representations and the forms constitute the ground of discussion underlying this book.

In 1593, Shakespeare interrupts his dramatic career to publish his first book of verse, *Venus and Adonis*, a poem of 1,194 lines in the popular and

---

[1] On Shakespearean art as a deep probe of trust, see Schwartz, "Contemporary Psychoanalysis." On Shakespeare's "epistemological optimism about access to otherness," see Krier, *Birth Passages*, 69. On Shakespeare as a godly playwright with a sacramental art, see Knapp, *Shakespeare's Tribe*.

erotic Elizabethan genre of the Ovidian epyllion or minor epic (Hulse, *Verse*). This "first heir" of his "invention," as he calls it (*Riverside*, 1799), is complete with a prose dedication to Henry Wriothesley, the young earl of Southampton, and is signed by "William Shakespeare," in what turned out to be his most popular printed work during his lifetime (*Riverside*, 1798). In 1594, he followed with *The Rape of Lucrece*, a 1,855-line poem also in the genre of minor epic, again prefaced by a dedication to Southampton, and signed "William Shakespeare," in what also became one of his most popular works printed during his lifetime. Accordingly, in 1599 William Jaggard tried to capitalize on Shakespeare's popularity by publishing a book of verse titled *The Passionate Pilgrim* with Shakespeare's name on the title page, a volume that includes some poems known to be by Shakespeare and some still unattributed poems that could be by him, especially a group on the myth of Venus and Adonis (Roe, ed., *Poems*, 1, 54–60). Shortly thereafter, in 1601 Shakespeare wrote the enigmatic sixty-seven-line philosophical poem, "The Phoenix and Turtle," as a special contribution to Robert Chester's *Love's Martyr*, for reasons to which we are still not privy (Roe, ed., *Poems*, 1–2, 41–54). Even more enigmatically, in 1609 Thomas Thorpe published a work titled *Shake-speares Sonnets*, dedicated to one "Mr W. H.," in a volume that includes 152 Petrarchan sonnets, two Anacreontic sonnets, and the 329-line *Lover's Complaint* – with the first work in this collection, the Sonnets, today "regularly outsell[ing] everything else he wrote" (Evans, ed., *Sonnets*, 1).[2]

Contrary to popular opinion, the publication of Shakespeare's poems coincided throughout his career with the staging of his plays and even the printing of his plays in quartos (see Figure 3). Around 1600, Spenser's friend Gabriel Harvey intimates as much: "The younger sort take much delight in Shakespeare's Venus and Adonis; but his Lucrece, and his tragedy of Hamlet . . . have it in them to please the wiser sort" (*Shakspere Allusion-Book*, 1: 56). Harvey here divides Shakespeare's works not between poems and plays (the way modern editions of Shakespeare's works popularly do) but rather by audience appeal or moral effect. During Shakespeare's lifetime, Harvey appears quite comfortable conjoining one of Shakespeare's printed minor epics, *Lucrece*, with one of his stage tragedies, *Hamlet*, and in then seeing both works as opposed to another minor epic, *Venus*. The early

---

[2] In *Norton*, Cohen remarks that Shakespeare's "Various Poems" were "composed from the early 1590s *until shortly before Shakespeare's death*" (1991; emphasis added). These poems, some of which may or may not be by Shakespeare, include "Shall I die?" discovered by Gary Taylor (see S. Wells, *Life* 31, 126–27); "Verses upon the Stanley Tomb at Tong"; "On Ben Jonson"; "An Epitaph on Elias James"; two epitaphs on John Combe; "Upon the King"; and an "Epitaph on Himself." None of these poems bears significantly on the topic at hand, and so will not be discussed further.

Year	Plays	Poems
1593		Q1 *V & A*
1594	Q1 *Tit.*, Q1 *2H6*	Q1 *Luc.* Q2 *V & A*
1595	O1 *3H6*	O1 *V & A (?)*
1596	Q1 *E3*	O2 *V & A*
1597	Q1 *LLL*, Q1 *R2*, Q1 *R3*, Q1 *Rom.*	
1598	Q1, Q2 *1H4*, Q2 *LLL*, Q2, Q3 *R2*, Q2 *R3*	O1 *Luc.*
1599	Q2 *Rom.*, Q3 *1H4*, Q2 *E3*	O1, O2 *PP*, O3, O4 *V & A*,
1600	Q1 *H5*, Q *2H4*, Q1 *Ado*, Q1 *MND*, Q2 *2H6*, Q1 *3H6*, Q2 *Tit.*, Q1 *MV*	O2, O3 *Luc.*
1601		Q1 *Love's Martyr*
1602	Q1 *Wiv.*, Q3 *R3*, Q2 *H5*	O5 *V & A (?)*
1603	Q1 *Ham.*	
1604	Q2 *Ham.*, Q4 *1H4*	
1605	Q4 *R3*	
1606		
1607		O6 *V & A (?)*, O4 *Luc.*
1608	Q1 *Lr.*, Q4 *R2*, Q5 *1H4*	O7 *V & A (?)*
1609	Q1 *Tro.*, Q1, Q2 *Per.*, Q3 *Rom.*	Q *Son.*
1610		O8 *V & A (?)*
1611	Q3 *Tit.*, Q3 *Ham.*, Q3 *Per.*	Q2 *Love's Martyr* [*Britain's Annals*]
1612	Q3 *Tit.*, Q3 *Ham.*, Q3 *Per.*, Q5 *R3*	O3 *PP*
1613	Q6 *1H4*	
1614		
1615	Q5 *R2*	
1616		O5 *Luc.*
1617		O9 *V & A*
1618		
1619	Q3 *2H6*, Q2 *3H6*, Q4 *Per.*, Q2 *Wiv.*, Q2 *MV*, Q2 *Lr.*, Q3 *H5*, Q2 *MND*	
1620		O10 *V & A*
1621		
1622	Q1 *Oth.*, Q6 *R3*, Q7 *1H4*, Q1 *Rom. (?)*, Q4 *Ham. (?)*	
1623	F1	

Figure 3. Shakespeare's poems and plays in print 1593–1623.

Notes: The present book concentrates on the years 1593 to 1612.
All editions that advertise Shakespeare's authorship are underlined. When the title page contains Shakespeare's initials, dotted lines are used. Dotted lines also indicate works where there are two title pages (one of which contains Shakespeare's name) or an entire edition is lost.

modern critical mind appears to differ considerably from the scholarly mind today.

Shakespeare's major poetic works emerged in three primary printed installments. One installment occurs early in his writing career, between 1592 and 1594, when he composes and publishes *Venus* and *Lucrece*; one occurs in the middle, between 1599 and 1601, when others print poems on his behalf, sometimes to his dismay; and one occurs later, between 1600 and 1609, when he composes many of the Sonnets and *A Lover's Complaint* and witnesses their publication (with or without his consent; see chapters 7 and 8). Scholars even believe that Shakespeare worked on the Sonnets throughout his career: "several of the Sonnets are very likely to have been composed at the start of Shakespeare's career, and the whole sequence should be thought of as something approaching Shakespeare's life's work" (Burrow, "Life," 17). This provocative idea deserves pause, because it discovers Shakespeare's "life's work" not where we might expect it (in the plays) but in one of his "non-dramatic" works. Equally of note, Shakespeare's interest in narrative poetry spans the two halves of his career: his "concern with the writing of narrative poems did not abort with *Venus and Adonis* (1593) and *Lucrece* (1594) but extended through the time of *The Phoenix and Turtle* (1601) to within four years of the end of his career as a dramatist [through *A Lover's Complaint*]: he was occupied with writing non-dramatic poetry for a much longer time than we have imagined" (Hieatt, Bishop, and Nicholson, "Rare Words," 220). The repercussions of this idea are also worth pausing over, because it tries to get at an important yet neglected historical phenomenon.

Following up on such ideas, we might begin by looking into what would today seem to be a paradox at the core of Shakespeare's career: he is the consummate "man of the theatre" who simultaneously produces some of the most remarkable poems in the English language. While serving for nearly twenty-five years as a committed playwright, actor, and shareholder in the Lord Chamberlain's Men and later the King's Men, he maintains a second or shadow career in the art of poetry. How are we to explain this paradox?

Clearly, it could be no paradox to Harvey. Yet it has become one to many subsequent generations. Between the late seventeenth and the early twenty-first centuries, the prevailing historical explanation has been prone to look back at the poems through the lens of the plays. Relying on a posterior lens, scholars have approached the poems in one of three principal ways. First, they have largely neglected the poems, producing that overwhelming bulk of studies devoted exclusively to "Shakespearean drama." In this approach, Shakespeare is virtually equated with drama – his writing with theatre – so much so that his poems quickly lose their voice, as this from a recent catalogue published by a prestigious university press: "Shakespeare was essentially a man of the theater who intended his words to be spoken and acted out on stage. It is in this context of dramatic realization that his plays are best understood and experienced."[3] Much recent criticism and textual scholarship emphasizes the *constructedness* of "Shakespeare," including the texts we read and perform, but rarely does it acknowledge that the situation is more complicated than we might imagine: the "Shakespeare" that scholarship constructs for the world-audience today is fundamentally a "dramatic" Shakespeare.

In a 1986 essay strategically printed in Stanley Wells, edition of *The Cambridge Companion to Shakespeare Studies*, Harry Levin helps us to understand the profession-wide energy required to produce this modern version of Shakespeare, when announcing the successful completion of the twentieth-century project: "Our century . . . has restored our perception of him to *his genre, the drama*, enhanced by increasing historical knowledge alongside the live tradition of the performing arts" (228; emphasis added). In announcing the success of this restoration project, Levin is responding to what he considers an earlier phase of modern Shakespeare criticism (the actual topic of his essay): the Restoration, Augustan, Romantic, and Victorian reduction of Shakespeare's performative genre to "Dramatick Poesy."[4] If critics from the late seventeenth century through the nineteenth tended to read Shakespearean drama as poetry (while largely neglecting the poems themselves), critics in the twentieth century finally succeeded in detaching Shakespearean drama from poetry, preferring to view it purely as theatre. During the thundering applause, the poems could find little room, if any. Indeed, the *dramatic, performative* model of Shakespeare as a "man of the theatre" has recently been institutionalized in *The Norton Shakespeare: Based on the Oxford Edition*, where the most influential critic of his generation,

---

[3] *Cambridge Shakespeare* (Cambridge UP, 1999). Cambridge University Press has just published Erne's *Literary Dramatist*, which argues that Shakespeare was not simply a playwright who wrote theatrical texts for the stage but also a literary dramatist who produced reading texts for the page. Several recent books take up the cue of Berger, *Imaginary Audition*, to combat or sometimes complement performance criticism: Duncan-Jones, *Ungentle*; Bruster, *Quoting Shakespeare*; Bednarz, *Poets' War*; Freinkel, *Shakespeare's Will*; S. Roberts, *Reading Shakespeare's Poems*; Hyland, *Introduction*; Schalkwyk, *Performance*.

[4] Dryden, reprinted B. Vickers, ed. *Critical Heritage*, 1: 136. Evidently, this first phase does extend into the twentieth century, since Mullaney for one reports that he has been "trained . . . to regard plays as poems, and drama as . . . a literary phenomenon" (6–7).

Stephen Greenblatt, opens his General Introduction by speaking of "Shake-speare the working dramatist."[5]

Occasionally, scholars following this first approach do acknowledge the poems, but almost always they see *Venus*, *Lucrece*, and the Sonnets as the product of forced circumstance: the exigencies of time and the misfor-tunes of chance compelled Shakespeare to become something that he was not.[6] The most famous specific version of this approach has become one of the most stubborn yet unexamined staples of Shakespearean biography, endlessly repeated yet rarely pursued: Shakespeare wrote *Venus*, *Lucrece*, and a draft of the Sonnets because the theatres closed due to plague in 1592–93.[7] As we shall see, the story behind Shakespeare's poems is more complicated than this popular formulation allows. Biographers have been content simply to approach Shakespeare's writing of poetry during the plague years in terms of a principle of authorial intention. They thereby have neglected not so much the recent contradiction of this principle, "social construction" (generally recognized now as equally simplistic), but even a more balanced principle that acknowledges both authorial inten-tion and social construction as contributing to the production of literary work.[8]

Like the first approach, the second one asserts Shakespeare's standing as a working dramatist, but it argues that Shakespeare came to London to be a poet. Scholars following this approach see the poems as the abandoned genesis of Shakespeare's career in the theatre, with the most detailed argu-ment coming from Gary Schmidgall in his 1990 study, *Shakespeare and the Poet's Life*: Shakespeare "cease[d] in his efforts to combine the professions of courting poet and dramatist, and turn[ed] more exclusively to the world of the theater" (1). Scholars who subscribe to this approach thus tend to view the poems as a "dramatic" apprenticeship – "a proto-sketch for . . . [the] drama" (Vendler, ed., *Art of Shakespeare's Sonnets*, 3) – so that "connections [among *Venus*, *Lucrece*, and the Sonnets] suggest . . . how this group of works came to be the foundation of the mythic form of the Tragic Equation as it appears in the mature plays" (Hughes, *Goddess of Complete Being*, 50). The most recent, authoritative statement comes from Frank Kermode, *Shake-speare's Language*, who reports that he is "writing against the current, since

[5] *Norton*, 1. The phrase "man of the theatre" comes from *Oxford*: "he was himself, supremely, a man of the theatre" (xxxvi).

[6] For Shakespeare as a "playwright and occasional poet," see Thomson, *Professional Career*, 106.

[7] For the commonplace, see McDonald, *Bedford Companion*, 15–16. For recent consolidation of such *plague theory*, see Duncan-Jones, *Ungentle*, 54–81.

[8] See Dubrow, "Twentieth-Century Shakespeare Criticism," *Riverside*, 38.

for many years now we have been urged to think of Shakespeare as above all a professional man of the theatre who was required to be a poet because in his time plays were mostly written in verse" (3): "it seems at least as reasonable to suggest that he arrived in London intending to make his way as a poet not of the theatre but of the page" (17).[9] Kermode's demonstration of Shakespeare's dramaturgy in *Titus Andronicus* as fundamentally that of a working poet imitating an Ovidian text (the Philomela story) is persuasive, but it does not explain why Shakespeare resurrects this same text twenty years later in *Cymbeline*. Finally, then, this second approach supports the first in its fundamental assumption of a Shakespearean dramatic paradigm, with the distinction that it gives to the poetry a primacy in the origin, structure, and motives of Shakespeare's professional career.

Both approaches, however, are fundamentally anachronistic, because they peer back at the few surviving poems through the overwhelming "genius" of some forty plays – a quite unnatural perspective to Harvey, to Shakespeare, and to their contemporaries. By putting history backward, these approaches posit a misleading set of nonhistorical relations between Shakespeare's poems and plays. Neglecting the coincidence of plays and poems throughout his career, they do not examine the simultaneity of cultural pressures and personal ambitions that together most likely produced the precise, peculiar contours of Shakespeare's actual career.[10]

The third approach has been by far the most valuable, for during the last few years an intrepid band of editors and critics has been searching for a more accurate classification of Shakespeare as an early modern author – one that accounts affirmatively for the presence of the poems. Recently, for instance, in his important Chatterton Lecture on Poetry, Colin Burrow assembles "facts" that "give strong grounds for putting the poems at the front of our thinking about Shakespeare, and perhaps even at the front of collected editions of his works. It also should prompt us to ask why we do not think of Shakespeare as primarily a non-dramatic poet" ("Life," 17).[11] The recent proliferation of editions of Shakespeare's poems, supported by a surge of important monographs and articles, has done much to put the poems back in the professional and even the public eye, with most of

---

[9] Earlier versions can be found in Cruttwell, *Shakespearean Moment*, 38; Hubler, ed., *Songs and Poems*, xii.

[10] De Grazia, *Verbatim*, argues that our Shakespeare is foundationally a late eighteenth-century construct of Malone; Stallybrass, "Sexing," argues that "Shakespeare is a central nineteenth-century author" (130).

[11] Others who have also been instrumental to the recuperation of the poems include Fineman, Kerrigan, Duncan-Jones, Dubrow, De Grazia, Roe, D. Kay, Cousins, S. Roberts, Hyland, and Schalkwyk (see works cited).

the effort arguing for the value, complexity, and relevance of the poems. While this third approach has been an important historical counter to the "dramatic" Shakespeare, it nonetheless joins the first two approaches in needlessly separating the poems from the plays and thus in removing the poems from their vital context within Shakespeare's professional career. Overwhelmingly, that is, the defenses, for all their intrinsic merit, appear in editions, books, and articles devoted exclusively to the poems; structurally, they end up reinforcing the very separation they resist.[12]

Consequently, the opening of the twenty-first century seems a ripe occasion to take the enterprise one step further, to its next Hegelian step: to probe the precise equation of poems to plays in Shakespeare's career, and to do so by recalling the original historical moment in which this equation emerged. As indicated previously, however, the vastness of the topic has necessitated an originally unforeseen design feature: the use of the poems to specify the larger argument about Shakespeare's standing as an author of both poems and plays. Space and time warrant this decision, but further justification comes from the structural principle, employed throughout, of attempting to embed the poems in the context of Shakespeare's dramatic practice; from the need of a full study of the poems along these lines, including analysis of both poetry and theatre in the discourse of the text; and from the critic's plan to follow up with a volume devoted to the plays. One advantage to concentrating on the poems here is to enter this part of the corpus more centrally into the ongoing conversation about Shakespeare and nationalism.

EARLY MODERN "PLAYS AND RHYMES"

Rather than attempting to sever the poems from the plays, or seeing Shakespeare initially as a poet but finally as a playwright, or viewing his poems anachronistically through the lens of the drama, we might peer through what is best characterized as an anterior lens. This lens follows the twin arts of Shakespeare's production – both poems and plays – as they originate in antiquity, migrate through the Middle Ages, and enter early modern Europe in the 1590s.[13]

---

[12] The notable exception is Schalkwyk, *Performance*, which has just appeared.

[13] Cf. Bristol, *Big Time Shakespeare*, who identifies "two different and in some sense fundamentally opposed forms of production [in Shakespeare's career]: theatrical performances and printed books" (30). The printed books he has in mind tend to be plays, so he says little about Shakespeare's poems (cf., e.g., 3–4). Nonetheless, Bristol's chapter on the theatre and the print shop (30–58) sketches out the social, political, and economic context within which we might situate Shakespeare's works.

The intertwined-production of these two arts does not trace to the Greek dramatists but to the Greek poets, Homer and Hesiod; it includes the Greek dramatists, but it insists on the combination of poems and plays especially in classical Rome (Virgil as well as Seneca, Horace as well as Plautus). This double-production emphasizes the closing of the Western theatre in late antiquity and the subsequent authorizing of a largely poetic profession during the late Middle Ages, most famously articulated in its leading writers, none of whom specialized in the writing of plays: Dante, Jean de Meun, Chaucer, Petrarch, Boccaccio.[14] While acknowledging the survival of the theatrical tradition in the medieval plays (mystery, miracle, morality), the double-production I follow emphasizes the rupture of the mainstream medieval poetic profession by that decisive dramatic event of the 1560s and 70s: the re-opening of the commercial public theatres in England and Spain (see Cohen, *Drama*,). This rupture joins another, the sixteenth-century consolidation of the printing press, to play a decisive role in the birth of a new Western author who is both a poet and a playwright. The new historical model that I propose witnesses the formation of a distinct sixteenth-century phenomenon neglected in modern scholarship: the emergence around Europe – in England, Italy, France, Spain, and elsewhere – of a new type of author who pens both poems and plays as part of a single literary career: an author we might call a poet-playwright.[15]

By "poet," I mean simply a writer of poems; by "playwright," I mean simply a writer of plays. In distinguishing between poet and playwright, I am introducing terms that Shakespeare may not himself use. He and his colleagues are more likely to use the term "poet" to designate the writer of both poems and plays; they frequently call a play "a poem," as Polonius does when he speaks of theatre as a "poem unlimited" (*Hamlet*, 2. 2. 399–400); and they are more likely to emphasize another distinction: between the writer of a play and the actor of a play, as Hamlet does when he speaks about "the poet and the player" going "to cuffs in the question" of "money" during the allusion to the War of the Theatres (2. 2. 354–55).[16] Perhaps Shakespeare

---

[14] Petrarch did write one play (Germaine Warkentin, personal communication, 23 March 1999). William J. Kennedy says that Petrarch "did fess up to having written a Latin comedy at Avignon in his 20's, sometime between his return there from the university at Bologna (1326) and his first trip to Italy (1336). It was called *Philologia*, but it is now lost. We know about it from a letter . . . in Aldo Bernardo's translation of the *Familiares* 7.16" (personal communication, 15 January 2003).

[15] Critics use the term "poet-playwright" to talk about the playwright as a poet; see Goddard, *Meaning*, I: 55–67; Bloom, *Shakespeare*, 720; Dutton, *Licensing*, III. In a brief statement, Wilbern, *Poetic Will*, comes closest to my model of Shakespearean authorship (94).

[16] See Bednarz, *Poets' War*. Cf. Maguire, who distinguishes between poem and play within drama itself, relying on Webster's preface to *The Duchess of Malfi* (155); and Weimann, who concentrates on writing and playing in Shakespeare's plays (see esp. 61).

would have been unwilling to distinguish between the writer of poems and of plays for many of the same reasons that critics today are: he writes much of his drama in verse, thereby automatically rendering plays "poetical" (to borrow a term from Viola in disguise as Cesario [*Twelfth Night*, 1. 5. 195]); he even enfolds about 130 songs into his plays, some of them original, some borrowed; and he lends to his poems a corresponding "theatrical" mode, as in the opening to Sonnet 23, when Will imagines himself "As an unperfect actor on the stage, / Who with his fear is put besides his part" (1–2; see chapter 7).[17]

Perhaps the line of investigation I am outlining has escaped notice because we have been too unwilling to see Shakespeare's writing career as a historically important ratio between poems and plays – or, to borrow Thomas Dekker's phrase for Ben Jonson's compound production, "Plays and Rhymes" (*Satiromastix*, 5. 2. 292; quoted in Bednarz, *Poets' War*, 216). Admittedly, the ratio in Shakespeare is balanced in favor of plays, but it does not follow that we should erase the poems or the idea of a ratio altogether. If we do, we efface a literary history that plots Shakespeare along a continuum featuring such important contemporary rivals as Marlowe and Jonson, both of whom produced canons with more balanced ratios, with Jonson even printing his poems alongside his plays in the folio edition of his works the year Shakespeare died (*Works*). In the present book, the intent is not to argue that Shakespeare wrote more poems than plays, or to assert that his poems are more important than his plays, or even to claim that we should give poetic credit where poetic credit is due. Rather, the intent is to plot Shakespeare historically, in his own contemporary moment, as a writer of his time producing both poems and plays for complex cultural reasons, and then to express as accurately as possible this particular version of the Shakespearean factor. The aim, in other words, is not to deny Shakespeare's standing as a "man of the theatre" but to *complete* it: he is a supreme theatrical man who wrote poems of matchless value, for his time as for ours.[18]

Once we re-classify Shakespeare in this compound form, we are free to distinguish between Shakespeare's poems and plays while simultaneously

---

[17] Thus, I use *poetical* primarily to refer to the mode and form of Shakespeare's poems, and *theatrical* to refer to the mode and form of his plays. In no way do I wish to deny the "theatrical" quality of the poems or the "poetic" quality of the plays, but recall that these qualities are much discussed elsewhere.

[18] Shakespeare's work in the theatre and in print culture is not all of a piece (see Dutton, *Licensing*, 110–11). Moreover, there are larger institutional reasons for the divide today between "poetry" and "drama," since critics tend to specialize in one or the other, supported by various rubrics of the Modern Language Association, as well as by university curricula and other institutions and practices.

seeing poetry and theatre as an intellectual dyad vital to his signature as an author. This critical operation has a long tradition. The *locus classicus* remains the *Republic*, wherein Plato writes,

there is one kind of poetry and taletelling which works wholly through imitation . . . tragedy and comedy, and another which employs the recital of the poet himself, best exemplified, I presume, in the dithyramb, and there is again that which employs both, in epic poetry. (*Republic*, 3. 394c)

Here Plato divides literature into three "kinds": drama, which itself divides into tragedy and comedy; the dithyramb, which today corresponds to lyric poetry; and epic poetry. To distinguish among the three kinds (two of which are "poetic," one "dramatic"), Plato relies on the principle of narrative technique or voice: drama works through imitation of an action or mimesis; lyric poetry works through the poet's "recital" of his own (first-person) voice; and epic poetry combines the two. Poetry and drama are distinct kinds yet simultaneously interlocked: separate yet alike. Hence, in the *Poetics* Aristotle can distinguish between "Epic Poetry" and "Tragedy" in terms of their objects of imitation, privileging the latter over the former, yet simultaneously viewing them as twin forms "imitat[ing] . . . serious subjects in a grand kind of verse" (1449b. 9–11). By calling Shakespeare a poet-playwright, then, I am constructing a critical abbreviation, necessary in today's critical climate, for distinguishing between Shakespeare's poems and plays, for classifying his career dyad as a signature achievement, and for taking the cue of critics such as Burrow to put the poems at the "front" of our thinking about Shakespeare the working dramatist.

The primary purpose of this book, then, is to argue that we can most accurately historicize Shakespeare's achievement as an early modern author – and more satisfactorily account for the presence of both poems and plays in his writing production – by attending to the historical model of the newly emergent European poet-playwright as it enters sixteenth-century England. As we shall see, Shakespeare's generation was the very first to consolidate this new type of author, when it capitalizes upon a complex cultural dynamic that includes the emergence of both a print and a theatre culture.[19]

---

[19] On the sixteenth-century emergence of print culture, see especially Marotti, *Manuscript, Print*; Wall, *Imprint*. On Shakespeare, see de Grazia and Stallybrass, "Materiality."

THE OVIDIAN POET-PLAYWRIGHT

The new European poet-playwright is a reinvention of an older or Roman writer, and for Shakespeare's contemporaries this writer traces to the author traditionally glossed as "the poet" of the Orpheus story rehearsed by Lorenzo to Jessica in *Merchant*: Ovid. Studies of "Shakespeare's favorite poet" (*Riverside*, 1797) have been so numerous during the past hundred years that one can proceed here only with trepidation. Ovid is indeed "the poet" of "Shakespeare's favorite book," the *Metamorphoses* (McDonald, *Bedford Companion*, 160); but Ovid is also the poet of several other poems, especially the *Ars amatoria* and the *Heroides*, referred to and quoted from as early as *Two Gentlemen*, as well as the poet of the *Amores*, which Shakespeare quoted for his epigraph to *Venus and Adonis*. Yet Ovid was not merely a poet who wrote poems; he was also a dramatist, the author of *Medea*, a tragedy that is extant in two lines, that was famed in antiquity as the measure of Ovid's true genius, and that was known at least since the Renaissance to be the principal origin of Seneca's *Medea* (chapter 2). This last idea is important, because it suggests how naturally Shakespeare's contemporaries could "Ovidianize" the sixteenth-century Senecan movement so important to Elizabethan tragedy. Accordingly, Renaissance writers from Angelo Poliziano to Jonson identified Ovid as more than the author of erotic elegy or national epic; for them, he is also the author of dramatic tragedy. Thus, Poliziano includes the *Medea* in his inventory of Ovid's career, while Jonson opens *Poetaster* by presenting Ovid as the author of both *Amores*, 1. 15 and *Medea* (chapter 2). This "Ovid" – the poet and playwright, the author of light erotic verse and high tragedy – contributes a missing chapter to the story of the "Renaissance Ovid" and specifically of "Shakespeare and the Renaissance Ovid" (*pace* Bate, *Ovid*, 1–47).

I hypothesize that humanist scholars working on the recovery of classical learning during the European Renaissance became interested in Ovid the poet-playwright. Recurrently for them, he functions as a primary source of information on the Roman theatre – more widely cited than Horace – and nowhere better on display than in Thomas Heywood's 1612 *Apology for Actors*, which lionizes the light Ovid rather than the heavy Seneca as the great tragedian. That Renaissance writers believed Ovid to have actually written a tragedy could only have lent credibility to the authenticity of his theatrical knowledge in such works as the *Ars amatoria*.

Further research on the role of this Ovid needs to be done, especially in the countless arcane Latin texts of humanists around Europe.[20] But initial research allows us to hypothesize that Ovid could be seen to function as a primary classical model for the new early modern author who pens both plays and poems – certainly for Shakespeare, but also for such disparate European authors as Marlowe in England, Tasso in Italy, Marguerite de Navarre in France, and Cervantes in Spain, all of whom combine poetry and drama within a single writing career.[21] In the wide gap of time, such a phenomenon, exhibited in so many authors over such a large geographical space, had never been witnessed, not even in antiquity, where its appearance was merely intermittent and today sadly fragmented, initially in Ovid's two great predecessors, Livius Andronicus and Ennius (Farrell, "Careers"; see chapter 2). Historians and literary historians have yet to identify the sixteenth-century Ovidian poet-playwright as a salient contribution of the Renaissance as a period concept (cf. Burckhardt, *Civilization*; W. Kerrigan and Braden, *Idea*; and Burrow, "Sixteenth Century").

"SCALD RHYMERS" AND "QUICK COMEDIANS"

Evidence from within Shakespeare's works suggests a secondary purpose to the present book: to examine Shakespeare's poems and plays for his own idiosyncratic register of the relation between the two literary forms, between poetry and theatre, and between the poet and the playwright. In general, we shall discover that he inscribes the poetry-theatre dyad in his ingrained thinking process, and in the myriad-minded way that Coleridge for one has long led us to expect. Consequently, we can extend more recent work (of Joel Fineman, "Shakespeare's Will," for instance) in looking into Shakespeare's language for evidence of his authorial "signature."

Shakespeare inscribes the poetry-theatre dyad most simply in single utterances within a work, as this encrusted deep in the discourse of *Antony and Cleopatra*, spoken by the Eastern Star herself, angry yet poised near the sign of her total eclipse:

---

[20] Cf. the several recent books on Ovid in the Renaissance, which tend to focus on the body, subjectivity, and so forth and do so usually with reference to the *Metamorphoses*: Stapleton, *Harmful* (which alone is on the *Amores*); Enterline; Lyne; A.B. Taylor, ed.; Stanivukovic, ed. By contrast, classicists are now viewing Ovid as an author along the lines laid out in Cheney, *Profession*; see Hardie, ed., *Cambridge Companion*, Hardie's introduction, and S. Harrison, "Ovid and Genre."

[21] This is not to say that such authors self-consciously modeled themselves on Ovid. In this group, I am confident only that Marlowe did.

> scald rhymers [will]
> Ballad 's out a' tune. The quick comedians
> Extemporally will stage us, and present
> Our Alexandrian revels: Antony
> Shall be brought drunken forth, and I shall see
> Some squeaking Cleopatra boy my greatness
> I' th' posture of a whore.
> (*Antony and Cleopatra*, 5. 2. 215–21)

Recent criticism has made a good deal of the splendid metadrama concluding the utterance, but typically it effaces the curious conjunction with metapoetry.[22] Cleopatra imagines her literary afterlife with Antony back in Rome, and she divides their joint representation into two forms of persecution: ballads and comedies; verse and drama. What is noteworthy in Cleopatra's utterance is the white space between the "scald rhymers" and the "quick comedians": there is no transition, for there is no need of one. The Eastern Star appears to fear each, for both are modes of public discourse that she considers dangerous to the representation of her dignity and the exhibition of her integrity.[23] While Cleopatra may fear the "quick comedians" more than the "scald rhymers," as the overbalanced ratio of discourse between the two forms implies, we would not be wise to forget that her discourse does record a ratio. Perhaps the discourse should compel us to look again at the play as a whole. Once we do, we may re-imagine Shakespeare's complete professional discourse as voicing an intriguing ratio between the more famous discourse of theatre and a less-noted discourse of poetry: "Hoo, hearts, tongues, [figures], scribes, bards, poets, cannot / Think, speak, cast, write, sing, number, hoo," thunders Enobarus (3. 2. 16–17). The "story" that he and others in this play are so self-conscious to "earn" a "place" in (3. 13. 46) is surely history itself, but also both drama and the "number" of the "poet."

Poets, bards, scribes, rhymers / number, sing, write, ballad: there is a lexicon here, and we need to see it jostling with the lexicon of those quick comedians who boy the greatness of Roman history's greatest queen. In particular, Cleopatra's fear of the scald rhymers singing their ballads turns out to

---

[22] See, e.g., Sprengnether, "Boy Actor"; Cook, "Fatal Cleopatra," 245–46. Schmidgall ends his book by discussing this passage but he neglects the "scald rhymers" (*Poet's Life*, 202).

[23] Cleopatra also fears "Saucy lectors," who will "catch" at her and Antony "like strumpets" (214–15), but she evidently puts the lawyers in the audience of her imagined spectacle. Cf. Nashe, *Pierce Penilesse* (in McKerrow, *Thomas Nashe*, 1: 197). Sir Thomas Hoby calls *The Song of Songs* a "book of ballats" (Rollins and Baker, eds., *Renaissance in England*, 534), suggesting that a ballad can mean more than the popular definition afforded by the *Oxford English Dictionary*.

haunt the Shakespearean dramatic corpus as a whole, and well it should, since recent scholarship emphasizes not simply the distinction between plays and ballads but their absolute interpenetration (see Maguire, *Suspect Texts*, 122). While the performative similarities help explain the recurrent presence of ballads and songs within Shakespearean drama, we also need to distinguish between them. On the one hand, ballads can be seen to perform a synecdochic role as theatre, but on the other they sound a synecdochic voice as poetic song.[24]

This last principle is important. Unless there is good reason not to do so, I shall take the texts' own cues to interpret song in Shakespeare as a form and metaphor for lyric poetry. There is critical, textual, and bibliographical warrant for doing so. Among critics, Heather Dubrow emphasizes the intimacy between song and lyric, music and poetry, during the sixteenth century: "connections between the Renaissance lyric and courtly music clarify debates about the workings of lyric in general, reminding us that in some important instances it is indeed linked with song – and, more significantly, linked as well with performance and courtly ritual" ("Lyric," 186). Indeed, the Shakespeare canon entreats us to see the intimacy of lyric and song that Dubrow articulates, making it a short step to seeing song as itself a form of lyric, as Spenser's glossarist E. K. does when foregrounding the concept of authorship for the poet-musician Colin Clout, who recites "a proper song, whereof [he] . . . was Author" (*August*, Arg.), the words "song" and "Author" here only appearing to be in opposition.[25] Luckily, Shakespeare makes the step himself; periodically, he represents an artistic process by which poetry turns into song. In *Twelfth Night*, for instance, he can be seen to represent the primary example of the courtly poet-musician to which Dubrow refers, when Feste sings lines from "an old song, a version of which is attributed to Sir Thomas Wyatt" (*Riverside*, 468): "Hey, Robin, jolly Robin" (4. 2. 72). Is this simply a song in a play, or a song recorded from a printed poem for rehearsal in a staged play, which itself we read in a printed work?

Earlier, Viola in disguise self-consciously echoes a Spenserian Orphic tradition of the pastoral "green cabinet," when she tells Olivia that if she herself were in love, she would

---

[24] Cf. Freinkel, *Shakespeare's Will*: "the lyric . . . [as] irreducibly theatrical" (70) is not early modern but Romantic and New Critical (71).

[25] The poet as a musician-singer is an Elizabethan convention, employed famously by Spenser to open his Virgilian career (*Calender*, "To His Booke," 8–9). For an "Ovidian" origin to the link between song and written poetry, see Enterline, *Rhetoric*, 188–97.

> Make me a willow cabin at your gate,
> And call upon my soul within the house;
> Write loyal cantons of contemned love,
> And sing them loud even in the dead of night;
> Hallow your name to the reverberate hills,
> And make the babbling gossip of the air
> To cry out "Olivia!"[26]
>
> (*Twelfth Night*, 1. 5. 268–74)

The details of Viola/Cesario's artistic process are precise (leaving aside here the comical tones and the homoerotic undertones). Note, for instance, the generic indicators; since the site of her imagined desire appears right on the divide between "willow cabin" and "house," she (or is it he?) moves the pastoral locus amoenus close to the epic domain, here the court world. Making her wood cabin at Olivia's "gate," she would miraculously "call upon" her own "soul within the house" – a considerable daemonic maneuver, it would seem. During the day, she would write a faithful canto of unrequited love, and then during the night she would sing her composition aloud, echoing Olivia's sacred name back to the pastoral hills. Viewed strictly as a representation of authorship, this is astonishing, not least because it so cleverly shows the harmony between "house" and "hills," court and country, epic and pastoral. Yet there is more. Shakespeare's own echoing of Spenser here reinforces the representation of poetry as an art form, even as the poetry conjoins subtly through transposition back with theatre during performance, rendered self-consciously again, for Viola plays before Olivia the part of Cesario.[27] Indeed, in nearly every work, poems as well as plays, Shakespeare inserts such compelling representations conjoining a discourse of poetry with a discourse of theatre.

Furthermore, recent work permits us to see a bibliographical rationale. Once we grant that Shakespeare wrote theatrical texts for the stage and reading texts for the page (Erne, *Literary Dramatist*), we can suggest that Shakespearean song in the plays more pristinely functions as lyric poetry in the printed versions of the text. When we read Shakespeare's songs on the page of the book, we experience song as lyric poetry: we literally see song laid out on the page as lyric; we read it as a textually marked off lyric unit.

---

[26] For Spenser's self-presentation as Colin Clout singing a "rurall song" in the "greene cabinet," see *December*, 17–18. For the green cabinet as "the *locus amoenus* of Greek pastoral poetry," see Rosenmeyer, *The Green Cabinet*, vii. For the Orphic dimension of Spenser's self-presentation, see Cheney, *Flight*, 23–76.

[27] Cf *Two Gentlemen*, 1. 2. 76–77. On the "tension . . . between lyric and dramatic" in drama of the period, see Bruster, *Quoting Shakespeare*, 56, 75–76; D. Henderson, *Passion Made Public*.

While it might be difficult to see song as lyric on the stage, it is perfectly natural to read song as lyric in the text. In fact, we might venture to say that readers do not experience song in the printed texts as anything other than lyric poem.

   Thus, it is a special discovery that many of Shakespeare's cherished characters resemble the authorial poet-playwright himself. Recurrently, they turn to song and disguise, poetry and theatre, to transact their comical, historical, tragical, or romantic plots. Hamlet is *not* "the English Renaissance's greatest tribute to the theatrical man" (Helgerson, *Laureates*, 159); rather, he is the English Renaissance's greatest tribute to the poet-playwright. Certainly Hamlet writes "some dozen or sixteen lines" (2. 2. 541–42) for *The Mousetrap*, but he also writes a love poem to Ophelia (2. 2. 116–19), and he typically complicates his famous discourse on the theatre with references to such poetic genres as the epitaph. In fact, it is remarkable to discover just how many characters resembling the poet-playwright people Shakespearean drama, in all four genres, from the beginning to the end of his career. The most significant include Joan of Arc in the first tetralogy; the collectivity of the four courtiers in *Love's Labor's Lost*; Bottom, Puck, and Oberon in *A Midsummer Night's Dream*; the bastard Faulconbridge in *King John*; Iago in *Othello*; Falstaff in his several plays, but especially *The Merry Wives of Windsor*; Benedick in *Much Ado about Nothing*; Viola and Feste in *Twelfth Night*; the Duke in *Measure for Measure*; Edgar and the Fool in *King Lear*; Autolycus in *The Winter's Tale*; and Prospero and Ariel in *The Tempest*. Throughout Shakespeare's works, we can indeed discern a recurrent fiction about the making of the new Ovidian poet-playwright in England. To my knowledge, the story of this fiction has never been told. The evidence of the works themselves suggests not simply that Shakespeare was a poet-playwright but also that he was deeply self-conscious about being one.[28]

   Generally speaking, in the history plays, the tragedies, and all of the major poems, Shakespeare represents ambivalence about the prospect of combining two careers and arts into one. In the comedies and romances, however, he appears more playful and detached, as perhaps we should expect. Throughout, we can observe the progress of the poet-playwright representation, through the poems and each of the four dramatic genres, from the early part of his career to the later part. While genre clearly affects all of the representations in important ways, the major inference to be

---

[28] This does not argue that Shakespeare intended to be an Ovidian poet-playwright, only that his works register a conflict between the two forms and roles.

drawn comes to this: early on, Shakespeare appears to have discovered the cultural importance of the Elizabethan competition between poetry and theatre, and thereby he made the two media the primary modes for his characters' thought, speech, and behavior. In Shakespearean art, poetry and theatre become primary expressions of identity, the principal forms of subjectivity, and thus the basic grid for one of the major dominants in the canon: the relation between "inner" and "outer."

For instance, in an earlier scene from *Twelfth Night*, Shakespeare alerts us to this important relation, at the same time that he shows us the genesis of Viola's interest in song and disguise. Here she is, first broaching her collaborative art to a new friend:

> There is a fair behavior in thee, captain,
> And though that nature with a beauteous wall
> Doth oft close in pollution, yet of thee
> I will believe thou hast a mind that suits
> With this thy fair and outward character.
> I prithee (and I'll pay thee bounteously)
> Conceal me what I am, and be my aid
> For such disguise as haply shall become
> The form of my intent. I'll serve this duke;
> Thou shalt present me as an eunuch to him,
> It may be worth thy pains; for I can sing
> And speak to him in many sorts of music
> That will allow me very worth his service.
> What else may hap, to time I will commit,
> Only shape thou thy silence to my wit.
> (*Twelfth Night*, 1. 2. 47–61)

In this remarkable speech, we catch Viola in the process of gauging the Captain's trust. She is reading him, and making judgments about his "character." This turns out to be crucial, because here an individual deploys Shakespeare's characteristic paradigm of *inward* and *outward* to seal the bond of faith so vital to a human relationship. Clearly, this is what Shakespeare wants his audience to see.

Viola begins the process of perception by noting the "beauteous wall" or material reality of the Captain's physical "nature" – what she terms his "fair behavior." Acknowledging the grim probability for such physical beauty to "close in pollution," she thus takes a real risk in her sudden leap of faith, choosing to "believe" that the Captain "hast a mind that suits" his "fair and outward character." *Suits* is an exquisite pun, detectable perhaps mainly to the (re-)reader or to those who have come across it elsewhere (*A Lover's*

Complaint, 79; chapter 8). Viola's leap of faith leads her literally to *dress* the Captain's "mind" – his inwardness – in the beauty of his "character" – his "outward[ness]." In him, she discerns a perfect *fit* between inner and outer beauty, mind and behavior, intellect and morality, psychology and ethics. The pun, however, turns out to be structural, for it leads Viola to the first part of her plan and request: to have the Captain "Conceal" her in a "disguise" in order to help her "become / The form of . . . [her] intent": to fulfill her purpose – "serve this duke." In her thought-process, that is, Viola establishes a connection between her own belief in the "suit" between the Captain's physical and moral beauty, on the one hand, and her strategy of service, on the other. On the surface, Viola's plans for deceptively disguising her own "nature" contrast with the evident probability for hypocrisy that in the Captain's case she wisely over-rules. She puts a personal technique of character-reading to work on the other, and then she reverses that technique with respect to the self.

Since a female is to disguise herself as a male to serve another male, the representation of subjectivity and identity quickly shifts into a gender register. Viola makes this explicit in her plan to disguise herself as "an eunuch." Not simply does she cross-dress her gender, but she then castrates her (performed) male sexual identity and relocates her power a bit higher up in her physiognomy, in her tongue and voice: "I can sing / And speak to him in many sorts of music." The gloss in the *Riverside Shakespeare* is conventional but hardly satisfying: "i.e. as a *castrato* or male soprano singer; thus her high voice will not be incongruous with her male disguise" (443). While Viola may select the disguise of a eunuch to "Conceal" the feminine nature of her high-pitched voice, Shakespeare is careful to show Viola as a strange hermaphroditic figure in the dual role of one who can "sing / And speak" in more than one form of "music." She will both sing songs to Orsino and perform a role before him in order to carry out her plan to survive on foreign soil after her unfortunate shipwreck. Viola concludes her speech when she requests the Captain to "shape" his "silence" to her "wit" – in yet a third application of her principle of correspondence, the suiting of outer to inner. Later, Viola will stage this theatre of song before the Duke's beloved, Olivia, writing and singing loyal cantons of contemned love, in what becomes one of the most recurrent representations of authorship in Shakespeare.

Shakespeare's use of disguise, costume change, and role-playing as a form of "metatheater" – "the study of how drama comments on itself" (Dubrow, "Twentieth-Century Shakespeare Criticism," *Riverside*, 41) – no longer needs much explanation, since it has been a regular feature of Shakespeare criticism from the 1960s forward (see, e.g., Righter, *Idea of the Play*) to the present day, including in the influential work of Stephen Greenblatt, and most famously in his essay on the Henriad, "Invisible Bullets" (*Negotiations*, 46–47, 64–65). One way to re-envision Shakespeare's sustained metadrama is to see it recurrently conjoined with a less discussed topic, his recurrent metapoetry.[29] Just as we shall frequently see song as metapoesis (when the text warrants it), so we shall see disguise, costume change, and role-playing as metatheatre (again, when the text warrants it).[30] In *Twelfth Night*, it is Sir Andrew Aguecheeck who first alerts us to this conjunction as performed by the great comedic figure who gets the play's final word, the clown Feste, who turns out to be the most important representation of the poet-playwright figure in *Twelfth Night*. "I had rather than forty shillings I had such a leg," says Sir Andrew,

and so sweet a breath to sing, as the fool has. In sooth, thou wast in very gracious fooling last night, when thou spok'st of Pigrogromitus, of the Vapians passing the equinoctial of Queubus . . . Excellent! Why, this is the best fooling, when all is done. Now a song. (*Twelfth Night*, 2. 3. 20–30)

As Sir Andrew reveals, Feste turns from his theatrical "fooling" to the singing of his first "song," the "love-song" (35) "O mistress mine, where are you roaming" (39–52). This clearly structured progression recurs in many variations throughout the Shakespearean dramatic corpus.

   Yet, as Park Honan allows us to see, Shakespeare's representation of song and fooling, poetry and theatre, or the poet-playwright figure, is not static during Shakespeare's career but intricately dynamic; it changes over time, due to certain exigencies that sometimes we can trace, sometimes not. For instance, Honan suggests that Act 4 of *Love's Labor's Lost* "seems to point Shakespeare away from a dramatic career and towards a lyric poet's one" (*Life*, 167), and he situates the change in terms of the early 1590s plague that closed the theatres and Robert Greene's famous attack on the upstart crow, which prompted Shakespeare's shame about his status as an "actor-poet," discussed in Sonnets 110–12 (161), and which prompted his turn to the publication of *Venus* and *Lucrece*. Perhaps more than any play in Shakespeare's corpus, *Love's Labor's Lost* takes as its topic the relation between lyric poetry and staged theatre, but it is important to recall that specific events may lie behind the representation. By contrast, *The Comedy*

---

[29] On poetry and the poems in Shakespeare's plays, see Hyland, *Introduction to Shakespeare's Poems*, 35–41; Schmidgall, *Poet's Life*, 123–60; Faas, *Poetics*; Schalkwyk, *Performance*.

[30] The text does not warrant seeing every representation of music as poetry; sometimes Shakespeare means music; see *Richard II* 5. 5. 41–66.

of Errors, which Shakespeare probably composed before the 1592–93 plague, is the only play in his canon that has no substantive representation of the dyad, concentrating as it does on the exuberance of Plautine theatre – an anomaly so puzzling it begs attention (although, alas, not here). *Richard III*, written just before the theatres closed, includes the dyad, but tends to split it up, introducing Richard as a man of the theatre but reserving the discourse of poetry for his brother, Clarence.[31] The switch from *The Comedy of Errors* to *Richard III* to *Love's Labor's Lost* via *Venus* and *Lucrece* thus appears to constitute a phase of Shakespeare's career, recording his developing interest in the relation between poetry and theatre, the career of the print poet and that of the stage dramatist: "With *Venus and Adonis* and *Lucrece*, he made a strong bid to be recognized as a poet by refined society" (Honan, *Life*, 169).

Subsequently, Honan adds, Shakespeare's Sonnets "partly account for a new lyricism in his plays, and also for the more individuated verse that he uses to give depth to his dramatis personae, and so, especially, in the 1590s, for his stunning progress as a dramatist": the Sonnets become a "rehearsal time" for Shakespeare's "theatre of the mind" (185). Thus, in *Hamlet*, "the first great tragedy to be written in two thousand years" (275), Shakespeare used "sonnet-writing" to solve "what has been called the most taxing problem in writing a revenge tragedy, or how to fill in the long interval between the commission of the crime which calls for vengeance, and the carrying out of revenge in Act V" (281). Effectively, Shakespeare brings the sonnet to the stage in a large-scale way. Not simply a literary form to be spliced into the drama, as in *Love's Labor's Lost* (or more famously, *Romeo and Juliet*), the sonnet becomes a central space for rehearsing psychological turmoil (Schalkwyk, *Performance*). With rare exceptions, poetry and theatre are not separate enterprises in Shakespeare's career or art, to be cordoned off as occasion warrants; they are ongoing interpenetrations, from beginning to end.

A TYPOLOGY OF INTERTEXTUALITY: MARLOWE'S
OVID, SPENSER'S VIRGIL

If we look more closely into Shakespeare's representation of the poet-playwright, we discover another paradox, to which we have only alluded and in which we can locate a tertiary aim. Within both his dramatic and his poetic fictions, Shakespeare presents the figure of the Ovidian author

---

[31] In fact, 4. 4. 507 and 5. 3. 306 intimate that poetry finally becomes the theatrical Richard's enemy.

singing songs and performing plays along a Virgilian path connecting the pastoral world to the world of epic. We should expect this paradox to be at the core of any Ovidian art, since Ovid himself casts his erotic poems of seduction, metamorphosis, and complaint in order to de-authorize the imperial power of Virgil.[32] More specifically, Ovid counters the Virgilian progressive *cursus* of pastoral, georgic, and epic through a *cursus* of amorous poetry, tragedy, and epic. This Ovidian career path is what we might imagine, playfully complex in ways that Virgil's is not, since it proclaims to be progressive in its mature trajectory even while it confesses to youthful oscillation.[33] Within Ovid's counter-Virgilian career, his inaugural work, the *Amores*, is important because it presents the fiction of an Ovidian author trying to write elegy, tragedy, and epic in order to counter the tripartite career of Virgil (see 1. 1, 2. 1, 2. 18, 3. 1, 3. 15).

Shakespeare often structures his fictions on the famed classical opposition between an Ovidian poetics and a Virgilian one. Yet he manages this structure with an early modern principle that I term the typology of intertextuality. According to this principle, a writer uses a clear imitation of texts from a preceding literary system in order to veil and target his rivalry with colleagues from his own literary system.[34] Perhaps the clearest instance of this typology in the Shakespeare canon occurs in *The Merchant of Venice*, when Shylock speaks an aside during the trial scene of Act 4:

> These be the Christian husbands.
> I have a daughter –
> Would any of *the stock of Barrabas*
> Had been her husband rather than a Christian!
> (*Merchant of Venice*, 4. 1. 294–97; emphasis added)

Here is the gloss in the *Riverside Shakespeare*: "Barrabas" is "a criminal (whose name is properly spelled *Barabbas*) whom the Jews asked Pontius Pilate to release in preference to Jesus (see Mark 15: 6–15); also the villainous chief character (*Barabas*) of Marlowe's *Jew of Malta*" (312). Shakespeare's double-voice requires pause. In the fiction of the play, Shylock refers to the biblical Barabbas, but outside the fiction Shakespeare uses his character's

---

[32] Ovid's critique of Virgil is a commonplace; see Hardie, *Epic Successors*. W. R. Johnson calls the Ovidian principle of critique "counter-classicism" ("Counter-Classical"): "Where classical poetry [such as Virgil's or Spenser's] attempts affirmations of man's capacities . . . counter-classical poetry attempts to stress man's limitations" (126).

[33] The information in this paragraph and the next is indebted to Cheney, *Profession*, 19–25, 31–48, 49–67.

[34] See Cheney, *Profession*, 18–19, 272–73n36. The principle mediates Bloom's focus on a single strong poet misreading a strong precursor and Roland Barthes' focus on multiple anonymous traces.

biblical reference to refer to a famous character in a rival's play, on which his own play is so clearly based (see, e.g., Charney, "Jessica's Turquoise Ring"). The literary working of the typology of intertextuality is supported by three features in the passage. First, Shakespeare's speech occurs in a self-reflexive theatrical moment, when a character on the stage steps forward to address the audience. Second, as the continuation of the *Riverside* gloss indicates ("Here and in Marlowe the name is pronounced with main stress on the first syllable"), Shakespeare uses meter to move the biblical reference into a Marlovian allusion – a feature that would quite literally be *pronounced* in performance. Third, Shakespeare's witty phrase "stock of Barrabas" refers to those in the blood-line of criminal Jews, but simultaneously it alludes to those in the literary line of Marlowe's Jew, with Shylock himself standing in the front. In a passage about origin and succession, parent and child, Shakespeare uses Shylock's aside to process his own complicated relation with a literary rival.

Similarly, Shakespeare's recurrent allusions and references to Virgil and Ovid work not just to evoke past writers from a preceding literary system but specific writers from his own system. No doubt Shakespeare's imitative practice coheres with one that Douglas Bruster calls, borrowing a term from Lévi-Strauss, "*bricolage*" – a system of un-cited quotation from a large and often heterogeneous collection of works and forms of cultural media (*Quoting Shakespeare*, 22). Yet, as Bruster emphasizes, within the complex texture of quotation we can still trace threads from recognizable authors and texts. Bruster himself places this practice within a massive scholarly project that has worked long to identify various "sources" and resources for Shakespearean intertextuality. Since so much work has been done on a large number of early modern authors – e.g., Nashe, Sidney, Daniel, Drayton, Marston, Jonson, and Fletcher – the present book acknowledges the *bricolage* of Shakespearean "quotation" even as it attends to those authors most pertinent to the topic of English nationhood and Shakespeare's writing of it: the Ovidian Marlowe and the Virgilian Spenser.[35]

Spenser, the New Poet, was the Elizabethan leader in the fictional writing of nationhood, called by Nashe "the Virgil of England" (McKerrow, ed., *Thomas Nashe*, 1: 299). Yet Spenser was followed by a group of patriotic or

---

[35] Most readers would accept the classification of Marlowe as Ovidian. But increasingly scholars are emphasizing Spenser as Ovidian (e.g., Hulse, *Verse*, 242–78). Nonetheless, even though we today may see the Ovidian dynamic of Spenser's poetry, a rival like Marlowe stubbornly did not (Cheney, *Profession*, 15). Such a notion is a specific version of what Bloom calls "misprision" – the strong author's inevitable "misreading" of his precursor (*Anxiety*, 7, 5).

"laureate" poets, principally Daniel, Drayton, and Chapman – later, modeling himself on Horace, by Jonson (Helgerson, *Laureates*). It was in opposition to Spenser that Marlowe presented himself as the Ovid of England. Probably in the mid-1580s he produces the first complete translation of the *Amores* into any European vernacular language. Thereby, he makes the counter-Virgilian Ovidian career fiction available to English contemporaries. Marlowe translates the Ovidian *cursus* not simply to participate in the Renaissance recovering of classical texts, but more particularly to contest the national authority of England's Virgil. Not surprisingly, Marlowe imitates Ovid in penning both poems and plays: "The Passionate Shepherd to His Love" and *Tamburlaine*; *Hero and Leander* and *Doctor Faustus*; *Lucan's First Book* and *Edward II*. Marlowe uses the two forms to write a counter-nationhood, a non-patriotic form of nationhood that subverts royal power with what Ovid calls *libertas* (*Amores*, 3. 15. 9) and Marlowe translates as "liberty" (*Ovid's Elegies*, 3. 14. 9). Thus, what Leo Braudy says of Ovid, we may extend to his great Elizabethan translator: "the poet begins to assert himself as the true nation" (135). In other words, what is at stake in Marlowe's competition with Spenser is the writing of English nationalism itself, the form the national poet is to take.

While recalling other resources where pertinent (e.g., Lodge and Daniel in Shakespeare's three narrative poems, Sidney and Daniel in his Sonnets, Kyd and Marlowe in *Titus Andronicus* and *Hamlet*), we need to foreground Shakespeare's debt to Spenser, because it is this intertextual relationship (more than any other) that decisively helps us complete the profile of Shakespeare as a man of the theatre: in his rivalry with England's Virgil, we can witness the great theatrical man competing with the author Richard Helgerson calls Renaissance England's first national poet (*Laureates*, 100). While it is well known that Shakespeare competed with Marlowe, the many studies on this topic neglect Spenser in the competitive equation. Especially overlooked is the idea that Marlowe rivaled Spenser before Shakespeare did, as well as that Shakespeare soon became implicated in his colleagues' rivalry. In practice, this means that a criticism seeking to understand the historical narrative about the printing of Shakespeare as national poet-playwright must come to terms with the authors who competed so forcibly for national authority, primarily Spenser, then Marlowe (and after these, the rest).

As an aspiring Elizabethan author of the 1590s, I believe, Shakespeare inherits the competition between Marlowe and Spenser, but among contemporaries he alone appears to have made this rivalry into something like the main frame of his art. Thus, there is an intimate link between his double-production of poems and plays as literary forms, his representation of the poet-playwright and of the poetry-theatre dyad generally, and his rivalry with these two leading writers.

To date, we possess numerous short studies that examine Shakespeare's intertextual rivalry with either Marlowe or with Spenser, with Ovid or with Virgil, but not a single book-length study of both English authors or both Roman writers – and certainly none that combines all four.[36] The state of criticism on Shakespeare's dual rivalry with Spenser and Marlowe is especially surprising, since Shakespeare's fictional representation of the poet-playwright is so clearly indebted to both these leading authors – but initially to Spenser. In *What is Pastoral?*, for instance, Paul Alpers observes in passing that "All the court figures in *As You Like It* can be seen as playing out Spenser's metaphor for himself as a pastoral poet: 'Lo I the man, whose Muse whilome did maske, / As time her taught, in lowly Shepheards weeds' (*Faerie Queene*, 1. Proem 1)" (74). This idea is worth exploring, especially in the context of two neglected points.

First, in the Proem to *Faerie Queene*, 1, Spenser does not simply use the metaphor of the theatrical mask to present "himself as a pastoral poet"; he situates his donning of the pastoral mask as the first stage of a career pattern that begins with pastoral and then turns to epic; the lines following the two that Alpers quotes read: "Am now enforst a far unfitter taske, / For trumpets sterne to chaunge mine Oaten reeds, / And sing of Knights and Ladies gentle deeds." Spenser thus presents himself as a court figure who at first dons the disguise of a shepherd to write pastoral but who then takes off that disguise to write epic. Herein lies an Elizabethan genesis to the Marlovian and Shakespearean author as theatrical agent, the Ovidian author who moves along the Virgilian path, playfully disguising himself in order to move through a generic hierarchy as part of a self-advertised literary career.[37] In his story of the Redcrosse Knight in Book 1 and of Calidore in Book 6 of *The Faerie Queene*, Spenser frames his Virgilian epic on precisely this narrative structure. Redcrosse begins as "a tall clownish young man . . . unfit through his rusticity for a better place," but then he manages to persuade Gloriana, the Faerie Queene, to let him "put upon him the dew furniture" or armor of "knighthood" (*Letter to Ralegh*). By contrast, Calidore begins as

---

[36] Cf. Shapiro, *Rival*; Helgerson, *Laureates*; Bate, *Ovid*; Bono, *Literary Transvaluation*; D. Hamilton, *Virgil and "The Tempest"*; Suzuki, *Metamorphoses of Helen*; Tudeau-Clayton, *Jonson*; James, *Shakespeare's Troy*; Bednarz, *Poets' War*.

[37] On Spenser and the Ovidian *cursus* in the *October* eclogue, see Cheney, *Profession*, 61–65. On Ovidian drama in the *Amores*, see Davis, *Fictus Adulter*; on performance in the *Metamorphoses*, see Wheeler, *Wonder*.

a knight of Gloriana, but then, "doffing his bright armes, himselfe addrest /
In shepheards weed" (6. 9. 36. 3–4). In framing *The Faerie Queene* on this
Virgilian-based plot with its Ovidian "maske," Spenser is certainly taking
cues from Philip Sidney in the *Old* and *New Arcadia*; but Sidney, in turn, is
most likely taking cues from Spenser in *The Shepheardes Calender*. In that
Virgilian pastoral, Spenser presents himself as "Colin Clout," a shepherd
who is an antic or clown (as his name advertises) but also, paradoxically,
the "sovereigne of song" (*November*, 25). Thus, Spenser recurrently uses the
figure of the clown to represent pastoral in preparation for epic: "Abandon
then the base and viler clown, . . . / And sing of . . . Knights" (*October*,
37–39). Spenser's colleagues, such as his friend Harvey, typically represent
the New Poet in these terms, even picking up the theatrical metaphor of
the "maske":

> Collyn I see . . . thy new taken taske [writing *The Faerie Queene*] . . .
> leades thy muse in haughtie verse to maske,
> and loath the layes that longs to lowly swaynes.
> That lifts thy notes from Shepherdes unto kings.
> (*Commendatory Verse*, 3. 1–5 to 1590 *Faerie Queene*)

Among his contemporaries, Spenser was famous for having disguised
himself as a shepherd-king and for narrating fictions in which characters
"play out" the role that he had assigned to himself.

Second, Marlowe was the first Elizabethan author to stage dramatic
characters playing out the Virgilian role that Spenser had assigned to himself (cf. Greenblatt, *Fashioning*, 224). This is virtually the topic of the
two *Tamburlaine* plays, whose protagonist is a "Scythian Shepherd" who
becomes a "Mighty Monarch" (1590 title page to *Tamburlaine*); however,
the Ovidian Marlowe turns to this Spenserian narrative fiction in nearly
all of his plays and poems, from *Dido, Queen of Carthage* to "The Passionate Shepherd to His Love" (Cheney, *Profession*, 18–19). Marlowe's Ovidian appropriation of Spenser's Virgilian persona helps explain why both
Marlowe and Ovid show up so directly in the Spenserian landscape of *As
You Like It*. In Act 3, scene 3, Touchstone tells Audrey about "honest Ovid"
(8) during an exchange that alludes to Marlowe's death: "a great reckoning
in a little room" (15) – a clear imitation of a famous line from *The Jew of
Malta* ("Infinite riches in a little room" [1. 1. 37]). In scene 5, Phoebe then
eulogizes Marlowe as the "Dead shepherd" and quotes the "saw of might"
from *Hero and Leander*: "Who ever lov'd that lov'd not at first sight?" (81–82;
see the Play Scene to Part 3). Significantly, Shakespeare dresses Marlowe in
Spenser's pastoral "maske" yet imitates works that reveal Marlowe to be the

writer of both a play and a poem – a revelation reproduced in *The Merry Wives* through both quotation of "The Passionate Shepherd" and reference to *Doctor Faustus*. We can profitably investigate the intertextual rivalry in the shepherd-king figure among Shakespeare, Spenser, and Marlowe.

From Julia in *Two Gentleman of Verona* and Venus in *Venus and Adonis* through the young courtier in *A Lover's Complaint* and Autolycus in *The Winter's Tale*, Shakespeare forges his writing career in the following way: onto a fiction of Spenser's Virgilian pastoral and epic, he superimposes a fiction of Marlowe's Ovidian poetry and drama. Repeatedly, that is, characters sing songs and perform roles along a narrative path connecting court to country. This intertextual representation forms the primary frame for Shakespeare's attempt to authorize himself as one of England's leading authors. Shakespeare's representation is fundamentally new, at least for the Elizabethans. Certainly, it has origins tracing to Odysseus in Homer's epic, but we cannot find it so lucidly or recurrently displayed in other works of literature – most importantly for our purposes, those by Spenser or Marlowe.[38] Because the origin of this characterization lies in the authorial self-presentations of his two Elizabethan rivals, we can discover here a valuable Shakespearean authorial representation. In today's critical conversation, such a representation is important to recognize, because it counters the notion that Shakespeare was a businessman so preoccupied with theatrical affairs that he had no time for the luxury of a literary career. To the contrary, the narratological frame derives from Renaissance notions of a literary career and is itself a literary representation of a career principle.

Shakespeare's frame may recur from *Love's Labor's Lost* and *A Midsummer Night's Dream* to *As You Like It* and *The Tempest*, but as this list of plays indicates, the figure of the Ovidian poet-playwright moving along the Virgilian path tends to appear in Shakespearean comedy and romance. In the history plays and in tragedy, the Ovidian poet-playwright most often moves along what we might call a displaced Virgilian path. Instead of a shepherd-courtier, the poet-playwright tends to appear in the guise of an antic-prince. Rather than leaving the court for the world of pastoral by donning the costume of a shepherd, a prince figure puts on the "antic disposition" (*Hamlet*, 1. 5. 172) of a fool, madman, or clown. Hamlet is certainly the most famous antic-prince in the canon, but it is astonishing to discover how many figures in the history plays and the tragedies participate

---

[38] Odysseus, in disguise as a beggar, narrates his marvelous adventures so that his song becomes virtually identical with Homer's. Virgil imitates this representation in the *Aeneid*, while in *Dido* Marlowe appropriates Spenser's Virgilian or shepherd-king fiction to provide intimations of the Ovidian singing player.

in this figuration. Like Hamlet, for instance, Edgar dons the theatrical disguise of an antic or madman, Poor Tom, in order to survive the tyranny of Lear's and Gloucester's world. Similarly, in the Henriad Prince Hal dons the disguise of a tavern wastrel in order to make his "reformation" more "wond'red at" (1 *Henry IV*, 1. 2. 213, 201). Thus, in *Henry V* the Constable of France permits us to see a link between this political ploy and that in Shakespeare's poems: "And you shall find his vanities forespent / Were but the outside of the Roman Brutus, / Covering discretion with the coat of folly" (2. 4. 37–38). The historical reference is important, for it recalls the conclusion to *The Rape of Lucrece*, wherein Lucius Junius Brutus "Began to clothe his wit in state and pride, / Burying in Lucrece's wound his folly's show" (1809–10). Not merely does Brutus anticipate Henry, Edgar, and Hamlet, but he models Shakespeare's portrait of Will in the Sonnets. Whereas in Sonnet 29 Will says, "I scorn to change my state with kings" (14), in Sonnet 110 he confesses, "Alas, 'tis true, I have gone here and there, / And made myself a motley to the view" (110. 1–2) – the word "motley" meaning "clown" (*Riverside*, 1863).

Shakespeare's recurrent representation of the antic-prince certainly betrays class consciousness, ambitions, and fantasies – his own perhaps but also those of most members of his writing generation, such as Spenser and Marlowe – but we might also recall that Shakespeare alone among his contemporaries quite literally wrote Ovidian poems and plays along the Virgilian path. As the son of a father who kept real sheep and real cows in a rural Warwickshire town, he left for the city of London to become a principal shareholder, actor, and writer for what later became The King's Men. Neither Spenser nor Marlowe could claim such Ovidian/Virgilian authenticity.[39] This biographical template and its manifestation in the poems and plays has never been articulated or probed as a major contribution to modern authorship.

To see Shakespeare structuring all four of his dramatic genres and all four of his main poetic genres on a primary frame relating Marlowe's Ovidian career with Spenser's Virgilian one is to alter our classification of Shakespeare as an early modern author. Evidently, he discovered in this frame a fundamental and versatile plot device, a rich technique of individual characterization, a shrewd intertextualizing strategy of literary imitation, and finally a powerful cognitive idea through which to foreground the concept of human metamorphosis, mapped within artistic, sexual, political, and

---

[39] On Shakespeare's knowledge of the "wool trade," see Honan, *Life*, 37. In *Greene's Groatsworth of Wit*, which Honan calls "virtually a rape of Shakespeare" (158), Shakespeare is called "'a country Author'" (159).

religious domains. While his plays and such poems as the Sonnets may obscure Shakespeare's intentions toward his art, this book finds an author with more interest in Renaissance ideas of a literary career than is usually acknowledged.[40]

THE MAKING OF THE NATIONAL POET-PLAYWRIGHT

During the past decade or so, critics have slowly been filling in the history behind what Michael Dobson calls the making of the national poet. As the subtitle to Dobson's book reveals – *Shakespeare, Adaptation, and Authorship, 1660–1769* – these histories tend to start after Shakespeare's death, including such important studies as Jonathan Bate's *Shakespearean Constitutions*; Margreta de Grazia's *Shakespeare Verbatim*; Gary Taylor's *Reinventing Shakespeare*; Hugh Grady's *Modernist Shakespeare*; and Richard Halpern's *Shakespeare among the Moderns*. The present book takes us back to the beginning of such a history, to the very making of the national author. It looks at Shakespeare during his active writing career, emphasizing the printing of the sixteenth-century Ovidian poet-playwright, and reads the double printing of Shakespeare's poems and plays through the lens of this historical moment. Central to the story about the printing of the "national poet" is Shakespeare's rivalry not simply with the dissident dramatist Marlowe; if Shakespeare eventually becomes the national poet, as so many recent literary historians observe, he does so by fulfilling ambitions he aired initially in his rivalry with England's Virgil, Spenser. The genesis of Shakespeare's emergence as national poet, that is, does not lie simply in later critical constructions but originally in his own literary practice.

At issue in the above literary histories – and in Shakespeare studies more broadly – is the question of just what kind of national author Shakespeare is. Does he write the nation along popular, royal, radical, or even commercial lines?[41] We can look profitably into this question by concentrating on Shakespeare's own representation of the poet-playwright, his most sustained

---

[40] Recent work by Suzuki, James, Hamilton, Bono, Bate, and others on Shakespeare's interest in Troy, Virgil, Ovid, and Rome can profitably be re-routed from matrices of politics, sexuality, religion, and general aesthetics to the Renaissance frame for this cultural project: the idea of a literary career. Cf. Alpers, *What is Pastoral?*, 9. I am grateful to Professors Colin Hardie and Helen Moore for inviting me to present a lecture titled "Did Shakespeare Have a Literary Career?" at the Third Passmore Edwards Symposium on "Literary Careers," at Corpus Christi College, Oxford, 2–4 September, 2004.

[41] See Patterson, *Voice*, on people power; Helgerson, *Forms*, 195–245, on royal power; Dollimore, *Radical*, 189–230, on radical power; and Bristol, *Big Time Shakespeare*, on commercial power. For the most recent overview, see Hadfield, *Shakespeare and Renaissance Political Culture*, who foregrounds a

representation of authorship within a national frame. What emerges is an anxious yet finally genial portrait of an English author, not so much with a clear and consistent political stance as with a quiet confidence about his own powers, able to use poetry and theatre to "frame" our "mind to mirth and merriment" (*Taming of the Shrew*, Ind. 2. 135), to "Mind . . . true things by what their mock'ries be" (*Henry V*, 4. Chor. 53), or simply to "obey" the "weight of this sad time" (*King Lear*, 5. 3. 324).[42] In this model, freedom is neither the monarchical problem that Spenser imagines in his role as England's Virgil, nor the political solution Marlowe inherits from Ovid (and Lucan), but rather an authorial space of released consciousness created by the communal dynamic of art itself: "As you from crimes would pardon'd be, / Let your indulgence set me free" (*Tempest*, Ep. 19–20). In other words, what finally emerges from the canon of plays and poems is Shakespearean authorship itself, a literary voice of national authority, a form of national language.

THE LEGACY OF THE RENAISSANCE

Finally, *Shakespeare, National Poet-Playwright* suggests that the emergence of the poet-playwright in the literary careers of Shakespeare and his English and European contemporaries forms a hitherto missing part to the story about the Renaissance as a period concept. In his introductory essay on "The Sixteenth Century" in the recent *Cambridge Companion to English Literature 1500–1600* (edited by Arthur F. Kinney), Burrow suggests that the "chief legacy" of the period was the "development of a form of authorship which was located in London life and articulated through the medium of print" (26). This is a lucid judgment – worth extending. The chief legacy of the English Renaissance may be the development of a double form of authorship articulated through the medium of both printed poetry and staged theatre: a compounded form of literary production, both poems and plays, *Lucrece* as well as *Hamlet*, which we may find legibly registered in the fictional representation of the Shakespearean poet-playwright. Resembling Will in such sonnets as 23, Feste presents himself to the beleaguered

---

republican author during the Elizabethan era. On Marlowe as the inaugural author of the Elizabethan republican imagination, see Cheney, "Introduction," *Cambridge Companion*. The complex dialogic presence of both Spenser and Marlowe as mighty opposites in Shakespeare's art may help account for the debate about the political working of his poems and plays.

42 This view of Shakespeare as author is consistent with that of Bednarz, *Poets' War*, 18.

Malvolio by using one of his endearingly witty songs as the printed figure of performed theatre:

> I am gone, sir,
> And anon, sir,
>   I'll be with you again;
> In a trice,
> Like to the old Vice,
> Your need to sustain;
>
> Who with dagger of lath,
> In his rage and his wrath,
>   Cries, ah, ha!
> (*Twelfth Night*, 4. 2. 120–28)

CHAPTER 2

Francis Meres, the Ovidian poet-playwright, and Shakespeare criticism

In 1598, Frances Meres prints a valuable portrait of an author largely lost since the early seventeenth century:

As the soule of Euphorbus was thought to live in Pythagorus: so the sweete wittie soule of Ovid lives in mellifluous & hony-tongued Shakespeare, witnes his *Venus and Adonis*, his *Lucrece*, his sugred Sonnets among his private friends, &c.

As Plautus and Seneca are accounted the best for Comedy and Tragedy among the Latines: so Shakespeare among the English is the most excellent in both kinds for the stage; for Comedy, witnes his *Gentlemen of Verona*, his *Errors*, his *Loves labors lost*, his *Loves labours wonne*, his *Midsummers night dreame* & his *Merchant of Venice*: for Tragedy his *Richard the 2. Richard the 3. Henry the 4. King John, Titus Andronicus* and his *Romeo and Juliet*. (*Riverside*, 1970)

The Meres miniature, as we might view it, is of particular value, because it helps us to restore some erased features to the critical portrait of Shakespeare in his original stature as an early modern author.

The Meres miniature is "justly famous," writes Jonathan Bate, for its inventory of Shakespeare's works at the mid-point of his career, but also for its portrait of Shakespeare as an Elizabethan Ovid. Thus, Bate opens *Shakespeare and Ovid* precisely with this portrait in order to answer the question: "what better model [than Ovid] for the ambitious young Elizabethan writer?" (2). "In support of Meres," Bate continues, "one could list many points of similarity," and from his list of six he singles out Ovid's and Shakespeare's shared "interest" in "the flexible self" (3). For Bate, in other words, the central point of connection between the English and the Roman author is that of subjectivity.

Bate makes two further remarks that merit emphasis. The first is that Meres' allusion to "the fifteenth book of the *Metamorphoses*" – where Euphorbus' soul does live in Pythagorus – is quite precise, since "Pythagorean metempsychosis . . . becomes a figure for the translation of one poet into another" (3). The second is that Meres' comparison of Shakespeare with Ovid should not be "restricted to Shakespeare's non-dramatic works, for the comparison with Plautus and Seneca is simply made in terms of shared excellence, whereas that with Ovid is phrased in such a way as to imply both stylistic and spiritual resemblance. The soul that has been metamorphosed into Shakespeare is that of Ovid, the poet of metamorphosis" (3).

Bate's first point specifies individual subjectivity as the author's subjectivity and suggests that authorial subjectivity originates in the subjectivity of an earlier poet. Here Meres self-consciously uses a model of literary relations to present Shakespeare as an Ovidian writer par excellence. Bate's second point shows the material productions of the author's translated subjectivity and suggests that an author's works originate in the works of a predecessor. Here Meres extends the Ovidian model beyond Shakespeare's non-dramatic works to include his dramatic ones. By combining the two points, we can infer how Bate understands the Meres portrait: Shakespeare is an author who self-consciously models himself on Ovid in order to discover his sweet voice and his flexible self in both his dramatic and his non-dramatic works.

What Bate does not say provides a point of departure for this chapter: that Meres is portraying Shakespeare as a new kind of European writer. More accurately, Meres is portraying Shakespeare as the reincarnation of an ancient Roman writer. This reincarnated, Ovidian writer pens both poems and plays. He is the author of both *Venus and Adonis* and *A Midsummer Night's Dream*; *The Rape of Lucrece* and *Richard III*. In fact, by 1598 Shakespeare has penned three important poems and twelve important plays – six "comedies" and six "tragedies." The symmetrical numbers look deliberate – an equation that balances comedy and tragedy and then puts the drama into a ratio with the poems: a one-to-four ratio. According to Meres, Shakespeare writes more plays than poems, but Shakespeare still writes poems, and what is more his poems are to be introduced before his plays, and they are to be classified according to the Roman author whom Meres and Bate see living most vitally in all of "mellifluous & hony-tongued Shakespeare." This new author is an Ovidian poet-playwright.

In this chapter, we shall look into the genealogy and reception of this author, from antiquity to today. The chapter divides into five sets of evidence external to Shakespeare's works, each of which suggests a need to redraw his portrait as an early modern author; collectively, the evidence may make the need imperative. Since the scope of the material is vast, with each set warranting a study in itself, a broad map will need to suffice. Hopefully, readers will bring their own examples, qualifications, and refinements.

POEMS AND PLAYS, HOMER TO TASSO

A historical survey of poems and plays from Homer to Tasso reveals the need to re-identify Shakespeare as a poet-playwright.[1] Within this survey, Shakespeare emerges as merely one author among many during the European Renaissance who helps recover and re-invent what was originally a Roman writing practice. The origins of this practice go even further back.

The clearest way to view the origins is to take Meres' cue and dust off the generic site of authorship, insofar as we can. When we do, we discover that almost all of the more famous authors, from classical Greece and Rome through late fifteenth-century Italy, France, and Spain, wrote either poetry or drama but did not write both together. Famous poets who bequeathed no plays to posterity include Homer, Hesiod, Pindar, Sappho, Callimachus, Lucretius, Catullus, Virgil, Horace, Propertius, Tibullus, Lucan, Statius, the medieval Troubadours, Guillaume de Loris and Jean de Meun, the Italian *stil novisti*, Dante, Petrarch, Boccaccio, Sannazaro, Boiardo, Chaucer, Lydgate, and Gower.[2] Famous dramatists who bequeathed no body of poetry to posterity include Aeschylus, Sophocles, Euripides, Aristophanes, Plautus, Terence, and Seneca (the only authors to whom the European Renaissance had access).[3]

For a few of these classical dramatists, we do possess scraps of poetry. For instance, we possess at least one poem by Aeschylus: his epitaph on himself (reprinted in *Oresteia*, 1). Richmond Lattimore refers to the legend by which Aeschylus "left Athens for Sicily in chagrin because he was defeated by Simonides, the great lyric poet, in a competition for writing the epitaph of the dead at Marathon" (Aeschylus, *Oresteia*, 2). This may be the earliest recorded instance of a phenomenon we will see arising nearly two thousand years later with respect to Shakespeare's "The Phoenix and Turtle": a famous dramatist turns his hand to poetry during a competitive environment. As Lattimore also records, the origins of tragedy trace to the "choral lyric," even though "the early phases of the course by which dramatic lyric was transformed into lyric drama are now invisible to us" (3). Finally, Lattimore observes that the origins of the *Oresteia* are themselves

---

[1] Cf. critics who examine lyric, drama, and narrative: e.g., Frye, *Anatomy*, 243–337; Hernadi, *Beyond genre*, chs. 2 and 3; Dubrow, *Victors*, 175, esp. n7.

[2] As indicated in chapter 1, Petrarch wrote one comedy, not extant; and certainly English authors like Lydgate were interested in theatrical art.

[3] On the Graeco-Roman tradition, see Farrell, "Careers," who confirms these statistics.

poetic, including works by Homer, Stesichorus, and Pindar (7). A version of the same complication characterizes Roman tragedy and comedy as well.[4]

The historical relation between poetry and theatre may be lost to us, but a study of their relation may profitably acknowledge the best scholarly conjecture: of an originary moment of generic succession, in which theatre grows out of poetry, staged drama out of lyric song. While the choral lyrics of Greek tragedy register a trace of this moment, we might be interested in representations that preserve such an origin. One appears in the portrait of Iphigeneia in Aeschylus' *Agamemnon* (239–47). When her father is offering her up for sacrifice, Iphigeneia's looks of "pity" are said to be "lovely as in a painted scene"; but in a subsequent use of the word "as," the playwright moves beyond simile into example:

> as many times
> at the kind festive table of her father
> she had sung, and in the clear course of a stainless maiden
> with love she had graced the song
> of worship when the third cup was poured. (Aeschylus, *Agamemnon*, 243–47)

This astonishing image presents Iphigeneia as a singer within a play. While it is traditional for a young girl to sing, in Greek as in Renaissance culture, we might be struck by the kind of girl being represented here. She bears an uncanny congruence with the form of the play itself: a tragic heroine is herself a singer of tragic song. Aeschylus does masculinize the representation, as when the male Chorus literally sings the choral origin of this tragedy: "Still the spirit sings, drawing deep / from within this unlyric threnody of the Fury" (990–01). But this "spirit" remains more powerfully feminine, and nowhere more hauntingly than in the doomed prophetess Cassandra, who voices it herself: "This pain flooding the song of sorrow is mine alone" (1137). The song Cassandra sings is that of the nightingale Philomela, as the prophetess sings her own "death song, the wild lyric" – what she also calls "the trebled song of [her] . . . agony" (1165) and "the death song of [her] . . . passionate suffering" (1176). At lines 1186–97, Cassandra locates the origin of this tragic song in the Eryines, later to be called the Eumenides (1186–92). Not all Greek tragedies are as self-reflexive as this, but some (Sophocles' *Electra* is another striking example) appear to represent their art through figures of tragic song that record a succession from lyric to tragedy as a form of continuity.

---

[4] On these origins, see Winnington-Ingram, "Origins of Tragedy"; Handley, "Earliest Comic Drama"; Gratwick, "Origins of Roman Drama."

By contrast, Seneca is notable for representing his art through figures that separate song and performance, poetry and theatre, creating discontinuity. In the play that Elizabethan writers singled out as typifying Senecan tragedy, *Thyestes*, Atreus self-styles himself as the play's tragedian.[5] More to the point, Atreus thinks he derives his plan of revenge against his brother Thyestes from reading the Greek tragedy of Philomela (2. 97–98; trans. J. Heywood), even though the audience knows differently, since the Fury has invented the plot in the opening scene (1. 56–57). Within the fiction, Atreus is recalling the dynastic history important to his own bloodline; but of his author we might wonder, who has Seneca been reading? The answer is surely compound: the great Greek tragedians like Aeschylus whom Seneca imitates – and who often included the Philomela myth in their plays – but also the most famous teller of the myth, Ovid, in his verse epic the *Metamorphoses*. Perhaps indebted to Ovid's interest in performance (Wheeler, *Wonder*; Hardie, *Poetics*), Seneca shows Atreus relying on deceptive strategies to triumph over his brother.

Atreus' self-conscious tragic show contrasts with Thyestes' drunken choral song, in which the younger brother sings happily – a song the audience views as hapless because the singer is ignorant about the tragedy quite literally within him: "To joyful state return thy cheerful face" (5. 2. 17). For Seneca, lyric is at odds with tragedy, as Thyestes rehearses what we experience as the impotence of affirmation. The irony of course is that Seneca's plays were probably never performed in the public theater; they were (we think) closet dramas, more book than spectacle. In a curious way, this historical phenomenon looks forward to the closing of the Roman theatre during the early Christian era, which in turn led to the fundamentally poetic profession during the Middle Ages.

In the works of St. Augustine, we can witness the changing of the cultural guard right where we might expect it. Augustine appears to have written both poems and plays. In *The City of God*, he preserved three lines of an evening hymn composed for singing at the lighting of the candle (15. 22). And in *The Confessions* he informs us that he has been writing for a "theatrical prize" (4. 2). As his autobiography reveals, he spent his sinful early life not simply stealing figs or sleeping with his mistress, but also reading Virgil (1. 13–14) and watching plays (1. 2).

While the dramatic profession survives most memorably in the miracle, mystery, and morality plays written to support Christian faith, it

---

[5] On "the ultimate theatricality of Senecan drama," see Braden, *Anger*, 61. On *Thyestes* for the Elizabethans, see Cheney, *Profession*, 286n34.

simultaneously goes underground in much of the great poetry of the Middle Ages. Consider the English case of Lydgate, who reduces the thirty-five short books of his source text for his 1420 poem, *Troy Book*, Guido delle Colonne's *Historia destructionis Troiae*, to five books, in "a gesture of acknowledgement and homage to Chaucer's 'litel tragedye'" in *Troilus and Criseyde* (Edwards, ed., *John Lydgate*, 1). Here we find a fundamental medieval configuration relating poetry to theatre: writers like Chaucer and Lydgate structure their long poems as plays (cf. Ganim, *Chaucererian Theatricality*). The most famous example is Dante's *Commedia*, a Christian epic in the form of a divine comedy designed to overgo Virgil's *Aeneid*, a Roman epic in the form of a human tragedy. Thus, at the end of *Inferno*, 20 the guide Virgil tells the pilgrim Dante, "a certain passage / of my high tragedy has sung" the story of Euryphus, too (112–13), while at the very beginning of the next canto, Dante reports that he and Virgil were "talking of things my Comedy is not / concerned to sing" (21. 2–3) – the juxtaposition of "my high tragedy" with "my Comedy" sounding the terms of this intertextual rivalry. In Lydgate's later version of Homeric epic, the English national poet is working in the Dantean medieval tradition – and perhaps crowning it, as his position in fifteenth-century England suggests.

During the English Renaissance, Sir Philip Sidney will extend this tradition by dividing his prose romance, the *Arcadia* (finished c. 1580), into five "acts" derived from the structure of Roman comedy, at about the very time James Burbage was building The Theatre (1576). In 1591, Thomas Nashe may be taking Sidney's cue when referring to *Astrophil and Stella* as a "tragicomedy of love . . . performed by starlight" (G. G. Smith, ed., *Essays*, 2: 223), but it is also possible that the new commercial theatre intensified such cross-generic discourse. This discourse is precisely what gives Nashe his voice during his famous preface to *Astrophil and Stella*: "here you shal find a paper stage streud with pearle, an artificial heav'n to overshadow the fair frame, & cristal wals to encounter your curious eyes" (G. G. Smith, ed., *Essays*, 2: 223). It is as if Nashe has just come from a performance at the Rose, the gorgeous architecture of the new commercial theatre providing the apt metaphor for entry into the luxury of Sidney's "paper stage," since Nashe finds in the Sidneian book the very spectacle of performance he has witnessed in the playhouse.

What we notice is that all around sixteenth-century Europe authors do not simply use theatre as a metaphor for poetry; they also regularly produce both poems and plays in a single career. In Italy, notable examples include Ariosto, Aretino, to some extent Machiavelli, all of whom wrote comedy alongside their verse, and of course Tasso, who wrote the tragedy *Torismondo* to complement such major achievements as the epic *Geruselemme Liberata*, the pastoral drama *Aminta*, and the vast collection of sonnets and lyrics, the *Rime*.[6] While none of the major French poets of the later sixteenth century – Du Bartas, Du Bellay, Ronsard, Desportes, or Marot – wrote plays per se, Ronsard did some dramatic experiments, and his lesser-known colleague Baif did write plays. As Anne Lake Prescott observes, the Pleiade included drama in its program, but in practice operated through "a sort of division of labor," with Du Bellay and Ronsard writing poetry and Jodelle and Garnier writing drama (personal communication, 10 June 1998), although in the end Jodelle published several collections of poems alongside his plays and Garnier penned an elegy on the death of Ronsard. Earlier in the century, however, Marguerite de Navarre did interweave drama not merely with poetry but also with prose fiction (the novella). She may be the first recorded woman writer to do so; certainly, she is the most famous. French drama does not achieve international prominence until the seventeenth century, first with Corneille, especially with Molière, and finally with Racine, all of whom were "men of the theatre." In Spain, after the opening of the commercial public theatres in the 1570s, such writers as Lope de Vega, Calderón, and (we have seen) Cervantes write both poems and plays. In fact, if we wish to find a literary scene analogous to that in England in the late sixteenth century, we must turn to Spain, where Lope and his colleagues are even more prodigious than their English counterparts, although Spanish dramatists of the Golden Age tended to limit their production to comedies (Frederick A. de Armas, personal communication, 15 June 1998). Around 1613–14, Leonard Digges made an inscription on the flyleaf of his copy of Lope's *Rimas* (1613): "this Booke of Sonets, wch [sic] with Spaniards here is accounted of their lope de Vega as in Englande wee sholde of o[u]r: Will Shakespeare" (quoted in Morgan, "Our Will Shakespeare," 118). The inscription makes sense only if we know that these two sonneteers were famous men of the theatre.

To my knowledge, only two major authors before the sixteenth century qualify as notable exceptions to this historical practice of generic exclusivity: Ennius and Ovid.[7] Ennius (239–169 BC) was famous as the author of both tragedies and comedies (especially tragedies), but he was best known for

---

[6] See Malago, "Shakespeare and Tasso," who contextualizes Shakespeare's poems and plays in terms of Tasso's combination.

[7] Livius Andronicus, the first Roman writer we know about (born c. 272 BC), is the author of poems and plays (Farrell, "Careers," 35–36). St. Hildegard (1098–1179), perhaps medieval Christianity's first woman poet-playwright, is the author of liturgical hymns and the first extant morality play, *Ordo Virtutum* (c. 1151; see Dronke, *Poetic Individuality*, 150).

his eighteen-book epic masterpiece on the history of Rome, the *Annales*. He also penned a number of minor works in various meters and forms (Farrell, "Careers," 37–40). Perhaps because Ennius' works existed only in fragments, but also surely because Ovid's genius managed to eclipse Ennius' generic eclecticism, the great Naso, we may hypothesize, emerged as the premier model of the poet-playwright for Renaissance writers and scholars.

Throughout the twentieth century, Renaissance scholars have understood Ovid to be only a poet (mostly of elegy, both amorous and exilic, but occasionally a poet of epic), and they have told a recurrent story: "Shakespeare lived during a period in which ways of reading Ovid underwent radical transformation, as a newly unapologetic delight in the poetic and erotic qualities of the *Metamorphoses* came to compete with the predominant medieval practice of moralizing and even Christianizing them."[8] What at least a few Renaissance scholars mention, most neglect: not merely that Ovid was a poet, but that he was a dramatist (Bate, *Ovid*, 28n53, 239; Miola, *Tragedy*, 102). In addition to elegy and epic, he wrote tragedy. As indicated in the last chapter, two lines of Ovid's historically priceless play have been preserved, while tributes to its genius exist in the Elder Seneca (*Suasoriae*, 3. 7), Quintilian (*Institutio oratoria*, 7. 5. 6, 10. 1. 98), and Tacitus (*Dialogus de oratoribus*, 12). Classicists believe that Ovid mentions his *Medea* at least three times: twice in his inaugural volume, the *Amores* (2. 18. 13–14, 3. 1. 29) and again in his valedictory work, the *Tristia* (2. 547–56).[9] In fact, classicists argue that Ovid's *Medea* served as the primary model for Senecan tragedy (Currie, "Ovid and the Roman Stage"; Tarrant, "Senecan Drama"), which Renaissance scholars agree served as the model for Renaissance tragedy, including Shakespearean tragedy (Miola, *Tragedy*). What we may wish to recall is the formal way in which the English Senecan movement is "Ovidian."[10]

Hence, on the title page to his 1648 translation of Seneca's *Medea*, Edward Sherburn includes an epigraph from Ovid's *Amores*: "Non estis teneris apta Theatra Modis" (1. 2). Accordingly, Ovid shows up often in Sherburn's "Annotations." Moreover, "Some" sixteenth- and seventeenth-century scholars, writes George Sandys, even "conjectred that Seneca's *Medea* belongeth to Ovid" (b3ᵛ), while others, like John Gower, think that Ovid wrote more than one tragedy: "He penned also some Tragedies: Of

---

[8] Bate, *Ovid*, 25. For bibliography on the Renaissance Ovid, see Cheney, *Profession*, 283n6.
[9] See Currie, "Ovid and the Roman Stage"; Tarrant, "Senecan Drama"; Nikolaidis, "Some Observations."
[10] Professor Robert Miola writes, "Everywhere I looked for Seneca I saw Naso's shadow in the period" (personal communication, 7 April 1997). On Seneca and Ovid, see also McCabe, *Incest*, 100–02.

which *Medea* is highly approved by Quintilianus and Corn. Tacitus, and not without desert" (B^r). In his 1612 *Apology for Actors*, Thomas Heywood even includes Ovid in his short list of excellent writers of "Roman tragedy," alongside Accius, Pacuvius, and Seneca (D1^v). In his *Refutation of the Apology for Actors* (1615), John Green articulates what archival research confirms and what remains a neglected feature of "Renaissance Ovid" criticism: "the next proofe of Antiquity for Stage-Plays by M. Actor alledged, is out of Ovids works" (*A Refutation*, 8). That is, like Heywood (also known as "M. Actor"), Renaissance commentators recurrently turn to Ovid as their primary authority on the theatre (see Gosson, *Schoole of Abuse* B3^r, B4^r, C1^r). Not surprisingly, Green reports that "Vives also writeth, that Ovid was most justly banished as an instrument of wantonesse, for making love bookes, enterludes, and such amorous trumpery" (*A Refutation*, 50).[11] Evidently, since only two lines of Ovidian drama formally survive, English Renaissance scholars felt inclined to invent an Ovidian dramatic canon. These seventeenth-century English scholars confirm the research of such Continental sixteenth-century scholars as Angelo Poliziano, Daniel Hensius, Martin Del Rio, and Giovambattista Giraldi Cinthio, all of whom speak about Ovid as the author of tragedy.[12]

Ovid, then, is not simply a poet of wit and eroticism but the first author to become famed as both a poet and a playwright. By recalling this fact, we supply a significant piece of information missing in literary histories of the Renaissance, including arguments about Shakespeare's role in the period. Most likely, Renaissance scholars and writers became interested in the original Ovid once the recovery of classical texts, Greek and Roman, increased the stature of drama in the literary system. The *Amores* is the key text here because it presents Ovid as an elegist-tragedian: "Horned Bacchus greater fury doth distil, / A greater ground with great horse is to till. / Weak elegies, delightful Muse, farewell."[13] Not simply does Marlowe translate Ovid's inaugural work (c. 1585), but he goes on to make the new Ovidian author as poet-playwright his model.[14] In terms of the English literary tradition up through the early 1590s, Marlowe's substantive combination of Ovidian poetry and drama within a single literary career is unique. The

---

[11] See also Stubbes, *Anatomie of Abuses*, lvii^r.

[12] See Poliziano's poem on Ovid, which refers to *Medea* (trans. Sandys, *Metamorphoses*, 10 and marginal notes); Hensius, ed., *L. Annaei Senecae*, 544–45, 552–53; Del Rio, ed., *L. Annaei Senecae Cordubensis*, prefatory poem titled "Ioan, Dominici Florentii Romani Carmen" (n.p.); Cinthio, *Discorsidi*, 222–23, 235.

[13] *Amores*, 3. 15. 17–19; in *Ovid's Elegies*, 3. 14. 17–19, trans. Marlowe. For Ovid as elegist-tragedian, see *Amores*, 2. 18 and 3. 1.

[14] This paragraph summarizes Cheney, *Profession*.

youth from Canterbury qualifies as the founding father of the new English author.

It is precisely Ovid the poet-playwright – the writer as both elegist and tragedian, author of the *Amores* and the *Medea* – whom "the legitimate heir of Marlowe" (Eliot, *Elizabethan Dramatists*, 75) puts on stage to open his 1601 *Poetaster*. While Ovid's servant, Luscus, speaks of Ovid's "songs, and sonnets" (1. 1. 5) and Ovid himself recites Jonson's own translation of *Amores*, 1. 15, his father accosts him with a paternal tirade: "Ovid, whom I thought to see the pleader, become Ovid the play-maker? . . . I hear of a tragoedie of yours comming foorth for the common players there, call'd Medea."[15] Perhaps because of such representations, at the end of the Renaissance, Milton models his figure of "Tragodea" in *Elegia Prima* (2. 37–46) on Ovid's portrait of Tragedy in *Amores*, 3. 1. 11–15 (Milton, *Complete Poems*, 8).

Certainly, the Humanist educational movement provided the greatest single impetus for the rupture of the poetic profession by the dramatic one. Thus a number of writers stage plays before the re-opening of the commercial theatre. Several other early modern movements also played decisive, integrative roles, including the change from a feudal to a capitalist society, but for the present argument the invention of the printing press proves decisive. Indeed, with the recovery, translation, printing, dissemination, study, and imitation of classical texts, Elizabethan school teachers combined poetry and drama in their curricula, so that students like Shakespeare, even through a grammar-school education, could see the literary tradition in a new light. They could see, for instance, Plautus and Terence seated alongside Virgil and Horace, with both groups contributing decisively to the formation of the Roman literary system. The building of the public theatres in the 1570s in both England and Spain joins the printing press to form the most powerful agents in this historical process.

THE ENGLISH POET-PLAYWRIGHT

A historical survey of the English poet-playwright in the late sixteenth and early seventeenth centuries also reveals the need to re-identify Shakespeare as a poet-playwright. For the first sustained time, in England (as in Spain, but not in Italy or France) individual writers combine poems and plays within a single literary career. Indeed, everywhere we look among Shakespeare's contemporaries we discover the presence of the new poet-playwright: "For

[15] Jonson, *Poetaster*, 1. 2. 8–11 (in Herford and Simpson, eds., *Ben Jonson*).

Bacchus fruite is frend to Phoebus wise," writes Spenser in 1579 (*October*, 106). In this important line, published just a few years after the building of The Theatre, Spenser calls on his colleagues to create a professional friendship between the god of tragic drama and the god of poetry, between tragedy and epic (Cheney, *Profession*, 61–64).

Certainly, English origins of the poet-playwright exist before the theatres open (as they do in Italy). The most notable examples appear in the writings of Skelton, Sackville, and Gascoigne, all of whom wrote at least one play and some significant poems. Only Gascoigne, however, wrote in more than one dramatic genre, combining comedy and tragedy, although his *Supposes* is a translation from Ariosto and his *Jocasta* a collaborative translation from Lodovico Dolce's *Giocasta*, which in turn draws from Euripides' *Phoenissae*. After 1576, writers of quite different stripes start to combine poems with plays, as if this were a natural practice (as we have seen, it is not). In addition to Spenser, Marlowe, and Shakespeare, writers penning both genres, men as well as women, include Watson, Lyly, Greene, Peele, Nashe, Lodge, Kyd, Greville, Chapman, Daniel, Drayton (whose tragedies have not survived), Mary Sidney, Marston, Jonson, Tourneur, Middleton, Webster, Ford, and Wroth. Between the opening of the theatres in the mid-1570s and their closing in 1642, this group constitutes the mainstream of influential writers at work in Elizabethan, Jacobean, and Caroline England. To this list, we can add Queen Elizabeth, who wrote a number of poems still extant, as well as translated Seneca's *Hercules Oetaeus* (*Collected Works*).

While all of these writers produced canons comprised of both poems and plays, we might be interested to see them representing the relation between poems and plays in their works. Such representations abound. To cite but one example, Daniel writes in his *Dedicatory Epistle* to Mary Sidney prefacing his 1602 *Works* that the Countess

> Call'd up my spirits from out their low repose,
> To sing of State, and tragicke notes to frame . . .
> I . . .
> Made musique to my self that pleasd me best,
> And onelie told of *Delia* . . .
> Madam, had not thy well grac'd *Antony* . . .
> Requir'd his *Cleopatras* company.
> (Daniel, *Dedicatory Epistle* to Mary
> Sidney, 7–16, in *Works*)

Here Daniel records his own generic history, together with its gender paradigm for artistic inspiration: left to himself as a young writer, Daniel wrote only amatory verse; but under Mary Sidney's inspiration, he turned to the higher form of tragedy. Daniel is not alone in presenting himself as a poet-playwright; his colleagues saw Daniel this way as well. Spenser, for instance, was alert to his younger colleague's combination; in *Colin Clouts Come Home Againe*, he encourages Daniel to move beyond "loves soft laies and looser thoughts delight" to "Tragick plaints and passionate mischance" (423–27).[16]

While versions of the poet-playwright appear in such treatises as William Webbe's *Discourse of English Poetrie*, such fiction as Sidney's *New Arcadia*, and such poetry as Spenser's *Faerie Queene*, it is the dramatists themselves who produce perhaps the most intriguing manifestation; they recurrently put the poet-playwright on the stage.[17] While Jonson's "Ovid" in *Poetaster* recalls the Roman origins of the new author for the Elizabethans, the most important early character is probably old Hieronimo in *The Spanish Tragedy*. Since Kyd's play is often regarded as one of the founding plays of English Renaissance tragedy, and since *The Spanish Tragedy* exerts a strong influence on subsequent drama, including *Hamlet*, we might recall Hieronimo's authorial career.

Most memorably, Hieronimo writes and stages two plays. At the end of Act 1, he presents a heroic "masque" about the martial victory of the English over Portugal and Spain (4. 137–74, in Tydeman, ed., *Two Tudor Tragedies*); then, at the end of Act 4 (scene 3), he resurrects the "tragedy" of Soliman and Perseda that he had written while he "studied" in Toledo (1. 70–77).[18] For this last play, he supplies a "book" (s.d.); he sets the stage for the play that he himself produces; he acts in it; and he serves as its principal commentator. While Hieronimo is best remembered as a "man of the theatre," Kyd also presents him as a student of "fruitless poetry" (1. 71) and even as the composer of a remarkable fourteen-line "funeral hymn" – a Latin "mish-mash of invented lines and selective quotations from Latin poets including Tibullus, Virgil, Ovid and Lucretius" (Tydeman, ed., *Two Tudor Tragedies*, 313). Thus, Kyd twice associates Hieronimo with the legendary founder of poetry, Orpheus: first, when Hieronimo tells the Senex, Bazulto, "be my Orpheus . . . The Thracian poet thou shalt

---

[16] Oram glosses "Tragick plaints" here with Daniel's *Cleopatra* (Oram, et al., *Yale Edition*, 542). On Daniel's "Senecan tragedies," see Hulse, *Verse*, 12.

[17] For Webbe, see *Discourse on English Poetrie*, G. G. Smith, ed., *Essays*, 1: 249–50, 300; Sidney, *The New Arcadia*, where Pyrochles and Musidorus sing songs and put on disguises to woo their respective beloveds, Philoclea and Pamela; and Spenser, Book 3, cantos 11–12 of *The Faerie Queene*, where the "vile Enchaunter" Busirane (12.31) functions as a critique of the poet-playwright, with his Ovidian tapestries and Masque of Cupid.

[18] Lukas Erne observes that both Hieronimo and Kyd, character and creator, wrote a play called *Soliman and Perseda* (personal communication, 9 May 2003; see also Erne, "*Spanish Tragedy*," 160–62). Effectively, Kyd offers a self-dramatization of his own authorship.

counterfeit" (3. 13. 116–21); and later, when the Ghost of Don Andrea says, "I'll lead Hieronimo where Orpheus plays, / Adding sweet pleasure to eternal days" (4. 5. 23–24). While Orpheus never formally writes plays in the classical myth(s) about him, Kyd's punning phrase "Orpheus plays" may register the great Bard of Rhodope as a type of poet-playwright.[19]

Somewhat surprisingly, the other candidate for the founder of Elizabethan tragedy does not represent the poet-playwright in his plays as clearly as does Kyd. Nonetheless, it is a commonplace that "Tamburlaine is a poet" (Hope, "*Tamburlaine*," 53). Hence, in Part 1 of *Tamburlaine* the Scythian shepherd's "talk [is] much sweeter than the Muses' song" (3. 2. 50), and during his only soliloquy he broods on "Beauty, mother to the Muses," who "comments volumes with her ivory pen" (5. 1. 144–45) – the same writing implement Tamburlaine soon identifies as "held" by the "poets" themselves (161). In Part 2, at Zenocrate's death, Tamburlaine attempts to outdo Homer, Catullus, and Ovid in memorializing his beloved (2. 4. 86–101), and throughout both parts he quotes, echoes, and revises "The Passionate Shepherd": "And if thou pitiest Tamburlaine the Great," he says to the departed spirit of his wife, "Come down from heaven and live with me again" (*2 Tamb.*, 2. 4. 117–18). Yet Tamburlaine is also a man of the theatre, as presented in Part 1 during his opening change of costume from Scythian shepherd to mighty monarch (*1 Tamb.*, 1. 2. 34–43) and during his closing costume change from warrior to husband (5. 1. 525). Thus he demonstrates superior power to "play the orator" (1. 2. 129), is attracted instinctively to the "mask" (*1 Tamb.*, 1. 2. 199, 4. 2. 108, 5. 1. 187; *2 Tamb.*, 5. 1. 78), and ruthlessly stages his political maneuvers as "our pageant" (*2 Tamb.*, 4. 3. 90) or what Zenocrate simply terms "another bloody spectacle" (*1 Tamb.*, 5. 1. 340). Tamburlaine may display an acute knowledge of martial action, but it is astonishing how much of his characterization derives from a learned discourse of both poetry and theatre.[20]

In early seventeenth-century drama, we can periodically witness the kind of representation that Marlowe and Kyd make available. In *Volpone*, enough time has passed for Jonson to display genuine self-consciousness about the representation. In one of the most famous scenes in Renaissance drama, the bed-ridden Volpone bolts from his couch to woo Celia: "I am now as fresh . . . / As, when, in that so celebrated scene, / At recitation of our comedy, / For entertainment of the great Valois, I acted young Antinous

---

[19] On Orpehus and tragedy, see DeNeef, "Poetics of Orpheus."
[20] On sonnets imbedded in Tamburlaine's dramatic speeches, see Kocher, "Sonnet"; Eriksen, "Petrarch." For details on Marlowe's representation, see Cheney, "Biographical Representations."

and attracted the eyes and ears of all the ladies present, / To admire each graceful gesture, note, and footing."

> *Song*
> Come, my Celia, let us prove
> While we can, the sports of love . . .
> (*Volpone*, 3. 3. 161–70, in Fraser and
> Rabkin, eds.)

In this comedy, Volpone appears as a sick man, throws off his disguise to make love to a beautiful young woman, recalls his past career as a comedic actor, and turns from theatre to song (in a recasting of Catullus' famous ode well documented to be modeled on Marlowe's "Passionate Shepherd"). Jonson's representation of Volpone as a playwright and a poet (as well as an actor for the comic stage) is among the most technically self-conscious in Renaissance drama. From Volpone to Hieronimo, Justice Overdo to Dr. Faustus, and even Dekker and Middleton's Moll Cutpurse to Tourneur's Vindice, the poet-playwright emerges as a significant artistic representation among English Renaissance dramatists. Their representations reflect a larger cultural formation emergent throughout sixteenth- and seventeenth-century discourse: not merely in drama, but in poetry and prose.

Shakespeare's status as an English poet-playwright is thus part of a broad European phenomenon. Yet his status remains unique, because he is the first (certainly in England) to make the imprint of poetry and theatre absolutely vital to his authorial signature.[21]

PLAGUE THEORY

A critical look into *plague theory* in the mid-1590s similarly reveals the need to re-identify Shakespeare as a poet-playwright. Such a look questions

---

[21] Here Lukas Erne helps us to distinguish Shakespeare from, say, Daniel: "Whereas Shakespeare is a poet-playwright who contributed plays to an entertainment industry, Daniel is a poet-dramatist who wrote closet drama for readers. What is remarkable is that Shakespeare was clearly a chief player in an entertainment industry, in a world of artistic production that seems far removed from that of the poet who pursues a career through print or manuscript publication and patronage. Thus, it seems less remarkable that Daniel, who wrote closet dramas for readers and prefaced them with dedications, also wrote collections of poetry like *Delia* (prefacing them with similar dedications) than that Shakespeare, who was working for the public stage, simultaneously continued to write poetry. In terms of the economics of artistic production, Shakespeare, contrary to Daniel, straddles the divide between the coterie and patronage system within which poetry circulates and an early modern capitalist entertainment industry. The dominant mode of production in the latter is collaborative writing. In a situation where two, three, or even more playwrights collaborated in order to produce theatrical fast food, the idea of a literary career must have seemed far-fetched to many. In short, Shakespeare, despite the socio-economic divide that separates the two realms of poet and commercial playwright in ways that Daniel did not, pursued a career as a poet-playwright" (personal communication, 9 May 2003).

the idea that Shakespeare became a poet *because* the theatres closed due to plague in 1592–93. That was the cause, but yet *per accidens*. Certainly, Shakespeare reacted to the plague to write poems, but this does not explain why our language's greatest writer also wrote poetry. Yet few critics go beyond recording the commonplace, which today remains one of the most unexamined staples of the Shakespeare biography: "It was probably during the months following July 1592, when London theatres had to close because of plague, that Shakespeare sat down for the only time in his life to extended bursts of writing not intended for the stage" (S. Wells, *Life*, 115). Plague theory cannot bear the burden of historical accuracy.[22]

For instance, in her recent biography Katherine Duncan-Jones writes, "Plague was a defining context for all of Shakespeare's writing, but above all for his non-dramatic writing" (*Ungentle*, 54). This is no doubt true, and Duncan-Jones alludes to her work on the Sonnets, in which she argues that Shakespeare turned to the Petrarchan genre during "four probable phases of composition" that are bound to plague years: before 1598; 1599–1600; 1603–04; and August 1608 – May 1609 (Duncan Jones, ed., *Shakespeare's Sonnets*, 12–13; see 1–28). Such an argument is factually true and simultaneously misleading; it neglects other forces at work. These include Shakespeare's interest in the art of poetry before 1592–93, evident in such plays as *Two Gentlemen* and *The Taming of the Shrew* (with their references to Ovid, as we shall see) or the *Henry VI* plays (with their foregrounding of the Spenserian shepherd-king), and perhaps a sonnet like 145, which Andrew Gurr believes is Shakespeare's earliest composition, dating to the mid 1580s. Such a scenario suggests that Shakespeare had long been interested in the art of the poet, and that he benefited from the closing of the theatres to pursue that interest.

Another (more plausible) explanation for Shakespeare's writing of poetry is that he was joining his generation as a practicing member of the new writing institution combining poems and plays in a single career, itself the product of a complex series of cultural events.[23] As the two *Dedicatory Epistles* to Southampton indicate, Shakespeare wishes to present himself as a poet in the English and European tradition – a tradition represented most prominently at this time by Spenser – and yet, simultaneously, he is compelled to become a poet by the closing of the theaters and the need for patronage. It makes little sense to say that Shakespeare wrote the Sonnets – arguably a world-class masterpiece – simply because he had nothing else to do. It makes more sense to see Shakespeare responding to and formed by

---

[22] On the plague and theatre during the Stuart era, see Barroll, *Politics, Plague*.
[23] Burrow agrees (Burrow, ed., *Sonnets and Poems*, 9–10).

specific cultural pressures: he is compelled to become a poet-playwright, and he takes a leadership role in forging a new kind of author that partly because of his genius establishes a new model of English authorship for the centuries to come.[24]

CONTEMPORARY REPORTS

The critical reports from contemporaries provide some of the most decisive historical evidence for re-conceiving Shakespeare as a poet-playwright. During his lifetime, his colleagues certainly referred to his plays or remembered him in passing as a "writer . . . for the stage" (Bolton, *Shakspere Allusion-Book*, 1: 213); only one of his contemporaries, however, wrote a commemorative portrait of a playwright (Sir John Davies in 1611; *Shakspere Allusion-Book*, 1: 219). The rest of the known theatrical "allusions" refer to a playwright but do not mention Shakespeare by name (such as Robert Greene in his notorious indictment in 1592; *Shakspere Allusion-Book*, 1: 2), and most simply report the staging of individual plays (as when Nashe refers to *1 Henry VI; Shakspere Allusion-Book*, 1: 5).

By contrast, during Shakespeare's lifetime many more commentators identify him in terms of his role as a poet, and several mention him by name; the extensive list includes Sir William Harbert in 1594; Thomas Edwards and W. Covell in 1595; Richard Carew in 1595–96; Richard Barnfield in 1598; John Lane in 1600; Robert Chester in 1601; Henry Chettle, William Camden, and I.C. in 1603; William Barkstead and Thomas Heywood in 1607; and Edward Howes and Sir William Drummond in 1614 (see *Shakspere Allusion-Book*, 1: 14–251). Many of these early reports place Shakespeare in the tradition of great Elizabethan poets. Edwards' roll call, for instance, includes Spenser, Sidney, Daniel, Watson, and Marlowe (*Shakspere Allusion-Book*, 1: 2), while Barnfield places *Venus* and *Lucrece* in the company of such "immortall Booke[s]" as Spenser's *Faerie Queene*, Daniel's "sweet-chast Verse," and Drayton's "Tragedies, / And sweet Epistles" (*Shakspere Allusion-Book*, 1: 51). Especially noteworthy here is Barnfield's coupling of Shakespeare's minor epics with two works in the higher genres, the epic of Spenser and the tragedies of Drayton. Several of such lists extend Shakespeare's achievement as a poet from contemporary England, to

---

[24] On social construction, see Greenblatt, *Fashioning*. In "What is an Author?," Foucault has done much to quell interest in intentionality (101–20); see Orgel, "Text"; Masten, *Intercourse* and "Playwrighting." Yet for post-revisionist commitments to intentionality, see Marcus, *Puzzling*, 19, 42, 68–70; Shapiro, *Rival*, 6; Bristol, *Big Time Shakespeare*, 49–58; Helgerson, *Forms*, 215; Montrose, "Domestic," 92.

medieval England, to ancient Greece. In the 1600 *Return from Parnassus, Part 1*, it is not completely a joke when Gull quips, "Let this duncified worlde esteeme of Spenser and Chaucer, I'le worshipp sweet Mr. Shakespere, and to honoure him will lay his Venus and Adonis under my pillowe, as wee reade of one . . . [who] slept with Homer" (*Shakspere Allusion-Book*, 1: 68). In fact, Shakespeare's contemporaries more consistently identify him as a great poet in the English and European tradition than they do as a playwright.

References to Shakespeare the poet form the cornerstone of most recent attempts to discuss the poetry in light of the plays. Such attempts are useful as a corrective to the paradigm of Shakespeare the working dramatist, but they miss the real point and drive the wedge further between the two forms. While some of Shakespeare's contemporaries do view him as a playwright, and more view him as a poet, both groups do not accurately map Shakespeare's complete writing career, as is attested to by yet a third group.

During his lifetime, Shakespeare's contemporaries also recurrently present him as a poet-playwright. The list includes an anonymous writer in 1593; John Weever in 1595; Gabriel Harvey around 1598; Meres also in 1598; the authors of the *Parnassus* plays between 1600 and 1602; I.C. in 1603; William Drummond in 1606 and 1611; an anonymous writer in 1609; and Thomas Freeman in 1614.[25] As we have seen, some, like Meres, even present Shakespeare as an Ovidian poet-playwright. To construct a more accurate portrait for Shakespeare's authority and identity as an author, we need to return to Meres and his colleagues, who do not simply praise Shakespeare's achievement as a poet but recurrently situate his poetry alongside his plays. Perhaps the most bizarre contemporary report occurs sometime between 1597 and 1603, when an anonymous writer scribbled a disordered series of words, phrases, quotations, and names on the title page to the Duke of Northumberland's manuscript of Bacon's "Of Tribute, or giving what is dew" (*Shakspere Allusion-Book*, 1: 40). As Figure 4 reveals, the titles of two Shakespeare plays – *Richard II* and *Richard III* – appear at the top of the page, along with Shakespeare's name, which is scattered in various forms down the page. The fragment toward the top left records line 1086 and part of 1087 from *The Rape of Lucrece*. Evidently, one did not have to be able to

---

[25] These all appear in the *Shakspere Allusion-Book*. Thus, Bradbrook is simply mistaken: "Falstaff, Othello, Desdemona, Brutus, Iago and Hamlet (in that order) were what Shakespeare's contemporaries and immediate successors thought, and spoke of whenever they thought of his art" (*Shakespeare*, 103). So is Schmidgall: "Harvey, Meres, Weever, and the *Parnassus* plays" indicate that "Shakespeare gained some considerable fame from his early poetical exertions" (2).

William Shakefpeare

Rychard the fecond   Shakefpeare

Rychard the third

hakfpeare reuealing
           day through
           euery Crany   by Thomas Nafhe & inferior places
           peepes and   *your*
               fee

William Shakefpeare
                     Sh
Shak   h   Sh   Shake   hakefpeare
Sh   h Shak *your*
            william Shakefpeare
            william Shakefpeare

        Willi   Shakfpeare

    william

    Shakefpe

      will Shak

Figure 4. Transcription of the title-page to the Duke of Northumberland's manuscript of Bacon's "Of Tribute, or giving what is dew," with scribbling about Shakespeare.

see straight to know that Shakespeare was a poet-playwright. (If this fellow can see it, why can't we?)

Toward the end of Shakespeare's life, Thomas Freeman pens a commendatory verse "To Master W. Shakespeare," prefacing his *Runne, and a Great Cast. The Second Bowle* (1614):

> Who loves chaste life, there's *Lucrece* for a Teacher:
> Who list read lust there's *Venus and Adonis*,
> True modell of a most lascivious leatcher.
> Besides in plaies thy windes like Meander:
> When needy new-composers borrow more
> Thence Terence doth from Plautus or Menander.
>   (*Shakspere Allusion-Book*, 1: 245)

Freeman's articulation is among the most priceless on record, and for two reasons. First, his verse appears after we think Shakespeare ended his professional career, when he had left London for Stratford. By 1614, the excitement over Shakespeare's narrative poems had had time to cool down, and the early seventeenth-century exuberance over his plays had had time to heat up. Yet Freeman "praise[s]" Shakespeare by balancing his poems with his "plaies" – specifically, his narrative poems and comedies, singling out *Venus* and *Lucrece* by name. Second, Freeman's representation of Shakespeare as a poet-playwright helps us counter the posthumous representation exhibited in the First Folio, where Jonson and company present Shakespeare as only a man of the theatre. Freeman's representation acquires primacy because it is the last extant one to be published before Shakespeare's death.

SHAKESPEARE CRITICISM, 1616–2003

The history of Shakespeare criticism from his death to the present moment supplies additional evidence for viewing Shakespeare as a poet-playwright. For this history reveals that the paradigm of Shakespeare the working dramatist is fundamentally a posthumous paradigm. Although surfacing intermittently during Shakespeare's lifetime, the paradigm becomes enshrined in the 1623 Folio; it gets formally articulated only toward the end of the seventeenth-century; it becomes the primary articulation of the eighteenth and nineteenth centuries; and finally it acquires the status of a critical assumption in the twentieth – remaining so today. A history of this paradigm is sobering, because our most authoritative histories of Shakespeare criticism show little if any self-consciousness about it, so deep-rooted it is as an assumption.[26]

A good deal has recently been written about the First Folio as a "book" or material text. Yet rarely do critics discuss how this important book effaces Shakespeare's achievement as a print poet, since it preserves only his plays.[27] The title page equates the "Picture" or "Figure" (Jonson, "To the Reader") called "William Shakespeare" with the theatrical profession; atop the famous Martin Droeshout etching is the heading *"Mr. William Shakespeares Comedies, Histories, & Tragedies"* (*Riverside*, 90–91). As readers move down the page, we realize that the general purpose of all the book is to imprint on the tablet of our memory Shakespeare's identity as a dramatist.

---

[26] Most notably, Dubrow's "Twentieth-Century Shakespeare Criticism" (*Riverside*, 27–54). See also Levin, "Critical Approaches"; Danson, "Twentieth-Century Shakespeare Criticism: The Comedies," Muir, "Twentieth-Century Shakespeare Criticism: The Tragedies," Berry, "Twentieth-Century"; M. Taylor, *Shakespeare Criticism*.
[27] Cf., e.g., Kastan, *Book*.

All subsequent items in the prefatory material confirm this impression. In the *Dedicatory Epistle* to the earls of Pembroke and Montgomery, Heminge and Condell refer to "Shakespeare" in terms of "his playes" (*Shakspere Allusion-Book*, 1: 313), while in their *Dedicatory Epistle* "To the great Variety of Readers" they refer to their readers as members of an audience "sit[ting] on the Stage at Black-Friers, or the Cock-pit, to arraigne Playes dailie," even as such readers are assured that "these Playes have had their triall alreadie" (*Shakspere Allusion-Book*, 1: 315). Subsequently, Hugh Holland titles his commendatory verse "Upon the Lines and Life of the Famous Scenicke Poet," referring to "Shakespeares . . . dainty Playes, / Which make the Globe of heav'n and earth to ring," and crowning Shakespeare "Poet first, then Poets King" by singling out his "Tragedies" (2–9; *Shakspere Allusion-Book*, 1: 317). By poet, Holland means playwright, as his pithy epithet "Scenicke Poet" conveys. Next, Leonard Digges writes a commendatory verse equating "Shake-speare['s] . . . Workes . . . Line . . . [and] Verse" with his "Stage," citing the "Passions of Juliet, and her Romeo" and "thy half-sword parlying Romans" (1–18; *Shakspere Allusion-Book*, 1: 318) – a quite different portrait, we have seen, than the one Digges presents in Benson's 1640 edition of the *Poems* or even on the flyleaf of his copy of Lope's *Rimas*.[28] The subsequent commendatory verse by I. M. relies on a theatrical metaphor to stage Shakespeare's immortality – "thou went'st so soone / From the Worlds-Stage, to the Graves-Tyring-roome" – and emphasizes that the publication of a play can extend a playwright's life: "An Actors Art, / Can dye, and live, to acte a second part" (1–6; *Shakspere Allusion-Book*, 1: 319).

Even Jonson's historically priceless "To the memory of my beloved, The Author" contributes to this project: "Soule of the Age! / The applause! delight! the wonder of our Stage! / My Shakespeare" (reprinted in *Riverside*, 97). Obedient to the First Folio's promotion of the theatre, Jonson traces Shakespeare's professional genealogy only in terms of the dramatic tradition: from the Greek tragedians, Aeschylus, Sophocles, Euripides, and the Greek comedian, Aristophanes; to the Roman comedians, Plautus and Terence, and the Roman tragedians, Pacuvius, Accius, and Seneca; to the sixteenth- and seventeenth-century English playwrights, Lyly, Kyd, Marlowe, and Beaumont. Moreover, the page listing "The Names of the Principall Actors in all these Playes" (including the first, "William Shakespeare"

---

[28] De Grazia observes that "Holland's and Digges's appropriative tributes [to Shakespeare in the First Folio are] drawn from Shakespeare's sonnets" (*Verbatim*, 22–23), and in a note she specifies: Holland's lines in the couplet of his sonnet "recall . . . Sonnets 16, 18, 74," while Digges's poem "draws" on Sonnets 55, 65, 81, 107 (23n30; see 37).

[*Riverside*, 105]) is headed with the title "The Workes of William Shakespeare, containing all his Comedies, Histories, and Tragedies" (*Riverside*, 105) – an emphatic equation between Shakespeare's "Workes" and the three dramatic genres. Finally, the opening page of the first work, *The Tempest*, prints its theatrical identity simply with its opening stage direction, centered immediately beneath the play's title, set off by print larger than that of the play itself, and enclosed between a set of horizontal lines: "*Actus primus, Scena prima*" (*Riverside*, 107).

We do not know why the First Folio excludes Shakespeare's poems. Colin Burrow speculates that the marketability of both *Venus* and *Lucrece* would have made it "difficult and expensive to obtain the right to print them" (Burrow, ed., *Sonnets and Poems*, 8). This is certainly possible, but Burrow is merely speculating ("this may be one reason" [7]); to my knowledge, the issue has never been studied in detail. If marketability is the "reason," why would Heminge and Condell not have said something about it in their prefatory material? Why are all the writers of commendatory verses silent about Shakespeare's poems, especially Digges, who is on record for praising both the poems and plays? Surely, it would not have been out of place to mention the poems, even in passing. And why were such authors as Daniel and Jonson able to get the right to print both their poems and their plays in editions of their works? One wonders, rather, whether the two members of Shakespeare's acting company, themselves men of the theatre, set about to memorialize their own profession – a worthy end in itself, but one that skews the historical record, momentous because of this very publication.

Perhaps because the First Folio prints Shakespeare as the working dramatist, subsequent commentators repeat or magnify the "Figure." In 1627, for instance, Drayton, who, like Jonson should have known better, sees Shakespeare as only a comedian and a tragedian: "Shakespeare thou hadst as smooth a Comicke vaine . . . / . . . and as Cleere a rage, / As any one that trafiqu'd with the stage" (*Shakspere Allusion-Book*, 1: 334; see Milton, *Shakspere Allusion-Book*, 1: 342). After the 1642 closing of the theatres and their reopening during the Restoration, Shakespeare appears almost exclusively as a "Dramatick Writer" (Nahum Tate, 1680 preface, *Shakspere Allusion-Book*, 2: 266). The key figure here is Dryden, for whom Shakespeare's plays became something of an obsession; his arch-project was to re-dramatize Shakespeare's plays, as revealed by the opening to his 1679 "Preface" for *Troilus and Cressida, Or, Truth Found too Late*: "The Poet Aeschylus was held in the same veneration by the Athenians of after Ages as Shakespeare is by us" (B. Vickers, ed., *Critical Heritage*, 1: 249).

From Rhymer in *A Short View of Tragedy* (1693), to Pope in his edition of Shakespeare (1725), to Samuel Johnson in his proposal for an edition of "The Dramatick Works" (1756), to Coleridge in his unpublished lectures on Shakespeare (1811–12), to Hazlitt in his *Characters of Shakespeare's Plays* (1817), the Bard is fundamentally a dramatic writer. However, Coleridge deserves special merit, because he reports that Shakespeare "had shown himself a poet, previously to his appearance as a dramatic poet" (quoted in Schmidgall, *Poet's Life*, 6), even though he sets the stage for commentary up to our own day:

> our *myriad-minded* Shakspear. I mean the 'Venus and Adonis' and the 'Lucrece;' works which give at once strong promises of the strength, and yet obvious proofs of the immaturity, of his genius . . . I think, I should have conjectured from these poems, that even then the great instinct, which impelled the poet to the drama, was secretly working in him . . . In Shakespeare's *poems*, the creative power, and the intellectual energy wrestle as in a war embrace . . . At length, in the DRAMA they were reconciled. (Kolin, ed., "*Venus and Adonis*," 69–72; Coleridge's emphases)

Through the nineteenth century, most commentators would not dispute the eighteenth-century hyperbole of Dr. Johnson – "his drama is the mirrour of life" (B. Vickers, ed., *Critical Heritage*, 5: 59–60) – or the exaltation of Pope: "he is justly and universally elevated above all other Dramatic Writers" (2: 403). But some, like Hazlitt, oppose Coleridge on even the developmental merits of the poems: "It has been the fashion of late to cry up on our author's poems, as equal to his plays: this is the desperate cry of modern criticism . . . The two poems of *Venus and Adonis* and of Tarquin and Lucrece appear to us like a couple of ice-houses. They are about as hard, as glittering, and as cold" (quoted in Kolin, ed., "*Venus and Adonis*," 14). The poles represented by Hazlitt and Coleridge characterize commentary up through the end of the millennium, even the recent spirited defenses of the poetry identified in the last chapter.

Nonetheless, for late nineteenth century critics, as for twentieth and early twenty-first-century critics, Shakespeare remains fundamentally the working dramatist. As most histories of Shakespeare criticism acknowledge, Bradley's 1904 *Shakespearean Tragedy* established the benchmark for commentary in the twentieth century; as Harry Levin put it in 1986, "In the vast sea of secondary studies that have grown up around Shakespeare, no single book has gained wider acceptance than Bradley's" ("Critical Approaches," 228). What is significant is that this most influential book should examine only the drama – and only one genre within it. While Bradley's project proves vast in influence, well justifying an "Age of Bradley" in Michael

Taylor's recent analysis of Shakespearean Criticism in the twentieth century (*Shakespeare Criticism*, 39–84), in fact Bradley narrows the generic scope of Shakespeare's genius considerably.

We might find it striking, then, to see the extent to which three important 1997 editions of Shakespeare's works reproduce the tradition from the First Folio to Bradley (and beyond). The new *Riverside Shakespeare*, *The Norton Shakespeare*, and the *Longman Shakespeare* all inscribe the "dramatic" paradigm that has controlled the "vast sea" of Shakespeare studies since the seventeenth century. What is more to the point, they do so unconsciously. *The Riverside Shakespeare*, for instance, prints its contents page with the following headings: "Comedies," "Histories," Tragedies," "Romances," "Poems." Evidently, the nonparallelism does not disrupt the reader's expectation; indeed, the theatrical paradigm is so widely held that no heading called "Plays" is required. Similarly, the opening sentence to Greenblatt's "Preface" in *The Norton Shakespeare* equates the theatrical principle of Shakespeare's career with the primary principle organizing his volume: "Since Shakespeare's principal medium, the drama, was thoroughly collaborative, it seems appropriate that this edition of his works is itself the result of a sustained collaboration" (xi). Moreover, the *Longman Shakespeare* relies on the conventional generic structure: "The Comedies," "The Histories," "The Tragedies," "The Romances," and "The Poems." David Bevington's "General Introduction" subtly equates Shakespeare's "Life" with Shakespeare's "Drama," as revealed by the titles of his first three units: "Life in Shakespeare's England," "The Drama Before Shakespeare," and "London Theaters and Dramatic Companies." *Life . . . Drama . . . Theatre*. In Shakespeare studies today, life *is* drama in the theatre.

This short history of Shakespeare criticism suggests that the notion of Shakespeare the working dramatist is the product of a partial taxonomy created seven years after the author's death, principally by the First Folio. Having looked into this history, we should not be surprised to see what has happened. We might be more surprised to discover that such seventeenth-century poet-playwrights as Jonson, Drayton, Milton, and Dryden could so misrepresent one of their kind. How do we account for this? One explanation is that Shakespeare turned out to be so much more gifted as a dramatist than as a poet. Although he wrote both poems and plays, he was so superior in talent as a dramatist that this achievement eclipsed his record as a poet and even his composite identity as a poet-playwright. If so, we can here see how futile was the enterprise of Benson, who in 1640 set about to print an edition of Shakespeare's poems that would do for the poet what the First Folio had done for the playwright. Had Benson succeeded in his venture

Figure 5. Frontispiece to *The Plays and Poems of William Shakespeare*, edited by Edmund
Malone (London, 1790).

on the scale of Heminge and Condell, or if they, rather than he, had been able to print both forms in the same volume, we might wonder, would the history of Shakespeare criticism be different?

While the history of criticism from the seventeenth through to the twenty-first centuries reveals the paradigm of the working dramatist to be an anachronism, we might take the cue of Coleridge to recall that in each century commentators periodically emerge with a more accurate historicism. In the late seventeenth century, for instance, Milton's nephew, Edward Phillips, presents Shakespeare at least as a playwright-poet: "William Shakespeare, the Glory of the English Stage . . . : from an Actor of Tragedies and Comedies, he became a Maker . . . ; and in all his Writings hath an unvulgar style, as well in his *Venus and Adonis*, his *Rape of Lucrece* and other various Poems, as in his Dramatics" (*Shakspere Allusion-Book*, 2: 222–23). Similarly, in the late eighteenth century Edmund Malone remarks: "All that is known with any degree of certainty concerning Shakespere, is – 'that he was born at Stratford upon Avon, married and had three children there, went to London, where he commenced actor, and *wrote poems and plays* – returned to Stratford, made his will, died, and was buried'" (quoted in De Grazia, *Verbatim*, 135; emphasis added).

Poems and plays: Malone emerges as the pivotal figure in a counter-history of Shakespeare criticism, since he is "the first editor of Shakespeare to publish the 1609 Sonnets in an edition of the works, first in 1780 as a supplement to the Johnson–Steevens 1778 edition and then in the final volume of his own 1790 edition": "The title of the 1790 edition reflected their [the *Sonnets'*] new status; while previous editors had called their editions either *The Works* or *The Plays*, Malone entitled his edition *The Plays and Poems*" (De Grazia, *Verbatim*, 152, 154). Accordingly, we might recall the frontispiece to his edition (Figure 5), where the author of the Chandos portrait oversees a three-panel display, the left one with its theatrical mask clearly evocative of the plays and the right with its musical instruments perhaps evocative of the poems. Finally, Malone joins Coleridge and Phillips in preparing us to restore Shakespeare to the contours of what we have called the Meres miniature: Shakespeare's original status as an English Ovidian poet-playwright in the European tradition.

PART TWO

1593–1594: the print author presents himself
Play scene: "Two Gentlemen" to "Richard III"

In 1593 and 1594, while the theatres were closed in London due to plague, Richard Field, from Stratford-upon-Avon, served as the printer of both *Venus and Adonis* and *The Rape of Lucrece*. The choice of this printer for Shakespeare's first published poems contributes an intriguing dimension to the story about the national poet-playwright. For, as Colin Burrow observes, "Field's shop produced books which . . . made claims to high literary status," such as John Harington's translation of Ariosto's *Orlando Furioso* (1591), yet "there is a striking lack of theatrical texts among the works he printed" (Burrow, ed., *Sonnets and Poems*, 6). Evidently, the printer's trade could participate in the kind of generic exclusivity that such authors as the print-poet Spenser exhibited, when he eschewed the new commercial theatre for the "high literary status" of the Virgilian pastoral *Shepheardes Calender*, printed by Hugh Singleton in 1579, or the epic *Faerie Queene*, published by William Ponsonby in 1590. Field's profile as a printer ends up mirroring Shakespeare's profile as an author, for, as is well known, in both *Venus* and *Lucrece* Shakespeare turns from the world of staged theatre to that of printed poetry. But the counter-Spenserian profile sharpens because, as Burrow adds, Field "was also an appropriate printer for an Ovidian poem," having inherited his shop from Thomas Vautrollier, who "had enjoyed a monopoly in the printing of Ovid in Latin." More than this, for back in 1589 Field had printed Vautrollier's text of the *Metamorphoses* and would go on in 1594 to reprint Vautrollier's edition of the *Heroides* (Burrow, ed., *Sonnets and Poems*, 6). Effectively, with Field as his printer, Shakespeare extends his Elizabethan reputation as the stager of plays to present himself as a print author of Ovidian poems.

We need to see Shakespeare extending this Ovidian persona from stage to page, rather than simply inaugurating it for the purpose of print, because this is what is attested to by those of his plays authored and performed before the closing of the theatres, none of which came into print until after the theatres reopened (insofar as we can tell). While the exact composition and performance chronology of these plays remains unknown, most scholars would consent to the list from *The Oxford Shakespeare*, even if they might quarrel about some of its details:

The Two Gentlemen of Verona
The Taming of the Shrew
2 Henry VI (*The First Part of the Contention of the Two Famous Houses of York and Lancaster*)
3 Henry VI (*The true Tragedy of Richard Duke of York and the Good King Henry the Sixth*)
The Most Lamentable Tragedy of Titus Andronicus
1 Henry VI
Richard III.[1]

Such a list is convenient for showing the young Shakespeare overgoing the tragedic Marlowe by ranging widely through the three available dramatic genres advertised years later on the title page to the First Folio: comedy, history, and tragedy. Already, the young Shakespeare is a formidable practitioner of dramatic form, in ways that Marlowe would never live to be. For purposes of the present discussion, therefore, it will be convenient to group *Two Gentlemen* and *Shrew* together as early comedies, the three *Henry VI* plays and *Richard* as early histories, and *Titus* as an early tragedy.

These three sets of plays all require detailed analysis beyond the scope of this book, but it might be useful to suggest briefly that the main frame of Shakespeare's art, as discussed in chapters 1–2, does not suddenly appear in *Venus* and *Lucrece*. Most of the early comedies, histories, and tragedies show an engagement with the Ovidian art of poetry and theatre in a Virgilian landscape; the frame is almost always inflected with the aesthetics of Spenser and Marlowe. Obviously, a comedy like *Two Gentleman* accomplishes this inflection differently than a history play like *3 Henry VI*, and both differ from a historical tragedy like *Titus*.

While only a full analysis could do justice to the complexities involved, we might remind ourselves that *Two Gentlemen* and *Shrew* have clear affinities with *Venus*, especially in their interest in Ovidian myths of authorship (including Orpheus), but also in their engagement with the works of Spenser and Marlowe. Similarly, *Titus* has clear links with *Lucrece*; not simply were both the play and the poem published in 1594, but the stage tragedy refers to the Lucretia myth several times, and the two works share

---

[1] Some editors would include *The Comedy of Errors* in this pre-plague group (see, e.g., *Riverside*), but the anomaly of this play has already been noted, and thus it proves convenient to put it aside here. Other scholars, such as Bate, would date *Titus* after the plague years (Bate, ed., *Titus Andronicus*, 3, 72, esp. 77–79), but the precise chronology is not necessary to the present argument.

important references to the Ovidian and Spenserian myth of the nightingale Philomela.[2] The intertextual system is more complex than this suggests, however, because the delightful romantic comedy in *Two Gentlemen* toys darkly with tragedy and rape, naturally embedding several references to Philomela, while *Shrew* refers to both Philomela and Lucrece. As a group, the early plays record some splendid generic disjunctions, as when Charles the Dolphin in *1 Henry VI* tells Joan de Pucelle that her "promises are like Adonis' garden" (1. 6. 6) – forcing an uneasy alliance between the history play and Shakespeare's first narrative poem, not to mention Spenser's *Faerie Queene*, 3. 6, which the play clearly evokes (*Riverside*, 640). Less surprisingly, the epic landscape at Troy, with Sinon at its center, shows up importantly in *3 Henry VI* (3. 2. 188–95), as in *Lucrece*.

Accordingly, the *Henry VI* trilogy does not simply refer to the Virgilian story of Aeneas and Dido (*2 Henry VI*, 3. 2. 116–18, 5. 2. 62–64); it showcases the sovereign as a Spenserian shepherd-king. This figure is playfully satirized in Christopher Sly during the Induction scenes to *Shrew*, a play that also alludes comically to Virgil's national epic and probably to Marlowe's burlesque staging of it in *Dido, Queen of Carthage*: "As Anna to the Queen of Carthage was, / Tranio," declares Lucentio, "I burn, I pine, I perish" (1. 1. 154–55). In particular, *Two Gentlemen*, *Titus*, and *Shrew* are clearly plotted along the Virgilian path of epic court and pastoral countryside, in a narrative pattern that becomes important in the later comedies and romances, from *Love's Labor's Lost* through *The Tempest*.

In the early plays, versions of the poet-playwright figure include Proteus in *Two Gentlemen*, Tranio in *Shrew*, Titus in his tragedy, and most intriguingly Joan in *1 Henry VI*, a shepherd's daughter who claims to be the daughter of a king, as she herself insists: "Not me begotten of a shepherd swain, / But issued from the progeny of kings" (5. 4. 37–38). As mentioned in chapter 1, in *Richard III* Shakespeare tends to separate poet and playwright in the characters of Clarence and Richard. Nonetheless, in almost all of these plays, we discover a dramatic conflict between two figures whose aesthetics resemble those of Spenser and Marlowe, from Valentine and Proteus in *Two Gentlemen*, to Talbot and Joan in *1 Henry VI*, to Lucius and Aaron in *Titus*. Without access to the Spenserian aesthetics of pastoral and epic and the Marlovian aesthetics of poetry and theatre, including their interpenetration, we cannot possibly account for a passage like the following, spoken by Shakespeare's earliest shepherd-king figure, Henry VI:

---

[2] For recent analysis of *Lucrece* and *Titus*, see Hadfield, *Shakespeare and Renaissance Political Culture*, ch. 3.

> So flies the reakless shepherd from the wolf;
> So first the harmless sheep doth yield his fleece,
> And next his throat unto the butcher's knife.
> What scene of death hath Roscius now to act?
>
> (*3 Henry VI*, 5. 6. 7–10)

What makes this speech unusual and important is its artistically self-conscious yoking of two different forms of authorial discourse, typically separated in the literary tradition: that of the Spenserian pastoral shepherd; and that of the Marlovian theatrical man.[3]

Equally to the point, poetry and theatre are recurrent topics of conversation in all of these plays – and not simply in the comedies or more memorably *Titus*, with its formal tragic staging of the Ovidian "book": "'tis Ovid's Metamorphosis . . . / This is the tragic tale of Philomel" (4. 1. 41, 42–47). In fact, this scene is of considerable importance for Shakespeare's career. When Lavina "*takes the staff in her mouth, and guides it with her stumps, and writes*" the words "*Stuprum* – Chiron – Demetrius" (s.d. after l. 76 and l. 78) – Shakespeare doubly dramatizes a momentous conjunction and finally a historic transfer in literary and cultural media: from the printed book of Ovid's poetry to the very Senecan-styled tragedic theatre that he himself scripts, as revealed in Marcus' subsequent reference to "the lustful sons of Tamora" as "Performers of this heinous, bloody deed" and in Titus' own Latin quotation from Seneca's *Hippolytus* (79–80).[4]

In the history plays, as perhaps more memorably in the comedies, characters repeatedly talk about poets and their art. If Proteus in *Two Gentlemen* can tell the Duke that "Orpheus' lute was strung with poets' sinews" (3. 2. 77), Clarence records his horrifying dream with like-minded reference: "I passed (methought) the melancholy flood, / With that sour ferryman which poets write of" (*Richard III*, 1. 4. 45–46). In contrast, Clarence's vicious brother, Richard himself, can confide in the audience that he is putting theatre to work: "Thus, like the formal Vice, Iniquity, / I moralize two meanings in one word" (3. 1. 82–83). The one Ovidian poem that so

---

[3] I have often thought that the present book and its sequel are an attempt to account for the peculiarity of this speech near the beginning of Shakespeare's professional career. In chapter 1, we saw how both Spenser and Marlowe themselves bridge the two discourses, but Shakespeare here overgoes both in his technical reference to the theatre and its profession of acting.

[4] Barkan is on the verge of this idea when he finds here "a myth about the competition amongst media of communication," which he initially generalizes as "words, pictures, book, signs, and more," but then specifies as Shakespeare's own theatre, "a new medium of communication . . . that marries the book and the picture" (*The Gods Made Flesh*, 246, 247): "But to this process Shakespeare adds more stages. First, Lavinia can point to the book, a compendium of words and pictures already made; second, she makes signs in the earth; finally, Shakespeare can embody the whole fable in a drama: words, pictures, book, signs, and more" (245).

historically crosses the divide between poetry and theatre, the *Heroides*, is quoted in comedy and history alike (*Shrew*, 3. 1. 28–29; *3 Henry VI*, 1. 3. 48). Ovid himself is occasionally a topic of conversation, as in *Shrew* when Tranio tells Lucentio that they should not "As Ovid be an outcast quite abjur'd" (1. 1. 33). If this comedy opens with Ovid, *Two Gentlemen* opens with England's Ovid, as Valentine and Proteus reveal that they have been reading the "love-book" of the great Elizabethan Ovidian minor epic, *Hero and Leander* – "some shallow story of deep love, / How young Leander cross'd the Hellespont" (1. 1. 21–22).[5]

All of this helps explain not simply why books are a recurrent topic of conversation in these plays ("this small packet of Greek and Latin books" [*Shrew*, 2. 1. 98]), but why books often end up conjoined with theatre – sometimes absolutely deftly, as in Queen Margaret's superb "flattering index of a direful pageant" in *Richard III* (4. 4. 85). These plays, it turns out, are nearly as obsessed with publication and print culture as we shall see in *The Rape of Lucrece*. In *Two Gentlemen*, for instance, Proteus performs his falsifying part by relying on a term that has received considerable notice in the minor epic (chapter 4): "For love of you, not hate unto my friend, / Hath made me *publisher* of this pretense" (3. 1. 46–47; emphasis added). Consequently, the early plays show a remarkable commitment to the concepts of artistic immortality and national fame, and do so through the terms of print culture itself:

> O peers of England, shameful is this league,
> Fatal this marriage, cancelling your fame,
> Blotting your names from books of memory,
> Rasing the characters of your renown,
> Defacing monuments of conquer'd France.
> (*2 Henry VI*, 1. 1. 98–102)

Recalling some of these general contours in the early comedies, histories, and tragedies, we may now to turn to Shakespeare's two minor epics to see how the fledgling national poet-playwright manages the transposition from stage to page. This second part to the book thus consists of two respective chapters designed to explore the Shakespearean authorial frame in works in which he presents himself as a print poet, in competition with such nationally visible rivals as Spenser and Marlowe: chapter 3, on *Venus and Adonis*; and chapter 4, on *The Rape of Lucrece*.

---

[5] *Hero and Leander* was entered in the Stationers' Register on 28 September 1593, but is believed to have circulated in manuscript; the first extant edition dates to 1598.

Authorship and acting: plotting Venus and Adonis along the Virgilian path

I did but act, he's author of thy slander.
(*Venus and Adonis*, 1006)

In the epigraph above, Venus complains to the dying Adonis that she is merely the "act[or]" of a fatal verse script about his calumny that the villain Death has tragically "author[ed]." The discourse and narration of authorship and acting here suggests that *Venus and Adonis* may be more than simply a retelling of the luscious and poignant Ovidian myth about "sexual violence or harassment" between unequal heterosexual partners (Crewe, ed., *Narrative Poems*, xxxiv). It may simultaneously be an Ovidian fiction about the relation between the twin arts forming the frame of Shakespeare's professional career.

Venus' term "act" is recognizable as a theatrical term. The *Oxford English Dictionary* cites *Hamlet*, 2. 2. 435 and *Cymbeline*, 3. 4. 26, but we could recall line 359 of *Venus* as well: "this dumb play had his acts."[1] Similarly, Venus' term "author" is recognizable as a term for the author of printed poetry, especially during the early 1590s, when Spenser had used it forcibly to present himself as England's New Poet in the 1579 *Shepheardes Calender* – "the Author" (*Dedicatory Epistle*) – and then followed with the 1590 install-ment of *The Faerie Queene*, to which is appended a famous "Letter of the Authors expounding his whole intention in the course of this worke" (*Letter to Ralegh*).[2] In this chapter, we might look into Shakespeare's curious 1593 jostling of these terms and the twin professional institutions surrounding

---

[1] See Righter, who quotes W. J. Lawrence: "'It is to be noted that Shakespeare . . . uses the word 'act' . . . rarely, if ever, without giving it some associated theatrical colouring'" (*Idea of the Play*, 90).

[2] On Spenser's invention of "a new Elizabethan author function," see Montrose, "Subject": Spenser's "'Laureate' authorial persona . . . not only professionalizes poetry, it authenticates through print the subjectivity of a writer whose class position might otherwise have rendered him merely the anonymous functionary of his patron. In claiming the originative status of an 'Author,' a writer claims the authority to direct and delimit the interpretive activity of that elite community of readers by whom he himself is authorized to write" (319). In *Hamlet*, Shakespeare's Prince speaks of "the author" of the play on Aeneas and Dido (2. 2. 443).

them – a jostling that recurs in the poem as a whole. *Venus and Adonis* is valuable in part because it is Shakespeare's "first . . . invention" (*Dedicatory Epistle*) in print of a fiction directly about the cultural function and social interchange between poetic authorship and stage acting, at the very time when the art of theatre is competing with the art of printed poetry.[3] In 1602, the anonymous authors of *The Return from Parnassus* capture the peculiar Elizabethan competition between these forms, when Ingenioso relies on clothing imagery to tell Gull, "We shall have nothinge but pure Shakspeare and threds of poetry that he hath gathered at the theators!," only to have Gull quote stanza 2 of *Venus and Adonis* (*Shakspere Allusion-Book*, 1: 67).

THE NARRATIVE OF POETRY AND THEATRE

The fiction in *Venus and Adonis* initially tells of the great goddess of love and beauty using the art of poetry to court the idyllic young hunter: "For to a pretty ear she tunes her tale" (74).[4] Indeed, Venus repeatedly tells her "story" (716) with its distinctively erotic "theme" (770). For instance, when Adonis escapes after accusing her of "Bewitching" him with a "tempting tune" sung "like the wanton mermaids' songs" (777–78), she "sings" in solitude "extemporally a woeful ditty" (836), a "heavy anthem" (839), however "tedious[ly]" she "outwore the night" (841). In fact, Venus sings this song in order to "mark" the "echoes" from "the neighbor caves," which "Make verbal repetition of her moans" (830–35). Such discourse identi-fies her specifically as an Orphic poet who wittily "redouble[s]" (832) the woods-resounding formula so central to the Renaissance Orpheus myth (Cain, "Orpheus," 28). Toward the end of *Venus and Adonis*, the goddess "stories" the "victories" of Death (1013–14), and "whispers" in the dying Adonis' ears "a heavy tale, / As if they heard the woeful words she told" (1125–26).

Yet Venus does not simply sing her songs of seduction to court Adonis "extemporally"; as this theatrical terms suggests, she performs them as an actor on the stage, drawing Adonis into her erotic theatre: "And all this dumb play had his acts made plain / With tears which chorus-like her eyes did rain" (359–60).[5] The theatrical metaphor measures the couple's failure

---

[3] Only Fienberg links *Venus and Adonis* with the theatre and the print shop ("Thematics of Value," 250). For the value and limitations of this essay, see below.

[4] Critics identify Venus as a "rhetor/orator" who deploys "talents/entrapments" (Kolin, ed., "*Venus and Adonis*," 34; see 34–35; Mortimer, *Variable Passions*, 1–35). But some critics do identify Venus as a poet, usually a Petrarchan poet or sonneteer; see Baumlin, "Birth"; Kiernan "*Venus and Adonis*," 93.

[5] Roe discusses the theatrical significance here (Roe, ed., *Poems*, 98). For *extempore* as a theatrical term, see, e.g., *1 Henry IV*, 2. 4. 280: "a play extempore." On "Venus' skill as a role player," see Kolin,

to perform perceptual reciprocity and to enact companionate desire: they appear on stage together, but Adonis is the silent speaker of a dumb show and Venus the chorus commenting on his tragic action with tears. Thus, Venus can only imagine the "twain" of them participating in Love's "revels": "Be bold to play, our sport is not in sight" (123–24). Here the language of theatre and the language of sex are indistinguishable – and that is the point.[6]

At the end of the story, Venus' arts of poetry and theatre fail to perform their desired end. Adonis loses his life in the hunt for the boar and metamorphoses into a "purple flow'r . . . check'red with white" (1168).[7] Here the great goddess performs the poem's climactic act: she "crops the stalk" (1175) and cradles the flower to her "bosom" (1173). In the words of Jonathan Crewe, "The only 'progeny' resulting from the relationship is the flower Venus maternally cherishes in the end; since flowers traditionally stand for poetic creations, the poem becomes the sole 'offspring' of this ill-fated love" (Crewe, ed., *Narrative Poems*, xxxix). In this version of the poem's fiction, Venus is the figure of (female) agency who initially uses the (masculine) arts of poetry and theatre to render the comedic denouement of sexual fulfillment, but who finally consoles herself with a tragic artifact that represents the very work we are reading.[8]

Yet Shakespeare complicates this Venerean fiction by presenting Adonis similarly as an artistic figure of agency associated with the art of poetry. While initially refusing to talk (427), Adonis eventually breaks into a "mermaid's voice" filled with "Melodious discord, heavenly tune harsh sounding" (429–31). The image of the mermaid here does not simply match the one associated with Venus (quoted above) but also functions as "the quintessential figure for poetry," from the *Odyssey* forward (de Vroom, 437).

---

ed., "*Venus and Adonis*," 37. Hyland considers how Shakespeare's "theatrical experience might have a bearing on how he imagined Venus and Adonis" (*Introduction to Shakespeare's Poems*, 82). Hardie, *Poetics*, traces the theatrical Venus to Virgil's *Aeneid*, 4 (13).

[6] On theatre and sex in Shakespeare, see Parker, *Margins*, 253; on "show" and "tell" in terms of theatre, see 253–54, 271.

[7] As we shall see in chapter 5, the author of Poem 4 in *The Passionate Pilgrim* picked up on Shakespeare's use of poetry and theatre as Venus' two courting techniques: "She told him stories to delight his [ear]; / She show'd him favors to allure his eye" (5–6).

[8] On how *Venus* "registers the birth of the aesthetic from the sexual," see Halpern, "'Pining,'" 386. Cf. Schiffer, "Desire," 359–76, esp. 374; Dubrow, *Victors*, 40–43. Fienberg's "feminist argument" anticipates my own literary one: Venus' "bargains may . . . be analogous to the strategies Shakespeare, already a man of the theater, would employ as he both 'immures' that multiple, shifting, subversive theatrical talent between the fixed covers of a published poem, and risks exposing his poetry to the commodification of the court marketplace. Then Venus represents the politically, sexually, and epistemologically subversive realm of the theater invading the realm of published poetry" ("Thematics of Value," 257). We may extend this idea to Adonis, historicize it in terms of the intersystemic intertexual rivalry with Ovid and the intrasystemic rivalry with other writers in the Elizabethan literary system, and finally see here more than simple analogy.

Like Venus, Adonis tells a "tale" (591), narrates a "story" (716), produces a "text" (806), and "recreate[s]" himself "when he hath song" (1095). Just as Venus redoubles Orpheus by echoing song through the neighbor caves, so Adonis' song here has the Orphic power to order nature harmoniously: "The tiger would be tame, and gently hear him . . . / When he was by, the birds such pleasure took, / That some would sing" (1096–1102; see Cain, "Orpheus," 25–28). For all their differences, these lovers share an Orphic vocation.

They do not, however, share a theatrical profession. In Shakespeare's lexicon, Adonis is never a theatrical agent. Instead, the youth becomes complicit in Venus' theatre *against his will*, both in Love's "revels" and in the "dumb play" that she has been scripting. Later, he finds himself haplessly performing a part in the "play" of Death, as Venus herself laments: "this foul . . . boar . . . / Ne'er saw the beauteous livery that he wore – / Witness the entertainment that he gave" (1105–08).[9] According to this second version of the fiction, Adonis himself is a figure of (male) agency who uses the (masculine) art of poetry to resist the allure of Venus' (feminine) arts of poetry and theatre, only to find himself an unwilling participant in a poem and its theater bent on turning him into a tragic artifact.

Perhaps the most concrete icon for Venus and Adonis as figures associated with poetry and theatre appears in lines 211–16, when Venus breaks into complaint at her unresponsive lover:

> Fie, liveless picture, cold and senseless stone,
> Well-painted idol, image dull and dead,
> Statue contenting but the eye alone.
> (*Venus and Adonis*, 211–13)

Critics rightly observe that Venus here compares Adonis "in all but name to Pygmalion's statue" in Book 10 of Ovid's *Metamorphoses* – an especially appropriate allusion since "Adonis is, according to Ovid, the great-grandson of Pygmalion and the transformed statue."[10] As Richard Halpern suggests, "Shakespeare's innovation with respect to the Pygmalion myth – as in *Venus and Adonis* generally – is to explore the 'comic' possibilities of reversing this situation. Hence he places Venus in Pygmalion's place, lusting hopelessly after an unresponsive image" ("Pining," 380). As Halpern also notes, Shakespeare cross-dresses Venus as a male artist figure who fails to effect the metamorphosis that Venus in Ovid's story secures. The allusion

---

[9] On theatre and the "livery guilds," see Stallybrass, "Worn."
[10] Halpern, "Pining," 379–80. See also Roe, who adds that in Ovid's story "it was appropriately Venus who gave the statue life in response to Pygmalion's prayers" (Roe, ed., *Poems*, 91).

to the Pygmalion myth compels us, then, to see Shakespeare's principals as more than figures of eros; they are also figures of art.[11] Most obviously, Venus presents herself as an artist figure and Adonis as her artifact; thus it is easiest to see Shakespeare here simply following Ovid in representing the poet and his poem. Yet, by taking Halpern's *dramatic* cues, we can discern that the imagery from the visual and plastic arts – "picture," "painted idol," "image" – brings us close to theatre, especially if we recall that Shakespeare's most famous use of the Pygmalion myth, the resurrection of the statue of Hermione closing *The Winter's Tale*, formally stages the Ovidian myth's original theatrical potential.[12] As we shall see, Shakespeare uses the Pygmalion myth to consolidate a complex Ovidian art that intertwines poetry and theatre in the agencies of both Venus and Adonis.[13]

SONGS AND SHOWS

To understand more fully the story about "songs" and "shows" – and in particular about the interaction between the two within a poem conventionally understood to be about the death of desire – we may take Shakespeare's cue about Ovid's Pygmalion myth and recall the poem's most immediate historical context: the new, fundamentally sixteenth-century writing institution discussed in Part one, the emergence in England at this time of a writer who combines poems and plays as part of a single literary career, the author as poet-playwright. As we may recall, the new English poet-playwright is "Ovidian."

While it is well known that Francis Meres in his 1598 *Palladis Tamia* presents Shakespeare as England's Ovid, we might glance at another contemporary – one who more clearly understands Shakespeare's production of both poems and plays to be an Ovidian enterprise. Spenser's friend Gabriel Harvey wrote marginalia on a 1598 Speght edition of Chaucer (c.1600) that

---

[11] See, e.g., J. M. Miller, who notes that traditional interpretations see the Pygmalion myth either as "a metaphor for the creative process: the artist creates a perfect work of art which then comes to life," or as a metaphor for religious "piety" rewarded, although she herself emphasizes its "clear undercurrent of eroticism" ("Pygmalion," 206).

[12] Cf. J. M. Miller, "Pygmalion," 211–12. Hulse, *Verse* (141–94), discusses the idea that for the Renaissance "painting is mute poetry and poetry a speaking picture" (143), and he goes on to link *Venus and Adonis* with comedy (173). In *Statue*, Gross describes Ovid's Pygmalion myth through a discourse of theatre (72–74); on the moving statue in *The Winter's Tale* as a parable of theatre, see 100–09. Hardie's chapter on Pygmalion in *Poetics* (173–226), which includes a section on *The Winter's Tale* (193–206), helps account for Shakespeare's transposition of Ovid's poetical Pygmalion to the stage: "The story of Pygmalion can be read as an *aition* of illusionist art" (190).

[13] Cf. Kolin's conclusion: "Poetic readings of *Venus* turn dramatic for many critics, while dramatic performances turn back to the work's poetic stubbornness" (Kolin, ed., "*Venus and Adonis*," 59).

bears importantly on *Venus and Adonis*, and here we may quote Harvey's commentary at greater length than we did in chapter 1:

> The younger sort takes much delight in Shakespeares Venus, & Adonis: but his Lucrece, & his tragedie of Hamlet, Prince of denmarke, have it in them, to please the wiser sort. Or such Poets: or better: or none.
>
>
>
> Vilia miretur Vulgus: mihi flavus Apollo
> Pocula Castaliae plena ministret aquae: quoth
> Sir Edward Dier, betwene jest & earnest.
>
>
> (reprinted in *Riverside*, 1965)

Harvey finds Shakespeare's combination of two poems and a play here so natural that he emphasizes the dialectic of audience affect discussed previously. But Harvey then quotes Ovid, *Amores*, 1. 15. 35–36. Edward Dyer may have quoted these lines, but if so the quotation has not (to my knowledge) survived. Yet one quotation has survived: the epigraph to *Venus and Adonis*, which in Marlowe's translation reads: "Let base-conceited wits admire vile things, / Fair Phoebus lead me to the Muses' springs" (*Ovid's Elegies*, 1. 15. 35–36). Although Harvey evidently uses the Ovidian quotation to distinguish between such "vile" works as *Venus and Adonis* and such Apollonian works as *Lucrece* and *Hamlet*, he includes both kinds of literary productions under an "Ovidian" rubric.

One way, then, to read Shakespeare's fiction in *Venus and Adonis* is as a self-conscious Ovidian narrative about the arts of poetry and theatre forming the Ovidian structure of his own career.[14] As in his other two experiments in narrative poetry – *The Rape of Lucrece* and *A Lover's Complaint* – Shakespeare makes his fiction about the separation of the sexes and the fatal nature of desire pertain to his professional career.[15] While both Harvey and Shakespeare quote the Latin from the *Amores*, most likely their contemporaries would have recognized a veiled intertextuality with the English author who had translated them in the first place, made them famous for English culture. For Shakespeare and his contemporaries, Ovid's *Amores* were also Marlovian.[16]

By taking this cue, we can consolidate Shakespeare's literary historicism one step further, labeling his Ovidianism of poetry and theatre Marlovian.

---

[14] Cf. the principal studies of Ovid in *Venus and Adonis*: Keach, *Erotic Narratives*, 52–84; Hulse, *Verse*, 141–94, esp. 143–75; Dubrow, *Victors*, 21–79; Bate, *Ovid*, 48–67. See also Froes, "Shakespeare's Venus"; Stapleton, "*Praeceptor*"; Murphy, "Wriothesley's Resistance"; Kiernan, "*Venus and Adonis*."

[15] On eros independent of career, see Kahn, "Eros"; Belsey, "Trompe-L'oeil"; Merrix, "Hollow Cradle"; Schiffer, "Desire"; Halpern, "'Pining.'" For a "queer reading," see Stanivukovic, *Ovid* (quotation on 103).

[16] On Marlowe and the *Amores*, see Pearcy, *Mediated Muse*; Stapleton, *Harmful*.

Since scholarship and criticism have emphasized the presence of Marlowe in the discourse of *Venus and Adonis*, we need not argue this classification in any detail.[17] Rather, we may foreground a neglected idea: it is the poetry and theatre of Venus (in particular) that resembles the art of Christopher Marlowe. In fact, Venus' double-genre art of tragedic desire looks to be a rather precise photograph of Marlowe's aesthetics, especially as exhibited in *Hero and Leander*.[18]

Shakespeare could have taken Marlowe's own cue, for the Canterbury native dresses his heroine in "garments" (9) artistically depicting the Venus and Adonis myth: "Her wide sleeves greene, and bordercd with a grove, / Where Venus in her naked glory strove / To please the careless and disdainful eies / Of proud Adonis that before her lies" (1. 11–14). Hero's complete attire – "myrtle wreath" (17) and "Buskins" (31) – reveals her to be a (feminine) figure for Marlowe's Ovidian art of elegy and tragedy; she is a figure for his own intertwining of poems and plays, an icon for the (feminine) role of the Ovidian poet-playwright (Cheney, *Profession* 243–45). Like Hero, Venus is not simply a titillating portrait of an erotically aroused female; paradoxically, she is also a figure for a masculine, Marlovian aesthetics that uses poetry and theatre to gain sexual gratification: "For men will kiss even by their own direction" (216).[19] While examining details of this historical portrait later, we may here observe that Shakespeare's well-known ambivalence towards Venus, together with her modulation from a comic to a tragic character, is deeply bound up with his equally well-known ambivalence toward his arch-Ovidian rival.

THE VIRGILIAN PATH

Significantly, Shakespeare plots his Ovidian narrative about Marlovian poetry and theatre in a landscape that is decidedly Virgilian. As readers have long emphasized, Shakespeare sets his scene initially in a pastoral landscape: on the "primrose bank" (151) – a bank of flowers ("blue-veined violets" [125]), beside a river.[20] While neither Venus nor Adonis is a shepherd,

---

17 On Marlowe and *Venus and Adonis*, see Leech, "Venus and her Nun"; Bradbrook, "Recollections"; Dubrow, *Victors*, 65–67. For my review on the Marlowe–Shakespeare connection between 1987 and 1998, see Cheney, "Recent Studies."

18 What Berger says about Spenser's Venus obtains with Shakespeare (and Marlowe): "I think of Venus only as a symbol, a kind of intertextual allusion" ("Actaeon," 112). For support, see Hulse, *Verse*, 158; Roe, ed., *Poems*, 66.

19 On Venus' gender reversal, see, e.g., Kolin, ed., "*Venus and Adonis*," 9, 12; Dubrow, *Victors*, 26, 34.

20 Critics neglect Virgil but for isolated references, see Hulse, *Verse*, 175; D. C. Allen, "On *Venus and Adonis*," 101, 107n4; Mortimer, *Variable Passions*, 154, 175, 166–67. On the pastoral setting, see Lee,

Shakespeare does insert a formal pastoral representation: "herdsmen and their lives" (Alpers, *What is Pastoral?*, 22). When Adonis opens his lips, they are "Like a red morn, that ever yet betoken'd . . . / Sorrow to shepherds, woe unto the birds, / Gusts and foul flaws to herdmen and to herds" (453–56). Moreover, hunting is a traditional activity in pastoral literature, as Spenser's Colin Clout reports in the *December* eclogue: "I . . . / . . . joyed oft to chace the trembling Pricket."[21] Equally to the point, the myth of Venus and Adonis has a long connection with pastoral; as Sir Sidney Lee observed in 1905, the origins of Ovid's version of the myth derive from his self-conscious emulation of "Theocritus and Bion, the pastoral poets of Greece."[22]

Just as Shakespeare's Ovidian combination of poetry and theatre has a deep connection with Marlowe, so his Virgilian dyad of pastoral and epic is connected with Spenser. Given Spenser's recurrent presence as an intertext both in modern editions of the poem and in recent criticism on it, this classification will also be easy to sustain.[23] Unanimously, critics have understood Shakespeare's homage to lie in his ideological response to Spenser's twofold representation of the myth of erotic desire in Book 3 of *The Faerie Queene*: the myth weaved into the tapestries of Malecasta's Castle Joyous in canto 1, and the appearance of Venus and Adonis in the Book's core canto, the famed philosophical Gardens of Adonis episode.[24] Yet A. C. Hamilton provides a clue that helps us to re-route the conversation from the characters' desire to the author's career: "It was inevitable that Shakespeare's first work, one in which he announced himself as a poet, should be dedicated to Venus. For the major poets in the English tradition, Spenser and Chaucer, were poets of love" ("*Venus and Adonis*," 13).

Shakespeare's inaugural self-presentation as a poet of Spenserian pastoral love is complicated by what we should expect: his inclusion of epic topoi.

"Introduction," 89–90; Bush, "*Venus and Adonis*," 91–92; D. C. Allen, "On *Venus and Adonis*," 101; Griffin, "Contraries," 46, 47, 52; Muir, "*Venus and Adonis*," 9–10; D. G. Watson, "Contraries," 58, 60; Yoch, "Eye of Venus," 61, 66; Dubrow, *Victors*, 52, 61–62; Kolin, ed., *Venus and Adonis*, 4; Merrix, "Hollow Cradle," 345, 348; Mortimer, *Variable Passions*, 50–51. Kiernan sees the Venus–Adonis conflict as one between Virgilian and Ovidian art ("*Venus and Adonis*," 84–85)

[21] Spenser, *December*, 25–27. On the hunt, including links with pastoral and with the Venus and Adonis myth, see M. J. B. Allen, "The Chase"; E. Berry, *Hunt*.

[22] Lee, "*Venus and Adonis*," 90; see Bush, "*Venus and Adonis*," 94–95; H. T. Price, "Function of Imagery," 110–11.

[23] As with Ovid and Marlowe, most critics mention Spenser; see, e.g., A. C. Hamilton, "*Venus and Adonis*," 6, 8–9, 12–13, 15; Muir, "*Venus and Adonis*," 4; D. G. Watson, "Contraries," 34, 41, 59; Williams, "Coming of Age," 772–73; Greenfield, "Allegorical Impulses"; Mortimer, *Variable Passions*, 56. Most would agree with Paglia that *Venus and Adonis* is a "homage . . . to Spenser" (194). Hyland recalls that Spenser had used the *Venus* sixain stanza in the opening and closing eclogues of the *Calender* (68).

[24] On Spenser, see Berger, "Actaeon"; on Spenser and Shakespeare here, see A. C. Hamilton, "*Venus and Adonis*," 7, 15; Greenfield, "Allegorical Impulses," 485–86.

For Spenser himself, pastoral is not an independent genre that the youthful poet pens simply in his idleness; it is the first phase of a laureate career leading to epic.[25] Accordingly, Shakespeare plots his Ovidian fiction of poetry and theatre along a Virgilian path, leading from the domain of pastoral to that of epic.[26]

When read in this literary context, Venus comes to represent, not simply the great goddess of beauty and desire from classical myth, but both Virgil's Venus from the *Aeneid*, the feminine fount appropriated for masculine empire, and her Spenserian guises in the Legend of Chastity. Not surprisingly, Shakespeare associates Adonis with the epic warrior. In lines 97–108, Venus appeals to Adonis' martial temperament when she cites the attraction to her felt by the "direful god of war, / Whose sinowy neck in battle ne'er did bow, / Who conquers where he comes in every jar, / Yet hath he been my captive, and my slave" (98–101). Her subsequent description of Mars reveals that she has seduced the great god into traveling down the Ovidian path, from epic achievement to elegiac dalliance:

> Over my altars hath he hung his lance,
> . . .
> And for my sake hath learn'd to sport and dance,
> To toy, to wanton, dally, smile, and jest,
> Scorning his churlish drum, and ensign red,
> Making my arms his field, his tent my bed.
> (*Venus and Adonis*, 103–08)

The references here to "dance" and especially to the "drum" sound a literary representation.[27] Moreover, Shakespeare shows Mars in terms strikingly similar to those with which Ovid had presented himself in the *Amores* (and Marlowe in his translation), especially 1. 1 and 2. 1, with line 106 constituting a formal listing of Ovid's (and Marlowe's) elegiac activity: *toy, wanton, dally, smile,* and *jest* (cf. Mortimer, *Variable Passions*, 59). Venus recalls her union with Mars precisely to entice Adonis to walk down the Ovidian path himself: "'Thus he that overrul'd I oversway'd, / Leading him

---

25 On Spenser's "pastoral of progression," see Cheney, "Pastorals."

26 Only Hulse places Shakespeare's "minor epic" along the "Virgilian path": "The minor epic was, in effect, the proving ground for lyric and epic . . . It was a genre for young poets ceasing to be young, a form somewhere above the pastoral or sonnet and below the epic, the transition between the two in the *gradus Vergilianus*" (*Verse*, 12; see 175). While Hulse plots *Venus and Adonis* on the Virgilian track, he supplies no detail.

27 See Kiernan, "*Venus and Adonis*": "Epic poetry has been reduced to the level of a love elegy" (90; see 92–93). Other critics referring to epic include D. C. Allen, "On *Venus and Adonis*," 105; Griffin, "Contraries," 52; Doebler, "Many Faces," 39; Hulse, *Verse*, 166; Dubrow, *Victors*, 52, 61–62; Mortimer, *Variable Passions*, 56. On the drum as a trope for counter-Virgilian epic, see Marlowe, *Lucan's First Book*, 6; Cheney, *Profession*, 29–32.

prisoner in a red rose chain'" (109–10). Venus of course fails to persuade Adonis to walk down the Ovidian path, for the hunter chooses to walk down the path of Virgil. But what is striking here is that Shakespeare would present their opposition as a dialogue between two established aesthetics and models for a literary career.

In lines 259–324, Shakespeare inserts the episode of the steed and the jennet – the only image of sexual reciprocity in the poem: "He looks upon his love, and neighs unto her, / She answers him, as if she knew his mind" (307–08). As Hulse observes, "Adonis's horse is an epic steed, fit for the fields of praise, yet he is also a descendent of Plato's dark horse, the emblem of license" (*Verse*, 166). Dressed in "rich caparisons, or trappings gay" (286) and even sporting a "compass'd crest" (272), Adonis' horse mirrors the god of war himself in marching down the path from epic warfare to elegiac desire: "The iron bit he crusheth 'tween his teeth, / Controlling what he was controlled with" (269–70). As F. T. Prince indicates, the primary source of Shakespeare's description of the jennet in lines 295–98 is "Virgil's description of the well-bred horse in the *Georgics*, III. 75–94" (Prince, ed., *Poems*, 19). The contrast between the male horse and its master, signaled when the epic steed "Breaketh his rein" (264) and hies him from the primrose bank "unto the wood" (323), may also function as a generic indicator.

Finally, in lines 595–98 Shakespeare applies the union of jennet and steed to the goddess and her lover, when metaphorizing the embrace of Venus and Adonis as a chivalric tilting joust: "Now is she in the very lists of love" (595). As Hulse remarks, Adonis "has a chance to reenact his horse's epic deed," although the "moment of union slips away, love's freedom and bondage still at strife" (*Verse*, 167). Shakespeare inserts epic topoi into his pastoral landscape, but he follows Marlowe in Ovidianizing the Virgilian/Spenserian representation.

The structure of *Venus and Adonis* helps support this argument. Robert P. Merrix divides the poem into two parts ("Hollow Cradle," 345): in lines 1–810, Shakespeare lays his scene in the "pastoral setting" of the "primrose bank" (151) in order to narrate the action of Venus attempting to seduce Adonis unsuccessfully; then in lines 811–1194 the author moves his scene to "an alien environment" in order to narrate the action of the Boar killing Adonis, of Adonis transforming into a flower, and of Venus prophesying misery for all future lovers. While Merrix joins many critics in locating the scene of the first part in the domain of pastoral (see also 348), he never quite says that the second part moves into epic: "In leaving the static primrose bank, Adonis enters the deadly world of the hunt – the world of militant chivalry" (350). He does follow Marcelle Thiébaux in identifying the boar with "dangerous militant activity as dangerous and exhilarating as warfare" (350), while Thiébaux himself notes the "epic magnitude in which boars loom . . . as adversaries . . . of heroes" ("Mouth of the Boar," 290; see Merrix, "Hollow Cradle," 351). For his part, Shakespeare structures *Venus and Adonis* via the twin domains of the Virgilian/Spenserian progression from pastoral to epic, but then he plots a Marlovian narrative in which Ovidian figures of poetry and theatre sing songs and perform dramatic roles along the Virgilian path.[28]

Hence, just as Shakespeare presents Venus' poetry and theatre as a form of Marlowe's Ovidian aesthetics, so he presents the Virgilian figure of pastoral and epic, Adonis, voicing an aesthetics that resembles Spenser's. Most obviously, Adonis is a figure of Spenserian chastity – what Venus scornfully terms "fruitless chastity" (751). Adonis prizes his virginity, like Spenser's Virgilian huntress Belphoebe, and refuses to participate in erotic play: "I know not love . . . nor will not know it" (409).[29] Specifically, Adonis imitates Spenser's chaste Neoplatonic aesthetics from Book 3 of *The Faerie Queene* (see Hulse, *Verse*, 165). Immediately after accusing Venus of voicing her "idle over-handled theme" in a "treatise" (770, 774), Adonis lapses into his own "text": "Call it not love, for Love to heaven is fled, / Since sweating Lust on earth usurp'd his name" (793–94).

Adonis has not just been reading Plato and his Renaissance philosophical heirs, "invoking the Platonic distinction, newly set forth by Ficino and others, between Venus Urania (or heavenly, chaste Venus) and the earthier Venus Pandemons" (Roe, ed., *Poems*, 119). He has also been reading an English poet like Spenser, who indicates that he himself has been reading Plato, Ficino, and others:

> Most sacred fire, that burnest mightily
> In living brests, ykindled first above,
> . . .
> Not that same, which doth base affections move
> In brutish minds, and filthy lust inflame.[30]
>
> (*Faerie Queene*, 3. 3. 1)

Like Spenser, Adonis distinguishes sharply between "love" and "lust," imagines love to be from "heaven," and chooses divine love over destructive "lust"

---

[28] According to Mortimer, "Shakespeare rewrites the relation between Venus and Adonis [from the Ovidian and Italian traditions] as a conflict" (*Variable Passions*, 195).

[29] Keach observes in passing that the epyllion poets of the 1590s "challenge Spenser's vision of the 'glorious fire' of love ideally realized in the creative chastity of marriage" (*Erotic Narratives*, 232).

[30] For support, see Hamilton, ed., *The Fairie Queene*, 326.

(see Belsey, "Trompe-L'oeil," 271). The "text" to which Adonis refers as "old" is almost certainly the "antique history" of *The Faerie Queene* (2. Proem 1). In short, while we can view the opposition between Venus and Adonis in sexual terms, we may also view it in terms of the 1590s clash between an Ovidian aesthetics of poetry and theatre, represented by Marlowe, and a Virgilian aesthetics of pastoral and epic, represented by Spenser.[31]

THE OVIDIAN EPIGRAPH AND THE *DEDICATORY EPISTLE*

The two prefatory items to the 1594 quarto of *Venus and Adonis* create the lens through which we view the poem. Specifically, the epigraph constructs a lens for an Ovidian career:

vilia miretur vulgus; mihi flauus Apollo
pocula Castalia plena ministret aqua. (Ovid, *Amores* 1. 15. 35–36)

Most often, critics read this epigraph as simple Ovidian eroticism – a philosophy of desire (see Hamilton, "*Venus and Adonis*," 7, 12). Ovid, however, distinguishes between his own elegiac verse and one that is "cheap" (Marlowe's translation, already quoted, and usually cited by editors). Thus the Roman poet foregrounds the difference in cultural value between his own higher form of poetry and a lower art practiced by others.

Yet long ago Muriel Bradbrook understood Shakespeare to be using the epigraph to "dissociat[e] . . . himself from [the] baseness . . . of popular playwrighting" and to turn to "courtly poetry," while recently a series of critics have followed suit.[32] We may add that Shakespeare's dialectic of poetry and playwriting originates in the *Amores* itself. In *Venus and Adonis*, the Ovidian epigraph functions as a career announcement for the famed man of the theatre's turn from stage to page.

If the epigraph constructs an Ovidian lens for viewing *Venus and Adonis*, the *Dedicatory Epistle* to Southampton introduces a corresponding Virgilian lens of lower and higher genres, pastoral/georgic to epic:

---

[31] Burrow sees *Venus and Adonis* "worrying about the risks of publishing and selling a poem" ("Life," 29; see 35). Dubrow, *Victors*, sees Venus as "the generic potentials of Ovidian mythological poetry," Adonis as "the pieties of *Ovide moralisé*," and their opposition as a "tension between two possible ways of imitating and adapting Ovid" (48). For an erotic understanding of the conflict, see Streitberger, "Ideal Conduct," 172; Kahn, "Eros," 182; Hulse, *Verse*, 165; Merrix "Hollow Cradle," 343. For the rhetorical opposition of selfhood, see Mortimer, *Variable Passions*, 27–32.

[32] Bradbrook, "Beasts," 62–63. See Bate, *Genius*, 18; Halpern, "'Pining,'" 377; Duncan-Jones, *Ungentle*, 60; Mortimer, *Variable Passions*, 1. These critics are not in dialogue with one another.

I know not how I shall offend in dedicating my unpolished lines to your Lordship, nor how the world will censure me for choosing so strong a prop to support so weak a burden. Only if your Honour seem but pleased, I account myself highly praised, and vow to take advantage of all idle hours, till I have honoured you with some graver labour. But if the first heir of my invention prove deformed, I shall be sorry it had so noble a godfather: and never after ear so barren a land, for fear it yield me still so bad a harvest. I leave it to your Honourable survey, and your Honour to your heart's content, which I wish may always answer your own wish, and the world's hopeful expectation. (*Riverside*, 1799)

Here Shakespeare relies on a broad European discourse originating in Virgil's *Eclogues*. In Eclogue 6, for instance, Tityrus reports that he "first" sported his Muse in the "strains" of the pastoral "woods," but that when he tried to "sing of kings and battles," Apollo warned him not to step beyond the bounds of the shepherd (1–10). Most critics believe that Virgil relies on the tradition of the *recusatio* to predict in a rather unspecified way the epic that turned out to be the *Aeneid* (Farrell, *"Georgics,"* 314; see 291–314). Ovid was among the first to imitate this discourse – and right where we might expect it, in *Amores*, 1. 15: "Tityrus and the harvest, and the arms of Aeneas, will be read as long as Rome shall be capital of the world she triumphs o'er" (25–26).

For Renaissance writers, the Virgilian discourse is characterized by the self-presentation of a youthful writer who admits the lowness of his present publication yet paradoxically predicts his ability to write a work of greater merit and higher literary form.[33] Here is Marlowe addressing Mary Sidney on behalf of his recently deceased friend, Thomas Watson, in the 1592 *Amintae gaudia*:

you who imbue my yet unripe quill with the spirit of a lofty rage; by whose aid, wretch as I am, I believe that I can achieve more than my unripe natural talents are accustomed to bring forth . . . So shall I, whose scanty riches are but the shore-myrtle of Venus and the evergreen tresses of the Peneian nymph [Daphne], call you to my aid on the first page of every poem. (Marlowe, *Dedicatory Epistle* to *Amintae Gaudia*, reprinted in Pendry and Maxwell, eds. *Christopher Marlowe*, 397)

Marlowe relies on the terms of the Virgilian progression, telling the Countess he will turn from works produced by his "yet unripe quill" to those penned in "the spirit of a lofty rage," but then he superbly Ovidianizes

---

[33] See Sannazaro, *Arcadia*: "he by nature having a genius disposed to higher things, and not contenting himself with so humble a strain, took in exchange that reed that now you see there, larger and newer than the others, to be the better able to sing of greater things" (ch. 10: 104–05; see ch. 7: 74–75).

(and Petrarchizes) the discourse, acknowledging that currently his "scanty riches" foreground Venus and Daphne but then promises to invoke the Countess' high standing "on the first page of every [future] poem."[34]

A year later, Shakespeare imitates such a Virgilian discourse in his poem on "the shore-myrtle of Venus." Thus, he addresses Southampton in the terms of husbandry ("prop," "burden," "labour," "ear," "barren a land," "yield," "harvest," "survey") in order to introduce *Venus and Adonis* as a lower verse form ("unpolished lines . . . weak . . . first heir . . . deformed"). But then he promises Southampton "some graver labour" – a higher verse form with greater "yield" in the "harvest."[35] While traditionally readers have found Shakespeare's "countryside" metaphors simply evoking his rural Warwickshire (here and in the poem itself), we need to recall that such rhetorical language was also part of the discourse of a young poet presenting himself as a Virgilian author of pastoral, including in competition with England's Virgil in the progression to "some graver labour." Thus, Shakespeare's rural metaphors underscore the author's need for maturation and his promise of it; they also signal his transference of this developmental model to the career of his patron, as the concluding (double) resonance of "hopeful expectation" entreats.

Together, the epigraph from Ovid's *Amores* and the *Dedicatory Epistle* to Southampton create the double lens through which to view the poem; that lens is not strictly erotic but literary. The two prefatory items present "William Shakespeare" as an "author" with a generically based literary career, in competition with other authors with literary careers. Specifically, the Ovidian and Virgilian career models in the epigraph and the dedication do not allude simply to the careers of the two great classical authors. In this Shakespearean typology of intertextuality, they allude to Elizabethan England's successors to each of them, especially the two most famous practitioners during the early 1590s: the Ovidian Marlowe and the Virgilian Spenser.

THE OVIDIAN INTERTEXT

The Ovidian and Virgilian career models from the prefatory material shed fresh light on the primary intertext of *Venus and Adonis*: Ovid's telling of the myth in Book 10 of the *Metamorphoses*. Critics have seemingly exhausted

---

[34] For details, see Cheney, *Profession*, 223–26.

[35] Roe notes "metaphors of human and natural growth" (Roe, ed., *Poems*, 78), while Lee notices "impressions of the country-side" ("*Venus and Adonis*," 89). The Renaissance does not always oust georgic from the Virgilian progression (Fowler, *Kinds of Literature*, 240); at times, it enfolds georgic into both pastoral and epic (Tylus, "Spenser").

this topic, but they tend to confine themselves to Shakespeare's reworking of Ovidian sexuality. Some recall the complex placement of the myth in Ovid's poem – as one of the songs of Orpheus. But we can add two features of Ovid's Orphic representation that are crucial to a fuller understanding of Shakespeare's Ovidian intertextuality.

The first is that Ovid presents Orpheus not simply as a poet who has lost his wife, but more precisely as an author with a literary career, enacting a progression of literary forms:

. . . he raised his voice in this song: "From Jove, O Muse, my mother – for all things yield to the sway of Jove – inspire my song! Oft have I sung the power of Jove before; I have sung the giants in a heavier strain. . . . But now I need the gentler touch, for I would sing of boys, beloved by gods, and maidens inflamed by unnatural love." (Ovid, *Metamorphoses*, 10. 148–53)

Orpheus tells how his loss of Eurydice leads him to turn from songs about Jove and his battle with the Giants to songs about amorous desire addressed to young men and young women. From the outset, Ovid's story of Orpheus posits an intimate link between sexual desire and literary production. Eurydice's death leads Orpheus to make a career change: from singing a higher form of song to singing a lower one – from epic to elegy.[36]

Orpheus' turn from Virgilian epic Gigantomachy to erotic elegy reverses – and probably evokes – Ovid's own career turn opening the *Metamorphoses* itself: "My mind is bent to tell of bodies changed into new forms. Ye gods . . . bring down my song in unbroken strains from the world's very beginning even unto the present time" (1. 1–4). In this opening, writes E. J. Kenney, "Ovid has been metamorphosed from elegist into epicist" ("Ovid" 137) – a metamorphosis confirmed later in Book 1 when Ovid narrates the Gigantomachy (151–60). Yet Ovid also reverses the career predicament he suffered back in the *Amores*, where he tried to write Gigantomachy but turned instead to elegy; in Marlowe's translation,

> I durst the great celestial battle tell,
> . . .
> Jove and Jove's thunderbolts I had in hand,
> . . .
> My wench her dore shut, Joves affairs I left,
> . . .
> Toys, and light Elegies my darts I took.
> (Marlowe, *Ovid's Elegies*, 2. 1. 11–21)

[36] See Sharrock: the Gigantomachy is "the theme which above all others epitomizes martial epic, which the most daring of literary exploits and exactly that attempted by Virgil" (*Seduction*, 115).

In Book 10 of the *Metamorphoses*, then, Ovid presents Orpheus as he had presented himself in the *Amores*: as a poet who turns from epic to elegy. This network of authorial representations suggests a new context for viewing Shakespeare's appropriation of the Venus and Adonis myth.

The second feature useful to recall is that Ovid presents Orpheus moving from epic to elegy by unwittingly participating in the genre of tragedy, as the theatre simile introducing the death of Orpheus in Book 11 makes clear:

Then these [the Maenads] turned bloody hands against Orpheus . . . and as when in the amphitheatre in the early morning of the spectacle the doomed stag in the arena is the prey of dogs. They rushed upon the bard and hurled at him their wands wreathed with green vines. (Ovid, *Metamorphoses*, 11. 23–28)

According to Stephen Hinds, the Ovidian *locus amoenus* here has "built-in associations . . . with performance" (*Metamorphosis*, 35). As the indirect representation of the Actaeon myth indicates, the performance is in the ampitheater of tragedy, as Orpheus undergoes a grim death enacting the biography of Ovid, who used the Actaeon myth to represent his predicament in the Augustan state – both before and after his exile.[37] Ovid's use of the topoi of tragedy reinforces his reference to the genre of tragedy: the Maenads are the priestesses of Bacchus, god of tragedy (17), and they kill Orpheus with the implement held by Dame Tragedy in *Amores*, 3. 1: the thyrsos. Structurally, the tragic death of Orpheus marks the end of the second part of the *Metamorphoses*, which Ovid divides into three parts – "thrice five rolls about changing forms" (*Tristia*, 1. 1. 117–18): Books 1–5 represent love elegy; Books 6–10, tragedy; and Books 11–15, epic.[38] Just as Orpheus' singing of both epic and elegy mirrors Ovid's self-presentation in the *Amores*, so does Orpheus' link with tragedy, since (as we have seen) the penultimate poem of Book 2 ends precisely with Ovid's self-presentation as a tragedian.[39]

The context of the Ovidian story is a complex one, as the reader literally experiences a series of poems within poems: Ovid tells the story of Orpheus proper (1–155), which then divides into five parts: Orpheus' marriage with Eurydice; the death of this beloved wife and his descent to the underworld to use his art to win her a second life; the failure of this artistic endeavor

---

[37] See Cheney, *Profession*, 164–65, 311nn17–20. For Actaeon in the simile, see N. J. Vickers, "Diana," 99–100; Enterline, "Embodied Voices," 127–28.

[38] Professor Joseph Farrell suggested this idea to me, and noted that the pattern has never been examined (personal communication, June 1998).

[39] On Orpheus and tragedy, see DeNeef, "Poetics of Orpheus," 22, 35; on Ovid's Orpheus and tragedy, see Segal, *Orpheus*, 55–56.

and his subsequent shunning of "love of womankind" in favor of the love of boys (79–80); his corresponding turn from epic to elegy, the gods to youths and maidens; and the series of five tales that he actually sings (143–739), the last of which is the story of Venus and Adonis (503–59, 708–39). Altogether, Ovid's Orphic story narrates the tragedy of desire – in large part, of marital desire: "Marriage . . . is a fatal thing" (621).

What the *Metamorphoses* shares with the *Amores* is a keystone of Ovidian aesthetics – the one that is more foundational than wit, eroticism, style, and subversion:[40] what we have called Ovid's elegiac attenuation of Virgilian epic. This principle forms the inaugural base of Ovid's career, since the very opening of the *Amores* responds to the opening of the *Aeneid* through attenuation. In the *Metamorphoses*, Ovid attenuates Virgil on a more global scale than he does in the opening to the *Amores* by condensing the narrative of the twelve-book *Aeneid* into a few scattered lines in Books 13–15. Within the fiction, Orpheus most fully represents the Ovidian poet par excellence, and his turn from epic to elegy narrativizes the principle of Virgilian attenuation, which the Orphic poet-figure Venus herself extends.[41] Thus, Ovid's self-reflexivity about his art and career creates an intriguing equation: between Ovid, Orpheus, and Venus as types of artist (male mortal, bisexual mortal immortalized, immortal female). Specifically, Ovid's attenuating Orphic *cursus* of failed epic, elegy, and final tragedy, scripted to oppose imperial nationalism – a replay of the very *cursus* from the *Amores* – counters the imperial Virgilian *cursus* of pastoral leading to georgic and epic.

Ovid's presentation of Venus as a cross-dressed Orphic-Ovidian author of poetry and theatre is deeply pertinent to Shakespeare's representation of the goddess in his amorous minor epic. Elizabethan authors, from Gascoigne and Spenser to Daniel and Shakespeare himself, use the genre of the female complaint to "cross-dress" their authorial voices, literally "taking on the voice of a fallen woman" (Wall, *Imprint*, 260).[42] As we shall see, by rewriting Ovid's elegiac myth of counter-Virgilian epic, Shakespeare only appears to follow Marlowe in scripting the Ovidian principle for the purpose of attenuating the imperial Virgilian project of Spenser.

---

[40] On these four traits as the cornerstones of Ovid, see Keach, *Erotic Narratives*, 29.

[41] On Orpheus as the arch-Ovidian poet, see Segal, *Orpheus*, 54–72, 81–94: "Ovid's Orpheus verges close to becoming a persona for Ovidian aesthetics, particularly for an aesthetics deeply conscious of the distance between the narrative of the *Metamorphoses* and [Virgil's *Aeneid*]" (93).

[42] Wall, *Imprint*, briefly discusses both the Sonnets (195–98) and *Lucrece* (214–20, 272–73), but not *Venus*.

SHAKESPEAREAN ATTENUATION

What more specifically is the attenuating fiction that Shakespeare tells in *Venus and Adonis* about the two rival Elizabethan aesthetics? Initially, it is the tragic story about their fatal separation; but finally it is the poignantly comedic story about their intimate Shakespearean interlock. A clue to this reading lies in the structurally mirroring representations of an arch-artistic symbol in both the opening and the closing stanzas: the chariot. For Renaissance readers, the *locus classicus* of Shakespeare's imagery is Virgil's self-presentation in Book 3 of the *Georgics*, where the poet imagines himself driving "a hundred four-horse chariots beside the stream" (18), during his triumphal entrance into Rome in the presence of Augustus Caesar (1–39). As we have seen, critics locate the Virgilian horse in Shakespeare's steed and jennet episode. For Virgil himself, the chariot is thus an icon of his poetic art's immortal power, the reward of fame for his georgic labor.[43] As we might expect, Virgil's rival successor appropriates the symbolic Virgilian chariot in order to conclude the *Amores*, which in Marlowe's translation reads:

> Tender Love's mother, a new poet get;
> This last end [*meta*: chariot racing post] to my elegies is set,
> . . .
> Horned Bacchus greater fury doth distil,
> A greater ground [*area maior*: race-track] with great horse is to till.
> Weak elegies, delightful Muse, farewell.   (*Ovid's Elegies*, 3. 14. 1–19)

With this projected "meta" or chariot turn on the literary race-track from lower to higher genres, elegy to tragedy, the poet concludes his elegiac collection.[44]

In *Venus and Adonis*, Shakespeare's opening stanza introduces a superb two-line miniature of the sun and the morn in order to establish a temporal setting, with a core idea of erotic and artistic separation. Yet we peer at this miniature through the lens of the Ovidian epigraph, which features Apollo, god of the sun and god of poetry:

> Even as the sun with purple-color'd face
> Had ta'en his last leave of the weeping morn.
> (*Venus and Adonis*, 1–2)

[43] See also *Georgics*, 2. 541–42; Hardie, *Epic Successors*, 100–01.
[44] On Ovid's chariot as a symbol of his poetry, see Kenney, "Poeta," 206; for details applicable to the Ovidian Marlowe in rivalry with the Virgilian Spenser, see Cheney, *Profession*, 50–51, 283n5.

Shakespeare's little narrative inscribes the dynamic the poem will enlarge: the sexes are intrinsically separate, because the male departs from the domestic space of the female to perform his daily work (see Roe, ed., *Poems*, 79). As Prince notes, the identification of the sun as the lover of the morn rewrites the myth of the aged Tithonus as the lover of the Dawn (Prince ed., *Poems*, 3). One justification for Shakespeare's revision may be the link between the Ovidian erotic action of the poem and the Ovidian career model featured in the epigraph.

The remaining lines of the opening stanza help us to measure the import of this link:

> Rose-cheek'd Adonis hied him to the chase;
> Hunting he lov'd, but love he laugh'd to scorn.
>   Sick-thoughted Venus makes amain unto him,
>   And like a bold-fac'd suitor gins to woo him.
>   (*Venus and Adonis*, 3–6)

Since the opening phrase of the poem, "Even as," can also mean "just like," we may discern a simile that likens Adonis' hying him to the hunt to the sun's taking his leave of the morn (Roe, ed., *Poems*, 79). Moreover, the phrase suggests that Adonis follows the sun in his daily course. In both cases, a male abandons a female: the sun, the morn; Adonis, Venus. Evidently, Shakespeare identifies both a cultural problem and its cause: men and women remain separate because men "take . . . and leave," as the country maid laments in *A Lover's Complaint* (305).

Prince glosses "purple-colour'd" with *The Faerie Queene*, 1. 2. 7, which reads:

> Now when the rosy fingred Morning faire,
>   Weary of aged Tithones saffron bed,
>   Had spred her purple robe through deawy aire,
>   And the high hils Titan discovered,
>   The royall virgin [Una] shooke off drowsy-hed.
>   (*The Faerie Queene*, 1. 2. 7)

Spenser's myth for the time of day is the opposite of Shakespeare's: for Spenser, the female morning is the aggressive figure of separation, actively spreading her robe because she is "weary" of her elderly mortal husband. As Hamilton observes, "the mortal Tithonus . . . was granted immortality but not eternal youth" (Hamilton, ed., *Fairie Queene*, 45). Morning has made a mistake, and here she pays the price through her impatience. As Hamilton also observes, "To connect the virgin Aurora and Una, the classical and Christian day-stars, S. provides a pastiche of classical sources: **rosy-fingred** is the stock Homeric epithet, **saffron bed** is Virgil's *croceum cubile* (*Aen.* iv 585), **purple robe** is Ovid's *purpureae Aurorae* (*Met.* iii 184)" (Hamilton, ed., *Fairie Queene*, 45). In other words, Spenser's passage derives from the epic tradition. We can add that Shakespeare's meteorological report opposes Spenser's, wherein the Redcrosse Knight, under the spell of the evil magician Archimago, has fled from Una (1. 2. 6), who arises in the morning to seek him out. On the one hand, Spenser simply versifies the coming of day, but on the other he invests the weather with philosophy. Anticipating Shakespeare, he links the morning miniature with the action of his poem; unlike Shakespeare, Spenser does so through a principle of opposition: whereas Aurora is weary of Tithonus and leaves his bed, Una is faithful to her lover, who has abandoned her. At stake for Spenser is the importance of faith, both erotic and religious, but also the romantic matrix of his epic action celebrating "mery England" (1. 10. 61).

According to John Roe, Shakespeare's phrase "purple-color'd" means "red, blushing," and has "classical origins": "It also occurs in the classical derived genres: in tragedy or epic poetry, it describes the colour of blood (invariably shed in a noble action), whereas in lyric or erotic poems it may denote passion or even voluptuousness. Here it may carry several shades of meaning from regality down to embarrassment, especially through associations of debauch, purple being the colour of the grape which signifies the god of excess, Bacchus" (Roe, ed., *Poems*, 79). Thus the purple-colored face of the sun god constitutes a site for both generic and philosophical anxiety; it is a locus of conflict between the high genres of tragedy or epic and the low genres of lyric or erotic elegy, as well as that between the heroic action of regal duty and the shameful action of sexual indulgence.

Both Roe, *Poems*, 79 and Prince, *Poems*, 3, gloss the related phrase in the opening stanza, "Rose-cheek'd Adonis," with the identical phrase in *Hero and Leander*, where Marlowe describes the occasion for the poem's initial action: "The men of wealthy Sestos, every year, / For his sake whom their goddess held so dear, / Rose-cheeked Adonis, kept a solemn feast" (1.91–93). This occasion helps explain the dress Hero wears, which is embroidered with the Venus and Adonis myth. Hero is a priestess of Venus, and her love for Leander enacts the Goddess' love for Adonis. The rose-colored cheek of Adonis may echo the Elizabethan pronunciation of Wriothesley, Rosely or Risely, but it also links Adonis with the sun god, imprinting his face with both the sexual and generic stamp we have identified. Like Marlowe, Shakespeare writes an Ovidian epyllion, and like him he uses the genre to represent the inherent separation of the sexes. The matching imitations of Spenser and Marlowe in the opening stanza announce Shakespeare's rivalry with these two titans of the literary scene during the early 1590s.[45]

If the opening stanza implies an image of the authorial chariot moving along its path, the concluding stanza makes the image explicit:

> Thus weary of the world, away she hies,
> And yokes her silver doves, by whose swift aid
> Their mistress mounted through the empty skies,
> In her light chariot, quickly is convey'd,
>   Holding their course to Paphos, where their queen
>   Means to immure herself, and not be seen.
>   (*Venus and Adonis*, 1189–94)

This final image mirrors the opening one by representing a pattern of separation between the sexes; in both cases, the female is alone within her own domestic space, in a state of grief over the loss of her male lover. The primary difference is that at the end the female is the agent of her own immuring (cf. Hamilton, "*Venus and Adonis*," 15).

The concluding chariot image also evokes an author's literary career (cf. Doebler, "Many Faces," 42; Baumlin, "Birth," 204–05), presenting not an Apollonian *cursus* but a Venerean one, as the goddess uses her chariot to fly from "the world" to "Paphos." Venus' turn from earth to heaven suggests a turn from a lower to a higher form, mirroring the conclusion to Ovid's *Amores* and Marlowe's translation, in which the Ovidian poet tells Venus that she needs to "get" a "new poet" because he is turning from elegy to tragedy.[46]

Shakespeare's detailed narrative of Venus' courting of Adonis represents the precise contents of their opposing aesthetics. In the most famous part of the "tale" that Venus "tunes" to the "pretty ear" of Adonis, she relies on a richly embroidered language of sexual metaphor:

> "Fondling," she saith, "since I have hemm'd thee here
> Within the circuit of this ivory pale,
> I'll be a park, and thou shalt be my deer:
> Feed where thou wilt, on mountain, or in dale;
>   Graze on my lips, and if those hills be dry,
>   Stray lower, where the pleasant fountains lie.

---

[45] In his edition, Burrow briefly discusses Shakespeare's rivalry with both Marlowe and Spenser here, including the principle that authors of epyllion "loved to miniaturize the poems they were imitating" (*Sonnets and Poems*, 17).

[46] Macfie ("Ovid's Poetry") suggests that the chariot image closing Marlowe's *Hero and Leander* deploys the conventional image concluding classical tragedy, and we may re-route the idea to the closing of Shakespeare's *Venus*.

> "Within this limit is relief enough,
> Sweet bottom grass and high delightful plain,
> Round rising hillocks, breaks obscure and rough,
> To shelter thee from tempest and from rain;
>   Then be my deer, since I am such a park,
>   No dog shall rouse thee, though a thousand bark."
>   (*Venus and Adonis*, 229–40)

The great goddess uses the deer park metaphor to versify a Venerean aesthetics of desire, an eroticized poesis. Presenting herself as a figure for sexual love, she equates her body with the land in order to voice a piercing philosophy of desire.

Although this passage is famous for its titillating power to arouse erotic desire (see S. Roberts, *Reading Shakespeare's Poems*, 73), it manages to voice a philosophy of eros tracing to Plato's *Symposium*. Certainly, Shakespeare pens a masculine fantasy in which the goddess of love and beauty – Plato's Venus Pandemos rather than Venus Urania – invites a young man to come live with her and be her love – a fantasy that would appeal to Shakespeare's youthful patron and friends. Yet Venus' use of poetic metaphor suggests that she is not simply opening her body to pleasing recreation; she is making an argument. The image of the lone deer feeding where it wills, "on mountain, or in dale," appeals to the appetite, even as it offers the freedom of native nourishment. The deer's freedom within the "ivory pale" further promises security and protection – of a maternal nature. Specifically, Venus claims that she can open her body as a park to "shelter" Adonis from life's vicissitudes, "from tempest and from rain." Her physiological park will allow her dear to mature freely, pleasurably fenced off from the masculine warfare of the hunt: "No dog shall rouse thee, though a thousand bark." In short, Venus versifies the deer park to compel Adonis into believing that her female body – with all its nutritive pleasures – can protect him from time and death: love can fence off suffering and tragedy in a recreative park of eternal youth. Unlike Plato's Venus Pandemos in the *Symposium*, this Venus Pandemos philosophizes desire as a principle and force of immortality (see Cheney, "Alcestis"). Significantly, Venus' philosophy is that of Marlowe's "Passionate Shepherd" – with its discourse of "boy eternal," a phrase used by Shakespeare in *The Winter's Tale* (1. 2. 65; see Cheney, *Profession*, 82–85).

Since Venus is voicing her philosophy of boy eternal as part of the song she sings rhetorically to Adonis, her *locus amoenus* functions as a *locus poeticus*.[47] Generic indicators may lie in the *high/low* imagery of "mountain" and

---

[47] See Burrow, ed., *Sonnets and Poems*, 26: "The scene is a playwright's reading of a playwright's poem."

"dale," familiar as a central trope of pastoral/epic from Spenser's *Calender*,
as this from Hobbinol in some professional advice to Colin Clout in the
June eclogue: "Leave me those hilles . . . / And to the dales resort" (19–21).
Moreover, the "pleasant fountain" is not merely the female womb but also
the Ovidian *fons sacer*, the site of Ovid's professional confrontation with
Dame Elegy and Dame Tragedy in *Amores*, 3. 1. 3, as well as the "Muses'
well" introduced in the Ovidian epigraph to Shakespeare's poem. Venus
becomes Shakespeare's arch-representation of Marlowe's Ovidian aesthetics
of invitational desire.[48]

In a subsequent passage, Shakespeare stages the tragedic reality of Venus'
aesthetics, when he returns to the foraging metaphor after Venus and Adonis
"fall to the earth" (546):

> Now quick desire hath caught the yielding prey
>
> . . .
>
> > Whose vultur thought doth pitch the price so high
> > That she will draw his lips' rich treasure dry
>
> . . .
>
> With blindfold fury she begins to forage;
> Her face doth reek and smoke, her blood doth boil
>
> . . .
>
> > Planting oblivion, beating reason back,
> > Forgetting shame's pure blush and honor's wrack.
> > > (*Venus and Adonis*, 547–58)

No sooner does Venus fulfill her wish to hem her dear within the circuit of
her ivory park than the goddess undergoes an Ovidian metamorphoses into
a bird of prey, a "vultur" filled with the "thought" of "blindfold fury." Venus
begins to "forage," even as her landscape erupts like a volcano, smoking
and reeking, depleting the fountain on Adonis' lips. In this astonishing
photograph of the female in the throes of desire, Shakespeare emphasizes
the subjective and moral consequences. Rather than nurturing immortality,
she "plants oblivion," the arch-fear of Western (masculine) "thought," a
dark condition of forgetfulness and of being forgotten, the total erasure
of identity and achievement, the loss of consciousness – a kind of psychic
and reputational blackout.[49] In the process, Venus' oblivious fury beats

---

[48] Dubrow begins *Victors* with the deer park passage (21–24), but even though she sees Venus "twisting
Petrarchism," she calls the passage "a charming rendition of the playful sexual fantasies in which
lover's indulge" (22–23). We might see in Venus, however, a localized version of the "Tudor aesthetics"
emphasized by Hulse in his essay by this title: "the debate about the nature of imitation is itself
represented by Tudor writers through metaphors of the human body, so that Tudor aesthetics can
with justice be called an aesthetics of the body" (30).

[49] On memory and forgetting in Shakespeare, see Sullivan, "Forgetting."

reason back, holding at bay the mind's martial might to order recalcitrant desire temperately. Venus' intemperance has immediate social and moral consequences: the fury of sexual desire obliviates "shame's pure blush and honor's wrack," causing Venus to lose her female modesty, maternal instinct, and feminine identity. Her loss is dangerous – physiologically, subjectively, and morally – because it erases the sanctity of identity, smothering the intellectual faculties and their ethical character – what the maid in *A Lover's Complaint* calls "sober guards and civil fears" (298). Shakespeare dramatizes the full effect of Marlowe's Ovidian aesthetics.

The contents of Adonis' "text" turn out to have a similar doubleness of representation – at once idealized and criticized:

> Call it not love, for Love to heaven is fled,
> Since sweating Lust on earth usurp'd his name.
> . . .
> Love comforteth like sunshine after rain,
> But Lust's effect is tempest after sun.
> Love's gentle spring doth always fresh remain,
> Lust's winter comes ere summer half be done;
>   Love surfeits not, Lust like a glutton dies;
>   Love is all truth, Lust full of forged lies.
>   (*Venus and Adonis*, 793–804)

Adonis' text is certainly Neoplatonic, but of a Spenserian printing. Adonis uses his text to critique that of Venus, identifying her desire not as she idealized it in the deer park passage but as we realize it in the "vultur thought" passage: "'You do it for increase: O strange excuse! / When reason is the bawd to lust's abuse'" (791–92).

In the first stanza above, Adonis counters Venus by arguing that Lust is a tyrannical, "sweating" usurper to the kingdom of Love, who has been forced to seek asylum in heaven. If Love had not fled, he would have been devoured by a parasitical Lust, who is like the caterpillar that blots, stains, and bereaves the (rose's) "tender leaves." Yet the terms of Shakespeare's career are intimated through imagery of the "flowers of poetry" from "Apollo's garden."[50] Shakespeare's word *blotting* is usually glossed as a moral term ("making it shameful" [Roe, ed., *Poems*, 119]); but Colin Burrow has shown how Shakespeare worries over print publication in the poem, which Burrow terms "a study in the materialities of work and print."[51] The discourse from the print shop merges with a theatrical representation in the image of Lust

---

50 Sidney, *An Apologie for Poetrie* (G. G. Smith, ed., *Essays*, 1: 105).
51 Burrow, "Life," 35; on "blotting," see Valbuena, "Reproduction."

disguised "Under . . . simple semblance" – wearing the garb of an actor who impersonates Love in order to "usurp" Love's "name."

In the second stanza above, Adonis relies on the seasonal and meteo-rological imagery familiar from Spenserian pastoral to reveal Lust for the imposter he is. Love, Adonis insists, brings comfort, renews the body and spirit, never satiates himself, and commits himself to "truth." By contrast, Lust storms the body and spirit, brings coldness prematurely, feeds glut-tonously, and commits himself to falsehood.

Even though this is "the most serious passage in the poem" (Putney, "Venus *Agonistes*," 137), Shakespeare clearly critiques Adonis' aesthetics of desire, not simply through Adonis' comical admission of its oldness and of his own (pastoral) greenness (806), but also through the poem's fatal conclusion: Adonis' philosophy fails to protect him as haplessly as does the philosophy of Venus. Shakespeare pinpoints the idealistic shortcomings of Spenser's Virgilian aesthetics in opposition to the Ovidian aesthetics of Marlowe.

"SHE CROPS THE STALK": BEYOND OPPOSITION

What are we to make, then, of Shakespeare's retelling of the story of Venus and Adonis along the lines we have examined? First, he appears to be using the Ovidian myth to bring into print a literary history of his own professional environment during the early 1590s. *Venus and Adonis* registers the decisive point of entry of Marlowe's Ovidian aesthetics of poetry and theatre into a literary scene dominated by Spenser's Virgilian aesthetics of pastoral and epic. Although certainly not an allegory of this literary rivalry, *Venus and Adonis* does appear to process the rivals' authorial projects. Second, Shakespeare could simultaneously be representing the effect of this rivalry on his culture – on those who have read Marlowe and Spenser. According to this second possibility, *Venus and Adonis* would explore not simply "the obligations and power, burdens, and mystery of readership" (Kolin, ed., "*Venus and Adonis*," 23; see 23–30) but a very particular historical form of readership. And if so, Shakespeare would be processing the literary consequences of his two competing colleagues' work.[52]

A final possibility exists, for the climactic act of the poem also suggests a personalized version of this literary history of reading and writing:

---

[52] On readers of *Venus*, including contemporary dramatic fictions of characters reading the poem, see Prince, ed., *Poems*, 16; S. Roberts, "*Reading Shakespeare's Poems*," 20–101. For contemporary reaction to the poem generally, see Duncan-Jones, "Much Ado."

> She bows her head, the new-sprung flow'r to smell,
> Comparing it to her Adonis' breath,
> And says within her bosom it shall dwell,
> Since he himself is reft from her by death.
>   She crops the stalk, and in the breach appears
>   Green-dropping sap, which she compares to tears.
>
> "Poor flow'r," quoth she, "this was thy father's guise."
>   (*Venus and Adonis*, 1171–77)

In a way that no longer should surprise us, Venus' repetition of the words "Comparing" and "compares" shows her performing the poetic process of similitude, as when Will in Sonnet 18 famously writes of the young man, "Shall I compare thee to a summer's day" (1).

For her part, Venus bows her head to smell the flower, pausing to compare it to the breath of her deceased lover, and speaking, evidently to herself quietly so that the text does not record her words, what is surely one of the most stunning representations of the immortality of subjectivity in the canon: "And says within her bosom it shall dwell," since Adonis has been "reft from her by death." As the goddess voices the transposition of death into physiological immortality, she enacts the transposition decisively, cropping the stalk in preparation for her departure to Paphos. But in the process Shakespeare opens his text to something like the origin of literary production itself, the exquisite "breach" showing the "Green-dropping sap," which Venus compares to tears – Adonis' certainly, and her own, but also perhaps the green of pastoral liquid from the Ovidian *fons sacer*. When Venus does speak so that we can hear her, she introduces a remarkable temporalization of Ovidian poetry and theatre: "Poor flow'r . . . this was thy father's guise." Quite literally, the text grafts the cropped poetical flower to the costumed "guise" of theatre, rehearsing a process that looks like the author's own "move from stage to page" (Mortimer, *Variable Passions*, 1): Adonis may have once "act[ed]" in the "dumb play" of Venus' "chorus-like" tears, but now he becomes the poor flower within the goddess' eternal bosom.

Taking the cue of Crewe and others, we can say that when Venus crops the flower, Shakespeare grafts the stalks of his two rivals' careers. Whereas previously Venus and Adonis clashed and were separated, now they act out a process not of unity but of succession, as Venus bears away the metamorphosed Adonis in her chariot. The moment of grafting that produces the artifact of the poem models more than the rivalry between Marlowe and Spenser, Ovid and Virgil, or even their Elizabethan readers; it models one particular reader who happens to be an author. In *Venus and Adonis*,

Shakespeare can be seen to represent his own entry into the authorial list: he grafts the two aesthetics – "mighty opposites, poised in antagonism" (Greenblatt, *Fashioning*, 222) – into a single yet hybrid art of dramatic poetry. When Coleridge observed that "'Venus and Adonis' seem at once the characters themselves, and the whole representation of those characters by the most consummate actors" (reprinted in Kolin, ed., "*Venus and Adonis*," 70), he appears to intuit the fusion of poetry and theatre that here we witness iconographically.

If the boar who kills Adonis represents "nature's arbitrary violence," as Anthony Mortimer argues, so that "the death of Adonis remains an accident" (33), Shakespeare shows how two very different principles of immortality, Spenser's "eterne in mutabilitie" (*Fairie Queene*, 3. 6. 47) and Marlowe's boy eternal, become subjected to a higher power in the new print of their rival: the tragic randomness of time and "mad mischances" (738) "cross the curious workmanship" not simply of "nature" (734) but of art.

Venus' "prophe[c]y" that "Sorrow on love hereafter shall attend" (1136) does seem to identify *Venus and Adonis* as "an etiological poem," which is often understood to be about "how the tribulations of mortal lovers originated" (Crewe, ed., *Narrative Poems*, xxxiv). Yet Venus' bearing of the flower of Adonis to her royal palace also constitutes a new Elizabethan icon, a figure for a hybrid literary career and its driving aesthetics: Shakespeare imprints an etiological poem about the origins of *Venus and Adonis* itself. Specifically, Shakespeare's inaugural narrative poem is born out of his perception of a fatal clash being waged at this time between the twin arts of England's two great contemporary authors. In *Venus and Adonis*, Shakespeare manages to record his own literary genealogy as the youthfully competing heir of two interlocked, violently opposed literary aesthetics, both forcefully transacted through the cultural opposition between the twin media of poetry and theatre. Presenting himself in print for the first time, Shakespeare uses the amorous minor epic to sing extemporally about the birth of the new Ovidian poet-playwright within his own historical moment.

CHAPTER 4

Publishing the show: The Rape of Lucrece *as Lucanian counter-epic of empire*

> They did conclude to bear dead Lucrece thence,
> To show her bleeding body thorough Rome,
> And so to publish Tarquin's foul offense.
> (*The Rape of Lucrece*, 1850–52)

Even more than *Venus and Adonis*, *The Rape of Lucrece* is imbued with the discourse of both the theatre and the print shop. The epigraph above constitutes a 1594-version of the conjunction, as Brutus, Collatine, Lucretius, and the emergent founders of the Roman Republic bear the "dead Lucrece" in order to "show" her "bleeding body" as a spectacle through Rome and to "publish" Tarquin's "foul offense." In the last line, the word "so" puts the conjunction in motion: the "show" leads to "public[cation]"; the bearing of the dead female's deflowered body allows the men to publish the criminal's action. The community of surviving men becomes the agent of the show, the dead female its object, and the masculine perpetrator its prime suspect. The publicity occurs within a nationalist environment, "thorough Rome," the product of a shared, rational judgment by – and a government decision among – men: "They did conclude." The words *show* and *publish* nominally refer to political behavior with subjective origins, but jostling here in the poem's final stanza, they consolidate two sustained strands of literary discourse from Shakespeare's professional career, cut along clear lines of gender.

Show was a standard Elizabethan term referring to performances in the theatre, and was used as such by Shakespeare habitually, as in this self-conscious display during the actors' performance of *The Mousetrap* from *Hamlet*:

OPH. Will a' [the Prologue] tell us what this show meant?
HAM. Ay, or any show that you will show him. Be not you asham'd to show, he'll
not shame to tell you what it means.[1] (*Hamlet*, 3. 2. 143–46)

---

[1] On "show" in Shakespeare, see Parker, *Margins*, 252–71; on "show" and "tell" and the "links between dramatic show and female show" here, see 253.

The word *show* occurs in its cognate forms fourteen times in *Lucrece*, from beginning to end (81, 115, 252, 296, 395, 402, 807, 953, 1507, 1514, 1748, 1761, 1810, 1851). *Publish* meant "proclaim" or "make public," but at this time it was also coming to mean *put into print*, and, as several recent critics point out, the narrative that concludes with this term also opens with it: "why is Collatine the publisher / Of that rich jewel he should keep unknown" (33–34).[2] Thus, for recent critics interested in the materiality of the text, Shakespeare's use of the word as bookends to his narrative signals his own anxiety about "shifting from the sphere of theatre to that of print[ed poetry]," brought about when a man of the theatre turns from drama to verse, as the theatres close in 1592–93 due to plague.[3]

Admittedly, *The Rape of Lucrece*, like *Venus and Adonis*, does not go as far as *A Lover's Complaint* in telling a story in which the author's twin literary forms play a role in the plot, the way the young courtier's "deep-brain'd sonnets" and "tragic shows" do in Shakespeare's third and final narrative poem (209, 308). Tarquin and Lucrece remain the legendary (semi-historical) Roman prince and Roman matron that they had been since Livy's *History of Rome* and Ovid's *Fasti* (or even Chaucer's *Legend of Good Women*); they are not, that is, Elizabethan practitioners of poetry and theatre. Nonetheless, Shakespeare does suffuse his re-telling of the West's arch-myth of sexual violation, personal reputation, and political formation (see I. Donaldson, *Rapes*, 7–9) with a formulation suggested by the poem's final stanza: in this poem, the author is also processing his own (afflicted) standing as an emergent English poet-playwright.

The Rape of Lucrece remains "one of the most exhaustively discussed poems in the English language" (Crewe, ed., *Narrative Poems*, xli), yet critics who represent three major groups – sexuality, politics, and art – neglect the discourse of both poetry and theatre *in the text*. Neglected as well is the nationalist context for understanding this discourse: the counter-Spenserian movement mounted in the early 1590s when Marlowe composes two minor epics in opposition to *The Faerie Queene*: the Ovidian *Hero and Leander*; and a translation of Book 1 of Lucan's epic, the *Pharsalia*, known as *Lucan's First Book*, "arguably one of the underrated masterpieces of Elizabethan literature" (Martindale, *Redeeming the Text*, 71).

---

[2] See, e.g., Dubrow, *Victors*, 89–90; Breitenberg, *Anxious Masculinity*, 97–100, 115–24. See Barkan: "The word *publish* in Shakespeare's time was finely poised between the pre-Gutenbergian general meaning of 'make public' and our more limited sense of 'one who publishes a book'" (*The Gods Made Flesh*, 347n8).

[3] Wall, *Imprint*, 217; see Burrow, "Life," 29–33; cf. Breitenberg, *Anxious Masculinity*, 97.

Critics who emphasize the poem's sexuality tend to read *Lucrece* as a work about rape, brooding over a cultural problem in which men abuse women, over questions such as "consent," over debates regarding the extent to which rape corrupts the flesh of the victim while preserving the purity of her soul, and finally over Shakespeare's representation of his characters' interiority, first in the rapist Tarquin, then in his victim Lucrece.[4] Critics emphasizing the poem's politics read *Lucrece* as either a-political or more often today as deeply political, with the latter dividing between those who see a "royalist" poem in support of the Tudor monarchy and those who see a "republican" poem in support of individual freedom, as critics attempt to get at the poem's contribution to a 1590s conversation about matters of government and state policy.[5] Finally, critics emphasizing art or the literary read the poem variously for its genre as an Ovidian minor epic, narrative poem, complaint, or tragedy; its intertextuality with the principal sources, Livy and Ovid, but also Virgil, Petrarch, Chaucer, Gower, and other medieval and Renaissance authorities; its distinctive (for some, overbearing) rhetoric and striking tropes – what Jonathan Crewe terms its "figurative overload" ("Writing Rape," 154); and its clear two-part structure (before and after the rape) and other formal features.[6]

In a recent edition of the poem, Crewe helps us see a critical genealogy for the three groups, reminding us that "it took a succession of feminist critics, writing in the 1980s and 90s, to gain attention for the poem as one of sexual violence against a woman rather than, say, as a literary-historical, rhetorical, or aesthetic phenomenon only" (Crewe, ed., *Narrative Poems*, xxxv). Thus, Crewe himself goes on to emphasize a sexual and political reading: "It is rape . . . in Shakespeare's *Lucrece* and elsewhere that brings

---

[4] See Hynes, "Rape"; El-Gabalwy, "Ethical Question"; Kahn, "Rape"; Bromly, "Lucrece's Recreation"; Cousins, *Shakespeare's Sonnets*, 48–110; Baines, "Effacing Rape"; Ziegler, "My Lady's Chamber"; Newman, "Mild Women"; P. Berry, "Woman, Language"; Willbern, *Poetic Will*, 76–96; Dubrow, *Domestic*, 15–61; Hendricks, who gives a recent overview of feminist criticsm ("A word," 104–07). See Belsey, "Consent," on the feminine agency of Lucrece's important utterance (327–28). See also Jed on the humanist interpretation of the myth, *Chaste Thinking*.

[5] For an a-political reading, see Tolbert, "The Argument." For a royalist reading, see I. Donaldson, *Rapes*, 40–56; for republican readings, see Patterson, *Reading*, 304–09; Platt, *Rome*, 13–43; Dzelzainis, "Political Thought," 106–08. Nass sees a critique of monarchy ("Law," 311n28). On the poem and Elizabethan historiography, see Dubrow, "Clio"; on Rome, see Miola, *Rome*, 18–41.

[6] On genre, see H. Smith, *Elizabethan*, 113–17 (on Ovidian verse); Hulse, *Verse*, 175–94 (on minor epic); Dubrow, "Mirror" and "Narrative and Lyric" (on these genres and complaint); Walley, "Tragedy." On intertextuality, see Lanham, "Ovidian Shakespeare"; Newman, "Mild Women"; Bate, *Ovid*, 65–82; Enterline, *Rhetoric*, 152–97, who emphasizes Ovid and Petrarch; M. A. Wells, "Rape," who emphasizes Virgil and Petrarch; Hillman, "Gower's Lucrece," who emphasizes Gower. On rhetoric and tropes, see French, "Badge of Fame"; N. J. Vickers, "*Lucrece*" and "Heraldry"; Maus, "Tropes." On formal features, see R. M. Frye, "Composition"; Kramer and Kaminsky, "Contraries."

into the fullest possible view the systemic nature of unequal power-gender relations in Western culture" (xliii). Published in 1999, Crewe's edition in a popular series (The Pelican Shakespeare) might be seen as valorizing sexual and political commentary at the expense of the "literary-historical." Neglected in this genealogy, however, is the most recent phase of commentary (already evoked): indebted to Joel Fineman and Nancy J. Vickers in particular, a phase represented by Wendy Wall and Colin Burrow, who emphasize *Lucrece*'s subtle representation of (male) authorship and the poem's self-conscious role within and representation of manuscript and print culture.[7]

Despite an evident return to a literary emphasis, most important recent work does move across the boundaries of the sexual, the political, and the literary. To these three groups, we probably need to add a fourth – one touched on by most commentary: the religious or philosophical, which shows the poem foregrounding human rather than divine agency and thus emphasizing questions of name, fame, and reputation.[8] What most critics in all four groups share is a strong sense that Shakespeare's *Rape of Lucrece* constitutes a complex yet crucial authorial intervention in one of our most enduring and troubling myths, evidently as important today as it was in classical Rome or Elizabethan England. By turning first to the immediate historical context of literary nationhood in which Shakespeare composed and printed the poem, and then to the combined discourse of poetry and theatre emerging from within it (both the prefatory material and the poem proper), we may extend the shared value of *Lucrece* as a decisive moment in English literary history. Specifically, we may more fully understand the tension between "show" and "publication" in the poem's final stanza only *inside* the contemporary scene of literary competition for the national rights to publish the historical show of the female's interpetively porous body.[9] In his 1655 edition of the poem, John Quarles intimates something of this national project, when his title page calls Shakespeare "The incomparable Master of our English Poetry," and his frontispiece presents the famed Droeshout dramatic author looking down on a theatrical scene right out of the poem: Lucrece stabs herself dramatically in front of a male figure whose shoulder bears a theatrical mask and who could be either her husband,

---

[7] Fineman, "Shakespeare's Will"; N. J. Vickers, "*Lucrece*" and "Heraldry." See also Crewe, "Writing Rape"; Enterline, *Rhetoric*, 152–97; M. A. Wells, "Rape."
[8] On human agency, see Maus, intro. to *Lucrece, Norton*, 638. On fame, see Dubrow, *Victors*, 145–47; Breitenberg, *Anxious Masculinity*, 96–97, 102–15.
[9] Thanks to Heather James for this formulation (personal communication, 25 June 2003).

Figure 6. Frontispiece to *The Rape of Lucrece*, edited by John Quarles (London, 1655).

Collatine, her rapist, Tarquin, or her successor as political activist, Brutus –
perhaps all three (Figure 6).[10]

Most recent critics would agree to classify *Lucrece* through some version of
Ovidianism, whether "Ovidian narrative poem" or "Ovidian minor epic"
(or epyllion).[11] The classification of Ovidian minor epic is more precise,
in part because *Lucrece* is "not really [a] narrative poem . . . at all": it does
"not do very many or very interesting things with temporal sequence, and
not very much happens" (Burrow, "Politics," 1); in part because the rhyme
royal stanza, the nationalistic frame, and the dominant military metaphors
show Shakespeare's attempt to enter the epic register.[12]

 Such Ovidian classification identifies the historical context of *Lucrece*,
like that of *Venus*, as lying in the author's attempt to walk down the Virgilian
path of pastoral and epic via the medium of printed poetry (cf. Hulse,
Verse, 12). While both poems deploy the Virgilian progression in their
topoi and in their landscape, we may observe how the forest scene of
Shakespeare's first minor epic more precisely identifies *Venus* as a version of
Ovidian pastoral, while the domestic or civic scene of his second minor epic
identifies *Lucrece* as a version of Ovidian epic, the "graver labor" advertised
in the *Dedicatory Epistle* to *Venus*. Together, the two publications present
the English Ovidian author progressing from lower to higher Virgilian
forms in order to "establish himself as a respectable poet" (Hulse, *Verse*,
175) – establish himself, we may add, in competition with other authors.
The paradox imprints Shakespeare's "signature" as an author: an Ovidian
author pursues a Virgilian career, in competition with other contemporary
authors. In turn, the paradox draws attention to the author's revision of the
Virgilian career model as his signal achievement in the Elizabethan literary
system.

[10] Thanks to Sasha Roberts for suggesting Collatine and Margreta de Grazia for suggesting Tarquin
(personal communications, 22 November 2003).
[11] In *Verse*, Hulse collapses the traditional division of "Ovidian verse" into "two major categories" in
order to discuss "minor epic": "the epyllion or minor epic, dealing with classical mythology; and
the historical complaint, drawing on English chronicles" (16). In addition to Hulse (and before him
Keach), the most important recent Ovidian analyses are by Bate, *Ovid*; Enterline, *Rhetoric*.
[12] Fineman suggests that "There is something momentous, both thematically and tonally, about the
way . . . [lines 1520–26 on Troy] call up the loss of everything the English Renaissance self-servingly
identifies with the bright light of Troy, something genuinely epic" ("Shakespeare's Will," 59). See
Dubrow, "Clio," 429–36; N. J. Vickers, esp. on the "heraldry in Lucrece's face" ("*Lucrece*," 64; see
"Heraldry"). Maus takes this line a (generic) step further: "in the elaborate description of Lucrece's
face . . . the (pastoral) field of flowers and the (epic) field of war strive for predominance in time-
honored Petrarchan fashion" ("Tropes," 78).

In the early 1590s, we do not have to look far to discern the authors with whom Shakespeare might most see himself in competition. At the wellhead, Marlowe's perturbed ghost has long been seen to haunt Shakespeare's two minor epics, especially in the form of *Hero and Leander*. Yet on 28 September 1593, within a few months of Marlowe's death on 30 May, *Hero and Leander* shows up back-to-back in the Stationers' Register with Marlowe's *second* "narrative poem": the 694-line *Lucan's First Book*. C. S. Lewis anticipates most scholars today in judging Marlowe's poem of "very great merit," even though he was "tempted" to deny that Marlowe wrote it (*English Literature*, 486) – a question no longer in dispute. Where we may classify *Hero* as a counter-national epic championing the freedom of the Ovidian author, we may classify *Lucan* as a new Elizabethan genre, a counter-epic of empire championing the freedom of the Lucanian author within a republican frame.[13]

As the name suggests, a counter-epic of empire is a poem in the epic mode that *counters* the politics of the normative epic of empire, Virgil's *Aeneid*, but also its European heirs, including Dante and Petrarch, Tasso and Ronsard, Spenser and Milton. In classical Rome, the first great authors of this subversive genre were two: Ovid in the *Metamorphoses* and Lucan in the *Pharsalia*. Both poets organized their epics to attack and resist Virgil's epic poem in service of the Augustine regime, and what they share is precisely a republican ethos of *libertas*. Yet Ovid and Lucan differ, and not simply because one wrote a mythological epic and the other a historical one. Ovid is a counter-national poet in the sense that he counters the concept of the nation as a political collectivity by asserting the authority of the poet himself.[14] By contrast, Lucan counters the national poet with a political form of nationhood, that of the Roman Republic. Hence, Ovid tells universal myths about the changing of the gods, subject to the power of desire, but Lucan narrates a historical battle between two political leaders, Caesar and Pompey, in the event that turns the Republic into the Empire. Lucan is *formally* a political author of Roman nationhood in a way that Ovid is not. To be sure, Ovid is a political author, from the *Amores* and *Ars amatoria* through the *Tristia* and the *Ex ponto*; but as Ovid makes clear in his later works, he foregrounds the poet's own competition with the Emperor, even in the very poem he writes to placate Caesar's wrath for relegating him to Tomis: "my mind is . . . my comrade and my joy; over this Caesar could have no right" (*Tristia*, 3. 7. 47–48). Back in the *Amores*, Ovid had written:

---

[13] See Cheney, *Profession*, esp. 221–26 (on Marlovian epic), 227–37 (on *Lucan*), and 238–58 (on *Hero*).
[14] On "counter-nationhood," see Cheney, *Profession*, 19–25.

"Verse is immortal, and shall ne'er decay. / To verse let kings give place, and kingly shows" (1. 15. 32–33; trans. Marlowe). If Lucan is a patriotic author in service of Rome, Ovid is not; he is patriotic to his own authorship. When Marlowe translates both the *Amores* and the *Pharsalia*, he shows his fellow Elizabethans alternative modes of literary subversion – Ovidian and Lucanian – which he re-deploys in his two minor epics of the early 1590s: *Hero and Leander* and *Lucan's First Book.*[15]

The Roman originators of the counter-epic genre did not simply create an alternative space, as many of the epyllion writers of the 1590s did with the allure of eros. Rather, the Roman counter-epicists of empire, like their Elizabethan heirs, composed political poems that confronted the imperial epic of empire decisively on its own ground, where the topic of freedom stands forcibly as its stronghold: freedom of thought, freedom of speech, freedom of action, and freedom of writing.[16]

Marlowe's translation of Book 1 of the *Pharsalia* is the first to be printed in English, and therefore it deserves to be moved to the front of any genealogy of the epic tradition pertaining to England. Although not published until 1600, it was almost certainly the inaugural poem firing the English Lucan revival in the 1590s, represented by Daniel's *Civil Wars* (1595), Drayton's *Mortimeriados* (1596), and Shakespeare's *Julius Caesar* (1599).[17] Marlowe did not translate Lucan simply to participate in the Renaissance project of recovering classical authors; he aimed also to attack and resist the great Virgilian epic of empire for his nation, *The Faerie Queene* (Cheney, *Profession*, 227). In this typology of intertextuality, Marlowe translates Lucan to counter Spenser's cultural authority. What is at stake in such a professional competition is the writing of English nationhood. Specfically, Marlowe counters Spenser's monarchical form of nationhood with a republican-based counter-nationhood, and this form narrates the author's oppositional freedom of voice and art. The Elizabethan Lucan revival, in its incipient, Marlovian form, counterpoises the Elizabethan Virgilianism championed by Spenser.[18]

---

[15] In *Epic*, Quint neglects this Elizabethan genealogy, distinguishing between "two rival traditions of epic" – "epics of the imperial victors and epics of the defeated" (8) – with Virgil and Lucan functioning as the figureheads.

[16] On *libertas*, see Cheney, *Profession*, 21–25, 273–74nn40–41.

[17] On Lucan in the English Renaissance, see Blissett, "Lucan's Caesar"; Hulse, *Verse*, 195–205, 210–14; McCoy, *Rites*, 103–26; G. M. Maclean, "The Debate," 26–44; Quint, *Epic*, 5–10, 131–60; Norbrook, *Writing*, 23–62.

[18] Dubrow, *Victors*, joins most critics in concentrating on those writers between Livy and Gower who told the Lucrece myth. Similarly, Enterline's study relating Ovid, Petrarch, and Shakespeare jumps over Shakespeare's contemporaries. The "literary history" she tells (*Rhetoric*, 176) is thus in need of supplement. The same applies to M. A. Wells on Virgil, Petrarch, and Shakespeare.

Since "Lucan was the central poet of the republican imagination" (Norbrook, *Writing*, 24), we may profitably call his first English translator the central Elizabethan poet of the republican imagination.[19] We may agree that republicanism does not become a decisive question of government until the English Civil War, but we might also recall the political context of the 1590s – what Patrick Collinson famously calls Elizabeth's "monarchical republic."[20] While *Lucan's First Book* joins other pre-1640s "dramatization[s] and publication[s] of the classics" in forming a largely "oblique" conduct of political debates between monarchy and republic, we need to give Marlowe credit, especially since the "first book of the *Pharsalia* was in fact much cited by two of the leading seventeenth-century theorists of republicanism, James Harrington and Algernon Sidney" (Norbrook, *Writing*, 13, 36–37).

Like Marlowe, Shakespeare composes two short epics in the early 1590s. Just as we commonly read *Venus* with *Hero*, so we might read *Lucrece* with *Lucan*. While these last two works seem to have little in common, they share a specific Elizabethan context: young authors of the same sex and generation, born in the same year and of the same middle-class environment, compose mid-length narrative poems on Roman political topics, at the same time (1592–93) and under the same cultural circumstances: the closing of the theatres due to plague.[21] Above all, both *Lucrece* and *Lucan* represent a Roman political narrative divided across the government line separating monarchy and republic. Whereas Marlowe follows Lucan in using the Civil War of Pompey and Caesar to represent the death of the Republic and call for its political reinstatement, Shakespeare uses his two principal source texts, Ovid and Livy, to show how sexual strife between Tarquin and Lucrece represents the birth of the original Republic. Consequently, we may wish to re-classify Shakespeare's work; it is not simply a second narrative poem but a specific version of the Elizabethan genre Marlowe had invented: a Lucanian counter-epic of empire, opposing the primary Virgilian epic of Elizabethan empire, Spenser's *Faerie Queene*.[22]

---

[19] Norbrook (*Writing*) recalls only incidentally that Marlowe was the first to be published as a translator of Lucan (41), and he never mentions *Lucrece* (or her myth), referring to Shakespeare only a few times in passing (12, 224, 373).

[20] For Norbrook's brief discussion of Elizabethan republicanism, including reliance on Collinson's paradigm, see, *Writing*, 11–14. For more detail in *Lucrece* on this paradigm, see Hadfield, *Shakespeare and Renaissance Political Culture*, ch. 3.

[21] On the dating of *Lucan's First Book* late in Marlowe's career, see Lewis, *English Literature*, 486; Shapiro, "Lucan," 323–24.

[22] Cf. H. Smith, *Elizabethan*: "No poet writing in 1594 could fail to be influenced by the achievement of Spenser's publication four years earlier" (117).

The gender dynamic at the center of *Lucan* and *Lucrece* does differ. Perhaps tellingly, Marlowe narrates a competition between two men, while Shakespeare narrates a competition between a man and a woman. Eros lies at the center of *Lucrece* in a way that it does not of *Lucan*.[23] Having said that, we may wish to peer in on what is probably Marlowe's most neglected representation of the female; it is also one of his most poignant, all the more so because it turns into an address to a woman who has died surrounded by men, right near the beginning of *Lucan's First Book*:

> for Julia,
> Snatched hence by cruel fates with ominous howls,
> Bare down to hell her son, the pledge of peace,
> And all bands of that death-presaging alliance.
> Julia, had heaven given thee longer life,
> Thou hadst restrained thy headstrong husband's rage,
> Yea, and thy father too . . .
> (*Lucan's First Book*, 111–17)

Who is this remarkable woman? She is the daughter of Caesar, Julia, who married Pompey to seal the attempted alliance of two men so narcissistic that "Pompey could bide no equal, / Nor Caesar no superior" (125–26). Caught tragically between her father and her husband, this young woman, as Marlowe powerfully renders, goes to hell giving birth to the child who would be heir to the two huge men in her life, so much so that Julia can hold their largeness at bay, although not even she is strong enough to endure the "ominous howls" of "cruel fates," who grimly determine that such a "pledge of peace," with its political-marital "bands," must become a "death-presaging alliance." So much, we might say, for the vagaries of having to translate someone else's poem, yet the young man is not to be chastised for voicing so powerfully this tragically youthful icon of the dead mother and her child, sacrificed to the fatal engine of masculine politics. We might wonder what Shakespeare would have thought.

Whatever he thought, he and Marlowe both end their counter-epic poems with a memorable female icon. Lucrece takes her life into her own hands to motivate exemplary future action not simply among chaste Roman matrons (1714–15) but also among powerful Roman men. Identifying her assailant, she states, "'He, he, fair lords, 'tis he, / That guides this hand to give this wound to me'" (1721–22), prompting outrage so charged it "changed" the Roman "state government . . . from kings to consuls" (Argument, 45).

---

[23] See Wheeler, "Lucan": "Lucan does not avoid Ovidian eroticism altogether: Caesar's love for Cleopatra recalls that of Pygmalion for his statue (cf. 10.71–72 and *Met.*, 10.252)" (379n57).

Similarly, Marlowe follows Lucan in cross-dressing his voice in the garb of the Bacchic Roman matron, who ends the book in a furious complaint – a poetic form important to Shakespeare's work (Dubrow, "Mirror").[24] "Disclosing Phoebus' fury," the matron addresses Apollo, "'Paean, whither am I haled? where shall I fall, / Thus borne aloft? . . . / Why grapples Rome, and makes war, having no foes? / . . . I have seen Philippi" (676–93).

That last reference is crucial, because *Lucan's First Book* ends with a double reference to two famous and interrelated battles that occurred on the same field in Macedonia. Philippi is "where Octavianus and Antony defeated Brutus and Cassius in the crucial battle of the Civil War, 42 BC. But the place was conventionally identified with Pharsalus, so that Lucan's [and Marlowe's] reference is in fact to both battles" (Orgel, ed., *Christopher Marlowe*, 259). The typology is even more precise for Shakespeare's minor epic, because, as he himself recalls no fewer than three times in *Julius Caesar*, there were two famous (and related) anti-imperial, pro-republican men named Brutus. As Marcus Brutus puts it in Act 2, scene 1, "My ancestors did from the streets of Rome / The Tarquin drive when he was call'd a king" (53–54; see 1. 2. 159–61 and 3. 2. 50), referring to Lucius Junius Brutus. In Book 5 of the *Pharsalia*, Lucan recalls this genealogy, when Apollo cuts off the voice of the Delphic priestess, prompting the poet's intervention: "You, Paean, Prince of Truth . . . / . . . Your silence meant to ensure that Fortune achieves / deeds with a righteous sword – ambition punished, tyranny / met once more by a vengeful Brutus" (199–208). Later, in the most infamous moment in Lucan's epic, the cadaver of the dead soldier re-animated by the witch Erictho narrates to Pompey's son Sextus, "'You, Brutus, first Consul after the kings' expulsion, / you were the only pious shade I saw rejoicing" (6. 791–92).[25]

While Lucan does not refer to Lucrece directly, he brings his epic to the threshold of her domestic story by recurrently evoking Lucius Junius Brutus. Not surprisingly, Lucan appears to supply potential origins to some of Shakespeare's most memorable moments in *Lucrece*.[26] Shakespeare's military metaphors, singled out by critics, are consonant with Lucan's military

---

[24] On Lucan's cross-dressing of his own voice here, see Hardie, *Epic Successors*, 107–08; Feeney, *The Gods*, 275.

[25] Lucan mentions Lucius Junius Brutus five times in the *Pharsalia*; see also 7. 37–39, 7. 440–42, and 7. 586–96. Lucan clearly thinks of Brutus as the inventor of Roman liberty, just as he thinks of Julia, who goes on to haunt the epic darkly, as its most harrowing female casualty, joining Pompey's surviving wife, Cornelia.

[26] Jones (*Origins*) shows persuasively that Shakespeare imitated Lucan in such plays as the first historical tetralogy, *Julius Caesar*, the second tetralogy, *Hamlet*, and *Antony and Cleopatra* (273–77), and that he knew Marlowe's translation in manuscript (273).

battle. Yet it is Shakespeare's photography of the "crimson blood" "bub-bling" from Lucrece's "breast" that looks Lucanian in all its macabre detail, betraying a shared fascination with violence to the body's deep interior – a fascination Lucan no doubt inherited from his uncle but one for which even Seneca could find no match. Even in Book 1, which pales by compar-ison with later books, we discover the augurer Arruns slaying a bull to read the text of a Roman prophecy, which reads in Marlowe's translation:

> from the yawning gash,
> Instead of red blood, wallowed venomous gore.
> These direful signs made Arruns stand amazed,
> . . . a dead blackness
> Ran through the blood, that turned it all to jelly,
> And stained the bowels with dark loathsome spots;
> The liver swelled with filth, and every vein
> Did threaten horror from the host of Caesar:
> . . . and from the gaping liver
> Squeezed matter; through the caul the entrails peered,
> And which (aye me) ever pretended ill,
> At that bunch where the liver is, appeared
> A knob of flesh.   (Marlowe, *Lucan's First Book*, 613–28)

We may look on in horror, but Lucan is simply warming up.

Lucan's fascination with blood, its modulating color, but also its theatri-cality, re-appears in Shakespeare's poem, albeit in more reticent fashion:

> Her blood, in poor revenge, held it in chase;
> And bubbling from her breast, it doth divide
> In two slow rivers, that the crimson blood
> Circles her body in on every side,
> . . .
> Some of her blood still pure and red remain'd,
> And some look'd black, and that false Tarquin stain'd.
> About the mourning and congealed face
> Of that black blood a wat'ry rigol goes,
> . . .
> And ever since . . .
> Corrupted blood some watery token shows.
> (*Rape of Lucrece*, 1734–48)

Both authors pause to brood over the metamorphoses of blood, the min-gling of "black" and "red" color, the "stain" it leaves, its theatrical character, and strikingly its afterlife: Marlowe's Lucanian blood "ever pretended ill," while Shakespeare's "ever since, as pitying Lucrece's woes, / Corrupted blood some watery token shows." We shall return to Lucrece's blood later, observing here only that Shakespeare's major source-texts record no origin for his representation.[27]

Unlike *Lucan*, however, *Lucrece* is much more difficult to plot along a clear political axis.[28] One way out of the difficulty is to return to the material facts of the poem's production. Shakespeare's much-discussed move from stage to page is not simply the occasion for the poem but its underlying obsession. In *Lucrece*, more anxiously than in *Venus*, we see what happens when a man of the theatre presents himself in print as a poet in the English and European tradition. While critics have situated *Lucrece* within the author's conflict between print and manuscript, drawing attention to the poem's use of terms from print culture, we might attend to a combined discourse of printed poetry and staged theatre. Not simply Dame Night but the printed epyllion itself is a "Black stage for tragedies" (766). Through the poem's self-reflexive language, its references to such arch-myths of the Ovidian author as Orpheus and Philomela from the *Metamorphoses*, and its complex Virgilian ekphrasis of the fall of Troy, Shakespeare can be seen to process not so much a clear political organization as a decisive authorial representation. Since *Lucrece* narrates the legend leading to the birth of the Republic, we may wonder whether Shakespeare is here addressing the origin not of republican government per se but rather of what we might call republican representation: the author's representation of a republican frame of art. Such an art may well learn to operate within the Elizabethan monarchy, and if so, *Lucrece* would find a natural home in Elizabeth's "monarchical republic." And so it did, being printed four times during that sovereign's reign (see Figure 3 above).

THE DEDICATORY EPISTLE AND THE ARGUMENT

Typically, editors and critics separate their discussion of the twin prose items prefacing the 1594 quarto. Such discussion tends to view the *Dedicatory Epistle* as one of two patronage documents extant in the Shakespeare canon, emphasizing that it is "notably warm[er]" than the dedication to *Venus* and thus suggestive of that poem's persuasive power (Burrow, ed., *Sonnets and Poems*, 13). The Argument has spawned considerably more discussion, including about its authorship, though today most scholars accept it as

---

[27] The following editions record no speculation: Prince; Wilbur and Harbage; Roe; Crewe; Burrow.
[28] Whereas Burrow suggests only that "Lucrece's words ask awkward and unanswerable questions about unregulated monarchy" (*Sonnets and Poems*, 54), Hadfield argues that the poem champions republicanism outright (*Shakespeare and Renaissance Political Culture*, ch. 3).

Shakespeare's composition; the best discussion sees it counterpoising the poem's Ovidian or erotic interpretation of the Lucrece story with a Livian or republican one (e.g., Burrow, ed., *Sonnets and Poems*, 45–54). Taking this cue, we might see the two prefatory items as also providing counterpoised forms of discourse, twin windows for viewing the poem itself.

Almost always, critics view the dedication as evidence for understanding *Lucrece* as "the 'graver labor' promised . . . in the dedication to *Venus and Adonis*" (Lanham, "Ovidian Shakespeare," 94), without stating the repercussions, especially for our view of Shakespeare as a "man of the theatre": in 1593–94, the author presents himself *in print* as a Virgilian poet moving from lower to higher forms, effectively from pastoral to epic. The main problem with the commonplace view is that it closes the year-long space between *Venus* and *Lucrece* when Shakespeare's readers were primed to expect a poem formally in the epic register.[29] This space is now lost to us – admittedly it was brief – but we might try to re-capture it. When we do, we discover an author neglected in modern criticism: Shakespeare the print-epicist. Not Shakespeare the minor epicist, but Shakespeare the major epicist. In 1579, Spenser had set the precedent for Elizabethan authors to present themselves as Virgilian pastoralists preparing for national epic, and Shakespeare in the pastoral-based *Venus*, complete with its prophesying dedication to his patron, could easily be construed as preparing himself for the kind of epic labor Spenser published in 1590 with Books 1–3 of *The Faerie Queene*. Critics have been too quick to lose sight of this moment; to regain it is to re-envision Shakespeare at a distinct time of his professional career.[30]

The fact is, however, Shakespeare is not Spenser, and *Lucrece* is not *The Faerie Queene* (just as *Venus* is not the *Calender*). Like the *Dedicatory Epistle* to *Venus*, the dedication to *Lucrece* maps out an Ovidian discourse, attenuating the Virgilian career model in a way that is consistent with a counter-epic of empire. When read in its proper historical context, the *Dedicatory Epistle* advertises its Ovidian author as a rival to the Virgil of England. By calling *Lucrece* a counter-epic of empire, we supply a generic classification that can help us better understand the complexity of Shakespeare's Marlovian maneuver.

Hence, the discourse of the dedication repeats the European Virgilian discourse of empire but then shoots it through with the discourse we have come to expect from an Ovidian author:

---

[29] In his edition, Burrow concurs (*Sonnets and Poems*, 173).
[30] As late as the first decade of the seventeenth century, Shakespeare is entertaining epicist phantasies of competing with England's great national poet (Cheney, "Sonnet 106").

The love I dedicate to your Lordship is without end: wherof this Pamphlet without beginning is but a superfluous Moity. The warrant I have of your Honourable disposition, not the worth of my untutord Lines makes it assured of acceptance. What I have done is yours, what I have to doe is yours, being part in all I have, devoted yours. Were my worth greater, my duety would shew greater, meane time, as it is, it is bound to your Lordship; To whom I wish long life still lengthened with all happinesse.

Your Lordships in all duety.

William Shakespeare

(*Dedicatory Epistle, Riverside*, 1816)

Critics explain "without beginning" by referring to Shakespeare's narrative strategy in the poem itself, which opens *in medias res* – that is to say, along epic "Lines." Yet the epicist thrust is advanced through the bold repetition in the opening phrase of the central concept of Virgil's *Aeneid*: "imperium *sine fine*" (1.279: empire *without end*; emphasis added). This Virgilian intertextuality helps explain Shakespeare's preoccupation with two other arch-concepts from the *Aeneid*: "duety" (twice voiced) and longevity or fame. In Shakespeare's lexicon, however, it is not empire that is without end but "love" – the author's love not of the nation but of the patron; and it is this love to which he shows duty and grants immortality ("without end"). The author wishes his patron a very long life indeed, wittily *lengthened* through the triple repetition of "*long* life *still* [=always] *lengthened*." By shifting Virgil's claim of poetic immortality for the Empire to long life for Southampton, Shakespeare attenuates the Virgilian register with Ovidian (homoerotic) desire.

Like the dedication to *Venus*, this one shows the author's prediction of future works, but it also recollects past works: "What I have done is yours, what I have to doe is yours." The next phrase, "Were my worth greater," seems to acknowledge the author's humble position, yet it wittily asks for further support. If Shakespeare had more money, of the kind Southampton can supply, his "duety would shew greater": he would continue writing works "greater" than *Venus* or evidently *Lucrece* itself. While some find it "tempting to think that he may be referring to the *Sonnets*" (Roe, ed., *Poems*, 140), more likely Shakespeare is imagining higher (no doubt finally Ovidian) work on Southampton's behalf; a Petrarchan or even a counter-Petrarchan sequence would probably not qualify. The fact that such a grave work was either not forthcoming or has not survived does not erase the advertisement. Again, this is the space over which we may wish to pause.

When Shakespeare goes on to designate his "graver labour" (*Lucrece* itself) with humble terms, he does not violate the Virgilian decorum. For,

throughout *The Faerie Queene*, Spenser presents himself as a humble pastoral poet writing a "homely verse" (6. 12. 41). Thus, even as Shakespeare
fulfills the Virgilian promise to write in a higher genre, he tactfully dimin-
ishes his stature through humble signs. The word "Pamphlet" suggests
diminishment; similarly, the word "Moity" means "trifle," with the phrase
"superfluous Moity" meaning that "although only half a poem, it is still too
much" (Roe, ed., *Poems*, 140).[31] Perhaps, too, we might see an allusion to the
"Castalia . . . aqua" or Muses' springs advertised in the Latin epigraph from
Ovid's *Amores* prefacing *Venus*: the feminine source of the male's poetic
inspiration – a masculine phenomenology of the literary womb. Finally,
the phrase "untutored Lines" pens (Spenserian) humility, denying the very
learning critics have read into the dedication.

While the Virgilian discourse predominates, Shakespeare subtly lets his
discourse from the (Ovidian) theatre infiltrate: "shew greater." The phrase
predicts the Coleridgean principle, that Shakespeare's two narrative poems
"give at once strong promises of the strength, and yet obvious proofs of the
immaturity, of his [dramatic] genius" (Kolin, ed., "*Venus and Adonis*," 69).
In effect, Shakespeare lends Coleridge his voice. As we may also see, it is
the word "shew" here that unleashes the theatrical stream into the poem
itself.

Similarly, the phrase "being part in all I have" anticipates the theatrical
concept of the actor's "part" that also recurs in the poem – five times to be
exact (1135, 1327 [twice], 1328, 1830). Only the intense triple repetition in
lines 1327–28 has warranted a theatrical gloss – "plays a part of woe" (Roe,
ed., *Poems*, 206):

> For then the eye interprets to the ear
> The heavy motion that it doth behold,
> When every part a part of woe doth bear.
> 'Tis but a part of sorrow that we hear.
> (*Rape of Lucrece*, 1325–28)

Long ago, Malone observed of this passage: "Our author seems to have
been thinking of *Dumb-shows*, which were exhibited on the stage in his
time. Motion, in old language, signifies a *puppet-show*; and the person who
spoke for the puppets was called an *interpreter*" (Prince, ed., *Poems*, 126).

Yet the word "part" also belongs to the musical discourse of song. Shakespeare repeats the related idea of *bearing a part* three times (1135, 1327, 1830).

---

[31] Fineman suggests that "this image is quite central to 'The Rape of Lucrece,' figuring not only the
rape but also its motivation and consequences, so it is significant that Shakespeare . . . associates his
poem with the phenomenology of the spurt" ("Will," 27).

For example, in the first instance, Lucrece tells Philomela, the nightingale, "against a thorn thou bear'st thy part." Then in the second instance, quoted above, the *Riverside* editors catch a double ring, of both poetry and theatre: "sings a woeful part (in the musical sense)" and "plays a woeful role" (1831).[32] Thus, when Shakespeare says that Southampton is a "part" in all he has, he implicates the patron's theatrical and poetic role in his own literary production.

A version of this conjunction appears in the Argument, albeit in brief form. While acknowledging that this strange composition may be viewed as a Livian counterpoint to the Ovidian poem (see Belsey, "Consent," 320–21), we may note its slender strand of both Ovidian Petrarchism and Ovidian theatricalism. The Petrarchism appears when "Collatinus extolled the incomparable chastity of his wife Lucretia" (12–13), which the poem itself will dilate on tragically when Tarquin visits the sleeping Lucrece in her bedroom. The theatricalism emerges when the wagering husbands find all their wives but Lucrece "dancing and revelling" (18–19), when Tarquin initially "smother[s] . . . his passions" for Lucrece in order to ensure that he is "royally entertained" by her (22–23, 26), and more directly when Lucrece reveals to her husband and the other men that Tarquin is "the actor" (36) who has become the very "cause of her sorrow" (934–35). Shakespeare's concern in the Argument with tragic causality, located in the theatrical rapist Tarquin but more subtly in her Petrarchan husband, creates an authorial lens for viewing the story as the printed product of the poet-playwright.

TARQUIN, BOOKS, AND THEATRE

The authorial imprint is embedded in the sexual conflict between Lucrece and Tarquin and in the tragic resolution of their story. In the first half of the poem, Shakespeare presents Tarquin not simply as a lustful prince ruining his reputation and his rule, but also as an author who has written a book and is committed to playing the part of an actor. When Lucrece first greets him, she

> Could pick no meaning from their parling looks,
> Nor read the subtle shining secrecies
> Writ in the glassy margents of such books.
> . . .
>   Nor could she moralize his wanton sight,
>   . . .

---

[32] Enterline sees a conjunction of music and theatre here (*Rhetoric*, 192).

> He stories to her ears her husband's fame,
> Won in the fields of fruitful Italy;
> And decks with praises Collatine's high name,
> Made glorious by his manly chivalry,
> With bruised arms and wreaths of victory.
> (*Rape of Lucrece*, 100–10)

The narrator's discourse of printed books here is striking – and constitutes one half of Shakespeare's signature in his handling of the Lucrece legend. Yet the narrator imposes his bookish discourse and its narratival point of view onto Lucrece, who intuitively perceives Tarquin's "looks" for what they are without being conscious enough to act on her instinct: a printed copy of a concealed truth that she needs to read carefully. Since she "never cop'd with stranger eyes" (99), she reads the text of the book but evidently fails to heed the more arcane secondary text, "the subtle shining secrecies" revealed in the book's marginal glosses, which direct the reader to the truth of the inner-text. When she cannot "moralize his wanton sight," she fails to interpret the moral or ethical character of Tarquin's "wanton" book.

Lucrece may read Tarquin's face as a book, and fail to interpret it accurately, but almost simultaneously, as if in literary collusion, the prince presents himself as the author of the book she longs to read: a romance epic about her husband's glorious chivalry. In this narrative, Collatine has fought manfully, suffering bruises to his martial arms, but he returns home heroically, wearing the laurel wreath of victory.

We need to historicize this representation of authorship and readership, because Shakespeare's terminology compels us to do so. The contents of the "book" that Tarquin "stories" to Lucrece are formally Spenserian.[33] Drawing on a virtual inventory of the central words of *The Faerie Queene* – the only chivalric English Renaissance epic available at this time – Tarquin presents a narrative to Lucrece of her husband's standing as an epic hero, just as Spenser does to Queen Elizabeth of Prince Arthur, the heroic lover of Gloriana. Collatine has used "manly chivalry" to win the "wreath" of martial "victory" in the "field" of national battle, and thus Tarquin uses a versified narration to celebrate his friend's (and kinsman's) heroic achievement through "praise" of his "name," "fame," and "glor[y]."[34]

---

[33] Cf. Hillman, "Gower's Lucrece," who quotes the second stanza to support a Gowerian influence.

[34] Shakespeare's "bruised arms" recalls Spenser's "helmes unbruzed" (*October*, 42), the New Poet's synecdoche for the (as yet) unwritten Elizabethan epic. Accordingly, in the opening stanza to Book 1 of the written epic, Spenser presents the Redcrosse Knight wearing bruised arms (1. 1. 1), although Christian reasons emerge for their condition.

For her part, Lucrece cannot "moralize" Tarquin's "wanton sight." The word "moralize" is the final term announcing the Spenserian project in the opening stanza to the national epic: "Fierce warres and faithfull loves shall moralize my song" (1.Proem 1). While Spenser emphasizes the ethical dimension of war and love in the conduct of "Knights and Ladies" (1.Proem 1), Tarquin hypocritically moralizes his song of the warrior Collatine to disrupt the faithful love between husband and wife. "Wanton sight" is also striking, because it shows not simply Lucrece's blindness to the storyteller's sexual hypocrisy but also Tarquin's brilliant performance of the Marlovian maneuver of opening up the "wanton voice" of Spenser's "ethical" art.[35]

Marlowe was indeed the first to have performed this maneuver on a grand scale, making it his most sustained strategy for deconstructing Spenser's national authority.[36] Shakespeare appears to have been attuned to Marlowe's maneuver, and accordingly he presents Tarquin as a Marlovian superhero appropriating the Spenserian ethos. Specifically, Tarquin appears before Lucrece as a Spenserian epic author of his friend's glory precisely to transact his "counterfeit profession" (Marlowe, *Jew of Malta*, 1. 2. 292).[37]

Accordingly, once Lucrece entertains Tarquin in her home, the narrator lapses into Spenserian diction and verse to describe the guest's self-conscious "show":

> He makes excuses for his being there.
> No cloudy show of stormy blust'ring weather
> Doth yet in his fair welkin once appear,
> Till sable Night, mother of dread and fear,
>   Upon the world dim darkness doth display,
>   And in her vaulty prison stows the day.
>   (*Rape of Lucrece*, 114–19)

Here Shakespeare provides a version of the Spenserian poetics of night that critics find later in the poem.[38] For instance, the word "blust'ring" is a favorite of Spenser's in both the 1579 *Shepheardes Calender* and the 1590 *Faerie Queene*, where it occurs, respectively, three and five times.[39]

---

[35] Paglia suggests that both an "ethical voice" and a "wanton voice" compete for authority in *The Faerie Queene*, and she argues that Spenser's historical achievement lies in the victory his poem grants to the latter (*Sexual Personae*, 190–91), not the former, as he himself proclaims in the Proem to Book 1.

[36] See Cheney, *Profession*, 116–17. Yet Paglia allows us to see that the origins of Marlowe's wanton appropriation of Spenser's ethical art lie in Spenser himself.

[37] Dubrow calls Tarquin "a Marlovian character" (*Victors*, 119). On desire and will more recently, see Belsey, "Consent," 323–26.

[38] Bush glosses lines 747, 764–70, 799 – all part of Lucrece's complaint to "Night"– with *Faerie Queene* 3.4.55–59, Arthur's complaint to Night ("Notes"; see Roe, ed., *Poems*, 179, 180, 182).

[39] In chapter 8, we shall see that Shakespeare associates the word "blusterer" with the Spenserian figure of the reverend man in *A Lover's Complaint* (58).

Specifically, Shakespeare's phrase "stormy blust'ring weather" appears to glance at the opening (Virgilian) tempest of the Legend of Holiness, described as "cloudes" of "hideous storme" (1. 1. 6. 5–6) and as a "blustring storme" (10. 2). Similarly, Shakespeare's line 118 – "sable Night, mother of dread and fear" – collects together two other passages in Book 1: after the Redcrosse Knight kills the dragon, the coming of "sad succeeding night, / . . . with her sable mantle gan to shade / The face of earth" (11. 49. 6–7); and the departure of "everlasting Night" as "The mother of dread darknesse," along with Duessa, from the underworld (5. 43. 5, 44. 5). The word "welkin," a "poeticism for 'sky'" (Roe, ed., *Poems*, 149), is also a favorite of Spenser's in the *Calender* and in the 1590 *Faerie Queene*, as is the conceit of dimming bright light; the juxtaposition of the two conceits here may well glance at *Faerie Queene*, 3. 10. 46.7, a memorable passage directing readers to the story of Hellenore and Paridell, Spenser's parodic rewriting of Book 2 of the *Aeneid*, the fall of Troy. As the satyrs "give a busse / To Hellenore . . . / . . . th'Earthes gloomy shade / Did dim the brightnesse of the welkin round" (3. 10. 46).[40] Yet infiltrating Shakespeare's Spenserian *bricolage* is a discourse of performance – not simply in "blust'ring" but also in "show," "appear," and "display." The thought of Shakespeare's stanza, as so much else in the poem, is difficult and oblique, as the reader struggles to determine whether the meteorology is actual or metaphorical. Inescapably, the pronoun in line 116, "his," compels us to see a connection between Tarquin's demeanor or action – his making of "excuses for his being there" – and the curious agency of the "stormy blust'ring weather," which makes no "cloudy show" until Night displays her "dim darkness." Shakespeare writes Tarquin's Marlovian hypocrisy through with the performative verse of England's Virgil.[41]

Scholars may not find Spenser lurking in Lucrece's bedroom, but they find Marlowe. They gloss the colonial image of Lucrece's breasts – "ivory globes" and "maiden worlds" – with *Hero and Leander*, 2. 273–76, where Leander scales Hero's "rising ivory mount," which is "with azure circling lines impaled, / Much like a globe (a globe may I term this, / By which love sails to regions full of bliss)." Effectively, Tarquin is a Marlovian reader and writer of Spenser. Rather than simply misreading Spenser or siphoning off a wanton voice contained by an ethical one, Shakespeare's rapist operates

---

[40] Spenser's conceit of "dim[ming] the welkin" caught Marlowe's eye in *Doctor Faustus* (1. 3. 4) as did the Hellnore/Paridell story, an important intertext for the Helen of Troy scene (Cheney, *Profession*, 209).

[41] Shakespeare also appears to have in mind Archimago's hermitage: "And everyone to his rest betakes, / Save thieves, cares, and troubled minds" (124–26). Cf., e.g., *Faerie Queene*, 1. 1. 39, where Archimago sets about to "trouble sleepy mindes." On "The Postures of [Spenser's] Allegory," including allegory's performative dynamic, see Gross' essay by this title.

under the influence of Marlowe; his counter-Petrarchan, counter-Virgilian aesthetics originates not only in *The Faerie Queene* but also in *Hero and Leander*.

Marlowe's presence helps to explain the theatrical discourse in this part of the poem. Thus, before Tarquin awakens Lucrece, he betrays the theatricality of his project:

> Then childish fear avaunt, debating die!
> Respect and reason wait on wrinkled age!
> My heart shall never countermand mine eye,
> Sad pause and deep regard beseems the sage;
> My part is youth, and beats these from the stage.
> (*The Rape of Lucrece*, 274–78)

A man about to rape a woman imagines himself as an actor on the stage. Tarquin metaphorizes an internal drama of generational strife in which he plays the "part" of an impetuous "youth" beating the wisdom of an old "sage" from "the stage." Yet Shakespeare's phrase suggests not merely internal but professional conflict, as if the mental habit of theatre were itself both an impediment to and an abetter of desire (Dubrow, *Victors*, 90). The violence contained in the metaphor shows Tarquin relying on an imaginative drama to "countermand" such rational arbiters as "Respect and reason," "Sad pause and deep regard."

We can see a specific theatricalizing of Tarquin's shameful interiority in the poem's central representation of the "impious act" (199):

> Thus graceless holds he disputation
> 'Tween frozen conscience and hot burning will,
> And with good thoughts makes dispensation,
> Urging the worser sense for vantage still;
> Which in a moment doth confound and kill
>   All pure effects, and doth so far proceed
>   That what is vile shows like a virtuous deed.
> (*The Rape of Lucrece*, 246–52)

Since "graceless" means "lacking or refusing divine aid" (Roe, ed., *Poems*, 156), we can read this photograph of the lustful man's subjectivity in terms of Reformation Humanism – perhaps of the Spenserian variety. Bereft of Christian grace, Tarquin is one of the elect; like Faustus, he has been elected for damnation. In the next line, the whole program of Reformation Humanism literally goes up in flames. In contradistinction to the teaching of Luther (or of Plato), Shakespeare shows Tarquin's "hot burning will" able to *freeze* "conscience." Later, Lucrece will make the exact opposite point:

"I sue for exil'd majesty's repeal, / Let him return, and flatt'ring thoughts retire; / His true respect will prison false desire" (640–42). Where Lucrece joins Plato and Luther in arguing that conscience can arbitrate conduct before the unruly powers of desire, Shakespeare's poem hauntingly disagrees. Rather than understanding conscience as a divine voice standing above the body's fray, Shakespeare imagines the interior faculty embedded darkly in the tissue of flesh, subject to the hot power of "Will" (495).[42]

The subsequent debate between Tarquin and Lucrece intertwines the theatre with the print shop – especially stage tragedy and printed epic (470–76). Despite Tarquin's awareness of the consequences of his act – "I know repentant tears ensue the deed" – he strives to "embrace" his own "infamy" (502–04); he continues to locate *literary authority* in his victim. If Lucrece does not submit to his desire, he will falsify the evidence by killing "some worthless slave" (515), whom Tarquin will pretend he caught sleeping with her, to the calumny of "every open eye" (520),

> And thou the author of their obloquy,
> Shalt have thy trespass cited up in rhymes,
> And sung by children in succeeding times.
> (*The Rape of Lucrece*, 523–25)

In this context, the word "author" is noteworthy. Referring to the adulterous betrayal Tarquin will proclaim that Lucrece has committed, the word nominally means "cause" (Crewe, ed., *Narrative Poems*, 71). Yet the passage refers to the literary consequences of Lucrece's sexual authorship, both written and oral: poets will commemorate her in "rhymes" and children will sing about her in songs. She will "author" the very infamy that Tarquin earlier admitted he invented for himself.

Tarquin's defacement of his "soul's fair temple" as a "spotted princess" (719–21) identifies one consequence of rape: the male thinks he rapes a woman, yet in the process he rapes himself (Hynes, "Rape"). Yet Shakespeare also pinpoints the destructive psychological consequences of an individual's reading and writing of a certain form of art – a Marlovian art of Ovidian desire, transacted through poetry and theatre: "Desire doth fight with Grace, / For there it revels" (712–13). Shakespeare rewrites Spenser's Castle of Alma episode along Marlovian lines, as if Prince Arthur, the human minister of divine grace, had not simply failed to protect the besieged

---

[42] As readers observe here, Shakespeare seems to sign this idea with his own name. See "will" also at 1299 and Fineman, "Will," 28, 49–51, 68. Tarquin's theatrical self-presentation helps to explain the theatrical terms that flood Lucrece's own perception upon her awakening (456–62).

castle but become its principal attacker.[43] Marlowe knew that Spenser was wrong about desire: "Love is not full of pity (as men say) / But deaf and cruel where it means to prey" (*Hero and Leander*, 2. 287–88). The feminine "temple" being "defaced" (719) is thus also the "heavenly image" of Lucrece within Tarquin's "thought" (288). The process of perceiving the female is now complete. In the first half of the poem, Shakespeare uses the discourse of both poetry and theatre to present the Marlovian Tarquin as an Ovidian author violating the Spenserian chastity at the heart of the Elizabethan nation's cult of the Virgin: "Pure Chastity is rifled of her store" (692).

BEARING THE AUTHOR'S PART: LUCRECE, ORPHEUS, PHILOMELA

In the second half of the poem, Shakespeare turns to the literary interiority of the victim. He does so initially to measure the resistance by the Spenser target under Marlovian attack. If the first half assigns agency primarily to Tarquin, presenting authorship as fundamentally Marlovian, the second half assigns agency primarily to Lucrece, presenting authorship as fundamentally Spenserian. Specifically, Lucrece emerges as a Philomela figure associated with Orphic power.

Perhaps appropriately, the paradox of Tarquin's strategy – he takes authorship and agency into his own hands yet assigns authorship to his victim – produces one of the most perplexing moments in the poem. The narrator identifies a Roman matron lying on the threshold of violation with the arch-poet of classical culture:

> when a black-fac'd cloud the world doth threat,
> In his dim mist th' aspiring mountains hiding,
> From earth's dark womb some gentle gust doth get,
> Which blow these pitchy vapors from their biding,
> Hind'ring their present fall by this dividing;
>   So his unhallowed haste her words delays,
>   And moody Pluto winks while Orpheus plays.
>   (*Rape of Lucrece*, 547–53)

This is a complicated stanza. Within the narrative, the reference is part of the narrator's multi-stanza "delay" in reporting the outcome of Lucrece's plea to Tarquin: "be compassionate" (594). Lines 1–4 use a meteorological

---

[43] Roe ed., *Poems*, comments that lines 708–11 "strike a medieval or Spenserian note in their personification of lust's aftermath as wastage"; specifically, I suggest, the "Spenserian note" derives from *The Fairie Queene*, 2. 11. 22, the description of Maleger, who besieges the Castle of Alma.

analogy to explain the delay – a gendered analogy in which a "gentle gust" of wind from "earth's dark womb" blows "black-fac'd clouds" that threaten to envelope "th' aspiring mountains." The analogy works, since it impedes Tarquin's action: "So his unhallowed haste her words delays." Nothing in the first six lines prepares for the emergence of Orpheus in the seventh, which conjures up the tradition of Orphic art.

The disjunction Shakespeare creates, between evoking this charged myth and delimiting its presence, produces a challenge to criticism.[44] Shakespeare, I suggest, cues the reader to witness in this story of rape an arch-story about Ovidian intertextual authorship. Thus the Orpheus reference precedes an allusion to the myth during Lucrece's apostrophe to Philomela later: "And for, poor bird, thou sing'st not in the day . . . / . . . we will unfold / To creatures stern, sad tunes to change their kinds; / Since men prove beasts, let beasts bear gentle minds" (1142–48). Here Shakespeare does not simply discuss the limits and strengths of the "female voice" or confine his representation to "lyric" poetry.[45] By 1594, the myth of Orpheus, like that of Philomela, had acquired a rather specific authorial genealogy. In the *Commendatory Verses* appended to the 1590 *Faerie Queene*, Sir Walter Ralegh identifies the New Poet as "Philumena," while R. S. calls him the "Bryttane Orpheus."[46] In Shakespeare's hands, the rape of the "Philumena" – like Lucrece is textualized historically in terms of the "Bryttane Orpheus."

Shakespeare goes on to spread his representation of the violated Orphic author in four stages: Lucrece's complaint to Night, Opportunity, and Time (764–1036); her identification with Philomel (1079–1211); her composition of a letter to her husband (1289–1316); and her viewing of the Troy painting (1366–1582). Leaving aside the letter for a moment, the other three self-reflexive literary moments correspond to complaint, pastoral, and epic. For Elizabethans, these three genres were practiced most famously by Spenser, who had published his pastoral *Calender* in 1579, his epic *Faerie Queene* in 1590, and his *Complaints* in 1591. The presence of the Chaucerian genre of complaint in Spenser's career does not invalidate his standing as England's Virgil but complicates and extends it.[47] While Shakespeare's three-genre order implies a progression from lower to higher forms, it scrambles Spenser's publishing chronology, perhaps simply to

[44] Nonetheless, there is very little on it; cf. Enterline, *Rhetoric*, 168–69; Bate, *Ovid*, 77; Roe, ed., *Poems*, 170.
[45] On "female voice," see Bate, *Ovid*, 76–77; on "lyric," Enterline, *Rhetoric*, 169.
[46] On Orpheus in Spenser, see Cain, "Orpheus"; Cheney, *Flight*, 22–76, including on R. S. (167, 294n22). On Philomela in Spenser, see Cheney, *Flight*, 77–110, including on Ralegh (134).
[47] Cf. Rambuss, *Spenser's Secret Career*, 78–95. See Cheney, *Flight*, 247n2, 257–58n18.

accommodate narrative. Yet Shakespeare might also be subtly deploying a principle Marlowe had practiced in *Ovid's Elegies*, when he disrupts Ovid's accurate ordering of Virgil's tripartite career by erasing georgic and putting epic before pastoral: "Aeneas' war, and Tityrus should be read" (1. 14. 25: "Tityrus et segetes Aeneiaque arma legentur" [1. 14. 25]). Jonson found this procedure unacceptable and restored the original idea: "Tityrus, Tillage, and Aeney shall be read" (see Cheney, *Profession*, 7–8). Shakespeare's evident scrambling of the Spenserian structure turns out to be consistent with the view of the Britain Orpheus exhibited subsequently.

In her complaint to Night, Opportunity, and Time, Lucrece clearly searches for a literary form of consolation. This form is not simply the Elizabethan complaint stemming from *The Mirror for Magistrates* (Dubrow, "Mirror"), but more particularly the genre that Spenser had inserted into his Virgilian career three years previously in his collection of complaints. The Spenserian provenance of Lucrece's complaint is clear from its opening lines: "O comfort-killing Night, image of hell, / Dim register and notary of shame" (764–65). As Bush observed long ago, "The apostrophe to Night . . . bears a special resemblance to a speech that Spenser puts in the mouth of Arthur" (*Mythology*, 153; Roe, ed., *Poems*, 180). Like Prince Arthur, Lucrece relies on complaint to bring consolation during a moment of intense suffering.[48] Yet the Spenserian faith in literary consolation ultimately fails Lucrece: "In vain I rail at Opportunity . . . / The remedy indeed to do me good / Is to let forth my foul defiled blood" (1023–29). In this failure, a lot is at stake – including, in 1594, for England's New Poet. As Lucrece's speech makes plain, she uses the complaint to locate blame for her defilement. Her complaint thus counters Tarquin's analysis, which locates "the fault" in her (482), constructing an elaborate etiology for her tragedy.

In Shakespeare's lexicon, Tarquin's contamination of Lucrece appears as a Marlovian contamination of her Spenserian project. If in *Venus* Shakespeare shows the mighty opposites poised in antagonism, here he shows the consequences. Shakespeare's real interest lies in the moment of contamination, and nowhere more telling than in the coloring of Lucrece's complaint by tragedy. Shakespeare's echoes of both Marlowe and Spenser in his portrait of Lucrece, like those in his portrait of Tarquin, catch the early modern author in a decisive moment of literary competition. It is only in the moment of contamination that we can witness Shakespeare's representation of his own

[48] Roe ed., *Poems*, cites three other Spenserian origins to Lucrece's complaint: lines 799 (182), 881–82 (186), and 956 (180).

authorial predicament as a new Ovidian poet-playwright, caught in the double act of shame: shame through having "gone here and there" and made himself "a motely to the view" (Sonnet 110. 1–2; see chapter 7); and shame through "publishing" a printed poem. In her histrionic complaint, Lucrece transacts her own author's historical moment.

Only at line 1079 does Shakespeare identify the myth underwriting Lucrece's complaint: "By this, lamenting Philomele had ended / The well-tun'd warble of her nightly sorrow" (1079–80). The introduction of Philomela has two functions. First, since the nightingale sings its song during the night, it marks the transition from night to day – the very time Lucrece fears. Second, and more importantly, the reference identifies Lucrece with Philomela, as "By this" indicates. Shakespeare's paradoxical aesthetic formulation, that the "warble of her nightly sorrow" is "well-tun'd," unfolds this latter function, which gathers force immediately. For Lucrece herself addresses Philomela during an intense moment of literary identification: "Come, Philomele, that sing'st of ravishment" (1128). Through Lucrece's identification with Philomela, Shakespeare can narrate an author's attempt to rely on the Spenserian aesthetics to cope with the tragic act of rifled chastity. As Catherine Belsey reminds us, "In Shakespeare's Poem Philomel is seen not in the act of vengeance but after her metamorphosis into a nightingale, and leaning her breast against a thorn to keep her woe alive for all to hear" ("Consent," 335). In this aesthetics, the singer can identify with Philomela in order to experience consolation. Thus, throughout the *Calender* Spenser presents his pastoral persona, Colin Clout, as a Philomela figure. *August* is especially important for *Lucrece*, because its aesthetics of consolation anticipates Shakespeare's lines 1079–1148. As Colin puts it, "cheerefull songs . . . can chaunge my cheerless cryes. / Hence with the Nightingale will I take part" (182–83).

In his pastoral, Spenser had understood the tragic mode of the Philomela story, when Colin in his role as "Nightingale . . . sovereigne of songe" begins his elegy for the dead Queen Dido by evoking "Melpomene" (*November*, 53), the goddess of tragedy. Indeed, the Greek tragedians and Seneca all adopt the Philomela myth as the ur-myth of tragedy (cf. Garrod, "Nightingale," 136). Thus, the Elizabethan Philomela traces via the Roman Ovid to the Attic tragedians. Readers may recognize the power of Philomela for the Greeks by recalling Cassandra'a climactic identification with the ravished nightingale in Aeschylus' *Agammemon* (see chapter 2). For Elizabethans, the missing link in this genealogical chain would be Seneca, who in his tragedies relies on the Philomlela myth to represent the heart of Roman political atrocity – including in *Thyestes* (1. 56–57). The Senecan matrix for the Philomela myth may help explain the presence of Shakespeare's theatrical terms discussed earlier: "bear'st a part." Not merely does Philomela sing her song and play a role; she also bears the phallic thorn of Tarquin within her. Effectively, Tarquin contaminates Lucrece with his compound art of poetry and theatre.[49]

PAPER, INK, AND PEN: THE PRINTING OF LUCRECE'S AUTHORSHIP

After failing to find consolation in Spenserian pastoral and complaint, Lucrece writes a letter to her husband. The passage leading up to this act of letter-writing uses authorial terms to describe the difference between the agency of men and women:

> For men have marble, women waxen minds,
> And therefore are they form'd as marble will;
> The weak oppress'd, th' impression of strange kinds
> Is form'd in them by force, by fraud, or skill.
> Then call them not the authors of their ill.
>
> (*The Rape of Lucrece*, 1240–44)

The last line suggests the very struggle of *authorship* we are examining. Women like Lucrece cannot be "authors of their ill" because they are made of "waxen" material – that which is "impress[ed]" rather than that which presses. Thus, only men can be the "authors" of women's ill, since men are "form'd" of "marble," able to "oppress" the "weak," whether "by force, by fraud, or skill." The syntax seems to grant women authorship only to take it away, placing it in the "minds" of "men." As before, authorship is a trope for agency and causality, yet here the narrator reverses Tarquin's earlier charge against Lucrece: he is not the cause of the rape. In fact, the passage does not take authorship away from Lucrece (or women); only from "their ill." In terms of the Elizabethan literary collision, Shakespeare appears to be assigning blame for the violence of the current literary climate to Marlowe, rather than to Spenser.

Accordingly, Shakespeare presents Lucrece as an author when she directs her maid to fetch her "paper, ink, and pen" (1289). In this representation of Lucrece as an author, we may discover Shakespeare's "primal scene of . . . composition" with regard to printed poetry (Willbern, *Poetic Will*, 94):

---

[49] Cf. C. and M. Martindale, *Antiquity*, 49–50; Enterline, *Rhetoric*, 170.

> Her maid is gone, and she prepares to write,
> First hovering o'er the paper with her quill.
> Conceit and grief an eager combat fight,
> What wit sets down is blotted straight with will;
> This is too curious-good, this blunt and ill:
>   Much like a press of people at a door,
>   Throng her inventions, which shall go before.
>   (*The Rape of Lucrece*, 1296–1302)

Lucrece does not write about the rape in her letter to Collatine, "Lest he should hold it her own gross abuse, / Ere she with blood had stain'd her stain'd excuse" (1315–16). Instead, at line 278 "Lucrece herself adopts what is in effect a theatrical image for her behavior: ironically, in order to convince Collatine of her honesty, she must play her part like an actress" (Dubrow, "Mirror," 407). Rather than choosing a staged play over a printed inscription, Lucrece combines the two forms that will lead to her climactic political act: the inscription and enactment of her suicide in service of the Roman Republic: "I am the mistress of my fate" (1069). In other words, Lucrece reverses her author's own turn from stage to page, using the page of her letter to stage her final scene, as well as to script the role of revenger for her husband and the other men.[50]

TO FIND A FACE: LUCRECE AND SINON AT TROY

To prepare for this final event, Lucrece searches out one artifact in particular – a painting that for Elizabethans models the Western epic enterprise: the fall of Troy. Writers from Homer and Aristotle to Chaucer and Lydgate had selected the Troy story as the arch-myth for the intersection of epic and tragedy. For Aristotle, the primary origins to tragedy and comedy are the epics of Homer, which themselves are produced "through the dramatic character of his imitations" (*Poetics*, 1448b.24–1449a.7). In classical Rome, Virgil had shown his Homeric-based epic hero Aeneas viewing the frescoes of the Fall of Troy, thereby placing his *Aeneid* in the tradition of "lacrimae rerum" (1. 462). In Dante's *Inferno*, the character Virgil calls his epic "l'alta mia tragedia" (20. 113), while Dante finally detaches himself from his great Roman mentor by calling his epic about Christian salvation the *Commedia*. Influenced by this tradition, Chaucer relies on the verse form of rhyme royal to call his *Troilus and Criseyde* "little myn tragedye" (5.1786), while Lydgate in *Troy Book* extends this tragedic tradition in epic

---

[50] Thanks to Doc Rissel for this point (personal communication, 14 February 2003).

form.[51] Yet for Virgil in the *Aeneid*, as for Spenser in *The Faerie Queene*, the fall of Troy begins as a tragedy about men and women but finally serves a comedic political goal for the nation. Whereas Aeneas escapes Troy to found Rome, so (yet another) Brutus founds Troynovaunt. Both works transpose tragedy into epic. For Shakespeare in 1594, the Troy myth would be most immediately filtered from "the olde famous Poet Chaucer" through "the new Poete" (*Calender, Dedicatory Epistle*, 1), especially Spenser's detailed representation of the Fall of Troy in Book 3, canto 9, of *The Faerie Queene*.

What, more specifically, is a painting of Troy's fall doing in Lucrece's house?[52] Since the painting is there, indeed the home's central artifact, Shakespeare would seem to be depicting a domestic version of the religious principle enshrined in the *Aeneid*: the Fall of Troy is the animating ideology in the home of Lucrece and her husband. As with the Trojan frescoes in the temple of Sidonian Dido, the Troy painting licenses and determines Tarquin's behavior, his false epic "rape" of a beautiful woman in a national setting. Lucrece's domestic artwork tells us that she is doomed from the start; her domestic space has been infiltrated by an intruder who represents the state.[53] That intruder is not only Tarquin but Virgil – more accurately, Virgilian art, and not just monarchy but monarchical art itself: Spenser's monarchical art, organized around a deterministic nationalist teleology. This becomes clearer when Lucrece locates Tarquin in the painting itself. In short, the Troy painting is the Virgilian epic ideology organizing Lucrece's domestic space.

Within Shakespeare's fiction, Lucrece turns to the painting of Troy as an alternative to complaint and pastoral mourning (1364–65). Although this "newer way" works temporarily, in the end epic art fails as sadly as does these other genres: "none it ever cured" (1581). Here the poem rejects one of the West's most enduring ideas, specified in terms of Spenser's Virgilian ideal: that art can redeem, that literature can supply the purgation and consolation for life's traumatic sadness. In *The Rape of Lucrece*, unlike in *The Faerie Queene* or the *Aeneid*, art leads grimly to death.

Shakespeare relies on the principle of Ovidian attenuation to contain and subvert the epic of England's Virgil – a principle Marlowe initially put into play, by translating the *Amores*, by Ovidianizing the Troy story in *Dido*, and finally by translating Lucan's first book from the *Pharsalia*. At stake in

---

[51] For this discussion, I am indebted to Robert R. Edwards; see his edition of *Troy Book* (1).

[52] This is the question Hexter asks about the frescoes in Virgil: what is a painting privileging a Trojan myth important to Aeneas' destiny doing in Dido's Carthaginian Temple of Juno, the arch-enemy of Troy? For Hexter, the oddity of this crux shows a deterministic universe championing the Pax Romana.

[53] Helgerson, *Adulterous*; see 30 and 39 on *Lucrece*.

Lucrece is just what type of foundational myth will serve the nation: Spenser's Virgilian-based dynastic myth supporting the Tudor regime; Marlowe's Lucanian-based republican myth negatively rehearsed in the civil war that ends the Republic; or Shakespeare's Ovidian/Livian-based republican myth affirmatively performing the birth of the republic within a monarchical frame. Shakespeare appears to be advancing the case for a new national myth, beyond Marlowe, beyond Spenser.

Thus one significance of the Troy painting lies in the colliding presence of Spenserian and Marlovian models, which merge not in the figures we might expect, Helen or Hecuba, but in Sinon, the painting's climactic figure. In Sinon, Lucrece finds what she is looking for: an artistic model of the actor who has blotted the princess. She indeed knows what she wants: "To this well-painted piece is Lucrece come, / To find a face where all distress is stell'd" (1443–44). Lucrece goes to the Troy painting to "find a face" – one that *stells* distress, a word usually glossed as "delineated, portrayed" (Roe, ed., *Poems*, 211) but perhaps also meaning *distilled*. She finds a face to activate the purgative principle the narrator identifies earlier: to *suffice true sorrow feelingly* through *sympathizing* with a *like semblance* (1111–13). As if to emphasize this process, the narrator repeats the word "feelingly" later: "Here feelingly she weeps Troy's painted woes" (1492).

To find a face: it is an engaging idea. The word *face* occurs no fewer than nine times during the 200-line Troy passage. Whatever else Shakespeare is doing, he is probing an aesthetics of the face, the cultural problem of the face, the artist's show of face. Like the word *face*, the word *show* and its cognates appears eight times in the Troy passage. While in five of them Shakespeare describes the painter's art as a form of theatrical performance, in four he expresses both the painter's and his subject's deceit, with three concentrated on Sinon. In line 1503, *show* and *face* jostle in a description of the arch-traitor: "His face, though full of cares, yet show'd content" (1503). Sinon's power lies in the show of face.

That Lucrece should pass over Hecuba to Sinon reveals where her interest in art lies: not in identification but in activation – revenge rather than sympathy:[54]

> At last she sees a wretched image bound,
> That piteous looks to Phrygian shepherds lent;
> His face, though full of cares, yet show'd content;
>   Onward to Troy with the blunt swains he goes,
>   So mild that patience seem'd to scorn his woes.
>   (*Rape of Lucrece*, 1501–05)

[54] Cf. M. A. Wells, "Rape," who focuses on Helen.

For evidence that "'Phrygian' . . . connotes fierceness" in contrast with "'piteous,'" Roe cites E. K.'s gloss from *October* (*Poems*, 214) – Spenser's eclogue on the "state of Poet" (97), including the New Poet's review of the *cursus* of "the Romish Tityrus" (55; see 55–60, 193–99). Yet the E. K. passage contains the artistic principle Lucrece enacts when finding the face of Sinon; for E. K., this principle derives from Orpheus, since it is Spenser's representation of Orpheus' use of music to "bereave" the "soule of sence" (*October*, 27) that E. K. glosses (153–62). Shakespeare sees Sinon from Book 2 of Virgil's *Aeneid* putting into play this Spenserian Orphic principle in order to bring about the Fall of Troy, wherein the traitor uses his face to secure the "compassion" of the Trojans only to destroy them. Accordingly, Shakespeare presents Sinon walking down the Virgilian path; using his "face" to create "piteous looks" in the "Phrygian shepherds," he moves through the pastoral domain of "blunt swains" until he reaches the epic city.

This panoramic view of Sinon strolling from shepherds to princes leads the narrator to focus on the traitor's art of face:

> In him the painter labor'd with his skill
> To hide deceit, and give the harmless show
> An humble gait, calm looks, eyes wailing still,
> A brow unbent, that seem'd to welcome woe,
> Cheeks neither red nor pale, but mingled so
>   That blushing red no guilty instance gave,
>   Nor ashy pale the fear that false hearts have.
>   (*Rape of Lucrece*, 1506–12)

Shakespeare virtually equates Sinon's pastoral pose – his "humble gait" – with the "deceit" of a "harmless show": an innocuous theatre of appearance. As critics observe (e.g., Fineman, "Shakespeare's Will," 58), Sinon's face "mingle[s]" the pastoral red and white that Tarquin reads into the chivalric heraldry of Lucrece's face earlier. Sinon is not cross-dressed, but his "harmless show" performs an effeminate pastoral version of masculine warfare.

In the next stanza, Shakespeare makes the tragic theatre of Sinon's pastoral face explicit: "He entertain'd a show so seeming just" (1514). So powerful is Sinon's (Marlovian) theatre that Lucrece cannot believe "So fair a form" could be "lodg'd" in "a mind so ill": "Such signs of truth in his plain face she spied, / That she concludes the picture was belied" (1530, 1533–34). She discerns the complicity between the painter's "craft" and that of Sinon, prompting her to witness a crossover from art to life, from the circumstances of Troy to those of Rome: "Tarquin's shape came in her mind the while" (1537). Concentrating on Sinon's face as a theatrical mask, she makes an astonishing discovery: that Tarquin has himself read Sinon clearly, that her own domestic artwork contains the seed of her destruction. The discovery prompts her final epiphany: like Sinon with his pastoral pose, the epic "Tarquin armed" came to her "beguild / With outward honesty, but yet defil'd / With inward vice" (1544–46). This recognition prompts her rage, as she uses "passion" to "assail" the art of Sinon's face with her "nails" (1562–64). Only temporarily does such violence allow her "sorrow" to "ebb and flow," wearying "time with her complaining" (1569–70), because this truant use of art also fails: "Losing her woes in shows of discontent, / It easeth some, though none it ever cured" (1580–81). Finally, Lucrece's rapt absorption in Sinon's "shows" cannot free her from the defilement of rape. Lucrece's attack on the Troy painting prints Shakespeare's own critique of the Spenserian nationalist myth. In the process, he clears a space for a new myth, organized not around a monarchical dynasty but around a monarchical republic.

THE ART OF PUBLICATION: BRUTUS, LUCRECE, AND THE BLOOD OF THE REPUBLIC

When Collatine, Lucretius, and Brutus arrive, Lucrece has reached her decision: "And now this pale swan in her wat'ry nest / Begins the sad dirge of her certain ending" (1611–12). Traditionally, the swan is a sign of lyric poetry. Callimachus attributes the origin of lyric poetry to the movement and song of the swan at the birth of Apollo:

with music the swans, the gods' own minstrels, left Maeonian Pactolus and circled seven times round Delos, and sang over the bed of child-birth, the Muses' birds, most musical of all birds that fly. Hence that child in after days strung the lyre with just so many strings – seven strings, since seven times the swans sang over the pangs of birth. (*Hymn IV*, "To Delos," 249–54)

The idea is so ancient that our earliest preserved lyre is in the shape of a swan (Cheney, *Flight*, 70–71). Shakespeare's unusual placing of the swan on "her wat'ry nest," a site not of transcendence but of succession, of birth and maternal power, suggests his interest in the Callimachean etiology.

Certainly, the swan is an apt symbol for Lucrece's final "dirge," since the swan was thought to sing sadly before its death, as Spenser records in a fragment: "The silver swan doth sing before her dying day / As shee that feeles the deepe delight that is in death." The fragment is published by

E. K. in his gloss (242–43) on Spenser's resounding swan image in *October*, where the shepherd Cuddie claims that "Colin fittes such famous flight to scanne: / He, were he not with love so ill bedight, / Would mount as high, and sing as soote as Swanne" (88–90). Here Spenser uses the swan to predict his eventual transcendence of the Virgilian career model with a hymnic or non-courtly form of contemplative poetry (Cheney, *Flight*, 16, 29–31, 228–29). By recognizing this Spenserian genealogy, we can better discern in the swanlike Lucrece a striking figure of male poetic authorship. Because Shakespeare is publishing the representation in a poem, he is presenting Lucrece's final swanlike "dirge" as the product of the lyric print poet. Whereas Spenser's authorial swan flies into the beyond to acquire fame, his own Lucrecian swan stays earthbound, singing her song from her position on her nest. This is swansong with an attitude: out of her death, she will create life – in this world, not the next.

The lyric image of the swan jostles with Lucrece's turn to theatre to perform the final act of her last scene. When Collatine arrives, he "finds his Lucrece clad in mourning black" (1585), and immediately he recognizes the histrionics behind her unusual (Hamlet-like) costume: "'Unmask, dear dear, this moody heaviness, / And tell thy grief, that we may give redress" (1602–03). *Redress* is among the finest puns in the poem, and yet it is challenging to interpretation, since it forces the reader to temper this moment of obvious characterological "grief" with the author's hidden wit. The theatrical terminology also anticipates the sudden re-dressing of Lucius Junius Brutus. Lucrece's histrionics turn out to have a curious role in the afterlife – both spiritually, when "Her contrite sighs unto the clouds bequeathed / Her winged sprite, and through her wounds doth fly / Live's lasting date from cancell'd destiny" (1727–29) – and physiologically, when her blood divides into pure and impure streams of red and black: "And ever since, as pitying Lucrece' woes, / Corrupted blood some watery token shows" (1747–48).[55]

In the combined representation of her swan-dirge and performed suicide, Lucrece appears to be linking poetry and theatre in a new way, marshalling art back into constructive political action, for her act compels the "astonish'd" (1730) men to revenge her tragic death, spurred by Brutus, who alone "pluck'd the knife from Lucrece' side" (1807). When Brutus "throws that shallow habit by, / Wherein deep policy did him disguise" (1814–15), we witness a form of succession. Yet it is not simply political – the succession from monarchy to republic or, as the Argument concludes,

---

[55] Hadfield sees Lucrece's blood as "a symbol of freedom" (unpublished manuscript, 147).

"from kings to consuls." Nor is it even characterological, from "cheva-
liers" to "bounty hunters" or those who are straightforwardly "trusting,"
"idealistic," and "artless for survival in a post-Saturnian world" to individuals who are "mysterious pragmatists" and have in their heart a "motivational
riddle" (Majors, "First Brutus," 345–51). Finally, the succession is artistic
and professional, from the aesthetics of Spenser and Marlowe to that of
Shakespeare himself.

It is certainly easiest to see Brutus as a figure for the Shakespearean
actor/playwright, as the discourse describing Brutus is so clearly theatrical. Indeed, when Brutus throws aside his "habit" and "show," he recalls
Marlowe's Tamburlaine changing from Scythian shepherd to mighty
monarch. Yet Wendy Wall, *Imprint*, helps us see a more dynamic version of authorship, which allows us to include poetry: "Formerly regarded
as a jester, Brutus makes his debut by taking advantage of the outrage generated by the tale of the violated woman. He thus becomes a figure for
Shakespeare, whose emergence as an author rested, in part, on his creation
of *Lucrece*" (273). Wall goes on to relate this representation to Shakespeare's
"career trajectory" (273) from *Venus and Adonis* to the "graver labour" of
Lucrece, the equivalent to "Gascoigne's transformation from amorous lover
to didactic writer" (273). Something of this poesis in its relation to the
theatre of Brutus emerges when the former fool addresses "Courageous
Romans" in the marketplace of the city: "kneel with me and help to bear
thy part, / To rouse our Roman gods with invocations" (1830–31). "Bear
thy part" suggests theatrical enactment, but "rouse . . . with invocations"
suggests the tradition of poetry. As such, Brutus proves himself Lucrece's
legitimate heir, a theatrical hero with an interest in publication.

As the epigraph to this chapter intimates, the poem ends with this very
conjunction of poetry and theatre:

> When they had sworn to this advised doom,
> They did conclude to bear dead Lucrece thence,
> To show her bleeding body thorough Rome,
> And so to publish Tarquin's foul offense;
> Which being done with speedy diligence,
>   The Romans plausibly did give consent
>   To Tarquin's everlasting banishment.
>   (*Rape of Lucrece*, 1849–55)

According to Heather Dubrow, the double use of the word "publish" at the
beginning and end of the poem "signals the movement from the private
sphere of home to the public arena of the marketplace, from complaint

to epic" (*Domestic*, 59). With Philomela perched outside, Dubrow calls the private sphere a "pastoral home" (48). *The Rape of Lucrece* registers a cultural shift from poetry to theatre, print publication to staged show, the Virgilian career model of pastoral and epic to the Ovidian career model of amorous poetry and tragedy. If late-Tudor literature written in the reign of Queen Elizabeth comes to settle on an "aesthetics of the body" (Hulse, "Aesthetics," 30), Shakespeare can be seen to conclude his poem with a stirring icon. When the people "show" the dead body of the chaste matron in order to "publish" it throughout the nation, the author weds poetry and theatre to create a new hybrid form of republican aesthetics.[56] No word better represents this wedding than "publish," which in its early modern resonance catches the very transfer, from the meaning of "make public" to *put into print* (Burrow, ed. *Sonnets and Poems*, 338, 245).

To seal the aesthetics of publication, Shakespeare uses the two closing lines to represent a final form to the authorial conjunction. The word "plausibly" in the penultimate line means "with applause" (*Riverside*, 1836), suggesting that the Romans give their consent by applauding Tarquin's banishment. The printed poem ends with a version of the theatrical convention closing a play, in which the presenter figure steps forward to ask for the audience's applause, as Puck will do at the end of *A Midsummer Night's Dream* and Prospero at the close of *The Tempest*.[57] By ending his poem with the Romans applauding the Tarquins' banishment, Shakespeare gestures to his own reading public, subtly lending consent to a republican frame of art within the queen's monarchical republic, which will also be "everlasting" – *without end*. Finally, Shakespeare's "graver labour" is about – and is brought about by – the Marlovian invasion of the Spenserian domestic domain. We see an etiology not so much about the formation of the Roman Republic as about the printing of the national poet-playwright. Capturing a decisive moment in English literary history, Shakespeare's counter-epic of empire tragically publishes the author's national show.

---

[56] As we have seen, Vickers equates Lucrece with *Lucrece*.
[57] Thanks to Dustin Stegner for this point (personal communication, 14 February 2003).

PART THREE

1599–1601: the author brought into print

Play scene: *"Love's Labor's Lost"* to *"Troilus and Cressida"*

"How many tales to please me she hath coined."
"W. Shakespere," *The Passionate Pilgrim*, Poem 7

In his monumental 1790 edition, titled *The Plays and Poems of William Shakspeare*, Edmund Malone performs a curious editorial procedure. As the final poem to William Jaggard's *The Passionate Pilgrim* (1599, 1612) he prints "The Phoenix and Turtle," lifted from Robert Chester's *Love's Martyr, or Rosalin's Complaint* (1601). Malone's procedure may obscure the textual independence of these two volumes of early modern poetry, but it nonetheless highlights a shared genealogy for them: the genre of the printed miscellany.[1] In bringing the two volumes together, Malone makes available a set of comparisons between two works of erotic verse printed at about the same time.

Together, the printing of *The Passionate Pilgrim* and "The Phoenix and Turtle" near the mid-point of Shakespeare's professional career represents a second phase of the national poet-playwright in print. Unlike the 1593–94 *Venus* and *Lucrece*, however, these works do not show the author presenting himself as a poet through the medium of print, but rather they are works that show a manuscript poet brought into print by others. The nature of the appropriation differs, as do the roles of Jaggard and Chester in Elizabethan culture. Jaggard was a publisher and businessman on the look for a market success; Chester, an "obscure poet" in search of a patron (Burrow, ed., *Sonnets and Poems*, 82). As a savvy marketeer, Jaggard takes the liberty of collecting together a miscellany of verse and putting Shakespeare's name on the title page. Chester (we believe) commissioned Shakespeare as a popular author – famed from "both poems and plays," *Venus*, *Lucrece*, and *The Passionate Pilgrim* as well as the plays cited by Francis Meres the year before (Duncan-Jones, *Ungentle*, 107), to write a poem for a special volume.

---

[1] On the Elizabethan miscellany and authorship, see Wall, *Imprint*, 95–108, including on *The Passionate Pilgrim* (98–100). The forms of the two miscellanies do differ, and neither is a true miscellany, a collection of work by various hands: *The Passionate Pilgrim* is advertised as written by one hand (Shakespeare's) when in fact it is by several; and *Love's Martyr* is written nominally by one hand (Chester's) but is acknowledged to be augmented by others.

Nonetheless, as the epigraph above intimates, the two publishing enterprises cohere in their timely minting of "Shakespeare's name as an author."[2]

By examining the two volumes together, we can discern a story about Shakespeare at the very mid-point of his career. As Katherine Duncan-Jones reminds us, "professionally, the year 1599 was another *annus mirabilis*, one in which Shakespeare rose by bending" (*Ungentle*, 107), and she reminds us that the year saw a conjunction at the center of the present argument: the opening of the Globe Theatre (including the staging of *Julius Caesar*) and the printing of the first extant edition of *The Passionate Pilgrim*. To locate Shakespeare's poems within this theatrical time is to refine our knowledge of his professional career.

According to the *Oxford Shakespeare*, between the printing of the 1594 *Lucrece* and the 1601 *Love's Martyr*, Shakespeare composed eighteen plays, in the following order:

The Comedy of Errors
Love's Labour's Lost
Love's Labour's Won
A Midsummer Night's Dream
The Most Excellent and Lamentable Tragedy of Romeo and Juliet
The Tragedy of King Richard the Second
The Life and Death of King John
The Comical History of the Merchant of Venice
The History of Henry the Fourth
The Merry Wives of Windsor
The Second Part of Henry the Fourth
Much Ado About Nothing
The Life of Henry the Fifth
The Tragedy of Julius Caesar
As You Like It
The Tragedy of Hamlet, Prince of Denmark
Twelfth Night, or What You Will
Troilus and Cressida.

As with the first phase, here the chronology is anything but certain, and scholars have long debated with intense scrutiny the exact order of composition and performance. The *Oxford* chronology is useful here primarily

---

[2] S. Roberts, *Reading Shakespeare's Poems*, 158, citing Marotti, "Property" on this name "becoming important as a cultural phenomenon" (153), but for both critics with reference only to *The Passionate Pilgrim* and thus in need of extension to *Love's Martyr*.

to get a general sense of the kind of work Shakespeare was doing after the theatres reopened in 1594 and up through 1601. During this second phase, he continues his remarkable foray into the three primary kinds of drama, composing ten comedies, five histories, and three tragedies.[3] Once more, the boundaries between the genres are anything but stable. For instance, not simply are *Richard II* and *Julius Caesar* historical tragedies, but most notoriously *Troilus and Cressida* is problematic as a comedy, and already in *Twelfth Night* the generic darkness is falling.

The task of summarizing the presence of poetry and theatre in these eighteen plays within a few pages challenges the figure who turns out to inherit the discourse of "The Phoenix and Turtle": "Reason" itself. Yet the general conclusion is mercifully straightforward: in the comedies, histories, and tragedies during the middle of his career, Shakespeare does not abandon poetry in favor of theatre; he absolutely intensifies their conjunction, so much so that 10 of the plays easily sustain full-scale analysis: *Love's Labor's Lost, Dream, Romeo, Merchant, Merry Wives, Much Ado, Caesar, As You Like It, Hamlet*, and *Twelfth Night*. Most of the rest of the plays contain enough intriguing material to contribute important representations. In chapter 1, we saw the form of this conjunction especially in *Twelfth Night* through Viola and Feste, and we attended more briefly to such plays as *Merchant* and *Hamlet*. In particular, we followed Park Honan in noting how during this dramatic phase Shakespeare appears rather intently to be entertaining the possibility of a career as a print poet. That makes Jaggard's presentation of Shakespeare in *The Passionate Pilgrim* not simply a dubious marketing ploy cashing in on the author's capital but a rather shrewd reading of Shakespeare's own interests, commitments, and self-representations. Chester's commissioning of this author to pen a poem for *Love's Martyr*, then, is not a professional anomaly but a natural consolidation of the authorial facts. In the next chapter, we shall pause to look at the most formal conjunction of poetry and theatre during this phase, the printing of three songs and sonnets from *Love's Labor's Lost* in *The Passionate Pilgrim*. In the subsequent chapter, we shall likewise draw attention to links between *Hamlet* and "The Phoenix and Turtle." In this phase of Shakespeare's career, other links happily abound.

Here, we may note simply that several of the plays represent the Ovidian art of poetry and theatre in a Virgilian landscape, and again the representation is often inflected with the aesthetics of Spenser and Marlowe.

---

[3] Of the eighteen plays, only *Love's Labor's Won* is not extant, although some speculate that the title may refer to *Much Ado* (Erne, *Literary Dramatist*, 82n18).

A brief analysis of one play toward the end of this phase may indicate that Shakespeare continues his early interest in this complex professional project. In *As You Like It* (1599–1600), he relies on Spenser's Virgilian career discourse to identify the biography of the exiled Ovid with that of the dead Marlowe (and throws Jonson in to boot[4]). In Act 3, scene 3, the clownish courtier Touchstone woos the shepherd lass Audrey while the melancholic Jaques looks on under cover:

> *Touchstone.* I am here with thee and thy goats as the most capricious poet, honest Ovid, was among the Goths.
> *Jaques.* [*Aside.*] O knowledge ill-inhabited, worse than Jove in a thatch'd house!
> *Touchstone.* When a man's verses cannot be understood, nor a man's good wit seconded with the forward child, understanding, it strikes a man more dead than a great reckoning in a little room. Truly, I would the gods had made thee poetical. (*As You Like It*, 3. 3. 7–16)

In his first speech, Touchstone presents himself as an Ovidian author by identifying his pastoral sojourn in the Forest of Arden with Ovid's exile in Tomis, the "goats" of his pastoral world with the Goths of Ovid's exhilic landscape. In the aside, the Jonsonian figure of Jaques expresses his contempt for such illiterate scholarship, comparing Touchstone's "ill-inhabited" knowledge with a representation that appears to conflate two passages from the *Metamorphoses*: Jove's disguise as a shepherd before Mnemosyne (6. 114) and Mercury and Bacchus' disguise as mortals in the cottage of Baucis and Philemon (8. 611–724).

Yet the conflation may derive less from Ovid than from Marlowe, whose Scythian shepherd Tamburlaine reports both how "Jove sometime masked in a shepherd's weed" (*1 Tamb.*, 1. 2. 198) and how "the tempest of the Gods" felt "the lovely warmth of shepheards' flames, / And [maske(d)] in cottages of strewed weeds" (5. 1. 184–87).[5] Accordingly, in his second speech Touchstone expresses a further predicament for the Ovidian author, when he imagines his reader failing to understand his "verses," committing him to a state that is death itself. Grammatically speaking, the "man's verses" are Ovid's poetry and the "man" he claims is struck "more dead than a great reckoning in a little room" Ovid himself. Yet Shakespeare equates Ovid with Marlowe by echoing a famous line from *The Jew of Malta* ("infinite riches in a little room" [1. 1. 37]), representing Marlowe's death in that

---

[4] On Jaques as the Elizabethan satirists in the late 1590s, especially Jonson, see Bednarz, *Poets' War*, 108–11.

[5] Fuller cites Ovid's Jove and Mnemosyne for the first passage (Fuller, ed., *Tamburlaine the Great*, 5: 177) and Ovid's Jove/Baucis/Philemon passage for the second (5: 219). For scholarship on the textual crux of "mask" at *1 Tamb.*, 5. 1. 187, see Cheney, *Profession*, 301n26.

"little room" in Deptford over who would pay the "reckoning" or the bill for the day's meals and lodging. In his complex comedic representation, Shakespeare identifies Marlovian tragedy as an art originating in the poetry of Ovid. Shakespeare's subsequent allusion to Marlowe, in Act 3, scene 5, quotes a line, not from one of his tragedies but from *Hero and Leander*: "'Who ever lov'd that lov'd not at first sight?'" (*As You Like It*, 3. 5. 82; *Hero and Leander*, 1. 176). In this way, Shakespeare's pastoral classification of Marlowe as a "Dead shepherd" (81) spans both Marlowe's poems and his plays, at once recalling the Scythian shepherd Tamburlaine from the tragedy and the Passionate Shepherd from the lyric poem.

In this comedy, Shakespeare neither names nor quotes Spenser, but critics have discerned the omnipresence of England's Virgil. As we have seen in chapter 1, Paul Alpers suggests that the courtiers in this comedy "play . . . out" Spenser's metaphor for himself as a pastoral poet masking his muse in rustic shepherd attire (*Fairie Queene*, 1. Proem 1) (*What is Pastoral?*, 74). The metaphor is distinctly that of the pastoral man of theatre, the theatrical pastoralist, and figures like Rosalind and Orlando are merely among Shakespeare's most memorable imitations of this Spenserian authorial figure. To catch Shakespeare deploying this figure, we may turn to Act 5, scene 1, the "William" scene. Recently, James P. Bednarz has seen Shakespeare rewriting Spenser's pastoral interlude in Book 6 of *The Faerie Queene* (cantos 9–12), when Calidore sojourns among the shepherds and woos the shepherdess Pastorella, loved by the foolish shepherd Coridon. Thus, Spenser tells how Calidore, "doffing his bright armes, himselfe addrest / In shepheards weed, and in his hand he tooke, / In stead of steele-head speare, a shepheards hooke" (6. 9. 38–40). For his part, Shakespeare stages Touchstone stealing Audrey from William, the author's cheerfully playful self-portrait, who "shares both the author's first name and his birth-place," the forest of Arden (*Poets' War*, 117).[6] According to Bednarz, "Shakespeare comically reconfigures Sir Calidore's pastoral interlude . . . in Touchstone's violation of the knight's exemplary performance . . . Shakespeare's rewriting of Spenser's pastoral episode on the lowest mimetic level is one of the plays' better literary jokes" (119). In this joke, Shakespeare redeploys Spenser's authorial strategy of self-critique in order to indict his chief rival at this time, Jonson, represented in Jaques: "Using the pastoral convention of self-reference, Spenser and Shakespeare thus make brief appearances near the ends of their works, in scenes specifically created to

---

[6] For the possibility that Shakespeare acted the role of William alongside Robert Armin's Touchstone, see Bednarz, *Poets' War*, 117.

show them being deprived of the pastoral happiness their fictions celebrate. Unlike Spenser, however, Shakespeare fashioned this episode of dramatic self-effacement to demonstrate the Socratic paradox that the admission of ignorance is the securest form of knowledge" (120). For Bednarz, the point of the "William" scene, as for the play as a whole, is to challenge Jonson during the Poets' War. We may add that Shakespeare manages this challenge by evoking a recently deceased rivalry, aligning his own art with Spenser's and Jonson's with Marlowe's.

This brief discussion of scenes from *As You Like It* merely intimates the kind of authorial intertextuality that requires further analysis to sort out more fully. Between 1594 and 1601, Shakespeare may have concentrated on the writing of plays, but he continued to conjoin a discourse of poetry with a discourse of theatre in them. The four courtiers of *Love's Labor's Lost*; Peter Quince, Oberon, and Puck in the *Dream*; Richard II; Falstaff in his several plays but especially *Merry Wives*; Benedick in *Much Ado*; Hamlet; Viola and Feste: these are only the most recognizable figures for the poet-playwright during this phase. Figures like the Bastard Faulconbridge, Marcus Brutus, and Prince Hal (later Henry V) are splendid variations. Sometimes, the plots of these plays are structured by characters siding primarily with either poetry or theatre; we have mentioned Richard III and Clarence, but we could add a comedic version in Rosalind (a supreme woman of the theatre) and Orlando (a Petrarchan poet fond of hanging his sweet verse on pastoral trees). In the plays of this period, we find poems embedded in plays, as in *Love's Labor's Lost* or the sonnets of *Romeo and Juliet*, not to mention the recurrent presence of lyric in a wide array of songs, often sung by professional singers, like Amiens in *As You Like It* or Balthasar in *Much Ado*; formal portraits of the poet, as with Cinna in *Julius Caesar* but also Orlando, Benedick, and Hamlet himself; extended rehearsals of plays based on books of poetry, as in the Mechanical's staging of Pyramus and Thisby from the *Metamorphoses*, or of Virgil's (and Marlowe's) retelling of "Aeneas' [tale] to Dido . . . of Priam's slaughter" (*Hamlet*, 2. 2. 446–48). One play, *Troilus and Cressida*, performs this poesis on a grand scale, staging the Homeric and Virgilian epic of the Trojan War itself, parodically; in fact, the "Armed Prologue" to this play constitutes one of Shakespeare's most decisive attempts to enter the epic list, indicating that his epicist urgings had not flagged since the printing of *Lucrece*.

Throughout this period, Shakespeare does not separate theatre from books but implicates the one in the other. "Read on this book," Polonius tells a daughter too eager to entertain her father's theatre of intrigue, "That shows of such an exercise may color / Your [loneliness]" (*Hamlet*, 3. 1. 43–45).

Rather than turning away from print culture because of his dramatic production, the author literally absorbs himself in it, to discover the form of truth itself: "The story . . . is printed in her blood," claims Leonato in *Much Ado*, judging his fallen daughter Hero to be a whore by the blush on her cheek (4. 1. 122), only to have Friar Francis perform a radically different interpretation of the virgin's physiognomial text: "Trust not my reading, nor my observations, / Which with experimental seal doth warrant / The tenure of my book . . . / If this sweet lady lie not guiltless here" (4. 1. 165–69). Not surprisingly, the author continues his obsession with artistic immortality, nowhere more potent than in Hamlet's counter-Christian commitment. Standing on the threshold of annihilation, the Prince does not concern himself with Spenser's New Jerusalem (*Fairie Queene*, 1.10) but with an altogether different form of afterlife: "tell my story" (5. 2. 349), he says to his friend Horatio: "Report me and my cause aright / To the unsatisfied" (339–40). Maybe for the Prince, but hardly for his cause and story, is the rest silence.

Remembering these and other contours in the middle comedies, histories, and tragedies, we may turn to the two books of poetry in which Shakespeare is brought into print by others. This third part thus divides into two respective chapters: on *The Passionate Pilgrim* and "The Phoenix and Turtle."

CHAPTER 5

"Tales . . . coined": "W. Shakespeare" in Jaggard's The Passionate Pilgrim

[William Jaggard was] an infamous pirate, liar, and thief [who pro-duced a] worthless little volume of stolen and mutilated poetry, patched up and padded out with dirty and dreary doggerel.

Algernon Charles Swinburne, *Studies in Prose and Poetry* (1894), 90

With the 1623 First Folio and the 1599 and 1612 editions of *The Passionate Pilgrim*, William Jaggard had printed the first collections of both Shakespeare's plays and his poems.

Margreta de Grazia, *Shakespeare Verbatim* (1991), 167

The above epigraphs pinpoint changing critical perceptions of William Jaggard's role in Shakespeare's professional career. At the end of the nineteenth century, Swinburne works from a "Romantic" view of the autonomous author to judge Jaggard morally and *The Passionate Pilgrim* aesthetically. Jaggard is a cheat and the poetry poor. Since the poems' only begetter is a pirate, liar, and thief, and his little volume stolen, mutilated, patched, padded, dirty, dreary, and worthless, who could find interest in the enterprise? A hundred years later, de Grazia helps us begin to under-stand why. Even if we condemn Jaggard, he occupies a historic position in the printing of the national poet-playwright. He is the first to anticipate modern editors, including Malone, in the publication of both "the plays and poems of William Shakspeare." In between Swinburne and de Grazia, William Empson gets at the crux of the historical matter when he remarks, "*The Passionate Pilgrim* (1599) is a cheat, by a pirate who is very appreciative of the work of Shakespeare" ("Narrative Poems," 11).

The Passionate Pilgrim migrates to the center of a study of Shakespeare as a national poet-playwright because it prints a challenging historical enigma at the mid-point of his career. Without question, what is at stake, now as then, is the question of authorship.[1] *The Passionate Pilgrim* is a collaborative production presenting itself as a single-author work. What this should tell

---

[1] Much of the commentary in Rollins' *Variorum: Poems* is on this topic (538–58).

us is not just that Jaggard was a crook, or Shakespeare simply a collaborator, but that *The Passionate Pilgrim* is a site of transition between early modern and modern notions of authorship. The marvelous history of this volume's reception narrates a story of more than purely entertainment value.

TEXTUAL SCHOLARSHIP

We speak of "The Passionate Pilgrim," yet only to announce the difficulty. Which "Passionate Pilgrim"? By 1612, there are four distinct versions (extant): three separate editions – printed in 1598–99?, 1599, and 1612 – and two versions of the last edition, each having a different title page. What editors between the mid-seventeenth century and the early twenty-first do with this textual fracturing is part of the marvel. Today, a scholarly consensus protects it: we continue to be ignorant about the historical facts. This admission is somewhat belated, since it took much of the last century to become clear about what we do not know. The situation facing the critic of the new century is severe, since a long tradition of distinguished editors, starting with Malone in 1790, and continuing with Edward Dowden in 1883, Sir Sidney Lee in 1905, and "the all-but-infallible [Hyder] Rollins" in 1938 (Burrow, ed., *Sonnets and Poems*, 74n2), got it wrong. Yet with each new generation the narrative of candid ignorance continues to improve.

Today, for instance, we may not know the date of the first edition, but until World War II we did not even recognize it as a first edition. Housed in the Folger Shakespeare Library, it exists in fragment, signatures A3–A7 and C2–C7 (Poems 1, 2, 3, 4, 5, 16, and 18). In 1939, Joseph Quincy Adams proved that this fragment was not what Rollins thought, a scrap from the second edition, but rather the first edition itself. Since the fragment lacks a title page, we cannot date it definitively, but speculation ranges between September 1598, when the printer, T. Hudson, set up his press, and 1599, before the second edition emerged. This latter edition does bear a title page, but does not identify itself as "The Second Edition":

THE | PASSIONATE | PILGRIME. |*By W. Shakespeare.* |[Ornament] |*AT LONDON* | Printed for W. Iaggard, and are | to be sold by W. Leake, at the Grey- | hound in Paules Churchyard. | 1599.

The title page identifies Shakespeare as the author of the twenty lyric poems in the octavo, yet editorial tradition, tracing to Malone, determines that only five are written by him: Poems 1 and 2, which are versions of Sonnets 138 and 144 from the 1609 quarto; and three songs and sonnets

(3, 5, 16) from *Love's Labor's Lost.*[2] Malone was the first to delete poems that belong to other writers: Poems 8 and 20 by Richard Barnfield, and Poem 19, which includes the first printed (and abbreviated) copy of Marlowe's "The Passionate Shepherd to His Love" and (an even more abbreviated copy of) Ralegh's "The Nymph's Reply." Subsequent editors have attributed Poem 11 to Bartholomew Griffin. The authors of the remaining eleven poems are still unknown. Over the centuries, editors have wondered whether some might be by Shakespeare, but recent editors – notably John Roe and Colin Burrow – have emphasized our lack of evidence for doing so.[3] We can, then, easily determine what outraged Swinburne: under Shakespeare's name, Jaggard published a volume that contained poems written – and presumably were known to be written – by at least five writers and probably more, most of whom were still alive in 1599: Shakespeare (the author of five poems), Barnfield (two), Griffin (one), Marlowe and Ralegh (a combined one, with Marlowe deceased back in 1593), and then the anonymous poets (the remaining eleven).

What do we do with such a compounded portrait of print-authorship? The scholarly judgment today is helpful: rather than attributing authorship to "W. Shakespeare," we can see W. Jaggard *presenting W. Shakespeare as an author.* Yet the judgment quickly divides, between those like Swinburne who accuse Jaggard of piracy, and those like Edwin Willoughby who defend him. Today, most would follow the version articulated by Empson, acknowledging the dubiousness of Jaggard's enterprise but allowing for the different, pre-modern notions of authorship.[4] Recent work on collaborative authorship (Orgel, "Text"; Masten, *Intercourse*, "Playwrighting") warns us not to impose on Jaggard (or on Shakespeare) a modern notion of authorship. Since William Leake owned copyright to *Venus and Adonis,* Jaggard was probably "trying to ensure that book-collectors picked up copies of *The Passionate Pilgrim by W. Shakespeare* as a companion volume to the narrative poem" (Burrow, ed., *Sonnets and Poems,* 75). Marketing, rather than piracy, most likely drove the afflicted production of the 1599 *Passionate Pilgrim.* The volume was afflicted, for, as editors have long pointed out,

[2] The versions of the poems from the play that Jaggard prints do not derive from the first extant edition of 1598. See Freeman and Grinke, "Four New Shakespeare Quartos?"
[3] Thus the argument of Hobday has been either ignored (Roe, ed., *Poems*) or rejected (Burrow ed., *Sonnets and Poems,* 79n2). Hobday argues that the Venus and Adonis sonnets are by Shakespeare. The *Oxford Shakespeare* includes the following poems as possibly by Shakespeare: 4, 6, 7, 9, 10, 12–15, 17, and 18 (777–82). Five poems – 7, 10, 13, 14, and 18 – "are all in six-lined stanzas, the metre of Shakespeare's *Venus and Adonis*" (Lee, ed., *Passionate Pilgrim,* 39).
[4] See Roe, ed., *Poems,* 55. Roe concludes, first, that it is "most likely" that Jaggard either printed a commonplace book or assembled manuscript versions of several poems, and second, that it is "less likely that Jaggard commissioned them 'to look like Shakespeare', since . . . he probably did not intend to perpetrate an outright hoax" (56–57).

the octavo is rare in its printing of individual poems on rectos only, as if Jaggard did not have enough material to make up a complete volume.[5] Since Jaggard violated the economy of the day's printing practice, we can glean just how important he considered the Shakespearean venture to be. Empson was indeed on to something. Jaggard's motives might have been dubious but his savvy business judgment anticipates modern constructions of the Bard by at least two hundred years. If we look for an only begetter to "big time Shakespeare," we might do well to move William Jaggard into the spotlight.

Scholars call this edition the second one because in 1612 Jaggard printed what both extant title pages call "The third Edition." One of these title pages continues to bear the attribution "By W. Shakespere," but the other does not. While the two 1612 title pages differ in attribution, they share the printing of two new, related advertisements. The title page with Shakespeare's name on it reads:

THE | PASSIONATE | PILGRIME. | OR | *Certaine Amorous Sonnets,* | *betweene* Venus and Adonis, | *newly corrected and aug-* | *mented.* | *By W. Shakespere.* | The third Edition. | Where-unto is newly ad- | ded two Loue-Epistles, the first | from *Paris* to *Hellen,* and | *Hellens* answere backe| againe to *Paris.* | Printed by W. Iaggard. | 1612.

The first new advertisement, about the sonnets between Venus and Adonis, no doubt intensifies the strategy noted, of Jaggard trying to capitalize on Shakespeare's fame as the author of *Venus and Adonis,* but it also singles out those four poems as a special group (4, 6, 9, 11). We shall return to them presently. The second piece of new advertisement is damning, because, as Malone first pointed out, the two "Loue-Epistles" were not written by "W. Shakespere" but by Thomas Heywood, who was so outraged that he objected to Jaggard's falsification in print. In a postscript to his 1612 *Apology for Actors,* Heywood accused Jaggard of dishonestly printing poems that Jaggard himself had published earlier in Heywood's own *Troia Britanica.* Heywood added that he knew Shakespeare to be "much offended with M. Jaggard (that altogether unknowne to him) presumed to make so bold with his name" (Rollins, ed., *Variorum: Poems,* 535). Heywood's objection probably prompted Jaggard to cancel the original 1612 title page and to print a corrected form, without Shakespeare's name. The situation, however, was worse than Heywood imagined, because he appears to have taken the title page at its word, assuming that Jaggard had printed only the two "Loue-Epistles" announced, when in fact Jaggard printed nine. In either version,

---

[5] At the end of the volume, the printer abandons this plan (Burrow, ed., *Sonnets and Poems,* 76).

the third edition does not so much clarify authorship as further compound it. Insofar as we can tell, during his lifetime Heywood never did receive the proper recognition for producing the overwhelming bulk of the 1612 *Passionate Pilgrim*. In a curious paradox that might have made Jaggard smile (for he alone discerned it), today it is Shakespeare, not Heywood, whose name most famously benefits from versions of *The Passionate Pilgrim* printed in collected editions of his works.

Despite this predicament, the volume (in all three editions) continues to be marginalized by the Shakespeare community. While editors now commonly print the whole of the second or 1599 edition, *The Passionate Pilgrim* still fails to produce its own literary criticism, having fallen almost exclusively under the watchful eye of editors – and more recently, of those interested in copyright and intellectual property (see Thomas, "Eschewing Credit"). (As we shall see in the next chapter, this situation contrasts sharply with that for "The Phoenix and Turtle.") Indeed, there is a real gap between the marginal role that the volume plays in modern Shakespeare studies and the visible role that it played during Shakespeare's career. We still lack a detailed analysis of the volume's poems as poems.[6] Between 1598–99 and 1612 – the latter part of Shakespeare's career – three different editions ascribe to Shakespeare authorship of a collection of poems. When we add this printing history to that of his other printed poems – the ongoing editions of *Venus and Adonis* and *The Rape of Lucrece*, as well as the 1601 "Phoenix and Turtle" and the 1609 Sonnets and *A Lover's Complaint* – we can account for a considerable poetic print presence (see Figure 3 above). Finally, we need to combine this print history of the published poet with that of the published playwright in order more fully to grasp the compound identity of "W. Shakespere" at this time.

W. SHAKESPERE AS PASSIONATE PILGRIM

Concentrating on the poetry here, we can examine how Jaggard presents Shakespeare between 1598–99 and 1612 as an author of printed poems. The phrasing of the 1599 title page suggests that he presents Shakespeare *as a passionate pilgrim*: "*The Passionate Pilgrim. By W. Shakespere.*" The title intimates that the author has a distinct persona: W. Shakespeare *is* the passionate pilgrim. We do not know the origin of the alliterative title. It could have come from a commonplace book that Jaggard printed (Roe, ed.,

---

[6] The best commentaries are in the editions of Roe, *Poems*, and Burrow, *Sonnets and Poems*, and in S. Roberts, *Reading Shakespeare's Poems* (154–58).

Poems, 58n1; Rollins, ed., *Variorum: Poems*, 524), or it may have derived from Jaggard himself, who could have picked up on Shakespeare's reputation among contemporaries. As Edward Dowden suggested long ago (Dowden, ed., *"Passionate Pilgrim,"* iv), the title evokes the memorable metaphor Romeo puts into play the first time he speaks to Juliet during the Capulet feast – to quote the first quatrain of this "Shakespearean" sonnet embedded in a tragedy:

> If I profane with my unworthiest hand
> This holy shrine, the gentle sin is this,
> My lips, two blushing pilgrims, ready stand
> To smooth that rough touch with a tender kiss.
>   (*Romeo and Juliet*, 1. 5. 93–96)

The drama continues when Juliet addresses her future husband as "Good pilgrim" and again as "pilgrim" (97, 102). By presenting Romeo as a pilgrim who loves a lady, Shakespeare puts a passionate pilgrim on the stage. Since Romeo co-performs the self-conscious literary form of the sonnet in the theatre, we can note his resemblance to his author, as Juliet entreats: "You kiss by th' book" (110). Jaggard's 1599 title page, then, presents Shakespeare as a poet of desire within a religious cult of love.[7]

Yet Malone expressed puzzlement about the title: "Why the present collection of Sonnets &c. should be entitled *The Passionate Pilgrim*, I cannot discover . . . Perhaps it was so called by . . . Jaggard" (Rollins, ed., *Variorum: Poems*, 524). Rollins agrees, suggesting that Jaggard "had in mind a man who journeys a long distance as an act of devotion to his sweetheart; but, in any case, the alliteration of 'passionate pilgrim' led buyers to expect an anthology of love songs" (*Variorum: Poems*, 524). Judgments about the success of the marketing strategy once more divide. Characteristically, Swinburne judges the title "senseless and preposterous": *"The Passionate Pilgrim* is a pretty title, a very pretty title; pray what may it mean? In all the larcenous little bundle of verse there is neither a poem which bears that name nor a poem by which that name would be bearable" (Rollins, ed., *Variorum: Poems*, 524). Sir Arthur Quiller-Couch acknowledges Swinburne's objection regarding the facts but finds meaning elsewhere: "as a portly and attractive mouthful of syllables *The Passionate Pilgrim* can hardly be surpassed" (Rollins, ed., *Variorum: Poems*, 524).

---

[7] See Burrow, ed.: "The title probably alludes to the sonnet exchanged between Romeo and Juliet in 1.5.94–9" (*Sonnets and Poems*, 341). The first quartos of *Romeo and Juliet* appeared in 1597 and 1599, but Shakespeare's name did not appear on the title page.

The title's deployment of a metaphor draws attention to its self-conscious literary character. The pilgrimage is not real but figural, as the "attractive" alliteration implies. In doing so, the title evokes a literary heritage, for the religion of love stems from the courtly love tradition of the Middle Ages and later from Petrarch and the Petrarchan tradition.[8] In the words of Lisa Freinkel, Petrarch is the "eternal pilgrim"; his sequence of songs and sonnets, the *Rime sparse*, foregrounds "unconsummated desire": "In Petrarch's poetry, the flesh is never fulfilled" (*Reading*, 49). As Freinkel points out, Abel was the first pilgrim, becoming a type for Christ the great pilgrim, and the concept of pilgrimage suggests *peregrination, course, travel*. The pilgrim is always an exile: "The Christian is he who lives on the road" (16). We can then discover an affinity between pilgrimage as an action and the traditionally major genre of travel, epic, as depicted not simply by the authors of the *Odyssey* and the *Aeneid*, but by the pilgrim-authors of *The Divine Comedy* and *The Canterbury Tales*. During Shakespeare's day, Spenser places himself in this tradition by making his holy Palmer the guide of Sir Guyon in the great Elizabethan travel epic, Book 2 of *The Faerie Queene*.[9]

A "passionate" pilgrim is a particular type of (epic) traveler; he is, as Lee emphasizes, "amorous" (Lee, ed., *Passionate Pilgrim*, 20). Thus the title Ovidianizes the epic and religious metaphor, opening up another affinity: between the Christian (and Petrarchan) pilgrim and the Ovidian (pagan) exile. Both live – or write – on the road. Critics typically emphasize the Ovidian nature of Jaggard's collection, calling the poems in it "lascivious" (Roe, ed., *Poems*, 56) and designating Shakespeare "an Ovidian writer" (D. Kay, "Shakespeare," 228). The title page to the third edition makes the Ovidian content explicit, referring to Venus and Adonis, a myth made famous in the *Metamorphoses*, and to the love-epistle genre of the *Heroides*, where indeed Helen and Paris exchange letters (*Heroides* 16 and 17; see Burrow, ed., *Sonnets and Poems*, 78). Yet the title page also fuses the Ovidian to the Petrarchan: "Amorous Sonnets, betweene Venus and Adonis." A "passionate pilgrim" does not actually traverse the terrain of epic so much as occupy the room of eros. Lee goes a step further: "'Passionate' . . . was a conventional epithet of 'shepherd' and 'poet' in pastoral poetry" (Lee, ed., *Passionate Pilgrim*, 20), as in Marlowe's "The Passionate Shepherd

---

[8] S. Roberts agrees: "Above all, literary skill and artifice becomes the real subject of *The Passionate Pilgrim*" (*Reading Shakespeare's Poems*, 156).

[9] See Quint, "Anatomy of Epic": "When we think of *The Faerie Queene* as an epic poem . . . we do so because of Book II, for it is there that Spenser's poem primarily attaches itself to the epic tradition" (28).

to His Love," a version of which shows up in the volume. In this way, the title to *The Passionate Pilgrim* transacts a crossover between Virgilian and Ovidian/Petrarchan career grids, and locates that cross-over in "W. Shakespere."

What appears to have escaped notice is just how such an authorial persona at this time appears to challenge Spenser's self-presentation. In his 1595 *Colin Clouts Come Home Againe*, the "Virgil of England" (in Nashe's phrase) presents himself as an Ovidian exile who is authorized by the "shepheards nation" of Ireland (17), where he acts as a Neoplatonic priest of love. Spenser's pastoral minor epic indicts the corruptions of courtly love (775–94) and narrates the magnificent hymn to Love (795–894), "religiously . . . esteemed," which prompts the shepherd Cuddie to declare Colin "Priest" of that "God" for such "deep insight" (830–32).[10] *Colin Clout* offers an inventory of twelve Elizabethan poets, one of whom is named "Aetion," often identified as the Shakespeare (444–47) who wrote *Venus* and *Lucrece* (Rollins, ed., *Variorum: Poems*, 568–72; Oram, *et al.*, eds., *Yale Edition*, 532, 541–42), but the poem has a specific intersection with Shakespeare's first narrative poem, when Colin plots the nursery of Love "in the gardens of Adonis" (804). As we shall see, *The Passionate Pilgrim* is unique in the Shakespeare canon for mentioning Spenser's name. Since England's Virgil had died on 13 January 1599, the publication of Jaggard's volume that year may have had a specific literary resonance for its first readers.

Without question, the persona of *The Passionate Pilgrim* – whom we might call Will (after Sonnet 136.14) – emerges as a different kind of passionate pilgrim than Colin: he is a counter-Spenserian priest of desire within a religious cult of love. Spenser's passionate shepherd is a communal figure; even though in exile, he belongs to a "nation." Indeed, Colin's standing as the high priest of love in his new Irish community constitutes a major change from the 1579 *Calender*, when Colin had withdrawn from the shepherds of Kent after Rosalind betrayed him. Sixteen years later, transplanted across the Irish Sea, Colin is now an authority regarding the "mightie mysteries" of Love that the false shepherds of Cynthia's court have "prophane[d]" (788). Not simply does Spenser identify himself as the high priest of love for the English (and Irish) nation, but he attacks those who have challenged his cult – those "licentious" (787) writers of the epyllion tradition like Marlowe, who had blasphemed Love and his mother in such poems as *Hero and Leander*.

---

[10] Material in the next three paragraphs derives from Cheney, "Pastorals," 83, 97–100.

Spenser's colleagues responded to his passionate project. Michael Drayton presents his 1598 minor epic *Endimion and Phoebe*, itself a Neoplatonic chastening of the form, as a companion piece to *Colin Clout*: "Colin . . . my muse . . . rudely . . . presumes to sing by thee" (993–94, in Reese, ed., *Verse Romances*). And Barnfield identifies his 1595 minor epic, *Cynthia*, as the "first" to "imitat[e] . . . the verse of . . . [*The*] *Fayrie Queene*" (*Dedicatory Epistle*, 19). Spenser's Neoplatonic hymn fuses body and soul, and the poem ends with his generous tribute to Rosalind, a "shepheards daughter" who appears "of divine regard and heavenly hew" (932–33). In this way, *Colin Clout* stands between the *Calender*, with its portrait of the author as the failed lover of the beloved's body (*Januarye*, 49–53), and the 1595 *Amoretti* and *Epithalamion*, with its portrait of the author celebrating the sacral flesh of his wife, a "handmayd of the Faery Queene" whose "heavenly hew" raises his "spirit to an higher pitch" (*Amoretti*, 80.11–14).

By contrast, the W. Shakespeare of *The Passionate Pilgrim* is not the author of companionate desire, even as staged tragically in *Romeo and Juliet*; he is the failed pilgrim of passion that we have seen in *Venus* and *Lucrece*, and that we will continue to see in the Sonnets and *A Lover's Complaint* – even in "The Phoenix and Turtle," where the avian principals are criticized for "Leaving no posterity" (59). *The Passionate Pilgrim* coheres with the general project of Shakespeare's poetry, diminishing the representation of desire from the plays by viewing the relation between the sexes as fundamentally fatal: "Desire is death" (Sonnet 147. 8).

Fifteen of the twenty poems in Jaggard's octavo proceed in the first-person voice, encouraging Elizabethan readers to identify "The Passionate Pilgrim" with "W. Shakespere." Of the five that do not, 4, 6, and 9 are on the myth of Venus and Adonis, and employ the third-person narrative voice from Shakespeare's 1593 poem, and could thereby be construed as "Shakespearean." The other Venus and Adonis sonnet, 11, differs from the first three in that its couplet suddenly breaks out of the narrative mode into the lyric voice of the poet: "Ah, that I had my lady at this bay!" (13). The fourth poem, 16, is a song from *Love's Labor's Lost*, and is even more easily assimilated to a Shakespeare author-function. That leaves only one poem lying outside it: Poem 13 includes no personal voice and lacks a Shakespeare connection (Burrow, ed., *Sonnets and Poems*, 354); it does sound like the dramatic voice we have been reading, using the third-person to describe "Beauty" as "a vain and doubtful good" (1). As this opening line nonetheless indicates, the volume coheres in presenting the printed voice of a single authorial persona, singing a complaint against love, beauty, and the female sex: "Fair is my love, but not so fair as fickle" (7. 1).

Viewed in these terms, *The Passionate Pilgrim* may be a more interesting volume than Swinburne imagined. What infuriated him could well fascinate us: the printer's counterfeiting of Shakespeare's authorial persona. The volume does not simply counterfeit the voices and poems of other poets; it reflects on its own counterfeiting:

> How many tales to please me hath she coined,
> Dreading my love, the loss whereof still fearing!
> Yet in the mids of all her pure protestings,
> Her faith, her oaths, her tears, and all were jestings.
>
> (Poem 7. 9–12)

Here the poet links fiction with infidelity, presenting his beloved as both a storyteller and a jester who uses discourse and action – "pure protestings" – to falsify her faith. The word "coined" refers to counterfeiting, an economical and monetary falsification of the queen's image, but the word acquires literary value during the period, referring to false imitation or plagiarism (Thomas, "Eschewing Credit," 278–79). This charge haunted not merely Jaggard and his three octavos but Shakespeare, for in 1592 Robert Greene had used another traditional metaphor of literary rivalry to accuse his colleague of being "an upstart crow, beautified with our feathers" (*Greenes, Groatsworth of witte*, reprinted in *Riverside*, 1959). There is a likeness between the fiction Jaggard prints and the print he fabricates. Whatever Jaggard's intentions were, *The Passionate Pilgrim* presents W. Shakespeare coining tales from other poets, its author a deliciously failed priest of erotic love, victimized by the allure of feminine infidelity. As in the Petrarchan tradition broadly, here a paradox may well suffice: there is much sweetness in his suffering.

Jaggard's printing of two sonnets that appear in the 1609 quarto hints that his portrait of the author aligns with that in Shakespeare's Sonnets, the Petrarchan part of which ends with Sonnet 152: "thou art twice forsworn, to me love swearing; / In act thy bed-vow broke, and new faith torn" (2–3). If the Sonnets are about betrayal, *The Passionate Pilgrim* fixes on this event, albeit in a less disturbing version.[11] Vows, oaths, swearings, faiths – and their inversions – organize the octavo's thought, appearing directly in five poems (1, 3, 5 16, 17), and narrated in five more (2, 7, 13, 18, 20) – half the total. The majority of these appear early, setting the volume's topic and tempo.

---

[11] Cf. S. Roberts, who emphasizes that the volume narrative treats the subject of desire with less "sting" than that in the 1609 Sonnets (*Reading Shakespeare's Poems*, 155).

WILL'S AUTHORIAL DESIRE

In Poem 1, we witness a 1599 printing of the 1609 sonnet that is "perhaps the most terrible of the whole [1609] sequence" (Cruttwell, *Shakespearean Moment*, 13–14). "When my love swears that she is made of truth" (1) sets the terms for the representation of Shakespeare as a passionate pilgrim, "Outfacing faults in love with love's ill rest" (8). We do not know whether this poem represents an early version of Sonnet 138 or a memorial recon-struction, with recent editorial opinion divided: whereas Roe argues for the latter (*Poems*, 238–39), Burrow keeps options open for the former (*Sonnets and Poems*, 341). Roe calls line 8 quoted above the "most radical departure from *Son*. 138" (239) – which reads, "On both sides thus is simple truth sup-press'd." But the 1599 "Outfacing faults" is fine in itself, using alliteration to introduce the theatrical metaphor of the face, dominant in Shakespeare's poetry from *Lucrece* (as we have seen) to *A Lover's Complaint* (as we shall see). As the metaphor hints, from its opening line *The Passionate Pilgrim* is concerned with the language of falsified desire, wittily expressed by the male poet at the expense of the female: "When my love swears that she is made of truth, / I do believe her (though I know she lies)" (1–2). Yet in this scenario the female beloved is the active speaker, the linguistic maker of faith, while the male lover remains her thoughtful recipient, receiving her declarations and responding doubly: he believes in them and knows they are false. Belief, faith – masculine subjectivity – is detoured around truth. Such doubleness ensures the poet-lover's own complicity in feminine falsehood: "Therefore I'll lie with love, and love with me, / Since that our faults in love thus smother'd be." This is a grim parody of Spenserian com-panionate desire; the parodic doubleness helps explain a second theatrical metaphor, in line 11: "O, love's best habit's in a soothing tongue." For Will in 1599, as in 1609, love is no more than a falsifying actor strutting along in deceptive costume.

We shall discuss the 1609 version of Poem 2 in chapter 7 under the habit of Sonnet 144, but here we may note simply that it, too, employs theatricality, while moving the sensual into the religious sphere. (And here it must be noted that Swinburne exaggerated his case for the anomaly of the title; several of the poems do employ a religious representation, and all are passionate.) John Kerrigan helps us understand why this poem might be singled out for separate publication, calling the 1609 version "one of the strongest sonnets in the volume" (ed., "*The Sonnets*," 59). It is also distinctive for its summarizing narration of the triangular love affair between the poet, his dark lady, and their young man: the poet seeks to "know" truth from falsehood, only to "live in doubt" (13). Unlike Poem 1 – or such 1609 sonnets as 15 and 23 – Poem 2 does not use the language of theatre so much as rely on the morality play tradition, with its staging of a struggle between good and evil, especially as performed through Marlowe's *Doctor Faustus*. In Shakespeare's dramatic morality sonnet, corrupt humans replace good and bad angels to couple with each other, casting a grim cloud over the Christian sky. Not merely do two (basically) authentic Shakespearean sonnets open *The Passionate Pilgrim*, but both rely on theatre, foregrounding the authorial "I" in response to a dark lady's desire to be governor of the universe.

Poem 3, which recurs in *Love's Labor's Lost* (4. 3. 58–71), introduces a swerve into this narrative, for here the poet himself commits "false perjury" (3), persuaded by "the heavenly rhetoric of [the beloved's] . . . eye" to break a vow to another lady (1–3). As in the Petrarchan tradition, the new lady is not mortal but "a goddess" (6), and the poem transacts the poet's process of justifying his turn of faith: "My vow was earthly, thou a heavenly love; / Thy grace being gain'd cures all disgrace in me" (7–8). He concludes with a question that he does not answer: "If by me broke, what fool is not so wise / To break an oath, to win a paradise?" (13–14). If Poem 2 evokes the Christian narrative of desire within the morality play tradition, Poem 3 evokes this narrative within the tradition of Scripture itself, especially its genesis: a narrative of the creation of a divine woman in paradise. In Poem 3, the woman replaces the deity as a figure of "grace," curing man of his "disgrace" (8). The male's faithful love of a divinely born woman can redeem him from the sin of a previous fall into desire. While this poem maintains the theme of sexual betrayal from the first two, it changes the volume's mode from tragic to comic, emphasizing the regaining of paradise, a happy consequence of mutual desire. Occurring within a sequence of lyric poems, this sonnet from a play constitutes an intriguing 1599 conjunction of poetry and theatre.

As critics observe, the poet's reference to a "goddess" anticipates the group of sonnets on Venus and Adonis that unfolds with Poem 4. This group, like Poem 3, creates a pastoral oasis – literally a "paradise" – amid betrayal, or the "hell" (2. 12) introduced in the first two poems. Viewed in this way, these poems extend the lyric narrative of Christian desire – a paradox surely, since they deploy a classical myth. Here we can glean something of the intellectual complexity of "*The Passionate Pilgrim. By W. Shakspeare*": the opening set of poems – 1–7 – relocates redemption and relief in a space at once classical and pastoral. By moving from Christian to pagan, the fallen to the idyllic, a mortal to a goddess, the poet to his lady, we move from sordid history to idealized myth.

Of all the poems in *The Passionate Pilgrim*, the sonnets on Venus and Adonis have generated the most controversy. Recent editors reject these sonnets as authentic Shakespeare poems. Poem 11 appeared in Griffin's 1596 *Fidessa*, and the scholarly consensus runs that the "author of these four acts of homage to the nature of Venus is quite possibly Bartholomew Griffin" (Roe, ed., *Poems*, 56). Editors are not "certain," but they think "quite possibly" that Griffin rather than Shakespeare authored the poems of pagan pastoral retreat (Burrow, ed., *Sonnets and Poems*, 79–80). We have a rather curious situation here. If editors are so certain that Shakespeare did not author the Venus and Adonis sonnets, why do they devote space to them in their editions? The answer cannot be that they want readers to have access to the complete book in which some authentic poems circulated; if they did, presumably they would print the 1612 edition, which textually and in terms of reception, transmission, and authorship is and always has been more heated territory for thought and interpretation.[12] We might remain intrigued with the mystery of Shakespearean authenticity here.

If we do, we no longer would see the question of authenticity as the most significant to be asked, but rather its opposite, the question of counterfeiting. No longer would we be obsessed with whether Shakespeare wrote these poems; instead, we would submit to the *fiction* of Shakespearean authorship. This is what readers saw until the nineteenth century.[13] For over three hundred years, editors were intent to take the discourse of the title page at its word. Benson incorporated the poems in his 1640 edition of Shakespeare's *Poems*. Then, in 1709 Bernard Lintott made the first separate edition by reprinting the second edition in his *Collection of Poems*. Ignorant of the original three editions, Charles Gildon in 1710 rejected the Lintott edition and returned to the Benson version. Subsequently, Sewell (1725, 1728), Ewing (1771), Evans (1775), and others followed Gildon in printing the Benson text (see Figure 1 above). Not until Malone's editions (1778, 1790) does a critical edition appear; however, as we have intimated, it is a compromised edition. Malone does not print the two sonnets that appear in the 1609 quarto, since he has just published 138 and 144 in the previous unit of volume 10 on the Sonnets; nor does he print the three poems that he knows to be by other hands (the two by Barnfield and the compound poem by Marlowe-Ralegh); he divides Poem 14 into two poems; he inserts as Poem 19 some stanzas from Fletcher; he prints "The Phoenix and Turtle"

---

[12] In 1940, Rollins was the first to complain about this situation, which has not changed much: "Few scholars, indeed, appear to have examined it, in spite of its great importance in the biography of Shakespeare" (Rollins, ed., *"Passionate Pilgrim,"* ix).

[13] The following account draws from Rollins, ed., *Variorum: Poems*, 531–33.

as Poem 20; and finally he brings the Venus and Adonis sonnets up front as a unit. As Rollins observes, "From Malone to the present day, editors have felt some qualms about reprinting [the 1599 or second edition] . . . entire" (Rollins, ed., *Variorum: Poems*, 532). Not until 1843 does that other Shakespearean pirate, John Payne Collier, print the complete 1599 edition, establishing the practice that prevails today. While the conversation about attribution continues at a dizzying pace – it is recorded at length in Rollins' *Variorum Edition* – we might recall Malone: "Many of these pieces bear the strongest mark of the hand of Shakspeare." Of primary interest to Malone were the Venus and Adonis sonnets:

> The title-page above given fully [to the 1612 edition] supports an observation I made some years ago, that several of the sonnets in this collection seem to have been essays of the authour when he first conceived the notion of writing a poem on the subject of Venus and Adonis, and before the scheme of his work was completely adjusted. (Malone, ed., *Plays and Poems*, 1790 edition 10: 322)

Like recent editors, Malone is not certain; unlike them, however, he is willing to entertain the possibility. Let us take his cue.

If we want to see what the "early" or "young" Shakespeare looked like, perhaps we can do no better than read the Venus and Adonis sonnets. Whether they are the *young Shakespeare* or the *counterfeit Shakespeare*, they are still *Shakespeare*, for the simple reason that even in the worst case they are *Shakespeare intertexts*. This is exactly what Jaggard found and published. For thirteen years, no one objected to the book "*By W. Shakespere*" – not even Barnfield, a committed Spenserian poet of the nascent print form, nor Griffin. No one called the editions in; no one cancelled any title pages or removed the author's name. During Shakespeare's maturity, when his reputation was at its height, the poems associated with the myth of his youth continued to flourish – much as Spenser's youthful pastoral of 1579, *The Shepheardes Calender*, flourished with editions in 1581, 1586, 1591, and 1597 – even after the publication of *The Faerie Queene*. In Spenser's case, as in Shakespeare's, the printer, not the author, accounts for the phenomenon, since Spenser had no hand in the four post-1579 *Calender* editions. With Spenser more than with Shakespeare, we might wonder what the author thought: even after Spenser announced his mature move into epic with the 1590 *Faerie Queene*, publishers printed and readers bought his youthful pastoral work. As we have seen, Shakespeare self-consciously presented himself in Virgilian terms in his dedications to Southampton, promising "some graver labour" to the "first heir" of his "invention,"

Venus and Adonis. As with Spenser's youthful Virgilian pastoral, however, Shakespeare's youthful Ovidian pastoral continued to be reprinted, and it is within this textual history of reception that we might place Jaggard's octavo(s).

We can view the problem of *The Passionate Pilgrim*(s) along a continuum linking authenticity and plagiarism, pinpointing the problem as one of imitation.[14] From Malone on, we have not been able to determine whether Shakespeare imitates himself or whether a contemporary imitates him. When we recall that at this time imitation was a cardinal principle of English poetics, and that Shakespeare shows up in the historical record (thanks to Greene) accused of having gone over the line, we should probably back off from Jaggard and his venture. Is there not a rather similar profile between the Shakespeare who appeared in print as the plagiarist of Greene and Company and the Shakespeare who appeared in print plagiarizing Griffin and Company? In *The Passionate Pilgrim*, we see a coin of such authentic mint that it took over two centuries to determine it counterfeit.

Poem 4, the first of the Venus and Adonis sonnets, joins Shakespeare's three narrative poems in its Elizabethan strategy of identifying the locus of agency for the conjunction of poetry and theatre primarily in the figure of a female:

> Sweet Cytherea, sitting by a brook
> With young Adonis, lovely, fresh, and green,
> Did court the lad with many a lovely look,
> . . .
> She told him stories to delight his [ear];
> She show'd him favors to allure his eye;
> To win his heart she touch'd him here and there –
> Touches so soft still conquer chastity.
>
> (Poem 7. 1–8)

Still conquer chastity: this is the soft counter-Spenserian touch from *Venus and Adonis.* As in that minor epic, here Venus appears as an author-figure, using "stories" and "show[s]" as social courting techniques to affect Adonis' senses of "ear" and "eye." She uses her compound literary project of narrative poetry and erotic theatre to accomplish her persuasive end: sexual consummation. In this Venerean poetics, the literary arts do not delight and instruct, nor move the viewer to virtuous action (as Sidney promoted in *The Defence of Poesie* and Spenser in the *Letter to Ralegh* prefacing the

---

[14] On plagiarism, see Orgel, "Plagiarist"; Thomas "Eschewing Credit."

1590 *Faerie Queene*); emptied of their ethical content, poetry and theatre prepare the mind and body for saturation in the sensual.

Poem 5, also from *Love's Labor's Lost*, is even more explicit about the literary character of the seduction and its threat to fidelity:

> Though to myself forsworn, to thee I'll constant prove;
> Those thoughts to me like oaks, to thee like osiers bowed.
> Study his bias leaves, and makes his book thine eyes,
> Where all those pleasures live that art can comprehend.
>
> (Poem 5. 3–6)

Justifying his change of faith with a torturous logic, the poet finds a model for his infidelity in the scholar who abandons his learned "leaves," only to find his "book" in the beloved's eyes. The purpose of such scholarly "art" is to "comprehend" the full range of "pleasures" that the eyes offer. Hence the subsequent attention to the poet's "Well learned . . . tongue," which commends the beloved with the "soul" of divine "wonder" for the "Celestial" figure she is, and which identifies the poet as a divine singer (8–13). Like Poem 3, Poem 5 does something salutary to our view of Shakespeare the working dramatist: it makes explicit the comedy's poem *as a poem*, pulling it out of its dramatic context and giving it an independent identity in print.

Poem 6 narrates the pleasures that art offers in a lovely vignette, when Venus

> A longing tarriance for Adonis made
> Under an osier growing by a brook,
> A brook where Adon us'd to cool his spleen.
> . . .
> Anon he comes, and throws his mantle by,
> And stood stark naked on the brook's green brim.
> The sun look'd on the world with glorious eye,
> Yet not so wistly as this queen on him.
> He spying her, bounc'd in, whereas he stood;
> "O Jove," quoth she, "why was not I a flood?"
>
> (Poem 6)

Reversing the situation of Petrarch's sight of Laura bathing in the Sorgue, or of Sidney's Pyrochles spying Philoclea in a similarly compromising situation, this sonnet imagines Adonis bathing in the brook, the female voyeur moved to religious devotion by the masculine body standing "stark naked." Among editors, Roe helps us to see a representation about the Ovidian merits of Spenser and Marlowe (*Poems*, 242–43). He cites "the opening section

of *Venus and Adonis"* for "the use of the sun as onlooker and the combination of heat and lust"; "Ovid's story of Salmacis and Hermaphroditus"
in Golding's Book 4 of the *Metamorphoses* (430: "Scarce could she tarience
make") for "a verbal echo" of line 4; Spenser's *Faerie Queene*, 3. 36. 5–6
for "the detail of Adonis bathing under Venus's slyly watchful eye"; and
Marlowe's translation of Ovid's *Amores*, 1. 5 for the poem's "whimsical sen-
suality," especially Marlowe's rendering of lines 17–18 – "Starke naked as
she stood before mine eye / Not one wen in her body could I spie" –
but also the elegy's concluding line: "Jove send me more such afternoons as
this." The intertextuality among Ovid, Golding, Shakespeare, Spenser, and
Marlowe – the *Metamorphoses, Venus and Adonis, The Faerie Queene*, and
Ovid's Elegies – is rather impressive. Whoever penned it, the poem's intertextuality contrasts with its narrative textuality: in the narrative, a female
beholds a male body; but in the intertextuality of this narrative, the male
poet has his eye on other male poets – an instance of what we might
call inter-textual intercourse (cf. Masten, *Textual Intercourse*). The moment
even gives voice to the excitement generated, as the great goddess stares
at the naked youth and wittily critiques her father for not making her "a
flood."

As we have seen, Poem 7 completes the opening unit by presenting
the beloved as the coiner of tales in search of sexual desire. Once we
see the self-conscious literary nature of the first seven poems, Poem 8
seems less anomalous than it might otherwise. Formally discoursing on
the agreement between "music and sweet poetry" (1), it cites an actual harmony between two sixteenth-century artists, the musician John "Dowland,"
whose "heavenly touch / Upon the lute doth ravish human sense" (5–6),
and "Spenser," whose "deep conceit is such / As passing all conceit, needs
no defense" (7–8). The poem is important for showing the alliance between
song and poetry during the period, and for locating that alliance in
England's New Poet. As late as the eighteenth century, scholars such as
George Sewell assumed that Shakespeare here is praising Spenser in print:
"Shakespear took fire on reading our admirable Spenser . . . Be it to Spenser
then that we owe Shakespeare!" (Pope, ed., Preface, *Works*, ix). Even though
Sewell is mistaken, he helps us realize how compelling the fiction of *The
Passionate Pilgrim* was for a long time. The author's reference to Spenser
prompts the reader to view the fiction of the volume as a whole as in some
sense "Spenserian," for the poet prints the name of his literary model. We
may go further, and see here a printed sequel to what Shakespeare promised
Southampton in his two dedications: a pattern of lower and higher verse
forms, a typology that specifically relates *The Passionate Pilgrim* to *The*

Faerie Queene, amorous poetry to epic. Again, we might wonder what Spenser's reaction would have been (had he lived long enough to read the inscription; probably he did not). Presumably, England's New Poet would have been horrified to see his name validating an erotic project antithetical to his "Legend of Chastitie," with its core canto allegorizing the relation between Venus and Adonis as a myth of chastity making the individual "eterne in mutabilitie" (3. 6. 47). While the mention of "Spenser" seems to express debt and admiration, it simultaneously measures difference and subversion.

The remaining poems in the first part of the volume fill in details to the counter-Spenserian pastoral myth of Venus and Adonis. Poems 9 and 11 continue the mythic narration; Poem 10 uses Spenser's pastoral trope of the "rose" (1) from the *Calender*; Poem 12 relies on the trope of the "sweet shepherd"; and Poem 13 descants on the loss of "Beauty" as a form of death (1), including use of floral imagery: "A flower that dies when first it gins to bud" (3; see 8). All of this prepares the reader for Poem 14, which refers to "Philomela" (17), Spenser's arch-trope for the pastoral poet in preparation for epic. Burrow observes that here the "allusions to Philomel might have made attribution to the author of *Lucrece* plausible to the volume's first readership" (Burrow, ed., *Sonnets and Poems*, 355), but we need to extend the intertextuality to Spenser.

Poem 14 has long provoked editorial intervention. Malone divided it in two (after line 12) but only after Jaggard printed a heading after it, "*Sonnets to Sundry Notes of Music*," making this the last poem in a first part and drawing attention to its unique position in the volume. We can profitably understand this emphasis only after we turn to the last poem of the second part, which also refers to the Philomela myth. Here we may note that the myth functions to summarize the narrative printed so far: the poet is separated from his beloved, for

> She bade good night that kept my rest away,
> And daff'd me to a cabin hang'd with care,
> To descant on the doubts of my decay.
> (Poem 14. 2–4)

Unlike *A Lover's Complaint*, where the country maid will "daff" the "white stole" of her "chastity" under pressure from the young courtier's "art of craft" (295–97), here the female assumes the chaste habit of agency and power. This posture drives the poet into a Spenserian House of Care (*Fairie Queene*, 4. 5), a parody of the "greene cabinet" (*December*, 17) that is the central locus of the pastoral tradition (chapter 1), since it inspires a song of doubt and decay. The poet's lady is all theatre, but he cannot decipher her show, which is exquisite:

> 'T may be she joy'd to jest at my exile,
> 'T may be again, to make me wander thither:
>   "Wander," a word for shadows like myself.
>   (Poem 14. 9–11)

Among editors, Burrow catches the theatrical resonance of "shadows": "people of no substance; also used of actors" (*Poems*, 355). As Puck puts it in the Epilogue to *A Midsummer Night's Dream*: "If we shadows have offended, / Think but this, and all is mended" (5. 1. 423–24). In 1599, the word as used in Poem 14 – a shadow like the poet wandering in exile – could well evoke Shakespeare's role as an actor on the stage.

While waiting anxiously for the morning to arrive, the poet encounters the nightingale: "While Philomela sits and sings, I sit and mark, / And wish her lays were tuned like the lark" (Poem 14. 17–18). Editors have long found the passage garbled: line 17 with Philomela contains two extra syllables, while line 20 with the lark is missing two (see Roe, ed., *Poems*, 250). Acknowledging this crux, we may recall that the nightingale-lark dyad is conventional to pastoral literature, most famously emerging in the bedroom scene of *Romeo and Juliet* (3. 5). But where in the tragedy the avian pair evokes a transition from night to morning, in Poem 14 it evokes an authorial identity. First, the poet imitates the nightingale (they both "sit"); next he differentiates himself from her, as he "mark[s]" the nightingale's song; and finally he engages in a fantasy about the bird, as he wishes her song were like the lark's welcome to the day. The poem ends with the poet locked in this subjective condition, separated from his beloved but wishing he were not.

As the heading dividing the volume into two parts suggests, Poems 15–20 may have been "known to have musical settings which are now lost" (Burrow, ed., *Sonnets and Poems*, 357). Nonetheless, most of them continue to foreground the narrative of sexual betrayal and the separation of the sexes: "For now I see inconstancy / More in women than in men remain" (17. 11–12). While 16 is another song from *Love's Labor's Lost*, and 17, 19, and 20 are all in the pastoral mode, 15 sounds the note of national epic. A "lording's daughter" changes her affection from "her master" to "an Englishman": "Long was the combat doubtful, that love with love did fight, / To leave the master loveless, or kill the gallant knight" (1–6). Poem 18 introduces an interesting conjunction between epic and theatre. A worldly wise poet first offers advice to the (male) reader about how to deal with women, employing a conceit familiar from *Lucrece*: "And to her will frame all thy ways . . . / The strongest castle, tower, and town, / The golden bullet beats it down" (13–18). Men need to besiege women because women merely perform their chastity: "The wiles and guiles that women work, / Dissembled with an outward show" (37–40). Men have their own theatre, and in Poem 16 from *Love's Labor's Lost* the poet toys with the prospect of breaking his "vow" (13), while in Poem 19 he uses the Marlovian voice to seduce his beloved into living with him and being his love.[15] Poem 20, which prints the figure of Philomela, brings the second part and the volume to a close.

Barnfield is now recognized as the author of the final poem to *The Passionate Pilgrim*. In the context of the present argument, this conclusion is not an impediment but a directive: it allows us to see the poet's posture as formally one of Spenserian pastoral. Imitating Colin Clout from the *Calender*, Barnfield's poet appears "Sitting in a pleasant shade" (3) communing with the nightingale. Yet within the fiction of Jaggard's volume, W. Shakespeare emerges as a type of Spenserian pastoral poet with a (homoerotic) difference. The poet's communion with Philomela evokes the violence of rape:

> She, poor bird, as all forlorn,
> Lean'd her breast up-till a thorn,
> And there sung the dolefull'st ditty,
> . . .
> For her griefs, so lively shown,
> Made me think upon mine own.
> (Poem 20. 9–18)

Philomela's posture, her breast against a thorn, refers to the ruddy patch on a nightingale's breast, but it evokes the princess of Athens' rape at the hands of Tereus, the brother-in-law whom she defies in her complaint. The theatrical ring of her song in "lively shown" is worth underscoring, especially since the poem will end with a familiar Spenserian (and Shakespearean) pun that we have glanced at in *Lucrece*: "bear a part" – both join in song and perform a role. Burrow notes "Barnfield's vaguely *Lucrece* like plangency" here (*Sonnets and Poems*, 81) – suggesting that, just as the Venus and Adonis sonnets relate with Shakespeare's first minor epic, so the two Philomela poems relate with his second minor epic.

The male poet's identification with a raped female may help him process his shame over publication, but what is striking here is the way the author

---

[15] What we cannot quite see in the Jaggard version is the presence of Philomela here, since only the first stanza of "Love's Answer" or Ralegh's "The Nymph's Reply" is printed – perhaps, as Burrow and others speculate, because the printer ran out of space.

turns the myth of Philomela into a meditation on the infidelity of a "Faithful friend" (56) – a turn consistent with Barnfield's homoerotic verse but also with Shakespeare's Sonnets.

SHAKESPEAREAN INTRATEXTUALITY

The Passionate Pilgrim has become historically important for a number of reasons, not least (we have seen) for its intriguing intratextuality with several works in the Shakespeare canon, both poems and plays, from *Venus, Lucrece*, and the Sonnets to *Love's Labor's Lost*. In particular, the verse miscellany's intratextuality with the author's play provides a remarkable case study for the present project. Indeed, the re-production within the verse miscellany of three poems *presented as poems in the fiction* of *Love's Labor's Lost* draws attention to the special economy of poetry and theatre in late-Elizabethan England.

The three poems from the play all come from a single action, designated Act 4, scenes 2 and 3 in the *Riverside Shakespeare*. This action is not just any but constitutes the most striking instance in the entire Shakespeare canon of a play staging the writing and reception of poems. Whoever extracted the poems from the play, he registers Shakespeare's success in rehearsing the author's own special interest in this particular Elizabethan economy. Since Jaggard's volume attributes *The Passionate Pilgrim* to William Shakespeare, we can say that it presents the author printing the economy of poetry and theatre itself.

The origin of the printing, however, lies in the play. In 4. 2, Nathan reads Berowne's sonnet to Rosaline (105–18). In 4. 3, Berowne himself enters with his poem in his hand, only to withdraw and overhear the King read his sonnet aloud (25–40). Independently, Berowne and the King then withdraw to overhear Longaville read his sonnet to Maria (58–71). Finally, all three men independently withdraw to overhear Dumain read his poem to Katherine (99–118). Afterwards, Berowne self-consciously theatricalizes the staging of poetry: "O, what a scene of fooling have I seen" (161). Of the four poems recorded in the play, only the King's does not make it into *The Passionate Pilgrim*, perhaps because it alone addresses a queen who resembles Shakespeare's sovereign (see 4. 3. 226–27). In any event, the extended action in the comedy is central to the plot, since it forms the very moment of exposure, the revelation of the play's problem, the exact point wherein the audience joins with Berowne – and slowly the other courtiers – in seeing the folly of the masculine vow to study books in their academy at the expense of women.

The extended scene from *Love's Labor's Lost* forms the clearest instance from Shakespeare's plays of a phenomenon that we will see reversed in the next chapter. If in "The Phoenix and Turtle" Shakespeare uses the poem quite literally to print a (mini-)play or "Threnos," in *Love's Labor's Lost* he uses his play to perform a poem. The fact that Jaggard printed poems out of the play for Shakespeare's printed work of poetry registers acutely the fertile conditions for combining poetry and theatre at this time.

CHAPTER 6

"Threne" and "Scene": the author's relics of immortality in "The Phoenix and Turtle"

By attending to Shakespeare's role as an early modern author, we can discover a fresh response to what has long been recognized as a reader's paradox: "The Phoenix and Turtle."[1] John Middleton Murray declared this philosophical lyric "the most perfect short poem in any language" (Rollins, ed., *Variorum: Poems*, 566), yet I. A. Richards found it "the most mysterious poem in English" (*Poetries*, 50). So mysterious, Richards thought, that "the whole poem" tries to convey "an endeavor to apprehend a mystery . . . the mystery of being" (57). William Empson called it "exquisite, baffling, and exalted" ("Narrative Poems," 18), while John Masefield found it "strange" and "beautiful," a form of "Spiritual ecstasy" (Rollins, ed., *Variorum: Poems*, 564). G. Wilson Knight believed the poem exhibited "the mystery of . . . love-death intercourse," by which "a mystic paradox vitalizes . . . tragic joy" (Rollins, ed., *Variorum: Poems*, 581–82), and Richard Wilbur said it is "strange and masterly," leaving "an impression of complete vitality" (Introduction to Wilbur and Harbage, eds. *Narrative Poems*, 20–21). More recently, Katherine Duncan-Jones has called the poem "extraordinary . . . one of the most dense literary riddles of the period" (*Ungentle*, 135, 140), while Colin Burrow has drawn attention to its "growing thunder of metaphysical speculation" (*Sonnets and Poems*, 87–88). In a 2001 statement in *The Times Literary Supplement*, Barbara Everett summarizes this view for the new century: "'The Phoenix and Turtle' is . . . brilliant and beautiful, but its extravagant rhetorics and unusual formality bring about a real opacity" (13). Back in 1922, Middleton Murray was thus on to something when he declared that "*The Phoenix and the Turtle* is mysterious, but it is crystal-clear" (Rollins, ed., *Variorum: Poems*, 565).

For a long line of distinguished commentators mesmerized by the poem, the paradox results because the poem's perfect beauty is so exquisitely belied

---

[1] Cf. Burrow, ed.: this title "was first used in 1807, and has no connection with Shakespeare" (*Sonnets and Poems*, 82).

by the opaqueness of its allegorical content. We admire the pristine expression of the poetry, but we possess no certitude about what it means. As to be expected, such a paradox has intensified rather than eliminated controversy, yet today we may still marvel at how such a slender portion of the Shakespeare canon – a mere 67 lines – has generated such a massive and important history of criticism.[2]

The major interpretations are drawn along four lines, which variously cross and combine: politics and history; religion and philosophy; sexuality and gender; genre and literariness. By far, the political or historical interpretation has received the most press, as scholars and critics have vigorously debated the allegorical referents for the two avian principals. No fewer than eight major theses about the identities of the phoenix and turtle have been forwarded: (1) Queen Elizabeth and the earl of Essex (Grosart, ed. *Chester's Love's Martyr*; Matchett, "*Phoenix and the Turtle*"; Oakeshott, "*Love's Martyr*"; McCoy, "Love's Martyrs"; Tipton "Transformation"; Hyland, *Introduction to Shakespeare's Poems*); (2) Sir John Salisbury and his wife Ursula (C. Brown, ed., *Poems*; Buxton, "Two Dead Birds"; Honigmann, "*Lost Years*," 90–113; cf. Klause, "Phoenix and Turtle"); (3) Elizabeth and the English people (Axton, "Miraculous Succession"; Hume, "*Love's Martyr*"); (4) Elizabeth and Salisbury (T. P. Harrison, "*Love's Martyr*"); (5) Lucy, countess of Bedford, and her husband, the third earl of Bedford (Newdigate, ed., "Phoenix and Turtle"); (6) Elizabeth and Giordano Bruno (Eriksen, "Bruno"); (7) the martyred Jesuit poets Robert Southwell and Henry Walpole (Asquith); and (8) the martyred Catholic Ann Line and her husband Roger (Finnis and Martin, "Another turn").

Yet many critics have eschewed such historical allegory for religious or philosophical allegory, usually by emphasizing scholastic elements of Christian mysticism, especially regarding the three-in-one mystery of the Trinity in its Reformation context (Cunningham, "Essence"); or Platonic and Neoplatonic philosophy (Ellrodt, "Poet," "Anatomy"), especially regarding the two-in-one mystery of eros; but also "a vision of love's aspiring immortality" emphasized by Knight in his famous commentary: "the very theme of *The Phoenix and the Turtle*" is that "In death there is no unfaithfulness"; there is, thus, "an assurance of immortality, in terms of 'death' and 'love,'" the "blending of duality in unity, of life and death in love's immortality" (Rollins, ed., *Variorum: Poems*, 580–81).[3] This last

---

[2] Even so, "The Phoenix and the Turtle" remains outside the mainstream of Shakespeare criticism, even in works sympathetic to Shakespeare's poems – e.g., Bate, *Genius*; Miola, "Poems," in *Reading Shakespeare*; S. Roberts, *Reading Shakespeare's Poems*; Hyland, *Introduction to Shakespeare's Poems*.

[3] Critics surveyed by Rollins in the *Variorum: Poems* often mention the Christian and Platonic dimensions (570–83).

dimension shades easily into sexual or gender dynamics, with most critics (especially recent ones) attending to Shakespeare's representation of male and female lovers – or the feminine and the masculine – within the institution of marriage, or to love as an abstraction and idea (see Roe, ed., *Poems*, 50–54; Burrow, ed., *Sonnets and Poems*, 83–84). Finally, critics have labeled the genre of the poem variously as a philosophical poem, a funeral elegy, or a love lyric, emphasizing its mix of technical philosophical terms with language in the transcendent key, tracing its literary origins to the bird poem, including Ovid's *Amores*, 2. 6 on the death of Corinna's pet parrot (Rollins, ed., *Variorum: Poems*, 571), but especially Chaucer's *Parlement of Foules* (Rollins, ed., *Variorum: Poems*, 571), Petrarchism and Ovidianism more broadly (Ellrodt, "Anatomy"; Roe, ed., *Poems*, 49–50; Burrow, ed., *Sonnets and Poems*, 83–84), Sidney and elegies on him (Everett, "Golden Bough"); and even drawing attention to Shakespeare's self-reflexive concern with his own art and role as a poet during the Elizabethan era (Ong, "Metaphor"; Roe, ed., *Poems*, 52–55; Burrow, ed., *Sonnets and Poems*, 89–90).[4]

While the interpretations continue to be dizzying, a number of recent critics have luckily reached something of a consensus about what has seemed the eye of the storm – the identity of the conjoined avian principals. The phoenix and turtle, who love each other, die, leave no posterity, yet warrant civic mourning among the purified elect, appear to allegorize Queen Elizabeth and the earl of Essex, who have put the national succession in jeopardy through the unfortunate tragedy of their star-crossed conjunction.[5] The poem was first printed in 1601, the very year when Elizabeth signed the execution warrant for Essex, who had forged a rebellion against his sovereign and failed. Since we possess no entry in the Stationers' Register for the poem, we cannot identify whether it was published before or after Essex's public beheading in March, but it does not really matter, since neither Essex nor Elizabeth needed to be dead for Shakespeare to represent their "death" in symbolic terms; he "need only have seen the situation as past redeeming" (Matchett, "*Phoenix and the Turtle*," 191). However persuasive rationally, this intriguing political tenor speaks little to the poem's awe-inspiring vehicle, the absolute beauty of its formal perfection, which continues to leave readers today in an exalted state of joy. Unfortunately, most readers who have emphasized the poem's formalized beauty, thinking

---

[4] For a literary interpretation, see also Brooks, *Well Wrought Urn*, 14–16; Richards, *Poetries*; Knight, *Mutual Flame*. For criticism through the early 1970s, see Underwood, "*Phoenix*"; the inventory above is also indebted to Roe, ed. *Poems*, 41–49; and to Tipton, "Transformation," 59–60n3.

[5] Asquith, "Phoenix," and Finnis and Martin, "Another turn," have just complicated this conclusion, but it remains to be seen how seriously. Even though Shakespeare might be processing the martyrdom of Ann Line or Southwell and Walpole, the Essex–Elizabeth fallout remains the most durable historical context.

with Ralph Waldo Emerson that it must be "a lament on the death of a poet, and of his poetrie mistress" (quoted in Richards, *Poetries*, 50), or with Richards that it must be about "the poetic endeavor" and of "poetry" itself (50), have tended to eschew politics. What "The Phoenix and Turtle" seems to require is a hermeneutic that can account for both the political and the literary at once.

Such a hermeneutic can be found if we view the poem as a work about the politics of authorship itself. In "The Phoenix and Turtle," Shakespeare versifies the very predicament of the late-Elizabethan author who willingly voices dangerous political crises, like that of Elizabeth and Essex, whose emotional conjunction threatened national succession. What seems challenging today is figuring out just how the poem relates the literary to the political. Since several important recent critics agree on the political allegory (even if others dispute it endlessly), we might turn our historical scholarship back to the literary.[6] When we do, we discover that the poem rehearses another kind of conjunction that happily predicts a more fortunate succession – one that pertains both to the material printing of the poem in Robert Chester's *Loves Martyr, or Rosalins Complaint* and to the professional environment of Shakespeare's professional career.

THE PRINTED CONTEXT: *LOVE'S MARTYR*

Sometime in 1601, Chester's volume was printed by Richard Field, the Stratford-born friend of Shakespeare's who nearly a decade earlier had printed both *Venus and Adonis* and *The Rape of Lucrece*. The Chester volume has other connections with Shakespeare's first two printed poems, because, as Burrow points out, Chester's dedicatory poem "alludes to the semi-epic status of *Lucrece*: 'Of bloody wars, nor of the sack of Troy, / . . . Of Lucrece's rape, being ravished by a King, / Of none of these, of sweet conceit I sing.'" Burrow also finds a "reference to Ovidian tales of Lucretia on p. 16; and a reference which may be to Shakespeare's first poem, 'under this / Faire *Venus* from *Adonis* stole a kisse', occurs on p. 18" (Burrow, ed., *Sonnets and Poems*, 84n1). What might be striking to recognize, then, is just how *Love's Martyr* coheres with the printing of William Shakespeare's name between the early 1590s and the first years of the seventeenth century – including through the practice of William Jaggard in *The Passionate Pilgrim*.

---

[6] On this foundation, we may then account for the sexual and the religious.

Chester's volume is "one of the hardest books to make sense of in Elizabethan literature" (J. Kerrigan, "Poems," 76). The difficulty is virtually advertised on the title page to the first edition:

LOVES MARTYR: | OR, / ROSALINS COMPLAINT. *Allegorically shadowing the truth of Loue,* | in the constant Fate of the Phoenix | *and Turtle.* | A Poeme enterlaced with much varietie and raritie; | *now first translated out of the venerable Italian* Torquato | Caeliano, by ROBERT CHESTER. | With the true legend of famous King *Arthur . . .* | *To these are added some new compositions, of severall moderne Writers* | *whose names are subscribed to their severall workes . . .* | [Ornament] | LONDON | Imprinted for E. B. | 1601.[7]

In a single volume, the reader can find a remarkable array of material: a curious miscellany of works "by" Robert Chester, ranging from a very long (and widely maligned) poem on the phoenix and turtle and a long verse discourse on King Arthur; and *"some new compositions, of severall moderne Writers,"* two by an anonymous poet named "Ignoto" (perhaps John Donne [D. Kay, "Shakespeare," 230] or Sir Walter Ralegh [Oakeshott, *"Love's Martyr,"* 40–41]), one by "William Shake-speare," four by "John Marston," one by "George Chapman," and four by "Ben Johnson," all of which are introduced by two poems collectively written by the "Vatum Chorus" (chorus of poets). To complicate the whole matter, the title page declares that *Love's Martyr "Allegorically shadow[s] . . . the truth of Loue"* in its myth of the phoenix and turtle – the very spring to the torrent of allegorical interpretation in the nineteenth, twentieth, and now the twenty-first centuries, from Grosart in 1878 (who first identified Elizabeth with the phoenix and Essex with the turtle) to Alzada Tipton in 2002 (who most recently confirms this interpretation). Briefly put, *Love's Martyr* is hard to make sense of as an Elizabethan book because it operates at two removes from the stability so many readers require: that of authorial "meaning." The book is that strange bedfellow, a collaborative allegory, and it just happens that the world's most famous author, "William Shake-speare," lies deeply embedded in its printed sheets.[8] More precisely put: *Love's Martyr* prints the paradox at the core of the present book: "The Phoenix and Turtle" is a poem by the world's most famous theatrical man. As it turns out, Chester's

---

[7] Quotations from *Love's Martyr*, except from Shakespeare's poem, come from Grosart's edition. A second printing of *Love's Martyr* appears in 1611, with a different title page: "The Anuals [Annals] of Great Brittaine. Or a Most Excellent Monument" – printed by Mathew Lownes (Burrow, ed., *Sonnets and Poems*, 83).

[8] On *Love's Martyr*, see Grosart, ed., *Chester's Love's Martyr*; C. Brown, ed., *Poems*; Knight, *Mutual Flame*, 179–92; Matchett, *"Phoenix and the Turtle"*; Oakeshott, "Love's Martyr"; Axton, "Miraculous Succession."

printed volume, like Shakespeare's printed poem, emerges directly out of a theatrical environment. James P. Bednarz recalls that Marston "became Shakespeare's commentator, collaborator, and rival in print" (*Poets' War*, 198), and he notes that Shakespeare, Marston, Chapman, and Jonson "were considered 'the best' modern playwrights" (198). Bednarz adds that it is not "accidental" that Shakespeare, Marston, and Jonson "were currently involved in the Poets' War" (198). In other words, in its original material casing, "The Phoenix and Turtle" functions as a lyric poem embroiled within a theatrical competition.

In fact, critics have long situated the poem in the context of Shakespeare's dramatic career. In 1886, Fleay believed that "the appearance of Shakespeare's name, as fellow-contributor to Chester's *Love's Martyr* with Jonson, Marston, and Chapman, marks the conclusion of the theatrical quarrel, and the reconciliation of all the principal combatants, except Dekker" (Rollins, ed., *Variorum: Poems*, 562; see 564). More frequently, critics have compared the poem with the plays. Some, like Middleton Murray, boldly declare the poem's absolute superiority to the plays (reprinted in Rollins, ed., *Variorum: Poems*, 566), while others find the poem's "philosophy" of male and female desire suggestive of that in the romantic comedies (see Rollins, ed., *Variorum: Poems*, 573). Occasionally, critics have even found the poem "dramatic" in quality, especially the concluding Threnos, "perhaps originally intended for the epilogue of an allegorical masque" (Rollins, ed., *Variorum: Poems*, 568). Such a view recurs as a convention in most modern introductions on the poem (Prince, ed., *Poems*, xliv; Roe, ed., *Poems*, 49). Yet critics have also added one feature of intriguing specificity; as Everett puts it: "In the year of *Loves Martyr*, *Hamlet* first held the stage, its author recognized as master of the public theatre, but still open to dismissal by well-born or university-trained writers. But *Hamlet* is a court tragedy. And in 'The Phoenix and Turtle' the poet is perhaps making plain that he can equal or outdo the court makers of his time in their own mode" ("Golden Bough," 14).

While acknowledging this theatrical context, Everett joins most commentators in emphasizing the poetical context. She suggests Sidney's "Eighth Song" from *Astrophil and Stella* as an origin for Shakespeare's discovery of "a music he uses nowhere else" (14).[9] Later, Everett observes that in *Cymbeline* Shakespeare picks up the "unfinished" works of Sidney's *Arcadia* and Spenser's *Faerie Queene* – what she calls their "heroic love epic[s]" – and she notes that "The Phoenix and Turtle" has "a rhetoric and feeling

[9] In fact, critics have long cited Sidney and his song; see Roe, ed., *Poems*, 48.

perhaps closest, in of all the poet's work, to *Cymbeline*" (15). Since she pursues only the Sidney connection, we might wish to follow up on the connection with Spenser, and then situate this connection within the theatrical competition emphasized by Bednarz in *Poets' War*. When we do, we discover one important way that "The Phoenix and Turtle" lines up with Shakespeare's other poems already examined: here Shakespeare competes not merely with fellow "playwrights" but with England's national poet, in a printed poem that processes his own standing as a poet-playwright before a national audience.[10]

Chester's hopes for *Love's Martyr* are signaled not merely by his attention to the Elizabeth–Essex fall-out, but by two other features. The first is well known, and is doubly advertised, first on the title page in the announcement of "*some new compositions, of severall moderne Writers*" and again on a second title page prefacing these compositions:

HEREAFTER | FOLLOW DIVERSE | Poeticall Essaies on the former Sub | iect; viz: the *Turtle* and *Phoenix*. | Done by the best and chiefest of our moderne writers, with their names sub- | scribed to their particular workes: | *neuer before extant.* |

In other words, Chester has managed to assemble, not just ordinary modern poets, but the "best and chiefest" then living – a judgment that literary history has largely confirmed, at least with respect to Jonson and Shakespeare.

The second feature is less well known. Presumably, Chester could make the high claim for this particular group of writers because he knew that England's New Poet had died two years previously. Accordingly, his main title page advertises his debt to Spenser in the alternative title to *Love's Martyr*: "*Rosalins Complaint*." By 1601, both Shakespeare and Lodge had written works featuring a heroine named Rosalind: in 1590, Lodge had published the prose fiction *Rosalynde or Euphues' Golden Legacy*, while toward the end of the 1590s Shakespeare had put Lodge's heroine on the stage in *As You Like It*. What has escaped attention is not that Spenser had first used Rosalind as a heroine in his 1579 Virgilian pastoral, *The Shepheardes Calender*, and kept her before the reading public in such works as the 1595 *Colin Clouts Come Home Again*, but more precisely that the name "Rosalind" in English literature appears to be a Spenserian coinage, and thus came to be associated with Spenser and his national art.[11]

---

[10] See Oakeshott on Chester's high hopes for the volume: "Here was . . . the chance that if and when the revolution that he and others confidently expected took place *Loves Martyr* . . . would be launched on the world" ("Love's Martyr," 47).

[11] For this idea, thanks to Dustin Stegner. See Mallette, "Rosalind," 622. The genealogy of the three authors has been discussed but not with respect to Chester's volume; see, e.g., C. Kinney, "Feigning."

If, as Marie Axton suggests, *"Rosalin's Complaint* voices a monarch's reproach to her subjects" ("Miraculous Succession," 118), *Love's Martyr* shows Chester making a rather large-scale appropriation of the recently deceased national poet's project: he employs a genre Spenser had turned into a nationally significant form (see H. Maclean, *"Complaints"*) and identifies the beloved of Colin Clout with Queen Elizabeth. Throughout his career, Spenser himself had been careful to conceal Rosalind's real-life identity; in the gloss to the *Januarye* eclogue, E. K. says that "Rosalinde . . . is also a feigned name, which being wel ordered, wil bewray the very name of hys love and mistresse, whom by that name he coloureth," citing as the first of several literary precedents Ovid and Corinna (118–20). As this discourse suggests, E. K. invites readers to make their own guesses, and though most readers think first of Spenser's beloved, some identify Rosalind with the queen (Mallette, "Rosalind," 622). Chester may be the first on record to indicate such a (royal) reading.

Love's Martyr includes other Spenserian moments. Chester equates Rosalin and her complaint with Dame Nature: "Rosalins Complaint, metaphorically applied to Dame Nature at parliament held (in the high Star-chamber) by the Gods, for the preservation and increase of Earths beauteous Phoenix" (9). We cannot determine whether Chester had seen *The Mutabilitie Cantos* in manuscript (it was not published until 1609), but the link between Rosalind, the complaint form, Queen Elizabeth, and Dame Nature suggests such a possibility. All the more so since one part of the miscellany, as we have noted, narrates the story of Arthur (the hero of *The Faerie Queene* and the destined husband of Elizabeth/Gloriana), while another part, as Axton observes, is called "Britain monuments": "Nature identifies the ancient founders of noble civilizations by giving an account of 'Britain Monuments' reminiscent of the *Faerie Queene*, Book II canto 10" ("Miraculous Succession," 122). Axton also notes that "Nature calls [London] . . . Troynouant," the name Spenser had used in his national epic (2. 10. 46), and she is even more precise when suggesting that "A Spenserian contrast between kinds of love is taken up in song" when "Nature laments Cupid who beguiles men's senses, while Phoenix sings of perfect love which is pure beauty" (123) – presumably thinking of *Faerie Queene* 3. 3. 1.[12]

The Spenserian dynamic in *Love's Martyr* suggests how at home Spenser might be in Shakespeare's contribution to the volume. Yet in the long history of reception, England's New Poet occupies a rather paradoxical position:

---

[12] Buxton cites a 1595 poem by Chester that concludes with a Spenserian inscription: "Bould and to bould" ("Two Dead Birds," 47; see *Fairie Queene*, 3. 11. 54: *"Be bold . . . / Be not too bold"*).

he appears recurrently yet incidentally (e.g., Rollins, ed., *Variorum: Poems*, 570), although in 1903 Brandl fancied that Shakespeare's "feathered king," the eagle, represented Spenser (Rollins, ed., *Variorum: Poems*, 570). Occasionally, critics suggest something more promising – as when Knight observes that the phoenix's "flaming spirituality appears to cover the whole range of Spenser's four *Hymns* in honour of Beauty and Love, Earthly and Divine" (*Mutual Flame*, 153). Even though Knight adds that "the Phoenix would scarcely be at home within Spenser's *Epithalamion*" (153), William Matchett recalls Spenser's representation of the phoenix in the 1569 *Theatre for Worldlings* and its 1591 version in the *Complaints* volume ("*Phoenix and the Turtle*," 24). These comments are important, because they record a matter of literary history: during the last decade of Elizabeth's reign, Spenser was the supreme love poet within a nationalist setting.[13]

Finally, we might recall that in the last poem printed in his lifetime, the 1596 *Prothalamion*, the New Poet had consolidated his standing as England's poet of wedded love by championing the national heroism of Essex, who had just returned from the famed Cadiz expedition: "Great England's glory, and the Worlds wide wonder" (146). In this swan allegory about the poet's role in national destiny, Spenser presents Essex as the martial hero who can "free" the "country" from "forraine harmes: / And great Elisaes glorious name may ring / Through al the world . . . / Which some brave muse may sing / To ages following" (156–60). At the end of this "Spousall Verse" (title page), the martial Essex steps forward to preside over the marriage of the two Somerset swans, who have sailed down the Thames to Essex House to join with their husbands, "Against their Brydale day, which is not long" (179). It is hard to imagine that Shakespeare could not have had this memorable poem in mind five years later under very different national circumstances.[14] We may even wonder whether in "The Phoenix and Turtle" and *Love's Martyr* as a whole Shakespeare and company were not taking up Spenser's call, presenting themselves as the brave muses singing Essex's glory to ages following, precisely when the circumstances did change.

[13] Editors typically gloss "obey" in line 4 with *Faerie Queene*, 3. 11. 35 (Rollins, ed., *Variorum: Poems*, 324; Prince ed., *Poems*, 179, mistakenly citing 3. 2. 35). Bednarz suggests Spenser's Gardens of Adonis in *Faerie Queene*, 3. 6 as a model for Shakespeare's Neoplatonic representation of love (*Poets' War*, 199), while Burrow notes that Chester's *Love's Martyr* is "clearly indebted to Spenser and Samuel Daniel" (*Sonnets and Poems*, 84). Eriksen attributes the poem's "compositional technique" to Spenser ("Bruno," 211).

[14] Finnis and Martin ("Another turn") prepare us to see an unexplored connection between Spenser, Shakespeare, and Essex, since they link Shakespeare with the Lines through a report to Lord Burleigh in January 1593, in which Mistress Line attends Mass in the home of the earl of Worcester, father to the two brides Spenser celebrates in *Prothalamion*.

The Spenserian dynamic in "The Phoenix and Turtle," perhaps like that of *Love's Martyr*, pays homage to Spenser for his championing of Essex. Yet, in the New Poet's failure to predict great Eliza's inglorious execution of the world's wide wonder, we might simultaneously discover grounds for an eclipse of Spenser's national achievement. The precise strategy Shakespeare relies on turns out to be of some importance to the future of English literature.

"CO-SUPREMES": THE HISTORICAL ACHIEVEMENT

To understand the stakes of Shakespeare's politics of intertextual authorship in "The Phoenix and Turtle," we might recall how a distinguished line of commentators has rendered the extraordinary historical achievement of this tender little poem. As the interest of Emerson, Masefield, Richards, Knight, Empson, Wilbur, Duncan-Jones, and Everett alone testifies, "The Phoenix and Turtle" occupies a special place in the canon of English poetry. Everett articulates this place in terms at once eloquent and resonant: "The poem is in fact neither an event ('history') nor an idea ('philosophy') but something that begins with what has to be called a music, an extremely original sound heard nowhere else in the Renaissance. Once invented, it was, however, noted, remembered and imitated by a series of English poets, the last of them probably Tennyson, and all very different from each other except perhaps in the fineness of their ear" ("Golden Bough," 13–14). For 67 lines buried deeply in a potentially obscure volume, this is an extraordinary achievement.

Following up on Everett's contribution, Burrow brings us even closer to the present line of inquiry:

Shakespeare's poem is clearly pushing in the direction of an innovative and abstract poetic vocabulary . . . His poem feels as though it is coming from another world, and as though it grows from thinking, and thinking gravely, about sacrifice in love, and about where Elizabethan poetry might move next. But the difficulty of attaching his poem to particular circumstances may partly derive from the work which it is attempting to achieve: to keep the name of Shakespeare alive and to keep it associated with new forms. (Burrow, ed., *Sonnets and Poems*, 89–90)

For Burrow, as for Everett and others like Richards and Empson, "The Phoenix and Turtle" is astonishing because in such short metric space it crafts a distinctive historic place, not simply in the evolution of Shakespeare's "career," nor even in "Renaissance" literature, but in the long course of what Richards calls simply "English." In fewer than seventy verse lines, Shakespeare manages to create a "new form" – an original "music" – that preserves "the name of Shakespeare." "The Phoenix and Turtle" is historically priceless because it prints Shakespearean political authorship in an eternal register.

Along this line of distinction, one of the most recent statements comes from Frank Kermode: "The years 1599–1600 seem roughly the time at which Shakespeare, already the author of several masterpieces, moved up to a new level of achievement and difficulty. There was a turning point, I think, and I associate it with *Hamlet* and with the poem 'The Phoenix and Turtle,'" and it may have something to do with Shakespeare's move to the Globe Theatre (*Shakespeare's Language*, ix). This is Kermode's book-length thesis, and importantly for the present book, he locates Shakespeare's "turning point" in both a play and a poem, written at about the same time, one for the Globe, the other for a printed miscellany. In his brief analysis of the poem (69–71), Kermode finds a new "metaphysical" use of subjective language (70): "around 1600 a new inwardness, almost independent of dramatic necessity," emerges (71) – what he calls an "effort to represent intellection" (43; see Roe, ed., *Poems*, 52).

Recalling the historical context of Shakespeare's career, we might come to view the supreme "intellection" of this artifact as a decidedly sixteenth-century phenomenon, a playwright's poem, a printed lyric by the world's most famous man of the theatre. By doing so, we discern how the printing of Shakespeare's poem in *Love's Martyr* speaks directly to the material predicament of his professional career, long neglected in Shakespeare studies: Shakespeare is a famed theatrical man who pens some of the most astonishing poems in "any language." The historical context for viewing the literary dynamic in "The Phoenix and Turtle" lies in the Elizabethan authorial conjunction of printed poetry and staged theatre, together with the fact, uncannily predicted in the poem itself, that an authorized Spenserian (and Jonsonian) culture of printed poetry may be outstripped by an upstart (Shakespearean) culture of performed theatre.

THE PRINTING OF THE AUTHOR'S VOICE

Supporting evidence for this historical argument lies in the very structure of the poem itself, which commentators divide into three units, following markers within the printed text:

1. Stanzas 1–5 (lines 1–20) present an unidentified narrator who conspicuously avoids the lyric "I" but who uses the imperative voice to invoke a choir of birds assembling to lament the deaths of the phoenix and turtle.

2. Stanzas 6–13 (lines 21–52) then modulate the narrator's imperative voice into the lamenting voice of the avian choir itself, actually recording its funeral anthem.

3. Finally, stanzas 14–18 (lines 53–67) stage a theatrical "Threnos" sung by one of the personified abstractions from the anthem, "Reason" (47), who uses new emotional authority to call purified members of the public to mourn before the birds' funeral urn.

The poem's careful formal devices clearly demarcate this three-unit division: while units one and two share a four-line stanza in the unusual meter of "a seven-syllable line with four evenly-spaced accents" (Matchett, "*Phoenix and the Turtle*," 34) or what Everett terms "broken trochaics" ("Golden Bough," 14), rhyming *abba*, the stanzas divide at line 21 (the beginning of stanza 6) with the formal announcement: "Here the anthem doth commence." Even more clearly, unit three is set off from the preceding two units through three formal features: the inset title of "THRENOS"; the replacement of the four-line stanza with a three-line stanza; and the change of the rhyme scheme from *abba* to the tercets, *aaa*.[15] Perhaps the real mystery no longer lies in the identities of the avian lovers but rather in the strange elegiac voice itself, which modulates through the poem's three units.

Let us look at the elegiac voice from each unit in turn. The enigma of "The Phoenix and Turtle" begins with its opening word, line, and stanza:

> Let the bird of loudest lay,
> On the sole Arabian tree,
> Herald sad and trumpet be,
> To whose sound chaste wings obey.
> ("The Phoenix and Turtle," 1–4)

The first word, "Let," functions ambiguously, meaning not merely *allow* but also *suppose* (Axton, "Miraculous Succession," 126): an unidentified narrator tells an unidentified auditor to allow the bird of loudest lay to be the herald and trumpet; and (or) a narrator tells the auditor(s) to suppose that this bird performs such a role. The unnamed narrator or poet quietly orchestrates the avian congregation, functioning as its master of revels. If the narrator's command is double-voiced, the auditor is similarly doubled, being either (or both) the community of birds within the fiction and (or) the reader of the printed poem. The effect of such a compound operation

---

[15] Matchett offers the most persuasive formulation about the enigmatic structure: "we have three approaches to the death of the Phoenix and the Turtle, that of the poet . . . that of the 'chaste wings' [line 4] . . . and that of Reason . . . The poet's dividing of the symbolic birds leads into the anthem in which Reason, said to be undone, actually asserts itself to present its own view of the event" ("*Phoenix and the Turtle*," 53; see 33–36). See also Wilbur and Harbage, eds., *Narrative Poems*, 20–21.

is not merely to open language and meaning up, but more emphatically to draw attention to language itself, to the complex way the poetic voice speaks, and even to the complexity of its reception. This is our first hint that voice, agency, authorship, and the afterlife of the poet are to be the virtual subjects of this poem.

Today, we still do not know the identity of the loud-singing bird on whose behalf the initial complexity in part operates – either its species or its relation to the twinned principals of the poem's (modern) title. Until recently, commentators swung between two major arguments. First, the "bird of loudest lay" is a species other than the phoenix and turtle, with Grosart proposing the nightingale and others the crane and cock (Bates, "Phoenix and Turtle"; Prince, ed., *Poems*, 173; Roe, ed., *Poems*, 232; Burrow, ed., *Sonnets and Poems*, 373); or the "bird of loudest lay" is "*the phoenix itself*" (Knight, *Mutual Flame*, 202–03; his emphasis) – a theory that Richards rather likes (*Poetries*, 52–53), as do many others. Knight quotes "the old English poem based on Lactantius": "singing exultant," the phoenix produces a "trancing song," "Warbling melodies wondrous sweet, / . . . More winsome far / Than any music that men may make; / And sweeter than any earthly strain" (203). Critics have also long cited *The Tempest*, which presents "Arabia" as the site of "one tree, the Phoenix' throne" (3. 3. 22–23). More recently, however, commentators emphasize the indecipherability of the loud bird: "The fact that the bird is not named here . . . is significant: it leaves readers uncertain whether a second Phoenix has sprung from the death of the Phoenix and the Turtle . . . in order to act as herald in its own obsequies" (Burrow, ed., *Sonnets and Poems*, 373; see Bradbrook, "'Phoenix'"). Not merely the authorial voice and its auditor but the initial subject evades easy intelligibility. Even the bird's gender escapes grasp, being neither clearly male nor clearly female. In the play of the verse, the emphatic word "be," the verb in the syntactical construction delayed until the very end of line 3, quite literally leads to ontology, the "mystery of being" that many like Richards have found themselves brooding over; it also creates an uncanny point of touch with that play being performed at the Globe that this author was also composing: "Let . . . be" (cf. *Hamlet*, 5. 2. 224).[16]

Paradoxically, the ontologically sounding bird is of singular (even solitary) identity, power, and authority: it sings the "loudest" songs; it occupies the exalted position atop "the sole Arabian tree"; and it is the herald and trumpeter for the congregation of birds. It is, then, their leader, for it possesses the unique attracting quality of chaste sexuality: the "chaste wings" of the other birds "obey" its chaste "sound." The concept of obedience is

---

[16] See Bloom, *Shakespeare*, on Hamlet's "let be" as the summation of the Prince's philosophy (422).

important in Shakespeare; for instance, it shows up in the final speech of *King Lear*, when (in the *Riverside* version) Edgar says, "The weight of this sad time we must obey" (5. 3. 324), as if the whole concept of Jacobean obedience were being re-routed, and right where "The Phoenix and Turtle" is taking us: to the heavy "weight" and "sad time" of tragedy itself. In the poem, the word "obey" certainly suggests allegiance, and (in context) communal bondage, but, as in *Lear*, obedience is being defined in terms of what Patricia Fumerton (*Cultural Aesthetics*) calls "cultural aesthetics," as "sound" confirms. Whatever species the loud-singing bird might be, its authority lies in its song, as two other words emphasize: "lay" and "trumpet." Above all, the bird of loudest lay is a figure of authoritative song, chaste and august, able to bond the community to faith through voice itself.

Yet we can be even more specific. The bird of loudest lay has come to "the Phoenix's tree, at which the ceremony is presumably to take place" (Matchett, "*Phoenix and the Turtle*," 37). In other words, the loud-singing bird has taken up residence "On the sole Arabian tree" in order to become its heir and successor. Furthermore, not merely is the bird's trumpet the instrument of epic poetry (a point neglected in the commentary), but the sound of its chastity evokes amorous poetry, and the two together suggest the genre of "epic romance" (Burrow, *Epic Romance*, 1–10). Not surprisingly, Everett has drawn attention to "the antique sounding dialect of his first line" and characterized the "Invocation" here as being "in a Virgilian fashion" ("Golden Bough," 14). It is not a long step to suggest that in "The Phoenix and Turtle" Shakespeare's poetic voice summons a Spenserian authorial figure with an epicist-sounding role for the community.

That Shakespeare in this unit draws on the literary convention of the bird parliament should help us see that he strains to represent a poetic voice – someone else's poetic voice. As recent critics would remind us, here we need to historicize. Whereas some critics may wish to identify the voice as Chaucerian, harkening back to *The Parlement of Foules*, we might recall that in the 1596 *Faerie Queene* Spenser had trumpeted his career-long appropriation of the Chaucerian epic voice, as he communicates directly to the Old Poet himself:

> through infusion sweete
> Of thine owne spirit, which doth in me survive,
> I follow here the footing of thy feete,
> That with thy meaning so I may the rather meete.
> (4. 2. 34)[17]

---

[17] See Cheney, "Spenser's Completion" and "'Novells,'" including on Spenser's appropriation of Chaucer as an epic poet.

Relying on an English (and rather gentle) version of the typology of inter-textuality, Shakespeare may imitate Chaucer but he does so almost certainly to represent the art of Spenser.

Shakespeare's foregrounding of the author's voice in stanza 1 confirms what many have suspected about the remaining four stanzas of this first unit: Shakespeare draws on the avian trope to represent a community of poets. Just as critics have long struggled to identify the phoenix and turtle, so the birds in the choir. Among the charming treasures of the *Variorum: Poems*, Rollins particularly delights in lampooning Brandl, who believed the poem a lament on the death of Marlowe, with the eagle representing Spenser, the crow Nashe, the owl Harvey, and the swan Shakespeare (571). Mercifully, such days have (largely) passed us by. And yet: the return to historicism does prompt us to historicize birds other than the phoenix and turtle. The most obvious candidates would seem to be the modern writers whom Chester assembled in *Love's Martyr*: Jonson, Chapman, Marston, and Ignoto (Eriksen, "Bruno," 210). In a volume that brings famous authors to write poems on the deaths of the "phoenix" and "turtle," we discover a poem that appears to fictionalize this very event. Some such design may be intended, but the fact remains: in four hundred years, no one has succeeded in identifying any of the birds with the least degree of certainty, and most have happily given up trying.[18] We need try no more, beyond suggesting an intriguing, generalized Shakespearean literary history for late-Elizabethan England. For the purpose of the present argument, such a history locates leadership in the national authority of Spenser, and leaves (most of) the rest to silence.

In stanza 2, the narrator commands the "shriking harbinger," once more not identified but usually thought to be the screech-owl, to "come . . . not near" the "troop" of birds, because it sings cacophonously, functions devilishly as "Foul precurrer of the fiend," and serves as a false prophet or "Augur of the fever's end": death itself (5–8). By banishing the shrieking harbinger while commanding the bird of loudest song to stay, the narra-tor establishes an ethical dialectic of good and evil song, of chastity and its violation, lucidly underwritten by Christian authority. Such a dialectic recalls that from *The Rape of Lucrece*, and thereby is evocative of the oppo-sition of aesthetics we found there (chapter 4): between a Spenserian and a Marlovian aesthetics, with the rehearsal of death here perhaps suggesting the genre of tragedy and the procurement of the fiend possibly conjuring up *Doctor Faustus*. If so, rather than being a lament on the death of Marlowe,

---

[18] For other identifications, see Knight; Matchett 18, 105–35; Asquith; Finnis and Martin.

"The Phoenix and Turtle" intimates a Spenserian exorcising of Marlowe's spirit.[19]

In stanzas 3, 4, and 5, what we notice is a kind of double identification operating in the representations of the remaining birds, in which each species performs both a literary and a nonliterary role. Thus, in stanza 3, the narrator extends the ethical dialectic of the chaste Spenserian aesthetics to the political sphere of justice. On the one hand, Shakespeare's representation looks to be a rather perfect model for "Elizabeth's monarchical republic" (Collinson, "Monarchical Republic"), at once "interdict[ing]" all fowls from the "session" who are "of tyrant wing" and inviting the eagle, "feath'red king," because it can use its high office to "Keep the obsequy . . . strict" (9–12). On the other, Spenser himself had had something to say about the virtue of justice, making it the topic of Book 5 of his national epic. At issue here, then, is not simply the politics of justice but the aesthetics of justice.

Accordingly, in stanza 4 the narrator calls for the true prophet, "the death-divining swan," to preside as "the priest in surplice white," because he is skilled in "defunctive music" or funereal song – and besides, without this bird dressed in the habit of Elizabeth's moderate Protestant ministers (Burrow, ed., *Sonnets and Poems*, 74), the "requiem" would "lack his right" – both Christian truth and Christian rite. Yet the nature of the rite has raised eyebrows, because of the exquisite ecclesiastical contradiction: this swan suited in Protestant attire sings a Catholic mass for the dead, the word "requiem" being "the first word of the Introit in the Mass for the Dead, 'Requiem aeternam donna eis, Domine'" (Burrow, ed., *Sonnets and Poems*, 374; see also H. N. Davies, "Phoenix and Turtle"). Among critics, John Klause has shown how "Shakespeare follows Skelton [*Phyllyp Sparowe*] in at least alluding, if very discreetly, to parts of this [Roman] liturgy" ("Phoenix and Turtle," 216). Klause sees Shakespeare later in the poem moving beyond "hint" to an "explicit resort to Roman theology" in the "idealization of married celibacy," and he gets at the recusant principle here: "Prayer for the dead . . . is a Catholic practice, which the English church . . . removed from the Book of Common Prayer in 1552 and, in the Elizabethan Homily 'On Prayer,' officially condemned" (217–18).[20] Like *Hamlet*, the poem appears to register the trauma caused by the Protestant erasure of purgatory and the Catholic prayer for the dead, and to seek recompense, not merely in

---

[19] In finding Bruno in the poem, Eriksen cites Marlowe's reference to the Italian scholar in *Doctor Faustus* ("Bruno," 210).

[20] Klause does not refer to the work on this topic by Neill, *Issues*, Low, "*Hamlet*," and Greenblatt, *Purgatory*, all of whom neglect "The Phoenix and Turtle" but attend to that play being rehearsed over at the Globe.

the genre of tragedy (Neill, *Issues*), but also in the art of elegiac poetry. Shakespeare uses the word "requiem" only one other time in all his works, during the scene of Ophelia's burial (5. 1. 237), suggesting a precise linguistic bond between the funeral poem and the stage tragedy (McCoy, "Love's Martyrs," 194). Not surprisingly, there is aesthetic import here: Shakespeare makes "the Swan figure the poet's own *troth*; Apollo's bird, unlike the shrieking harbinger, prophesies at death 'prosperity and perfect ease'. The swan-poet *divines* death, perceives and foretells it, but his immortal song also makes death itself divine, revealing it as the cause of new life, so he is essential to the miracle" (Axton, "Miraculous Succession," 128). While we might see Shakespeare including a cameo of himself in the Spenserian choir of birds, as Jordan long ago thought (Rollins, ed., *Variorum: Poems*, 568), we may alternatively find simply a professional representation that reflects a theology consistent with the one thought to be voiced by the author himself (Eriksen, "Bruno," 210).

Finally, in stanza 5, the "treble-dated crow" is singled out to join the "mourners," evidently because of two innate qualities: it lives nine times as long as humans do (says Pliny of Hesiod in *The History of the World*, 1. 180; Burrow, ed., *Sonnets and Poems*, 373); and it procreates through the chaste touch of its mate's bill (Pliny, *History*, 1. 276; Burrow, ed., *Sonnets and Poems*, 373). As such, the crow is a fit emblem of an eternizing sexuality. Among the choir, the crow is distinctive for its role as an erotic maker: "thy sable gender mak'st."

Simply in terms of the narrative, then, in stanzas 1–5 the poet selects the avian participants for a funeral service, banishing two kinds of birds (the "shrieking harbinger" and the "tyrant wing"), and invites four birds to join the troop: the bird of loudest lay, who functions as herald; the eagle, who presides as judge; the swan, who serves as priest; and the crow, who marches as chief mourner. As readers often note, the discourse is at once enigmatic and precise, opaque and technical. It is also comprehensive, drawing in the nationalist domains of art ("lay"), government ("session"), religion ("requiem"), and community ("'Mong'st our mourners"). As a troop, the birds are associated with artistic sound, strict law, pure religion, and chaste duty; what they share is a faith in song to combat time, death, and corruption. Altogether, Shakespeare's parliament of fowls confronts death with a wondrous power: an enchastened song of immortality.[21] The

---

[21] Matchett notes that "Shakespeare's poem emphasiz[es] . . . the voices of the birds" (*"Phoenix and the Turtle,"* 190). Critics who emphasize "immortality" include Richards, *Poetries*, 54; Knight, *Mutual Flame*, 204; Wilbur and Harbage, eds. *Narrative Poems*, 20–21; Kermode, *Shakespeare's Language*, 69–71.

immortalizing function is clear in the bird of loudest lay, but also in the eagle, who keeps the "obsequy" strict; the swan, who sings its "death-divining" song before it dies; and the crow, who is "treble-dated" and makes offspring with its "breath."

The immortalizing function makes best sense if we identify it as a Shakespearean photograph of a Spenserian-orchestrated poetics. While Spenser had no monopoly on the funeral elegy, he was the first (and most famous) Elizabethan poet to adopt the form for a nationalist role, advertised initially in the Song of Dido in *November* and subsequently fulfilled through a series of career elegies, including on Sidney (*Ruines of Time, Astrophel*), the earl of Leceister (*Virgils Gnat*), and Douglas Howard (*Daphnaida*) (Cheney, "Dido"). In "The Phoenix and Turtle," Shakespeare appears to recognize Spenser for nationalizing the function of the elegiac form. In the poem's first unit, we read the voice of the Shakespearean poet calling on the Spenserian bird of loudest lay to assemble the "chaste wings" of the immortalizing choir for the funeral elegy honoring the phoenix and turtle.

In unit two (stanzas 7–13, lines 25–52), Shakespeare records the anthem that the assembled birds sing, marked in the text by the unit's opening line, which announces the commencement of the anthem. In other words, this unit records the actual contents of the avian song, opening the aesthetics up to "Adversity's sweet milk, philosophy" (*Romeo and Juliet*, 3. 3. 55). As commentary variously reveals, Shakespeare gathers in the philosophical terminology from scholasticism, Neoplatonism, and Catholicism to introduce the phoenix and turtle as figures of quintessential love:

> Here the anthem doth commence:
> Love and Constancy is dead,
> Phoenix and the Turtle fled
> In a mutual flame from hence.
>
> So they loved as love in twain
> Had the essence but in one,
> Two distincts, division none.
> ("Phoenix and Turtle," 21–27)

The complexities of Shakespeare's paradoxes have been widely examined, so we need not pursue them in detail. Suffice it to say that the poet succeeds in representing "a wonder" (32): the absolute miracle of two "distinct" figures having the "essence but in one." While most often attention is deflected to the "'ecstasy' poems" (Everett, "Golden Bough," 14) – Sidney's "Eighth Song," Donne's "The Ecstasy," and Lord Herbert of Cherbury's "An Ode upon a question moved, Whether Love should continue for ever?" – we might recall that among Elizabethans, Spenser had most sustained the hermaphroditic wonder of two in one.[22]

What has been less attended to than we might think is the theatrical dimension entering toward the end of the second unit. In stanza 11, the figure of "Reason" suddenly emerges as a character within the avian anthem; this figure has both a subjectivity and a voice, and he emerges with a complex art form – all controlled by the narrator's (or is it the avian choir's) witty self-reflexivity:

> Reason, in itself confounded,
> Saw division grow together,
> To themselves yet either neither,
> Simple were so well compounded:
>
> That it cried, "How true a twain
> Seemeth this concordant one!
> Love hath reason, Reason none,
> If what parts, can so remain."
>
> Whereupon it made this threne
> To the Phoenix and the Dove,
> Co-supremes and stars of love,
> As chorus to their tragic scene.
> ("Phoenix and Turtle," 41–52)

This representation is "the outstanding event of the poem" (Matchett, "*Phoenix and the Turtle*," 44). The character Reason undergoes an epiphany, moving beyond confusion to clarity when he "Saw division grow together." So affected is Reason that he articulates what he sees, announcing his loss of reason even as he animates a new form of reason, inspired by the miraculous unity of "distinct" erotic opposites. Here Reason functions to bring a tragic "balance" to the choir of birds' anthem of affirmation by rejecting "married chastity" or "the very idea of Platonic love" (Matchett, "*Phoenix and the Turtle*," 196, 200). As Matchett puts it, "Shakespeare insists upon reason in a time of violent emotional commitments," and his "discovery of the voice of Reason" is "for man the greatest triumph" (202). But Reason does not simply cry out in passion and triumph; he moves beyond autarchic to artistic expression, and he does so through a historic transposition of literary forms.

---

[22] Noted by Eriksen, "Bruno," 200. On Platonic elements, see Ellrodt, "Anatomy," who discerns Shakespeare's original Platonism (104). Hardie, *Ovid's Poetics*, reminds us of the Ovidian origin of Shakespeare's two in one here (25–26).

Critics have surprisingly passed over this historic moment, as if the working dramatist's turn to theatre within a lyric poem were a natural event.[23] The combined discourse of poetry and theatre is here at its most *formalized*. While the earlier words "lay" and "anthem" jostle now with "chorus" and "tragic," the last stanza represents a formalized conjunctive relation in the emphatic rhyme of "threne" and "scene." Shakespeare's meditation on a whole series of conjunctions, or "Single nature's double name" (39) – phoenix and turtle, love and constancy, two and one, division and unity, love and reason – comes around to voicing the very conjunction organizing the author's professional career. What he says of the other conjunctions thus provides a "chorus" on his own literary predicament as an Elizabethan author trying to combine two careers in one: *mutual flame . . . two distincts, division none . . . neither two nor one was called . . . division grow together . . . simple were so well compounded.* "The Phoenix and Turtle" may not be a formal meditation on the compound of poetry and theatre, but it nonetheless functions as Shakespeare's most precise and sustained grammar for such a meditation.

The word *scene* speaks for itself as an arch-term for the place of the stage (see *Henry V*, Prologue, 3–4). By contrast, the word *threne* is unusual in English and thus requires special comment. According to the *Oxford English Dictionary*, it is a transliteration of the Greek word for "funeral lament": "A song of lamentation; a dirge, threnody," with the first recorded usage in 1432–40, the second in 1593 (by Southwell), and the third in "The Phoenix and Turtle." As Malone long ago indicated, the word also appeared in Kendall's 1577 *Flowers of Epigrammes*, nestled with other poetical forms: "Of Verses, Threnes and Epitaphes" (Rollins, ed., *Variorum: Poems*, 330). In this way, the word "threne" evokes *song* or *lyric poetry*. Yet as a Greek word for funeral song, "threne" also acquires theatrical resonance, since it refers to the threnody of the Chorus in Greek tragedy. Shakespeare identifies the third unit of his poem, called a "THRENOS," as a "threne," and thus he presents this unit *as a play*. He makes the point explicit by saying that the threne functions "As chorus to their tragic scene"; a song is a chorus to a tragedy. Yet there is an actual representation of (Greek) tragedy in line 51: "Co-supremes and stars of love." As in the Prologue to *Romeo and Juliet*, with its references to "star-cross'd lovers" and "fatal loins" (5–6), here the "stars" suggest fate: the "stars of love" for "the Phoenix and the Dove"

---

[23] Typical is Ellrodt, "Anatomy," 107–08. More recently, see Burrow, ed., *Sonnets and Poems*, 88. The critic who most anticipates my argument is Bates, who confines his version to a final paragraph ("Phoenix," 30).

have been "fatal," locking them into a tragic universe that determines their annihilation.

The conjunction of poetry and theatre, "threne" and "scene," forms the very point of transition from unit two to unit three. The word *chorus* in line 52 is a superb Shakespearean pun, and its effect is to slow the verse down, right where it should, in the transitional line between the two units. According to the *OED*, the pertinent definition of *chorus* reads: "In English drama, imitated or adapted from the chorus of Attic tragedy . . . by Shakespeare and other Elizabethan dramatists reduced to a single personage, who speaks the prologue, and explains or comments upon the course of events" (def. 1. c). As such, the word *chorus* in "The Phoenix and Turtle" could have at least two meanings, and the point is that they operate simultaneously: metaphorically, the song *comes before* or *comments* upon the tragedy; but literally, the song precedes or glosses the tragedy. In all cases of meaning, what we see is the absolute interpenetration of poetry with theatre.

Shakespeare presents the verse "THRENOS" precisely as a dramatic form. He thus accomplishes the rather difficult maneuver of *presenting a play within a poem*; this constitutes a photographic negative of his more familiar maneuver, of presenting a poem within a play, as in *Love's Labor's Lost*, or in Hamlet's poem to Ophelia (2. 2. 116–19). Recalling that Shakespeare probably wrote his plays for the page as well as for the stage (Erne, *Literary Dramatist*), we might say that in this lyric poem the author imprints a model of theatrical authorship itself.

Two independent sets of evidence measure the uniqueness of what Shakespeare is attempting here. The first comes by comparing his poem with the other three "'ecstasy' poems," Sidney's "Eighth Song," Donne's "The Ecstasy," and Lord Herbert's "An Ode." While all four poems share a philosophy of erotic essence, and gesture to their status as poems, only Shakespeare's relies on formal theatrical discourse. Alone, "The Phoenix and Turtle" constructs a self-conscious "artefact" (Everett, "Golden Bough," 14) that uses the medium of print, with careful markers in the text, to transact a transposition from poem to play, funeral elegy to stage tragedy. The second set of evidence is closer to Shakespeare's martyred hand: none of the other modern writers in *Love's Martyr* – even those known to be fellow poet-playwrights, Jonson, Chapman, and Marston – attempt to formalize a compound generic representation expressed by their colleague.[24]

---

[24] Occasionally, theatrical terms do infiltrate: Ignoto speaks of "the foule-maskt Ladie, Night" ("The first," 2); Marston, of "Hard favor'd Feminines so scant of faire, / That Maskes so choicely" ("To Perfection," 6–7); Jonson, of "the stale Prologue to some painted Maske" of "the Ladies of the Thespian Lake" ("Praeludium," 20, 25).

Shakespeare is often understood to be the only one of the modern writers who veers from Chester's memorial program, but we may now understand another way in which he crosses into new territory. In "The Phoenix and Turtle," he pens his clearest "signature" for his status as an early modern author of poems and plays: his professional role as national poet-playwright.

Within the fiction of the poem, the figure who performs this role is "Reason," who thus joins a whole host of characters in the Shakespeare canon as a type of poet-playwright. It is this figure who transposes the two forms; he makes his threne as a chorus to the tragic scene. Yet Reason differs from all other characterizations of the poet-playwright; as his name intimates, here we find the subjective spring for the fusion of poetry and theatre itself. The representation acquires a distinctly Ovidian form, "the flexible self" (Bate, *Ovid*, 3), when Shakespeare catches the poet-playwright Reason performing a miraculous metamorphosis, from a perplexed rationality to a super-rationality in apprehension of a mystery.

In the verse "Threnos," we see the mysterious contents of Reason's tragedy:

> Beauty, Truth, and Rarity,
> Grace in all simplicity,
> Here enclos'd, in cinders lie.
>
> Death is now the Phoenix' nest,
> And the Turtle's loyal breast
> To eternity doth rest.
> ("Phoenix and Turtle," 53–58)

While "Beauty, Truth, and Rarity" fix the (Platonic) absolutes, "Grace" and "eternity" Christianize them.[25] "To eternity doth rest" is nearly as resonant as Hamlet's "the rest is silence" (5. 2. 358): does it mean that the breast of the turtle will rest until eternity, or is it that the turtle's breast will rest eternally in death? In both cases, the message of the Gospel is not certified: in the first possibility, the turtle's destiny is stretched out only *as far as* – "to" – eternity, while in the second the turtle enacts a Christian tragedy in which the promise of resurrection goes down un-phoenix-like in flames.

As commentators observe, the next two stanzas – when the phoenix and turtle fail to leave behind a "posterity" because of "married chastity" (59–61) – leave Reason standing on the threshold of the void, only to look down and see what death is doing: "Truth and Beauty buried be" (63). Reason perceives "death as annihilation" (R. Watson, *The Rest is Silence*),

---

[25] Cf. Matchett, *"Phoenix and the Turtle,"* 50. The *OED* reveals that "eternize" has Christian origins, citing the 1610 translation of Augustine's *City of God* (def. 1).

represented by the phoenix's once eternal "nest," now occupied by the dramatic figure of Death. Is this the promised end?

The final stanza suggests not:

> To this urn let those repair
> That are either true or fair;
> For these dead birds sigh a prayer.
>
> ("The Phoenix and Turtle," 65–67)

The poem does not end with the phoenix and turtle as simply "dead birds"; an audience, "those" who are "either true or fair," are invited to "repair" to the couple's "urn" to "sigh a prayer." There is loss ("dead"), and weariness ("sigh"), as well as the sad diminishment of Platonic forms ("either" truth *or* beauty is "buried"). Yet a community of mourners gathers around the well-wrought urn containing the avian ashes to deliver an affirmative response, as the pun on the emphatically placed word "repair" suggests – a word that means *move hither* but also *mend*. In the words of Everett, "the turtle's breast rests to eternity with an absoluteness that makes dying the most active experience of a life-time, a wordless reversal of that calming with which the poem begins" ("Golden Bough," 15). Knight and Richards agree: what Shakespeare immortalizes is not the Christian soul ascending to Spenser's New Jerusalem but the body's eternizing performance of death as annihilation. This versified performance becomes the most concentrated miracle and the poem's greatest achievement. Thus the final word is not "sigh" but "prayer," the anguished groan sounding the very utterance of faith. Neither two nor one was called.

RELICS AND THE URN

In "The Phoenix and Turtle," the elegiac voice modulates through the three units in a way that is at once strange and admirable:

1. from the singular lyric voice of the poet-narrator, who speaks outside the fiction to call the fiction to life (and death);
2. to the collaborative voice of the avian choir within the fiction, which values the philosophical mystery of the birds' (Neoplatonic) conjunction and mourns the passing of their "mutual flame";
3. to the loving voice of Reason, a character within the anthem who presents the "Threnos" as a Greek tragedy because the turtle and dove have chosen "married chastity" over offspring.

Yet, just as the authorial voice modulates from singular lyric author to collaborative choir to the choral voice of tragedy, so does the author's form modulate: from a lyric poem by a single author, to an inset funeral anthem sung by a collaborative troop, to a single chorus voiced within a tragic play.[26] In terms of the preceding analysis, Shakespeare's positioning of the Spenserian art and its heritage in the first two units is particularly noteworthy: the Ovidian poet-playwright pays his debt to the Virgilian New Poet but records the historic transition from an age of Spenser to a new age of (Shakespearean) theatre. If there is a phoenix who arises from the ashes in this poem, it is Shakespearean tragic art itself.

Shakespeare imprints the deaths of "this Turtle and his queen" (31) not by identifying his authorial voice but by *displacing* it. Yet this displacement does not evade responsibility for authorship but formally draws attention to it, *arguably erecting one the most self-conscious representations of authorship extant*. Significant to the current conversation in Shakespeare studies, the author's representation is not strictly about his plays – their "text and performance" – but rather about the relation those plays have to his poems, their staging and their printing. In a way that appears to be unique in the literary tradition, "The Phoenix and Turtle" represents the material marking of the boundary between lyric and tragedy, the lyric anthem supremely printing the tragic voice of the stage.[27]

Although "The Phoenix and Turtle" appears to voice the turmoil of a nationally significant political crisis, it manages to leave a priceless record of the historical moment within which the author's professional voice speaks. The voice the poem identifies is not just that of the lyric poet writing the poem but more precisely a lyric voice modulating into the deep cognitive reach of tragedy. Within the tragic "Threnos," the poet-playwright creates what Richard C. McCoy calls "relics" ("Love's Martyrs," 203). Following up on the work of Walter Pater (among others), McCoy seeks to rectify an omission in Shakespeare studies during the past twenty years or so: the downplaying of the affections (203–04). He acknowledges that "There is finally no 'sure and certain hope of the resurrection' for love's martyrs in Shakespeare," but finds that "The Phoenix and Turtle," like the Sonnets, does produce "poetic renderings" that "remain sacred objects of a sort,

---

[26] Krier finds a three-step movement in Chaucer's *Parlement*, with each step figuring a "different literary region": (1) the "Latin philosophical realm"; (2) "late-medieval, vernacular, courtly love poetry"; and (3) lyric song (112–13). In *Love's Labor's Lost*, Shakespeare represents especially the move from comedy to lyric: "Shakespeare contemplates his place as dramatist in *poetic* genre history: he opens a space which the catalogues demarcate as specifically literary" (Krier, *Birth Passages*, 143; her emphasis).

[27] Cf. Kastan, *Book*: "Shakespeare has become virtually the iconic name for authorship itself, but he wrote in circumstances in which his individual achievement was inevitably dispersed into – if not compromised by – the collaborations necessary for both play and book production" (16). Kastan does not say that what gets into print is a single voice, however collaboratively produced; it is this printed voice that we witness in "The Phoenix and Turtle."

not sacraments but relics" (203). Such relics are powerful not because they save the reader's soul but because they have the "capacity . . . to stimulate emotion," and such an affective subjectivity has the miraculous power to create what Pater called a "quickened sense of life" (quoted in McCoy, "Love's Martyrs," 204). These relics – the ashes of the phoenix's "nest," the "cinders" of the two dead birds, and especially their funeral "urn" – are not, then, sacraments of Christian redemption typologically promising a spiritual afterlife so much as pagan relics grounding "eternity" in the affective authority of human inwardness. For many readers today, this inwardness is the very signature of Shakespearean authorship. Shakespeare's poems and plays are his last relics of immortality.

In the end, "The Phoenix and Turtle" appears to leave readers with a mind-bending marvel, perhaps worthy of the author's affectively suited figure of Reason: the playwright's tragic performance is movingly immortalized by the print of the elegiac poet's voice.

PART FOUR

1609: imprinting the question of authorship

Play scene: "Measure for Measure" to "Coriolanus"

The year 1609 saw the first printing of two radically different books authored by William Shakespeare: *Shake-speares Sonnets* (containing the Sonnets and *A Lover's Complaint*) and *Troilus and Cressida*. This printing conjunction late in the author's career recalls the very first one, back in 1594, when both *The Rape of Lucrece* and *Titus Andronicus* appeared. Yet the quarto of *Troilus and Cressida* is prefaced with a *Dedicatory Epistle* notable for its marketing link with Shakespeare's first minor epic – and first publishing venture – printed in 1593:

So much and such favored salt of witte is in his Commedies, that they seem (for their height of pleasure) to be borne in that sea that brought forth Venus. Amongst all there is none more witty then this.[1]

We do not know the author of this *Epistle*, but Katherine Duncan-Jones speculates that it could be "a collaboration between Shakespeare and the publishers – or possibly even an insertion written by Shakespeare himself, designed to sell the work by drawing attention to its upmarket status" (*Ungentle*, 219). Be that as it may, the author does not simply link Shakespeare's "Commedies" with his minor epic, his "Stage" plays with his first published poem; he creates a "witty" and self-conscious etiological myth for their shared genesis: all spring from the salty sea of eros giving birth to the great goddess herself (a scene represented, for instance, in the famous painting of Venus on a half-shell by Botticelli).

No doubt the epistolary author was riding the printing wave of *Venus*, which had gone through perhaps eight editions by 1609, the most recent in 1607 and 1608, and would be printed again the year following (see Figure 3 above). The comedies and the minor epic of "William Shakespeare" share

---

[1] Reprinted in *Norton*, 1826: "This prefatory epistle . . . was added to the second state of the 1609 quarto of *Troilus and Cressida* (Qb). It is not found in the first state (Qa) or in the first folio (F)" (1826).

a distinct aesthetics governed by the fusion of passion and reason, the "height of pleasure" and the "edge of witte"; this fusion can metamorphose the viewer or reader into a higher state of being: "all such dull and heavy-witted worldlings, as were never capable of the witte of a Commedie, comming by report of them to his representations, have found that witte there, that they never found in them-selves, and have parted better wittied then they came" (reprinted in *Norton*, 1826). Consequently, we may not wish to underestimate the way in which the printing of Shakespeare's poems and plays became implicated in each other during his lifetime.

Duncan-Jones helps us extend this process by emphasizing that the "parallels between *Troilus* and *Sonnets* run wider still": both were printed by George Eld; they are "the product of revision"; and they contain epistles that "invite . . . comparison." Moreover, play and poem alike offer "a defamiliarizing re-fashioning" of literary tradition (the play, of Chaucer; the sonnet sequence, of Petrarch); and both are "deeply rooted in an awareness of death, and of the desperate struggle to make one's voice heard before disease destroys both pen and phallus" (*Ungentle*, 219–22). We could extend the thematic parallels to *A Lover's Complaint*, a poem also about a literary tradition (the complaint) and the struggle over voice, although now it is pure sex itself – the loss of virginity – that destroys the "concave womb" (1). Altogether, the links between the 1609 playtext and poems extending from 1593 to 1609 open up an intriguing line of investigation.[2]

For the third phase of Shakespeare's career (1602–1609), the *Oxford Shakespeare* identifies ten plays, in the following order:

Sir Thomas More
Measure for Measure
The Tragedy of Othello, The Moor of Venice
All's Well That Ends Well
The Life of Timon of Athens
King Lear
The Tragedy of Macbeth
The Tragedy of Antony and Cleopatra
Pericles, Prince of Tyre
The Tragedy of Coriolanus.

As before, the actual chronology is unknown, but we can still recognize the kinds of drama that characterize Shakespearean art in this phase. He continues his extraordinary combination of dramatic form, penning

---

[2] See Duncan-Jones: "Shakespeare . . . by the plague year 1609 was undoubtedly a celebrated and authoritative dramatist and poet" ("Called," 10).

(or co-penning) three comedies, one history, and six tragedies. The generic boundaries are as unstable as they were. This is especially the case with *Pericles*, traditionally labeled a "romance"; it would be convenient to place this textually troubling "play from hell" (*Norton*, 2709) in the final phase, with the other "romances," but such is the generic untidiness of Shakespeare's practice that we need to subscribe to it.[3]

It will come as no surprise that the plays in this phase continue to exhibit Shakespeare's career-long combination of poetry and theatre. Among the ten plays, *Measure for Measure*, *Othello*, *All's Well*, *King Lear*, and *Coriolanus* especially require detailed examination, while the others contain important representations – such as Cleopatra's speech on the "scald rimers" and "quick comedians" discussed in chapter 1. Several of Shakespeare's greatest plays occur in this phase (*Lear*, *Macbeth*, *Othello*, *Antony and Cleopatra*), and, combined with some of the more textually compromised (*More*, *Timon*, *Pericles*), it is even more difficult to survey the professional project briefly. Nonetheless, if we try, we find a number of important characters who put on plays and write poems or sing songs or otherwise engage in a discourse of poetry and theatre, including Duke Vincentio in *Measure*, both Helena and Paroles in *All's Well*, Edgar and the Fool in *Lear*, and (perhaps surprisingly) Coriolanus. In *Pericles*, the medieval poet Gower steps on stage to perform a tale out of his poem *Confessio Amantis*: "To sing a song that old was sung, / From ashes ancient Gower is come, / Assuming man's infirmities" (1. Proem 1–3) – the word "Assuming" being a fine theatrical pun, suiting Gower's costume to his antique age. In this phase, we also encounter Shakespeare's most disturbing portrait of the poet-playwright figure: honest Iago.

Like Macbeth and Cleopatra, Iago is a consummate figure of the theatre (as is well known). From the start, he professes to Roderigo that he indeed has a theatrical "soul" (1. 1. 54), an exquisitely performed interiority: "trimm'd in forms and visages of duty," he keeps his "heart" attending on himself, "throwing but shows of service" on his lord, does "well" by him, and when he has "lin'd" his "coat," does himself "homage" (50–54). Moreover, in soliloquy he informs the audience, "I play the villain": "When devils will the blackest sins put on, / They do suggest at first with heavenly shows, as I do now" (2. 3. 336; 351–53). What might be less known is Iago's deployment of (written) poetry. In Act 2, scene 1, he insinuates himself

---

[3] *Sir Thomas More* is even more a special case, since editions such as the *Oxford* and *Riverside* print only those parts thought to be written by Shakespeare. On Shakespeare as collaborator, including in *Pericles* and *Timon*, see B. Vickers, *Co-Author*.

into Desdemona's conscience as a Petrarchan poet, when she asks, "What wouldst write of me, if thou shouldst praise me?" ". . . my invention," he replies (118, 125),

> Comes from my pate as birdlime does from frieze,
> It plucks out brains and all. But my Muse labors,
> And thus she is deliver'd.   (*Othello*, 2. 1. 126–28)

Just as later Iago stages the scene with the handkerchief, here he formally produces a twelve-line poem in rhymed couplets to demonstrate his prowess in poetic invention, the opening lines of which read: "She that was ever fair, and never proud, / Had tongue at will, and yet was never loud" (148–49).

Yet we also discover something more startling here: in this tragedy, Shakespeare appears to privilege poetry over theatre. In contrast to Iago, Desdemona is associated only with the art of poetry; this divine woman becomes at once its object and its subject. Early on, Cassio tells Montano that Othello "hath achiev'd a maid / That paragons description and wild fame; / One that excels the quirks of blazoning pens" (2. 1. 61–63). Later, however, Desdemona herself sings the immortal "willow song," originally voiced by her mother's maid, Barbary, in a feminine Orphic register: "Sing willow, willow, willow; / Her salt tears fell from her, and soft'ned the stones" (4. 3. 45–46). In Desdemona's song, Kenneth Gross discovers a "visionary moment": "the song holds out a cure for the more infectious babble in this play, a noise that does not so directly bind or blind its hearers, or turn itself into the motive for murder. Whatever knowledge the song offers to us draws a lyrical circle around itself." Even so, the play as a whole, as Gross says, exhibits "a tragic breach" (*Noise*, 125). His terms "lyrical" and "tragic" suggest that in this play a serious and vital dialogue and confrontation occurs between lyric poetry and dramatic tragedy. Poetry provides a space different from tragedy, a place and time at once visionary and redemptive, however fragile. The play does not simply stage the death of Desdemona; it also rehearses something like the tragic death of lyric itself.

Hence, throughout this phase poetry continues to be a topic of conversation; the poet, a formal character in the fiction. *Timon* opens with the "Poet," and he turns out to be a print poet: "When comes your book forth?" the Painter asks (1. 1. 26). "Upon the heels of my presentment" (27), the Poet replies, indicating that he is a print poet who specifically requires a patron for publication, Timon himself. Indeed, by studying the Poet's discourse from Act 1 through Act 5 we can assemble a rather detailed poetics, however objectionable: "'When we for recompense have prais'd the vild, / It stains the glory in that happy verse / Which aptly sings the good'" (1. 1. 15–17). In these plays, Shakespeare also recollects his own poems in dramatic form. Even as late as *Coriolanus*, there are intriguing glances back to the famous image of the snail in *Venus* (4. 6. 42–46, *Venus* 1033–38), as well as across to the Sonnets, including Sonnet 23, to be foregrounded in the next chapter: "Like a dull actor now / I have forgot my part" (5. 3. 40–41). In this play, the author is still thinking about the myth of Tarquin and Lucrece (2. 2. 87–88, 5. 4. 42–43), as he is more famously in *Macbeth* (2. 1. 54–56). In this latter play, we find book and theatre brought into an alignment that otherwise might seem peculiar; the Old Man can remember, "Within the volume of . . . time I have seen / Hours dreadful and things strange," to which Rosse replies, "Thou sees the heavens, as troubled with man's act, / Threatens his bloody stage" (2. 4. 2–6). As such, Shakespearean drama is still driven by the Virgilian fantasy of textual fame. In *Coriolanus*, Menenius tells the first watchman about the hero, "I have been / The book of his good acts, whence men have read / His fame unparallel'd, happily amplified" (5. 2. 14–16).

Thus, Shakespeare's last great Roman tragedies – *Timon*, *Antony*, *Coriolanus* – extend the Virgilian matrix in complex ways. Timon begins in his house at Athens, but toward the end his feelings of betrayal lead him to relocate in "*the woods*" (4. 3. s.d.), where he indicts the "senator" for his "Rotten humidity" and praises the "beggar" for his pastoral serenity: "It is the paster lards the brother's sides" (2–12). Moving from court to country, Timon reverses direction on the Virgilian path, sadly destined never to make the famous Shakespearean return to court. By contrast, Mark Antony opens his tragedy rehearsing an Ovidian metamorphosis, in what constitutes one of Shakespeare's more powerful representations of the antic-king figure: "you shall see in him / The triple pillar of the world transform'd / Into a strumpet's fool" (1. 1. 11–13). Antony is, of course, subject to the Ovidian theatre of Cleopatra, as she herself directs: "Good now, play one scene / Of excellent dissembling, and let it look / Like perfect honor" (1. 3. 78–80). In this gorgeously debauched theatre, Egypt wears his "sword Philippan" (2. 5. 23) while Antony courageously finds himself entering the liquidating bliss of female space, as the female herself narrates: "Ere the ninth hour, I drunk him to his bed; / Then put my tires and mantles on him" (21–22). No wonder that, when the Eastern Star is ready to move beyond the ninth hour, she "perform'd the dreaded act" (5. 2. 331), death itself, with the serene skill of a consummate actor: "Give me my robe, put on my crown,

I have / Immortal longings in me" (280–81). But not before delivering one
of the most stunning counter-Petrarchan blazons on record,[4] complete with
the combined discourse of song and show:

> His face was as the heav'ns, and therein stuck
> A sun and moon . . .
> His legs bestrid the ocean, his rear'd arm
> Crested the world, his voice was propertied
> As all the tuned spheres . . .
> . . .   His delights
> Were dolphin-like, they show his back above.
> (*Antony and Cleopatra*, 5. 2. 79–84)

As to be expected, Shakespeare's Virgilian and Ovidian matrices are often
typologically related to Spenser and Marlowe. For instance, at the end of
this phase Coriolanus is as commanding a Marlovian figure as Richard III
was back at the beginning: "Being mov'd, he will not spare to gird the
gods" (1. 2. 256), for "Fame" is that "at which he aims" (263). In nearly
every scene, Coriolanus presents himself as a man of the theatre: "It's a
part / That I shall blush in acting" (2. 2. 144–45). Yet in Act 3, scene 2, we
encounter a more complex representation conjoining Marlowe's Ovidian
model of elegy and theatre with Spenser's Virgilian model of pastoral and
epic. Volumnia is instructing her son to play his role before the people and
the tribunes – the very unnatural scene that the Tamburlaine-like general
blushes to act. When she tells him to "perform a part / Thou hast not done
before" (109–10), he acquiesces:

> Well, I must do't.
> Away, my disposition, and possess me
> Some harlot's spirit! My throat of war be turn'd,
> Which quier'd with my drum, into a pipe
> Small as an eunuch, or the virgin voice
> That babies lull asleep! (*Coriolanus*, 3. 2. 110–15)

Reversing Tamburlaine's Spenserian exchange of shepherd's attire for the
armor of the warrior, Coriolanus announces his own Ovidian metamorphosis. Inspired by the elegiac spirit of a harlot, he will perform his dramatic
part as a figure of political harmony. In the process, he will "turn" his epic
"throat of war," which was once "quier'd" with the instrument of epic, the
drum, into the "pipe," the instrument of pastoral, small as an eunuch, or a
virgin voice.

---

[4] On Cleopatra as a Petarchan poet, see Schalkwyk, *Performance*, 47.

Yet one of the most interesting of such representations occurs in *All's Well*. Helena, in disguise as a pilgrim, writes a displaced Petrarchan sonnet along the Virgilian path, as read in her letter to the Countess by the steward Reynaldo:

> I am Saint Jaques' pilgrim, thither gone.
> Ambitious love hath so in me offended
> That barefoot plot I the cold ground upon
> With sainted vow my faults to have amended.
> Write, write, that from the bloody course of war
> My dearest master, your dear son, may hie.
> . . .
> I, his despiteful Juno, sent him forth
> From courtly friends, with camping foes to live.
> *(All's Well That Ends Well*, 3. 4. 4–14)

Effectively, Helena uses the Petrarchan form to re-write the epic war of the *Aeneid* into her own performed biography, in service of love and marriage. For in Virgil's epic, "despiteful Juno" is the enemy of Aeneas, responsible for sending him forth from courtly friends and living with camping foes. By presenting Helena as a poet-playwright figure, Shakespeare can bring about his comedic recuperation: the name of "Helen" itself.[5]

Nowhere is the discourse of poetry and theatre more sophisticated than in the play we should expect – "beyond question the greatest of all tragedies" (Kermode, introduction to *King Lear, Riverside*, 1297). The premier figure for this conjunction is the Fool himself, the professional actor who sings some of the most gifted songs in the language – a figure, we might say, in whom the distinction between poetry and theatre is no longer visible:

> The sweet and bitter fool
>   Will presently appear:
> The one in motley here,
>   The other found out there.
> *(King Lear*, 1. 4. 144–47)

Yet the play's other great poet-playwright figure wears his profession more on his sleeve. In disguise as the bedlam beggar, the aristocratic Edgar constantly reminds the audience that he is an actor in danger of betraying the script he has authored: "My tears begin to take his part so much, / They mar my counterfeiting" (3. 6. 60–61). When he does sustain the pressure,

---

[5] Even in this play, Marlowe's art is alive and well – in the Clown, Lavitch, for instance, whose song about "Helen" begins, "'Was this fair face the cause,' quoth she, / 'Why the Grecians sacked Troy?'" (1. 3. 69, 70–71). In his chapter on the name "Helen" in *All's Well*, Schalkwyk neglects Helen of Troy.

no one disappears more darkly into his authorial role, complete with mad snatches of ruined song, borrowed and invented: "The foul fiend haunts poor Tom in the voice / Of a nightingale" (3. 6. 29–30). Surely this is one of the most resonant neglected lines in the canon, reverberating throughout not merely Shakespeare but Western literature itself. In this late tragedy, as in the first, the specter of Philomela returns for revenge, haunting the tortured masculine psyche with Ovidian songs and plays too horrible simply to laugh off. In the end, the Fool evaporates from the play-world, like the Ghost in *Hamlet*, while Edgar, like the princely son of that Ghost, proves ineffective in his use of poetry and theatre to cure anyone of what Hamlet rather precisely calls "th' imposthume . . . / That inward breaks, and shows no cause without."[6]

Recalling such contours in these third-phase plays, we may turn to the 1609 quarto printing Shakespeare's last poems. This volume publishes the very question of authorship raised by the two sets of poems juxtaposed in the previous two parts of the book: are these final poems the works of a print or a manuscript poet, one who self-consciously presents himself as a national author or one who is presented as such by others? To probe this question, the final part of the book divides into two respective chapters on the 1609 quarto, the first on the Sonnets, the last on *A Lover's Complaint*.

---

[6] Edgar's bastard brother, Edmund, is clearly a Marlovian overreacher (Bloom, *Shakespeare*, 499). Correspondingly, Edgar emerges as a Spenserian chivalric figure, when he challenges his brother to a duel for rather high stakes: the nation itself. Spenser's story of King Lear in *The Faerie Queene* (2. 10) is a source for Shakespeare's play (*Riverside*, 1298), and Coyle ("King Lear") argues that Shakespeare models Edgar's staging of Gloucester's leap off Dover cliff on Malbecco's suicide (*Fairie Queene*, 3. 10). See also Tobin, "Parallels" and "Malbecco."

CHAPTER 7

"O, let my books be . . . dumb presagers": poetry and theatre in the Sonnets

William Shakespeare is a man of the theatre who wrote a sonnet sequence.

For the English Renaissance, this is an unusual profile. Almost exclusively, the writers who composed sonnet sequences were not the same as those who worked in the theatre. The sonneteers, rather than being professional dramatists, belonged predominantly either to an amateur class of poets (for example, Sir Philip Sidney and Richard Barnfield) or to a laureate class (Edmund Spenser and Michael Drayton).[1] By contrast, the main professional dramatists (from Thomas Kyd to John Ford) did not produce sonnet sequences, even though nearly without exception they wrote in other poetic forms, from love lyric and pastoral to epyllion and satire.[2]

Shakespeare's Sonnets therefore constitute an unusual site for viewing the intersection of poetry and theatre during the English Renaissance. Sonnet 23 illustrates succinctly the discursive form of that intersection, which the sequence as a whole sustains: "O, let my books be then the eloquence / And dumb presagers of my speaking breast" (9–10).[3] While we shall examine Sonnet 23 in detail later, for now we may note simply that these lines intriguingly conjoin the medium of printed books of poetry (editorial tradition suggests *Venus* and *Lucrece*) with that of staged theatre (the dumb show of a play). That these lines turn out to contain a long-standing textual crux could well make the examination more enticing.

---

[1] For this classification, see Helgerson, *Laureates*. Sonneteers belonging to the amateur class include Henry Constable, Barnabe Barnes, Giles Fletcher the Elder, Sir Robert Sidney, Bartholomew Griffin, William Smith, and Sir John Davies. According to Gabriel Harvey, Spenser wrote *Nine Comedies* (Letter III in G. G. Smith, ed., *Essays*, I: 115), while Drayton wrote tragedies, but in both cases the plays have not survived, and some question whether Spenser's ever existed (see Oruch, "Works, Lost").

[2] Other dramatists who did not write sonnet sequences include John Lyly, Christopher Marlowe, Robert Greene, Thomas Nashe, George Peele, George Chapman, Ben Jonson, John Marston, Thomas Dekker, Thomas Middleton, John Fletcher, Francis Beaumont, and John Webster. On Samuel Daniel, Thomas Lodge, and Fulke Greville as partial exceptions, see Cheney, "Poetry," 222–24.

[3] The *Riverside* notes that "books" "may mean these sonnets, or, if the addressee is Southampton, the two poems *Venus and Adonis* and *Lucrece*," and it glosses "dumb presagers" as "presenters, as in the dumb show of a play" (1847).

In this chapter, we will look further into the Sonnets' sustained conjoining of these two principal forms of production during Shakespeare's career.[4] Such an investigation can prove useful in itself as an analysis of a neglected topic, yet the analysis may prove especially profitable in the current critical conversation about Shakespeare as an early modern author. As we shall see, the Sonnets constitute an unexplored territory for viewing him as inextricably caught in the cultural predicament of conjoining the two forms that engaged him throughout his professional career.

THE CRITICAL AND HISTORICAL CONTEXTS

We can indeed profit from viewing Shakespeare's Sonnets as the product of the world's most famous man of the theatre, the writer or collaborator of forty-two known plays, an actor in a professional company, and a shareholder in a commercial, public theatre. Sometime between the mid-1580s and the early seventeenth century, the famed dramatist wrote 152 sonnets in the Petrarchan tradition, and they were finally published in 1609 (with or without his consent) in a quarto volume titled *Shake-speares Sonnets*. The volume includes two anacreontic sonnets (153, 154) and *A Lover's Complaint*, in what was then a familiar format for a printed volume of verse.[5] Shakespeare did not write his sonnets simply when the theatres closed due to plague in 1592–93; as recent scholarship has demonstrated, he worked on them throughout his career.[6] As we have seen, in 1598 Francis Meres encourages contemporaries to integrate Shakespeare's "sugred Sonnets" centrally into his profession as a public dramatist and a published poet (*Palladis Tamia*, reprinted in *Riverside*, 1970).

---

[4] To my knowledge, no one has done so. For different models relating poetry and drama, see Hunter, "Dramatic Technique"; Melchiori, *Dramatic Meditations*; Dubrow, *Victors*, esp. 190; Henderson, *Passion Made Public*; Wright, "Silent Speech," 137; Schalkwyk, "Embodiment," "Performative," *Performance*. While Schalkwyk characterizes Shakespearean self-representation in terms of the Austinian performative, I contextualize it in terms of Shakespeare's historical predicament of being an English author at this time, a man of the theatre who has turned to sonneteering. Schalkwyk looks com pellingly at sonnets representing theatre – notably Sonnet 23 – but we still lack a detailed investigation into the discursive presence of poetry and theatre *in the text* of the Sonnets as a whole.
[5] See Duncan-Jones, "Unauthorized?" and her edition, as well as J. Kerrigan, ed., *The Sonnets*. On the 1580s dating of Sonnet 145, see Gurr, "First Poem."
[6] As noted in chapter 1, Burrow, "Life," suggests that we think about the Sonnets "as something approaching Shakespeare's life's work" (17). For further details, see Hieatt, Hieatt, and Prescott, "When," 73–74. Duncan-Jones suggests "four probable phases of composition": before 1598; 1599–1600; 1603–04; and August 1608–May 1609 (Duncan-Jones, ed., *Sonnets*, 12–13; see 1–28). In *Ungentle*, she remarks, "Writing, revising and re-ordering sonnets was probably a regular activity throughout his adult life" (214; see 214–16). J. Kerrigan believes that "Shakespeare was consciously shaping a collection when he wrote *A Lover's Complaint* in c. 1602–5" (Kerrigan, ed., *The Sonnets*, 12; see 10–18). Finally, see G. Taylor, "Manuscripts."

Some readers might dispute that Meres refers to sonnets from the 1609 quarto, emphasizing instead the conditions of manuscript circulation and arguing that Shakespeare did not intend the Sonnets for publication.[7] Yet the Meres passage suggests a more complicated cultural milieu, since Meres situates the Shakespearean manuscript sonnets he has read in an authorial practice that includes both printed poems (*Venus*, *Lucrece*) and printed and/or staged plays (quartos began appearing in 1594, and in 1598 Shakespeare's name began to appear on them). Moreover, the recent work by Wendy Wall and Colin Burrow emphasizes how the Sonnets – in Burrow's formulation – "could have been designed to operate more or less exactly on the borderline between the published and the privately concealed": "What makes the volume of *Shake-speares Sonnets* unique is the extent to which its every element can be seen [to] . . . invite from its readers a deliberate interplay between reading the collection for the life as a private manuscript record of a secret love, and reading it as a monumental printed work" (Burrow, "Life," 38, 42). Wall finds the collection periodically brooding over the problem of print publication (*Imprint*, 197). Such criticism is important because it presents a Shakespeare whom critics are increasingly beginning to see: not simply the writer of plays who assiduously avoids print and bookish immortality, but rather the author of both plays and poems whose works as a whole show a fascination with – sometimes also a fear and distrust of – print publication. While acknowledging that the Sonnets are situated on the "borderline between the published and the privately concealed," we might then profit by looking into certain neglected features of the former, especially since recent criticism has emphasized the latter.

In fact, scholars writing on the Sonnets have long emphasized Shakespeare's presentation of himself as a poet – a writer of lyrics – in the very sonnets he is composing.[8] Indebted to Petrarch (and before him, Ovid) as well as his sixteenth-century English heirs (Sidney, Daniel, Spenser), Shakespeare's self-representation appears as the subject of the poet's verse in over twenty-five different sonnets (e.g., 18, 55, 60, 63, 106, 116, 130), including this from Sonnet 60: "to times in hope my verse shall stand" (13). To these sonnets, we need to add the Rival Poet sonnets (78–86), in which

---

7 See, e.g., Love, *Scribal Publications*; Marotti, "Property," esp. 170n30 on Meres. Marotti's essay is invaluable for re-historicizing Shakespearean authorship, yet we need to complicate his thesis, taking his own cue: "Despite the decision to publish two narrative poems early in his career . . . Shakespeare was . . . a professional actor, playwright, and theatrical shareholder" ("Property," 144).

8 For Shakespeare's signature as a poet, see Fineman, *Perjured*, 6. See also Leishman, *Themes and Variations*, 27–91; Muir, *Sonnets*, 30–44, 112–22; Hammond, *Reader*, 61–78, 95–110, 135–49, 195–213. On "Shakespeare's Petrarchism," see the essay of this title by Braden; and on Shakespeare's Ovidianism, see Bate, *Ovid*, 87–100.

this poet-figure presents himself as a rival versifier for the artistic affection of the young man: "Was it the proud full sail of his great verse . . . / That did my ripe thoughts in my brain inhearse" (86. 1–3). To these two groups, we can add still other sonnets that refer to the media of printed books or to the literary tradition (11, 25, 53, 59, 77, 117), as represented in Sonnet 59, "Show me your image in some antique book" (7), or in Sonnet 53, which refers to the literary images of both "Adonis" and "Helen" (1–8). We also need to add Shakespeare's use of the vocabulary from the print medium to reflect on sexual experience, as in Sonnet 11 when the speaker advises the young man to marry and procreate: "Thou shouldst print more, not let that copy die" (14). For readers today, as presumably for Shakespeare's first readers, the Sonnets present a speaker who quite literally speaks as a poet, the author of the very sonnets we are reading. As Burrow, Wall, and others help us see, the poet, who calls himself Will in Sonnet 136 (14), situates his own poems on the borderline between print and manuscript.[9] From the perspective of the present argument, he is therefore distinctly compelled by the career of the print poet.

Yet scholars writing on the Sonnets have noted that in at least a few sonnets – most notably, 110, 111, and 112, but also 25, 29, 72, and 87 – Shakespeare presents this same poet-figure or sonnet writer as a man of the theatre, as this from Sonnet 110: "I have gone here and there, / And made myself a motley to the view" (1–2).[10] Stephen Booth observes: "If this poem were not by a professional actor, the line would simply say, 'I have made myself a public laughingstock' . . . However, Shakespeare's profession is – and presumably always was – known to his readers (see 111. 3–4), and this line therefore is colored by (and colors the following lines with) its pertinence to the particular circumstances of its author's life. The fact of Shakespeare's profession operates – much as the accident of his first name does in the 'Will' sonnets . . . – to give witty, pun-like extra dimension to statements complete and meaningful in themselves" (Booth, ed., *Sonnets*, 354). We can extend this important principle of representation and reception to other sonnets referring to Shakespeare's theatrical career, as well as to many sonnets that rely on theatrical metaphors (5, 15, 23, 24, 33, 61, 70, 98, 113), which Will often uses to represent erotic experience, sometimes without fanfare or even note: "Mine eye hath play'd the painter and hath [stell'd] / Thy beauty's form in table of my heart" (24. 1–2). To these two groups, we can add a large number of sonnets that inscribe

[9] On the "name" of "Will," see Pequigney, "Sonnets," 298–301; Schalkwyk, *Performance*, 183–88.
[10] See H. Smith, *Tension*: "It is traditional to see references to Shakespeare's career as an actor in the little series 110–112" (26; see 26–28). See Hubler, *Sense*, 115–22; Honan, *A Life*, 128, 161.

Shakespeare's working vocabulary from the theatre, even though in many instances we would be wary to claim a specific theatrical evocation. This vocabulary includes the word "show" (e.g., 5. 14); "mask" (33. 12); "rehearse" (21. 4); "play" (5. 3); "part" (8. 8); "act" (152. 3); "action" (65. 4); "actor" (23.1); "entertain" (39. 11); "shadows" (43. 5–6); "mock" (61. 4); "trim" (66. 3); "case" (108. 9); and, perhaps taking a cue from Sir Philip Sidney, "dumb" (23. 10). Shakespeare's insertion of this theatrical discourse into his sonnet sequence, while not surprising, is nonetheless unusual enough during the period to warrant attention.

Despite Shakespeare's inclusion of a discourse of poetry and a discourse of theatre in his Sonnets, critics tend to separate their analyses of poetry and theatre. Most importantly, critics who see Shakespeare worrying about print publication in his Sonnets do not concern themselves much with the theatrical matrix of the sequence.[11] The inventory of both theatrical and poetic matrices, together with the practice among Shakespeare's contemporaries of separating sonnets from plays, pinpoints the historical significance of the Sonnets as lying partly in their unusual representation of the intersection of these two forms at a critical time in English literary history. During the last twenty years, critics have tended to locate the Sonnets' historical significance in terms of Shakespeare's representation of subjectivity and/or sexuality.[12] In a recent, seminal essay, Peter Stallybrass argues that "In the case of the Sonnets . . . we can read the inscription of a new history of sexuality and 'character'" ("Sexing," 92). Stallybrass adds, "But that new history emerges unpunctually, dislocated by its need to write itself over the culturally valued but culturally disturbing body of the Sonnets" (92–93). In Shakespeare's sequence, we can also read the inscription of a new history of authorship and "character," discovering this history to emerge in a similarly unpunctual and dislocated fashion.

According to such a history, Shakespeare's Sonnets are important because they present a new type of European author, memorably represented in the Meres passage: the author who pens both poems and plays. Shakespeare's Sonnets are noteworthy for lots of reasons but especially for their original representation of the interconnection between these two fundamentally

---

[11] Cf. Wall, *Imprint*, 197n51. Valbuena, "Reproduction," reveals that Shakespeare's language is suffused with the discourse of early modern writing practices.

[12] Most famously, Fineman has argued that the Sonnets invent modern subjectivity (*Perjured*; see Ferry). This view has been tempered by such critics as de Grazia, "Motive"; Schoenfeldt, *Bodies*, 74–95. Others, such as B. R. Smith, argue that in the Sonnets "Shakespeare improvised a new form of discourse": "Shakespeare seeks to speak about homosexual desire with the same authority that Petrarch assumes in speaking about heterosexual desire" (*Homosexual Desire*, 228–70; quotations from 265, 264).

nascent literary forms. More specifically, the Sonnets' new history of authorship and authorial character publicizes a cultural clash between printed
poetry and the even newer, more socially compromising medium of staged
theatre. No other English Renaissance sonnet sequence does so. To represent the clash of media, Shakespeare presents Will in deep introspection
suffering a personal dilemma between being a playwright-actor ashamed
of his profession and being a poet working hard to be affirmative about his
career as a sonneteer.[13]

David Schalkwyk classifies Will as an "actor-poet," presumably because
the theatre representations appear to pertain to Shakespeare's role as an
actor rather than as a playwright ("Performative," 252). This seems basically
right, but we might note two complications: first, it might be difficult, even
unwise, to disentangle Shakespeare's theatrical roles as actor and playwright,
not least because in the Sonnets a poet is literally writing about his role
as an actor; and second, we might come to see one of Shakespeare's major
contributions to the representation of authorship during the period to lie
in the fact that he presents the author also as an actor.[14] Such a new history
emphasizes the homology between the twin but typically separate topics of
much recent criticism on Shakespeare's plays and poems: cross-dressing in
the plays; and homoeroticism in the Sonnets.[15] Shakespeare, we might say,
countered the large-scale European convention of Petrarchism, through
which a male poet addressed a sonnet sequence to a female beloved, *because
he was a man of the theatre*; this sonnet author experienced the staging of
same-sex relationships in costumed disguise as a matter of daily professional
practice.[16]

Shakespeare's self-conscious deployment of homoeroticism, theatre, and
printed poetry appears to be unique. We might then attribute his "most

---

[13] Dubrow, "Politics," argues that the Sonnets are best viewed as "internalized meditations unconnected
to a narrative line" (123). For a recent rebuttals to Dubrow, see (e.g.) Traub, "Sex," 442.

[14] See *The Roman Actor* (1626), wherein Massinger uses the actor as a metaphor for the playwright (see
Butler's intro., x). Cf. Honan: "there was a possible tactical advantage, for Shakespeare's actors, in
having these elegant lyrics in print in London at a critical time in 1609" (*A Life*, 362). Schalkwyk,
Performance, demonstrates persuasively that the Sonnets concern themselves with Shakespeare's
career as a player-poet; however, by focusing on the Austinian performative, Schalkwyk turns away
from (in particular) intertextuality.

[15] On theatrical cross-dressing, see Orgel, *Impersonations*. On homoeroticism in the Sonnets, see
Pequigney, *Such*; B. R. Smith, *Homosexual Desire*, 228–70, "Politics"; Traub, "Sex." Critics neglect
the homology, even though they may discuss the Sonnets and plays (e.g., B. R. Smith, "Politics,"
414).

[16] One did not need to be an actor to write sonnets addressed to another man, as testified to by
Richard Barnfield's twenty sonnets in his 1595 *Cynthia* (Duncan-Jones, *Sonnets*, ed., 47). Unlike
Sidney, Daniel, Spenser, and others, however, Barnfield does not include a discourse of theatre. He
does present himself as a poet writing in a tradition of English and European poetry in service of
fame.

salient" alteration to the Petrarchan sequence – "that most of them are addressed to a young male" (de Grazia, "Scandal," 38) – not simply to the personal circumstances of his sexual biography, nor even to his character-istically witty and innovative overturning of convention, but also to his singular position in the theatrical world. In his Sonnets, Shakespeare can be seen to transpose the homoerotic gender paradigm from the theatre to the Petrarchan sequence. He is a man of the theatre writing sonnets, and he capitalizes on his unique position in the literary system to present Will precisely as the theatrical man turning his dramatic hand to non-dramatic poetry. It is in this context that we might usefully view Shakespeare's oppos-ing representations of his twin arts, conveyed through Will's public shame over the theatre and his bid for public fame through his poetry.[17] By claim-ing poetic fame for Will and his subject through his Sonnets, Shakespeare is not simply participating in the long tradition extending from Homer through Virgil, Horace, and Ovid, to Dante, Petrarch, and Spenser: he is simultaneously offsetting a public infamy acquired through his role in the new English theatre. If the Sonnets are "Shakespeare's life's work," we might come to see Shakespeare positioning himself in another European econ-omy besides that of the theatre: the economy of a literary career, designed principally to secure the high cultural authority of poetic immortality.[18]

While we might wish to hold off claiming that the Sonnets constitute an advertisement for Shakespeare's status as a new English and European poet-playwright, his sequence nonetheless constitutes a historically sig-nificant meditation on, inscription of, and register for an author who is fundamentally a sixteenth-century invention – or, more accurately, the re-invention of a Roman writer that for Marlowe, Jonson, and Thomas Heywood traces to Ovid (chapters 1 and 2). Recalling Meres' Ovidian comparison, we may understand the conjunction of poetry and theatre in the Sonnets precisely in Ovidian terms: Shakespeare plots Will's aes-thetic and subjective struggle for identity amid the triangulated love affair with the young man and the dark lady along a distinctly Ovidian path of amorous poetry and tragic theatre. Like Ovid in the *Amores* (and Marlowe in his translation), Will stages a narrative of the poet-playwright caught between claims of poetry's power to immortalize and love's power to produce shame. Distinctly, however, Shakespeare shifts the site of shame

---

[17] See Engle, "Shame"; however, Engle does not situate shame in the theatrical matrix of the Sonnets, even though he reports that "Markets and theaters are, for Shakespeare, the most prominent local instances of such economies" (187).

[18] See Duncan-Jones, *Ungentle*, for the assumption that poetic immortality in the Sonnets comes from "the printed book" (177).

from love and poetry in the Ovid/Marlowe dynamic to the place of the stage.[19]

It is difficult to determine just how we are to gauge Shakespeare in relation to the Ovid/Marlowe dynamic. For instance, it might seem peculiar that an English Renaissance writer such as Shakespeare could discover in Ovid a model for the poet-playwright, since the great classical writer left a canon decidedly tipped in favor of poetry over drama. Yet in order to take the cue of Marlowe, Jonson, Heywood, and others, we need not insist that Ovid balanced the two; we could simply acknowledge that Ovid achieved his combination in a way that was compelling in the late sixteenth and early seventeenth centuries. Consequently, we might see Shakespeare perfecting an imperfect Ovidian model that Marlowe had instigated yet had left incomplete when he died prematurely in 1593. With their intense interest in classical authors – and especially their shared passion for Ovid – Marlowe and Shakespeare together can be seen to realize a model of authorship that Ovid had advertised but had failed to realize. Although Ovid says he is better "apt" for the "high designs" of "tragedies" than he is for the low designs of love elegy (*Amores*, 2. 18. 13–18; trans. Marlowe), his chronic disposition for erotic entanglements recurrently impedes the success of this notable dramatic temperament. Effectively, Ovid invents a career path that Marlowe begins to traverse and that Shakespeare is left more fully to chart.

Like Marlowe's other heir, Ben Jonson, Shakespeare may have really "wanted to be a poet rather than a playwright" (Yachnin, *Stage-Wrights*, xii). We might find it striking, however, that Shakespeare does not use his poetry to erase his role in the theatre, but rather makes his shameful theatrical profession a part of his self-presentation. The Sonnets thus stage a kind of crisis: the new English poet-playwright – so popular that in 1599 Jaggard could pirate *The Passionate Pilgrim* under Shakespeare's name – is caught in a compromising predicament with a morally bankrupt young man and an equally bankrupt dark lady. Of this narrative, Michael C. Schoenfeldt has recently observed that Shakespeare's sonnets "[M]ust have struck the 1609 reader as a radical disruption of the conventional narrative of erotic courtship. In the early sonnets, woman is not the idealized recipient of the erotic aspirations of a male speaker but rather a means of biological reproduction, to be frequented so that men may lay claim to the fragile immortality of progeny; in the later poems, woman, now identified with a

[19] On this place, see Mullaney, *Place*. On the "presence" of Ovid in the Sonnets, in relation to the "absence" of Petrarch, see Braden, "Ovid, Petrarch," 99. On "shame" in the "Ovidian model," see Brown, "Breaking the Canon," 66–67. For a different view of the *Amores* and Marlowe's translation, see Stapleton, *Harmful*.

culturally derogated darkness, is the object of a wasteful, enervating, uncontrollable desire that contrasts markedly with the idealized love of a young man" ("Matter," 240). Schoenfeldt's view of Shakespeare's narrative of sexual physiology and subjectivity corresponds to a striking statistic pertaining to the narrative of authorship and authorial character: with very little exception, Shakespeare confines both his poetic and his theatrical vocabulary to the young-man sonnets (1–126), so that in the dark-lady sonnets (127–52) this vocabulary virtually disappears.[20] Altogether, Shakespeare presents a narrative in which Will, the new Ovidian poet-playwright, loses the voice of his profession to the engulfing swirls of a dangerous, triangulated sexual desire: "desire is death" (147. 8). Against such mighty rage, how can poetry hold a plea?[21]

Finally, we might wish to be cautious when gauging Will's authorial self-presentation as definitive of Shakespeare's own view of his career or even of his own personal predicament, because it so clearly resembles Spenser's famous presentation of his persona in the 1579 *Shepheardes Calender*, wherein Colin Clout abandons his career as a poet after Rosalind, his own distinctly rose-tinted Petrarchan mistress, rejects him. Like Spenser, Shakespeare presents a powerful narrative of artistic failure precisely to claim authority as a (national) author.[22] Without recalling Spenser's paradoxical use of his failed, clownish persona to present himself as England's great laureate poet, we might have some difficulty processing Shakespeare's presentation of a rather negative model of authorship that even Ovid (and Marlowe) had presented more positively. Just as we need not confuse Spenser with Colin, so we need not confuse Shakespeare with Will. Thus, we may apply to Shakespeare the principle critics find operating in Spenser's *June* eclogue: the "topos of inability or affected modesty is in effect an indirect tactic of self-assertion."[23] Because the Sonnets are today Shakespeare's best-selling book, and because Shakespeare eventually displaced Spenser as England's "National Poet," we may conclude that in terms of reception history the author of the Sonnets succeeded admirably in substantiating the claim.[24]

---

[20] The only significant uses occur in "compare" at 130. 14 and in "play" at 143. 12; see Sutphen, "Dateless," 210.

[21] On "Desire is Death," see Dollimore.

[22] De Grazia borrows her classification for Will's relations with the young man and the dark lady, not from "the post-Enlightenment categories of homosexual and heterosexual," but from E. K.'s note to the *Januarye* eclogue: pederasty and gynerasty, respectively ("Scandal," 46). According to Bednarz, *Poets' War*, "Shakespeare in *Troilus and Cressida* identifies failure as an essential condition of experience" (263).

[23] Cain, intro., *June* eclogue, *Shepheardes Calender*, in Oram, et al., eds. *Yale Edition*, 108.

[24] For the history of the Sonnets' publication from the seventeenth century onwards, see (in addition to Burrow, "Life," 17–21) de Grazia, *Verbatim*.

Here we might wonder how a work that was basically erased not simply from the First Folio but from the canon itself until the eighteenth century could prove so historically influential. Although we may not be used to viewing the Sonnets the way we are here, they nonetheless record, as countless critics have helped us see (not least Joel Fineman), a large-scale artistic project that matches and even exceeds that of Petrarch's in the *Rime sparse*. Thus, we may not wish to ignore but rather to marvel at just how the Sonnets have undergone a long, extremely complex historical process of reception that finally gets around to recognizing the achievement of this project.[25]

SONNET 15

While many sonnets present Will as a poet and several present him as man of the theatre, a substantial number show him bringing poetry and theatre into conjunction.[26] Let us begin by considering Sonnet 15, long recognized to be important for articulating the central theme of the sequence and for first presenting the art of poetry as a solution to the problem of time and death – those relentless stalkers of the young man's beauty.[27] Sonnet 15 is less often recalled as the first poem to employ a substantive theatrical discourse and thus the first to conjoin theatre with poetry:

> When I consider every thing that grows
> Holds in perfection but a little moment,
> That this huge stage presented nought but shows,
> Whereon the stars in secret influence comment;
> When I perceive that men as plants increase,
> Cheered and check'd even by the self-same sky,
> Vaunt in their youthful sap, at height decrease,
> And wear their brave state out of memory:
> Then the conceit of this inconstant stay
> Sets you most rich in youth before my sight,

---

[25] See N. Frye, "Twain": "Shakespeare's sonnets are the definitive summing up of the Western tradition of love poetry from Plato and Ovid, to Dante and Petrarch, to Chaucer and Spenser" (106).

[26] The longer version of this chapter, "Poetry," also discusses Sonnet 54. Others not discussed there or here that *conjoin* poetry and theatre in thought-provoking ways include Sonnets 5, 8, 17, 21, 26, 38, 53, 76, 103, and 105. All of these, like the ones discussed here, appear in the young-man sequence, except the special case of 144, to be examined presently.

[27] Schoenfeldt notes that line 9 contains the "theme that unifies this collocation" (*Bodies*, 89): "this inconstant stay." Evans observes that Sonnet 15 "first sounds the Horatian and Ovidian theme of immortality assured through poetry" (Evans, ed., *Sonnets*, 127; see Rollins, ed., *Variorum: Sonnets*, 1: 41–43). Herman adds that "The thematic emergence of poetry . . . overlaps with the emergence of homoeroticism" ("What's the use," 277).

> Where wasteful Time debateth with Decay
> To change your day of youth to sullied night,
> And all in war with Time for love of you,
> As he takes from you, I ingraft you new.
>
> (Sonnet 15)

This sonnet, a perfect instance of the "Shakespearean sonnet" of three rhymed quatrains and a concluding couplet, is relatively straightforward. Relying on his famous logical pattern, Will tells the young man that "When" he considers the decay and death of all natural things, "Then" he looks on the young man both to discover meaning and to write that meaning into poetry.

Yet Sonnet 15 is also important because it relies on an authorial narrative to represent the central cognitive paradigm of the sequence – what many have seen as the heart of its enduring value: the English Ovidian poet-playwright locates meaning both in the individual's meditation on beauty as a consolation for the tyranny of time and death and in the individual's verse inscription. The cognition itself is hardly new, tracing back to the *Iliad* and receiving famous forms in Virgil, Horace, and Ovid, and later in Dante, Petrarch, and Spenser (among others). Shakespeare certainly brings a rich intelligence and a fresh talent to the topics of subjective perception and poetic fame, but what may make the articulation historically new is the conjunction here of poetry with theatre. If we look carefully at the fiction, Will presents himself as an actor on a stage writing poetry to combat time and death.

In the first quatrain, Will presents his speaking subject, "I," as an actor on a stage performing a cognitive action, as if in soliloquy.[28] The simple syntax of the first line is paradigmatic: "I consider . . . thing." The speaking subject uses his mind to consider material reality – not just any material reality, but one that "grows." Thus, Will considers the natural world in its capacity to change and mature. In line two, his word "but" at the mid-point intimates a problem, as Will considers that natural things retain their perfection for only a "little moment." In line three, he introduces the theatrical metaphor (it is not a simile) to place himself, the perceiver of natural decay, on a "huge stage" that presents nothing but "shows." This is certainly a tautology – but it is worse, a cliché: the trope of the world as a stage presenting man as an actor and life as a show is so popular a formulation during the period – the very motto of the Globe Theatre itself

---

[28] In "Politics," B. R. Smith argues that "'I,' 'he,' and 'she' exist ontologically in these texts exactly as three principal characters might in a theatrical script" (424)

(*Totus mundus agit histrionem*) – that we might intelligently seek to bypass commentary here altogether.[29] Such a bypass, however, would commit us to erasing the historicity of Will's self-presentation, through which he locates intellectual consideration on the stage, his platform for materialist speculations in lines 1–3: the world is nothing but a show, while the show itself merely stages the world.[30] Yet in line 4 Will extends his materialist philosophy to the metaphysical domain, now framing his platform with a sky and its astral bodies, which indeed were displayed on the canopy overarching the stage at the Globe: "Whereon the stars in secret influence comment." For a Christian audience, this line is important and challenging: Will presents the stars "comment[ing]" on the "nought" of the "show" with "secret influence."[31] As Katherine Duncan-Jones observes, Will presents the stars "as audience to the theatre of the world, [which] comment on and guide human life, but in ways that are undiscernible to us (*secret*)" (Duncan-Jones, ed., *Sonnets*, 140). As G. Blakemore Evans reports, however, "Shakespeare's use of 'comment' has caused difficulty, since though spectators at a play may comment, the stars were believed to do much more than 'comment' in a passive sense" (Evans, ed., *Sonnets*, 128). Evans goes on to say that he has "assigned a meaning to 'comment' (with support from the *OED*) which suggests the action of a commentator or reviewer who makes crucial or 'critical' decisions that affect the future of a 'work'" (128; see Booth, ed., *Sonnets*, 286). Thus, Will frames his fiction of an actor on a stage considering the death of nature within a larger setting that includes the religious sphere. The play in which he finds himself is looking like a tragedy, especially one emphasizing the tragic hero's victimization by a metaphysical agent. For Shakespeare's Christian audience, the repercussions must have been – and remain – striking.

    In the second quatrain, Will registers the very strike of those repercussions. In line 5, he uses anaphora to consolidate and specify the materialist (and theatrical) consideration of the first quatrain, when he perceives that men "increase" the way "plants" do. In line 6, he metaphysics the subject (to adapt a phrase from the opening of *The Winter's Tale*) in the sonnet's most unsettling line: "Cheered and check'd even by the self-same sky." The line is unsettling because of the (Christian) implications of a single sky performing two opposed actions: this meteorological domain both encourages

---

[29] The trope was intriguing even to individuals who were not associated with the theatre; see Greenblatt, *Ralegh*.
[30] Engle, "Shame," focuses on the treatment of eternity in the Sonnets as social endurance rather than transcendence (186). See his "Certainty," which responds to Bernard's "Platonic" argument.
[31] On "nothingness" in Shakespeare, see Bloom, *Shakespeare*, 642–49.

and rebukes, empowers and impedes, offers hope and takes it away, creates
fortune and misfortune equally (cheers "and" checks). If read in the context
of the Sermon on the Mount to which Hamlet refers (5. 2. 219–20), or of the
Christian tradition from Augustine to Dante to Hooker, the line is not simply unsettling; it is blasphemous. In Will's tragic theatre, unlike in Dante's
divine comedy, the sky is not the lucid source of salvation or damnation, nor
does it offer a special providence for the fall of a sparrow.[32] Quite literally,
the sky overhanging Will has turned cloudy; no longer does the individual
perceive the divine clearly, and worse, no longer does the divine communicate clearly to the individual. Once more, Evans helps in understanding
the theatrical resonance of the religious representation: "Encourage, solaced
(by good fortune), or, possibly, applauded (as in the theatre . . .) and hin-
dered, cut short, reproved (by bad fortune), or cried down, taunted (as
in the theatre)."[33] Will's transposition of the cosmic drama to the stage is
an important register for the historical context of the Sonnets: the much-
discussed advent of science and philosophy and its effects on the truths
and authority of Christian teaching (see Cruttwell, *Shakespearean Moment*,
1–38). In Sonnet 15, Shakespeare presents Will as a man of the theatre acting out a tragedy of particular relevance to the early modern audience. As
editors note, both lines 7 and 8 retain theatrical imagery in Will's portrait
of men who "[v]aunt" in their youth only to "decrease" in their "height"
and who "wear their brave state out of memory" (Evans, ed., *Sonnets*, 128).
The image catches the sad (yet perhaps slightly humorous) perplexity of
this particular tragic individual: he is a young actor who vaunts his voice
in splendid costume even as he falls into oblivion, the terrorizing Western
alternative to poetic immortality. Moreover, in scripting himself as an actor
in a tragedy, Will presents himself simultaneously as the writer of that play.
His representation of himself as a playwright is thus identical with his role
as a sonneteer.

  If the octave uses theatre to represent the material and metaphysical problem of living in an uncertain universe, the sestet thus discovers a solution
to lie in the intertwined activities of philosophical vision and written verse.
In lines 9–10, Will reports that the "conceit" (both his conception and his
literary image) of this murky universe is richly offset by his "sight" of the

---

[32] Cf. Sir John Cheke, who, says Riggs, "coined the term 'Atheists' to describe people who do not 'care
whether there be a God or no, or whether . . . he will recompense good Men with good things, and
bad Men with what is Evil'" ("Marlowe's Quarrel," 20).

[33] Evans, ed., *Sonnets*, 128. He adds, "Booth notes that Jonson seems to echo the theatrical suggestion
of lines 3–6 in his poem 'To the Memory of . . . Shakespeare' in the First Folio (1623), line 78: 'Or
influence, chide, or cheere the drooping Stage'" (128).

young man. In lines 11–12, he locates this perception again on the stage, witnessing a "debate" between two other actors in a morality play, "Time and Decay," who struggle over the youth to "change" his "day of youth to sullied night" – to perform an Ovidian degenerative metamorphosis on him. In this tragedic Ovidian theatre, Will imagines Time killing Nature, as Heaven betrays man by passively standing by, simply "comment[ing]" on the hapless protagonist.

Only in the couplet does Will present his poetry as the solution to this tragic predicament: as Time kills the young man, Will "ingraft[s] him new" – makes him immortal through his verse. As Bruce R. Smith reports, "Many readers have noted the pun here on 'engraft': it suggests the Greek root *graphein*, 'to write,' at the same time that it sets up images of horticultural grafting in the next sonnet."[34] More locally, poetic ingrafting also solves the problem from the preceding quatrains, where the growing plant increases only to decay; the poet is himself the gardener who can intervene protectively in this process, extending the life of the dying plant. In this sonnet, only the poet-playwright, not any other cultural or cosmic agent, including a real gardener or a real deity, can say to Time what Will says in Sonnet 123: "Thy registers and thee I both defy . . . / I will be true despite thy scythe and thee" (9, 14). In sum, Sonnet 15 presents Will as an actor on the stage writing both drama and poetry to solve the West's most enduring problem, the tragic fact of human mortality. Will's idea of poetry is once again hardly new, but his opposition between poetry with its living fame and theatre with its illusory show is especially fresh and important, at least in the English sonnet tradition.[35]

SONNET 23

The representation of sonneteer and stage appears substantively next in Sonnet 23:

> As an unperfect actor on the stage,
> Who with his fear is put besides his part,
> Or some fierce thing replete with too much rage,
> Whose strength's abundance weakens his own heart,
> So I, for fear of trust, forget to say
> The perfect ceremony of love's [rite],

---

[34] Smith, *Homosexual Desire*, 247. Freinkel, "Rose," traces the grafting image to its religious sources in St. Paul (Romans 11: 19–23) and in Luther (*Lectures on Romans*) (244–45). On husbandry, see Greene, "Thrivers."

[35] On fame from classical through modern culture, see Braudy,

> And in mine own love's strength seem to decay,
> O'ercharg'd with burthen of mine own love's might.
> O, let my books be then the eloquence
> And dumb presagers of my speaking breast,
> Who plead for love, and look for recompense,
> More than that tongue that more hath more express'd.
>   O, learn to read what silent love hath writ:
>   To hear with eyes belongs to love's fine wit.
>   (Sonnet 23)

As in Sonnet 15, the general drift here is relatively straightforward. In the first two quatrains, Will employs a theatrical simile designed to explain to the young man why he has forgotten to declare his love to him. In the third quatrain, Will offers a substitute for such a declaration by telling the youth to view his "books" as the "dumb presagers" of his love. Finally, in the couplet Will summarizes this directive by encouraging the young man to learn to read in print what Will has been unable to say in person.

Like Sonnet 15, Sonnet 23 is important for its clear combination of theatre and books. What precisely is that combination? In terms of the literal fiction, Will relies both on a theatrical simile (the actor on a stage) to explain his silence and on a theatrical metaphor (the dumb presagers) to describe the function of his books. In effect, then, he doubles the representation of poetry and theatre, introducing considerable complication: in a sonnet, he likens himself to an actor; and in this sonnet he equates his books of poetry with a play. The complication helps make its own point: Shakespeare's ingrained thinking process both separates and intertwines the two modes of his professional career. Yet, by borrowing Booth's principle from Sonnet 110, perhaps we can see Shakespeare presenting Will as a (clownish) man of the theatre who nonetheless has managed to write poetry of educational value – and is saying so in a Petrarchan sonnet. At the core of Will's educational program is the idea that runs throughout the sequence as a kind of refrain: that true love is silent and does not speak a part. Printed verse, not public theatre, is the fit medium to display the integrity of this faith in silent desire; theatre, by its nature, is a shameful public profession because it violates that integrity.

Yet the combination of theatre and poetry in Sonnet 23 is both more detailed and more complicated than even this preliminary formulation allows, as recent scholarship reveals. The primary problem lies in the textual crux of the word "books" in line 9. In the eighteenth century, George Sewell emended the 1609 quarto's "books" to "looks," mainly because of the problem "books" creates for the meaning of "dumb presagers" in line 10. As Booth explains, the word "presagers" has "not been satisfactorily explained . . . No other instance of 'presager' or any form of 'presage' is known where the reference is not to foreshowing the future" (Booth, ed., *Sonnets*, 172). Evans adds, "since Shakespeare's 'books'" are "already written," they "cannot properly be said to prophesy or foretell" (Evans, ed., *Sonnets*, 136). The word "looks" makes more sense, some editors insist, because "looks" can function as "dumb presagers" of Will's "eloquence."

I confess that I do not understand this line of argument, since a similar thought appears famously in Sonnet 106 (Cheney, "Sonnet 106"). Referring to past writers, Will observes,

> I see their antique pen would have express'd
> Even such a beauty as you master now.
> So all their praises are but prophecies
> Of this our time, all you prefiguring,
> And for they look'd but with divining eyes,
> They had not still [or skill] enough your worth to sing.
> (Sonnet 106. 7–12)

Here Will engages in a similarly tortuous, hyperbolic writerly thought grounded in impossibility: writers of old wrote works that prophesy the young man; however, because such writers looked only with divining eyes (able to foretell the youth), they lacked the style or skill to sing his worth consciously.[36] In the context of Sonnet 106, the word "books" in Sonnet 23 makes perfect sense: Will asks that his books function as presagers, foreshadowers, of his current poems celebrating the young man. In effect, Will assigns to his own poetry the principle he later assigns to the poetry of others; in both instances, the young man's beauty warrants the time-bending conceit (this turns out to be one of the few things to the youth's credit).

Before turning to the question of which books Will has in mind, we may note something rather curious here; perhaps lines 9–10 construct a fable for modern Shakespearean scholarship: the text's conjunction of printed poetry and staged theatre is precisely what has baffled us. Yet it is such a conjunction that the text presents, and thus we might profitably submit rather than try to erase it. Through theatrical discourse in a sonnet that refers to his printed poems, Will presents himself as a new English Ovidian poet-playwright caught between two interconnected, clashing media, even

---

[36] All editors gloss the textual crux here of "style" versus "skill," but neither reading seriously affects the argument. All three 1997 editions of the complete works – *Riverside, Norton, Longman* – print "books" and follow up with notes on Shakespeare's reference to his printed poems or works. Moreover, Booth, J. Kerrigan, and Duncan-Jones all print "books," as does Rollins, ed., *Variorum: Sonnets*.

in his relationship with the young man. This clash is precisely the context for negotiating that relationship.

In the first quatrain, Will likens himself both to an actor in the theatre whose stage fright has compelled him to forget his part and to a wild "thing" (or animal) whose anger has weakened his wrath. As Booth helps us see, the phrasing is more complicated: "Before a reader comes to line 4 and sees that *Or* introduces a parallel construction that presents an alternative for the whole of lines 1 and 2, *Or* can seem to introduce an alternative only to *fear* in line 2, an alternative cause of the actor's lapse of memory" (Booth, ed., *Sonnets*, 171). This reading extends the theatre simile to the whole of the quatrain, making its topic fully professional. Will is identifying either two causes or two alternative causes or perhaps two interlocked causes to the problem he withholds until the second quatrain: the intersection of opposing emotions of fear and desire interferes with his ability to "speak." Facing the young man, Will feels like a fearful actor on the stage (and/or a powerful creature with great energy) unable to act out his desire.

In the second quatrain, line 5 supports the interlock of fear and desire as the emotions Will experiences on the stage, for here the two become one: "So I, for fear of trust, forget to say." *Fear of trust/forget to say*: the loaded line brings to bear on poetry and theatre two ideas central to the Shakespeare canon – the fear of infidelity and the problem of memory and forgetting.[37] Will's fear of trusting the young man, perhaps himself, impedes his ability to write poetry, just as his stage fright impedes his ability to act in the theatre. Will does not cordon his relationship with the young man off from his double life as a poet and dramatist but rather interlocks the two in a complex dynamic. The echo between "*unperfect* actor" in line 1 and poetry's "*perfect* ceremony of love's rite" in line 6 – noted by editors – reinforces the structural conjunction between Will's twin professional media, as Evans's gloss helps us see: "word-perfect 'performance' or observance (such as would be given by the 'perfect actor'" on the stage)" (Evans, ed., *Sonnets*, 136).

In the third quatrain, Will supplies a solution to his problem: let his "books" speak for him, as the dumb show speaks for the play the audience is about to view. We do not know which books Will has in mind, but editors have turned up three main possibilities: (1) the present sonnets; (2) Shakespeare's past printed books, *Venus and Adonis* and *The Rape of*

---

[37] Sonnet 23 confirms what Sonnet 152, the last in the Petrarchan part of the sequence, clarifies, that Shakespeare's Sonnets are fundamentally about the problem of infidelity – sexual, marital, philosophical, theological, and of course professional: "new faith torn" (152. 3). The problem of memory and forgetting is less often discussed; see Sullivan, "Forgetting."

Lucrece; and even (3) the "written text of a stage play."[38] Each of these possibilities contains an intriguing line of inquiry that we can only sketch in briefly here. Taking the three in reverse order: If the books are Will's written scripts for stage plays, in effect he is encouraging the young man to read Shakespeare's plays as prefigurations of his sonnets, the representation of dramatic characters functioning as presagers for the young man. This reading conjoins poetry and theatre in an important dyad that could lead the historical young man (who ever he was) to view those plays in terms of himself. What would be the effect of carrying out such an interpretive program, even for a single play published before 1609, such as *1 Henry IV* or *Hamlet*? (Has anyone ever devised a sounder strategy for securing patronage? It couldn't hurt box-office receipts either.) If, on the other hand, the books refer to *Venus and Adonis* and *The Rape of Lucrece*, we might ask, What do these poems communicate to that same young man (or even to readers viewing this scenario, such as Shakespeare's "private friends" or his public friends, ourselves?) Plotting the terms of an interpretative program here is easier to perform. *Venus and Adonis* might well encourage the young man to avoid the brutal fate of Adonis' narcissism by listening to the authority of Venus (169–74) – the same authority Will has urged on to the young man in Sonnets 1–17: the young man would free himself from the fatal danger of virginity by marrying and then procreating. By contrast, *The Rape of Lucrece* might entreat the young man to avoid the equally brutal fate of Tarquin's devouring lust – the very bestial desire that Will encounters (albeit with the dark lady's complicity) through the "sensual fault" of Sonnet 35 (line 9; see Sonnet 34). According to this possibility, then, Shakespeare's two minor epics would acquire the status of humanist manifestoes training a young man (and young men generally) in the art of sexual character, in the hopes of turning tragic fate aside. Finally, if the books are the sonnets we are presently reading, Will is simply telling the young man that his sonnets – at the least the first twenty-two – function as presagers of his interior voice: his "speaking breast."

That last phrase deserves a pause, for, as Naomi J. Miller nicely observes, Will employs the discourse of early modern "codes of maternity," and this topic bears intriguingly on our discussion:

"As an unperfect actor," the speaker fears the responsibility of the mother's part, and fears as well the "strength's abundance" of "some fierce thing." . . . The nursing

---

[38] Quoted in Booth, ed., *Sonnets*, 172. For the present sonnets and Shakespeare's two previously printed poems, see Kerrigan, ed., *The Sonnets*, 203; Duncan-Jones, ed., *Sonnets*, 156.

metaphor underlying the "speaking breast" allows the poet to establish a maternal dumb show, in which the sonnets "express" the milk of the poet's love. (N. J. Miller 347, 355)

Although Miller does not engage the theatrical metaphor (from her title), she prepares us to re-imagine Will as that "actor on the stage": he is (also) "play[ing] the mother's part" (143. 12), cross-dressed quite.

In the couplet, Will directs the young man to "learn to read" such milky books, for to "hear with eyes belongs to love's fine wit." Here Will finalizes the sonnet's obsessive dichotomy between promulgation and silence, publication and inwardness, speaking and feeling, writing and loving.[39] For his part, Shakespeare turns Will's attempt to explain his lapse in celebrating the young man into a forum on the problem "express[ing]" his twin career as an English Ovidian poet-playwright.

SONNETS 29, 55, 108

In Sonnet 29, one of the most well-known in the sequence, Will appears to locate his public "disgrace with Fortune and men's eyes" (1) in the theatre and his consolation to such disgrace once again in his thought of the young man and in the "hymns" about the youth that he sings at "heaven's gate" (12). Although we do not know for sure the misfortune to which Will alludes, readers often suspect the author's life in the theatre.[40] The opening quatrain, with its portrait of Will "beweep[ing]" his "outcast state" and "troubl[ing] . . . deaf heaven" with his "bootless cries," certainly has the feel of drama, especially tragedy, with its suffering actor strutting on the stage. Therefore, we may wonder whether to detect a pun in "bootless" (perhaps a reference to the *cothurnus* or boot of the tragic actor?).[41] Those who do read theatre into the first quatrain (in particular) would see Will

---

[39] For Will's "oscillation" between "subjectivity" and "civic temperament," see Martin, *Policy*, 134–36.

[40] See, e.g., Evans, ed., *Sonnets*, 141. Evans also links the reference to bad "Fortune" at 111. 1 with Shakespeare's life in the theatre, citing Sir John Davies' two references to Shakespeare, the theatre, and fortune (Evans, ed., *Sonnets*, 222; see Duncan-Jones, ed., *Sonnets*, 332). Kerrigan glosses line 4 ("And look upon myself") as follows: "The poet is not navel-gazing but has become the spectator of his own predicament (compare *3 Henry VI*, 2. 3. 25–8 . . .)" (Kerrigen, ed., *The Sonnets*, 210).

[41] According to the *Oxford English Dictionary*, the word *bootless* can mean both "Void of boot or profit" (first entry, def 3) and "Without boots" (second entry), citing *1 Henry IV*, 3. 1. 66–67, when Glendower says he has sent Bullingbrook "Bootless home and weather-beaten back," to which Hotspur rejoins, "Home without boots, and in foul weather too!" The *Oxford English Dictionary* notwithstanding, here Shakespeare brings the two meanings of the word together. In "To the memory of my beloved," Jonson dresses Shakespeare himself in this guise: "to heare thy Buskin tread, / And shake a Stage" (36–37; *Riverside Shakespeare*, 97).

locating "disgrace" in his public role as an actor. Consequently, in the third quatrain, when Will provides the consolation for such misfortune in the thoughts he has of the young man and in the "hymns" he sings, we may once more see Will opposing poetry to theatre: his present practice as a private sonneteer consoles him for his disgraceful public profession.

The details of the antithesis deserve further attention. In the theatre of the octave, Will presents himself as a disgraced sufferer who seeks recourse in "heaven," only to find that high locale "deaf" – as if tragic theatre had no access to Christian grace, bound by the pagan determinism of "fate." In the poetic expression of the sestet, however, Will's "state" of thinking on the young man is "Like to the lark at break of day arising," able to "sing . . . hymns at heaven's gate." Since the lark is the bird that can sing while rising in flight, sixteenth-century writers often used it as a symbol of the individual's intellectual ascent to God.[42] Here Shakespeare uses the lark to evoke Christian resonance for his art, as the word "hymns" confirms. While theatre leaves the individual bootless – in an impotent state of misfortune – poetry puts his soul in touch with the deity. The image of the lark-like hymn singing "at heaven's gate" is pristine in its theological precision, compelling us to situate Shakespeare's claim for poetry in a longer Western continuum that stretches from Virgil and Ovid to Dante and Spenser. Whereas Virgil and Ovid vaunted poetry's power to secure fame along a horizontal axis (on earth, in time, and in the ears of posterity), both Dante and Spenser vaunted poetry's power to secure Christian glory along a vertical axis (in heaven, for eternity, and in the ears of God, Christ, and the saints).[43] By contrast, Shakespeare appears to be claiming an intermediate power for poetry, spatially between Virgilian earthly fame and Dantean Christian glory: Shakespeare's hymn cannot get the individual *into* heaven to secure grace and salvation, but it can get the individual *to* "heaven's gate." The conceit of an art that can sound to the Day of Judgment occurs in a related form throughout the Shakespeare canon, in both poems and plays, including three times in the Sonnets and most importantly in Sonnet 55:

> 'Gainst death and all-oblivious enmity
> Shall you pace forth; your praise shall still find room,
> Even in the eyes of all posterity
> That wear this world out to the ending doom.
> So till the judgment that yourself arise,
> You live in this, and dwell in lovers' eyes.
>
> (Sonnet 55. 9–14)

---

[42] See Cheney, *Flight*, 88, 269n11.   [43] See Cheney, *Flight*, 7–10.

In the history of fame, Shakespeare's tender little words "to" and "till" acquire dramatic significance, segueing the relation between classical Virgilian fame and Dantean Christian glory. Will dramatically writes a verse in which the young man steps forth with great authority in the eyes of posterity "to" the "ending doom" – "till" the "judgment." Shakespeare is not as bold as Dante or Spenser, but he is bolder than Virgil or Ovid.[44] The final *telos* of Shakespearean poetry, we may speculate, is to prepare the individual's soul for this momentous occasion; this may well be the promised end of Shakespearean subjectivity in the Sonnets. In the plays, we witness the same *telos* most powerfully when the Eastern Star says to Charmian, in her characteristically theatrical way, "I'll give thee leave / To play till doomsday" (*Antony and Cleopatra*, 5. 2. 231–32).

An extended, even technical version of poetry and theatre appears in Sonnet 108:

> What's in the brain that ink may character
> Which hath not figur'd to thee my true spirit?
> What's new to speak, what now to register,
> That may express my love, or thy dear merit?
> Nothing, sweet boy, but yet like prayers divine,
> I must each day say o'er the very same,
> Counting no old thing old, thou mine, I mine,
> Even as when first I hallowed thy fair name.
> So that eternal love in love's fresh case
> Weighs not the dust and injury of age,
> Nor gives to necessary wrinkles place,
> But makes antiquity for aye his page,
> > Finding the first conceit of love there bred,
> > Where time and outward form would show it dead.
> > > (Sonnet 108)

This densely complex sonnet could be the topic of a separate essay. Duncan-Jones notes the significance of the sonnet's number: "Reaching 108, the total number of sonnets in Sidney's *AS* [*Astrophil and Stella*] . . . the poet takes stock of his achievements. He can find no new way of representing either himself or the youth in words, but is compelled to reiterate what he has often said before; in so doing he continually rediscovers his

---

[44] See also Sonnets 116. 2 and 122. 4, as well as *Lucrece*, 924, *Love's Labor's Lost*, 4. 3. 270, *Richard III*, 3. 1. 78, *Henry V*, 4. 1. 137. Cf. Engle, "Certainty," 837–38 on Shakespeare's commitment to contingency; Greenblatt, who ends *Purgatory* with a note on "the afterlife" in Sonnet 55 (313n1). In "Ovid, Petrarch," Braden traces Shakespeare's use of immortality in the Sonnets to Ovid's *Metamorphoses*, but he misjudges the historic significance of Sonnet 55 when he sees it showing merely "poetry's ability to defy time" (108).

first love and the young man's first beauty, revivified in language though vanished in nature" (Duncan-Jones, ed., *Sonnets*, 326). Sonnet 108 also needs to be situated historically in the context of both Plato and Scripture, as its discourse of philosophy and religion indicates, especially the Platonically precise "eternal love" but also the various echoes of Christian worship: "prayers divine" and "hallowed . . . name."[45] Most obviously, the sonnet is important for its reflection on the seminal challenge of Shakespeare's poetic art: to write "eternal love in love's fresh case"; to present the particular instance or thing of love so that it partakes of the eternal essence, thereby freeing it from the dust of death – in effect, to write verse that allows the young man to prepare for (or participate in) Christian immortality.

Shakespeare's inclusion of a discourse that pertains either to printed poetry or to staged theatre helps support this reading. While the word "show" has clear theatrical resonance, and "antiquity" clear resonance for printed books, most of the words straddle the borderline between the two forms: "character," "figured," "speak," "say," "express," "form."[46] The word "case" is a case in point. John Kerrigan identifies four different meanings for the phrase "love's fresh case": "(1) in the (constantly) fresh circumstances of (truly true) love; (2) contained in affection's sprightly (though *old*) argument (meaning 'my love poetry'); (3) covered by affection's youthful vigour (*case* suggesting 'skin', and thus the *wrinkles* of line 11); (4) clad in affection's sprightly garb (common meaning of *case* in the period)" (Kerrigan, ed., *The Sonnets*, 321). To these four meanings, Evans adds a fifth: "in the case of a newly conceived love" (Evans, ed., *Sonnets*, 219). To these five, we can add a sixth, prepared for by Kerrigan's fourth meaning – one that pertains to the theatre: "case" as dress, costume, as in *Measure for Measure*'s "How often dost thou with thy case, thy habit" (2. 4. 13), but specifically "case" as theatrical disguise, as in Hal's directive to Poins in *1 Henry IV* during the robbery at Gad's Hill: "Case ye, case ye, on with your vizards" (2. 2. 53).[47] According to the theatrical meaning of "case," then, Will can be seen to talk not just about an author's expressive challenge but also about the challenge facing a playwright and an actor: the challenge of staging "eternal love" freshly. The emphatic word "show" in the last line compels this theatrical ring for the sonnet as a whole. Characteristically, the verbal play of "show"

---

[45] Editors emphasize Scripture but neglect Plato. Duncan-Jones glosses "eternal love" as having "strong religious connotations, as in Sidney's *CS* [*Certain Sonnets*], 32: 13–14" (Duncan-Jones, ed., *Sonnets*, 326).

[46] On "character" as a print term, see Burrow, "Life," 24–25.

[47] See *Romeo and Juliet* 1. 4. 29–30; *1 Henry IV*, 1. 2. 179; *Henry V*, 3. 2. 4.

shifts to where we might expect it – the negative side of the poetry/theatre dialectic, allowing Will to "show" what will die: "outward form."

SONNET 144

Sonnet 144 is the final poem of Shakespeare's Sonnets to bring poetry and theatre into significant alignment. This sonnet is notable not simply because a version of it was published along with a version of Sonnet 138 in *The Passionate Pilgrim*, but also because it is (as we have seen) "one of the strongest sonnets in the volume," and the only one that summarizes the triangulated plot of sexual desire between Will, the young man, and the dark lady.[48] As Duncan-Jones adds, "The sonnet's number in the sequence, 12 × 12, known as a 'gross', may be especially appropriate to this enumeration of the speaker's amorous possessions, which prove to be 'gross' also in the sexual sense" (Duncan-Jones, ed., *Sonnets*, 402). That Shakespeare would conjoin poetry and theatre in such a significant sonnet makes it especially worth entertaining here.

Unlike Sonnet 55 or Sonnet 111, Sonnet 144 contains no explicit reference to either Will's role as a poet or as a playwright, nor does it employ overt poetic or theatrical discourse. Instead, it presents Will as a sonnet writer who deploys a religious metaphor evocative of the morality play tradition, especially as staged famously in Marlowe's *Doctor Faustus*.[49] The effect of the morality play metaphor – and perhaps even of the Marlovian one – is to present Will as a sonneteer staging and rewriting his morality play predicament in terms at once personal and erotic.[50]

The first quatrain stages a dialectic between the young man and the dark lady as types of "love," conveyed through several fields – gender, aesthetics, ethics, theology, and finally personal affect:

> Two loves I have of comfort and despair,
> Which like two spirits do suggest me still:
> The better angel is a man right fair,
> The worser spirit a woman color'd ill.
> (Sonnet 144. 1–4)

Thus the young man is (indeed) a "man," "fair," "better," and an "angel" who brings Will "comfort," while the dark lady is a "woman," "color'd

---

[48] Quoted in Kerrigan, ed., *The Sonnets*, 59. Evans quotes Leslie Fielder, who calls 144 "the thematic key to the entire sequence" (Evans, ed., *Sonnets*, 262).

[49] Kerrigan, ed., *The Sonnets*, 375; Evans, ed., *Sonnets*, 262; Duncan-Jones, ed., *Sonnets*, 402.

[50] On the morality play in *Doctor Faustus*, see Grantley, "Theatricalism," 234–35.

ill," "worser," and a sinister "spirit" who brings him "despair." As Booth
observes, "comfort and despair" are "both terms in theology, an area which
the poem immediately invades" (Booth, ed., *Sonnets*, 497). Through this
dialectic, Will converts his lyric expression into a theatrical event.

The second quatrain puts the dialectic into action:

> To win me soon to hell, my female evil
> Tempteth my better angel from my [side],
> And would corrupt my saint to be a devil,
> Wooing his purity with her foul pride.
> (Sonnet 144. 5–8)

Here we learn that the dark lady has seduced the young man in order to
carry out revenge against Will. Critics rightly see Shakespeare rewriting the
plot of *Everyman* or *Doctor Faustus*, since the bad angel turns her attention,
not to the mortal soul in the middle, but to her mirror opposite, the
good angel, effectively cutting Will out of the theological deal. Moreover,
lines 6–8 introduce the important blurring of boundaries between the two
halves of the dialectic, for the good angel is here subjected to the temptation
of the evil angel: Will's "saint" becomes a "devil," the young man's "purity" is
wooed by the dark lady's "foul pride." The distinction between masculine
and feminine, beauty and ugliness, good and evil, comfort and despair
begins to evaporate, to be replaced by a new murkiness that resembles the
atmosphere from Sonnet 15.

The third quatrain then shows Will's reaction to this atmospheric
murkiness; he loses his ability to see clearly:

> And whether that my angel be turn'd fiend,
> Suspect I may, yet not directly tell,
> But being both from me, both to each friend,
> I guess one angel in another's hell.
> (Sonnet 144. 9–12)

He can only suspect, not actually determine, whether the young man and
the dark lady betray him behind his back. In the end, he is left to "guess,"
thereby creating a mental fiction in which "one angel [enters] in another's
hell." The line is ambiguous, since it does not specify which spiritual creature and which afterlife are which: the dark lady and the young man have
become indistinguishable. Will's emphasis here on inwardness ("suspect,"
"tell," "guess") marks his dramatic progress during the three quatrains, from
his formulation of a dialectic, to his representation of a dialectical action,
to his own reaction to that action.

In the couplet, Will summarizes his inward condition as one of ignorance, and he gestures toward an end to the (Im)morality play he has been staging: "Yet this shall I ne'er know, but live in doubt, / Till my bad angel fire my good one out." As Booth puts it, he will live in doubt "'Until she gets tired of him and kicks him out' and 'Until he shows symptoms of venereal disease'" (Booth, ed., *Sonnets*, 500). At the close, Will reaches clarity, but only through perceiving the grim effects of a maliciously lustful sexuality.

Will's phrase "live in doubt" is among the most useful in the entire sequence for registering the historical context in which Shakespeare produced his Sonnets. The phrase anticipates Donne's more famous articulation, two years later in the *First Anniversary*: "And new Philosophy calls all in doubt, / The Element of fire is quite put out; / . . . / Tis all in pieces, all coherence gone."[51] While this view of "doubt" during the period is well known, what might be fresh is Shakespeare's portrait of a new kind of author as the mouthpiece to the deeply anxious expression of the age: the English Ovidian poet-playwright.

PASTORAL AND EPIC THEATRE

The presence of Ovidian poetry and theatre in the Sonnets is inflected by the Virgilian career dynamic outlined in earlier chapters. We may take the cue of William Empson, who titles his famous chapter on Sonnet 94 in *Some Versions of Pastoral* "They That Have Power: Twist of Heroic-Pastoral Ideas into an Ironical Acceptance of Aristocracy" (87–115). However influential Empson's essay has been, it remains oblique, so perhaps it should not be surprising to discover that his Virgilian paradigm of epic and pastoral has not taken root in subsequent discussions of either Shakespeare's most discussed sonnet or of the Sonnets generally.

Curiously, Empson's chapter title is the only explicit statement of his thesis, so we may need to recall his special "version of pastoral," emphasized in his larger study: pastoral is an ideological practice of "putting the complex into the simple," the gentleman-courtier into the shepherd-poet. In other words, Empson's famous version "piled the heroic convention onto the pastoral one" (12). While Empson analyzes the intersection of the plant or pastoral imagery and the class or epic imagery in Sonnet 94, he reminds us that such imagery is gathered in from elsewhere in the sequence – from Sonnet 15, for instance, but especially from the memorable "rose" sonnets.

---

[51] Donne, *First Anniversary*, 205–13. Critics often see Shakespeare in the Sonnets living in doubt (Dubrow, *Victors*, 256–57), and we may wish to lean on his phrase in Sonnet 144 to encapsulate this frame of mind.

Indeed, Shakespeare's sequence opens precisely with this version of pastoral, as Will uses recurrent metaphors from what Empson regards as pastoral simplicity to encourage the young man to marry and procreate: "From fairest creatures we desire increase / That thereby beauty's rose might never die" (1. 1–2). Georgio Melchiori well documents these opening sonnets' "concern with concrete principles of good husbandry: ploughing (Sonnet 3), the distillation of perfume from flowers (Sonnet 5 and 6), cattle-rearing (Sonnet 6), harvesting (Sonnet 12), grafting (Sonnet 15), the cultivation of flowers and plants (Sonnet 16)" (*Dramatic Meditations*, 27–28). Bruce R. Smith adds that "The pastoral images of the first twenty sonnets are replaced by chambers and closets (46), beds (27, 142), chests (48, 52, 65), mirrors (63, 77), and clocks (57). The delights of the *locus amoenus* give way to the confidences of the bedchamber" (*Homosexual Desire*, 254). In other words, a pastoral ideal gives way to a courtly one.

By taking these cues and that of Sonnet 94, we can extend Will's "pastoral" and "heroic" concern beyond the Procreation Sonnets in order to see Will, not simply as an Ovidian poet-playwright in the Marlovian vein, but also as a Virgilian pastoral-epicist in the Spenserian vein. Indeed, Will's representation in Sonnet 32 of his "poor rude lines" (4) introduces Spenser's humble pastoral style into the Sonnets.[52] Similarly, Will's representation in Sonnet 106 of "ladies dead and lovely knights" evokes Spenser's epic project:

> When in the chronicle of wasted time
> I see descriptions of the fairest wights
> And beauty making beautiful old rhyme
> In praise of ladies dead and lovely knights.
>
> (106. 1–4)

While each of the first three lines carries Spenserian weight, line 4 is a quite specific *imitatio* of the most important programmatic line in the entire *Faerie Queene*: "And sing of Knights and Ladies gentle deeds" (1. Proem 1). Spenser's line is the first articulation in his romantic epic of his persona as the Virgil of England. As suggested in chapter 2, he opens his epic by relying on a theatrical metaphor that may have interested Shakespeare:

> Lo I the man, whose Muse whilome did maske,
> As time her taught, in lowly Shepheards weeds,
> Am now enforst a far unfitter taske,

---

[52] For details, see Cheney, "Sonnet 106," to which the following discussion is indebted. "Rude" (with cognates) is Spenser's habitual word for his pastoral poetry (*Colin Clouts*, 363, 669; *Januarye*, 67; *June*, 77; *December*, 14; Envoy, 5; *Astrophel*, Proem 12) and for the pastoral poet writing epic (*Faerie Queene* 1. 12. 23, 3. 2. 3).

> For trumpets sterne to chaunge mine Oaten reeds,
> And sing of Knights and Ladies gentle deeds;
> Whose prayses having slept in silence long.
>
> (Spenser, *The Faerie Queene*, 1. Proem 1)

Here Spenser announces his Virgilian turn from pastoral to epic. If Shakespeare is imitating the penultimate line, he is imitating the very site of Spenser's generic progression. From this brief moment, we can discern that Shakespeare's Sonnets present the author as an Ovidian/Marlovian poet-playwright traveling along the Virgilian/Spenserian path.

Sonnet 102 offers a clear map to this authorial representation:

> My love is strength'ned, though more weak in seeming,
> I love not less, though less the show appear;
> That love is merchandiz'd whose rich esteeming
> The owner's tongue doth publish every where.
> Our love was new, and then but in the spring,
> When I was wont to greet it with my lays,
> As Philomela in summer's front doth sing,
> And stops [her] pipe in growth of riper days:
> Not that the summer is less pleasant now,
> Than when her mournful hymns did hush the night,
> But that wild music burthens every bough,
> And sweets grown common lose their dear delight.
>   Therefore like her, I sometime hold my tongue,
>   Because I would not dull you with my song.
>
> (Sonnet 102)

As in the previous sonnets we have examined, here we can clearly locate the discourse of both theatre ("show") and poetry ("lays"). Beyond this, however, the form of the conjunction is anything but clear.

In line 4, for instance, the word "publish" might seem to evoke an anxiety over printed poetry (see Burrow, ed., *Sonnets and Poems*, 584), except that Will himself aligns it with the shame of "show" from line 2 (cf. Wall, *Imprint*, 197). As in Sonnet 23, Will distinguishes between the loving poet's silence as a form of integrity and the prospect of over-broadcasting as the mark of only "seeming" to "love." Yet in Sonnet 102 the word "show" describes Will's praise of the young man through the art of poetry: "I love not less, though less the show appear." That is to say, Will's poetry in praise of the young man is a "show," even though it appears less now that it once did. In lines 3–4, Will employs the mercantile terms of both the counting-house and the print shop to distinguish between his reticence in expressing his love and his "merchandiz[ing]" of love through "publish[ing]" it "every where." Will

does not say "publish" *at all*; he says "publish every where." Thus, in the
first quatrain, while the word "publish" shows Shakespeare worrying about
print publication, it also associates publication with "show" as a shameful
form of publicity violating intimate truth. Unlike other sonnets we have
examined, here poetry and theatre are complicit in the economy of shame.

Only in the second quatrain do we begin to acquire more authoritative
direction. Line 5, "Our love was new, and then but in the spring," introduces
a change from the present of the first quatrain to the past, "When" Will
was "wont" to "greet" the spring with his "lays." Even though he no longer
praises the young man, in the past he was able to "publish" his love through
the "show" of poetry. As in the first quatrain, Will sees poetry as a type of
theatre, but here it is not shameful. The simile then comparing Will's
writing process with the singing cycle of "Philomela" clarifies a crucial
point: just as the nightingale sings in the spring but "stops [her] pipe in
growth of riper days" – in late summer – so Will enacts a human process.
He does not stop his pipe because he loves the young man "less," but rather
because he participates in a natural or seasonal cycle. He compares himself
with Philomela to convince the young man that his poetic process is natural
rather than merely theatrical.

Yet this is no more than a version of Shakespearean humor, since the
author evokes the ancient myth of Philomela. As Evans remarks, the word
"'mournful' reflects the tragic events surrounding Philomela," especially
as Ovid retold those events in Book 6 of the *Metamorphoses* (424–674),
but also as Shakespeare himself had adapted the events in *Titus Andronicus*
(Evans, ed., *Sonnets*, 211) – and, we may add, in *The Rape of Lucrece* and
elsewhere. While Philomela clearly has the "Ovidian" associations that
editors conventionally assign to it, we might recall that both before and
after Ovid Philomela appears as the arch-myth for both pastoral and tragedy.
For Shakespeare, we might say, unlike for Spenser, the nightingale becomes
the quintessential figure for the fusion of theatre with poetry.

In line 8, Will evokes the tradition of Philomela as the myth of pastoral from Theocritus to Spenser: "And stops [her] pipe in growth of riper
days." The importance of this line has escaped attention, for it is among the
clearest excavations in the English Renaissance of an ancient archaeological
artifact: the nightingale as a musical instrument of pastoral poetry.[53] While
drawing on an ancient tradition, Shakespeare also situates himself historically. Editors cite Nicholas Breton in Sonnet 1 of his 1604 *The Passionate
Shepherd* (Evans, ed., *Sonnets*, 211), Sidney in the *Old Arcadia* (66. 13–14;

---

[53] See Cheney, *Flight*, 69–70, 265n46; on the panpipe and birds, see 265n45.

Duncan-Jones, ed., *Sonnets*, 314), Petrarch in Song 311 (Burrow, ed., *Sonnets and Poems*, 584), and Barnabe Barnes in *Parthenophil and Parthenophe* (Burrow, ed., *Sonnets and Poems*, 584). While poet after poet during the period does present him or herself as a type of Philomela, Spenser's E. K., we have seen, traces English origins to Gascogine and identifies Spenser himself as the prime inheritor after Gascoigne's death in 1578. If we recall merely that the "Elizabethans, probably influenced by the Philomela story, usually associated the song of the nightingale with the female" (Evans, ed., *Sonnets*, 211), we erase this specific Elizabethan genealogy. Conversely, by recalling that Shakespeare's "*Philomel* resembles a sheperd(ess) playing pan-pipes in a pastoral landscape" (Kerrigan, ed., *The Sonnets*, 306), we profitably situate Will's pastoral self-representation along Spenser's Virgilian path.[54]

In fact, Will's phrasing in lines 6–8 clearly echoes that of Colin Clout in the *November* eclogue, where Spenser's persona is called "The Nightingale . . . sovereigne of song" (25) and where the shepherd himself refers to "Philomele" steeping her "song with teares" during his Song of Dido (141). Let us place the two sets of lines together:

> When I was wont to greet it with my lays,
> As Philomela in summer's front doth sing,
> And stops [her] pipe in growth of riper days.
> (Shakespeare, Sonnet 102. 6–8)

> The mornefull Muse [Melpomene] in myrth now list ne maske,
> As she was wont in youngth and sommer dayes.
> (Spenser, *November*, 19–20)

Perhaps Spenser's theatrical metaphor, "maske," attracted the theatrical man. In any event, here we discover another Spenserian link between poetry and theatre, pastoral and tragedy. In line 6, Shakespeare's phrase "was wont" is distinctly Spenserian, occurring no fewer than 238 times in his canon (with cognates), often in the context of both pastoral and poetry. Like Will, Colin Clout famously stops his pipe in "growth of riper days" (see *June*, 36).[55]

Thus, in a sonnet conjoining Marlowe's Ovidian discourse of poetry and theatre with Spenser's discourse of pastoral and epic, Shakespeare uses the Philomela myth as a point of intersection between the two literary representations. Effectively, Will presents himself as a pastoral tragedian singing "mournfull hymns." In the third quatrain, he then uses his identity with Philomela to detach himself from rival poets who have also been using "wild

---

[54] On Spenserian pastoral and Shakespearean dramatic pastoral, see Alpers, *What is Pastoral?*, 185–86.

[55] The phrase "mournfull hymns" recalls the "hymne" to Dido sung by Colin, who invokes Melpomene, "mournefulst Muse of nyne" (*November*, 53).

music" to "burthen . . . every bough."[56] Here Will justifies "stop[ping]" his
poetry through an ornithological process, in which countless birds eventually join with the nightingale in singing their songs. Consequently, in this
"riper" season the nightingale-poet ends his song to affirm his distinction
as the sovereign of song.

In the couplet, Will confirms his likeness to Philomela. Perhaps his
phrasing about "hold[ing] his tongue" and not "dulling" the young man
glances at Philomela's loss of her tongue through the brutality of Tereus.
As Wall reveals, Elizabethan poets like Spenser and Gascoigne recurrently
cross-dress their voices in the garb of a female, including Philomela, to air
their shame over printing their art (*Imprint*, 260–62). While Wall refers to
Sonnet 102 only in passing (262), we might extend her analysis about the
shame of publication to the twin domains of poetry and theatre, including
Shakespeare's pastoral theatre here.

MANUSCRIPT AND PRINT AUTHORSHIP

So far, we have discussed poetry and theatre in terms of the narrative
sequence that begins with the young-man sonnets and ends with the sonnets to the dark-lady. Recent textual scholarship, however, suggests that
Shakespeare's compositional practice reversed this narrative order: he wrote
the dark-lady sonnets first, c. 1591–95; and the young-man sonnets second,
c. 1595–1604 (Burrow, ed., *Sonnets and Poems*, 103–11, 131–38). This scholarship has intriguing implications for the present argument, because the
discourse of poetry and theatre occurs almost exclusively in the young-
man sonnets. While we can follow such critics as Fineman and Margreta
de Grazia in formulating a critical narrative based on the structure of the
1609 quarto, foregrounding subjectivity or sexual scandal, we can take the
editorial cue of Burrow to see how the Sonnets also register Shakespeare's
increasing interest in the twin forms of authorship itself, the conjunction
of poetry and theatre, from the mid-1590s through the first years of the
seventeenth century. The author did not abandon poetry for theatre but
came to see their conjunction as the central form of his art.

Having said so, we might acknowledge the challenge we confront in
reconstructing the historical context for the Sonnets, for Shakespeare's collection has long been at the eye of a critical storm over the issue of authorship. On the one hand, the 1609 quarto has been so mysterious that from the

---

[56] Burrow glosses "burthens" by recalling that the "noun 'burden' can mean *chorus* (*OED* 10)" (Burrow,
    ed., *Sonnets and Poems*, 584).

perspectives of both the bibliographer and the biographer we would not be unwise to abandon the category of the author altogether. The question was forcefully raised by Duncan-Jones in the title of a seminal essay, "Was the 1609 *Shake-speares Sonnets* Really Unauthorized?" Our answer to this question commits us to a series of critical positions – especially, in the current critical climate, our sense of the relation between a manuscript and a print Shakespeare. Those answering yes to the question, believing the Sonnets unauthorized, are compelled to identify the author as a manuscript rather than a print poet. On the other hand, the bibliographical (and biographical) work done by Duncan-Jones, Kerrigan, and others – those who answer that the Sonnets are indeed authorized – presents us with a radically different Shakespeare: not a private coterie poet in the mold of Donne but a public proto-national poet in the mold of Spenser. In these terms, the Sonnets would become not simply a manuscript poem circulated randomly among private friends but rather a carefully controlled collection that moves from scribal circulation to print publication.

Critics of differing professional temperaments will presumably suit themselves to whichever position they find comfortable, and few would be so unwise as to think rational argument could budge anyone either way. One suspects, however, that the truth lies elsewhere: that Shakespeare is neither Donne nor Spenser; the Sonnets are neither fully a manuscript-authored nor a print-authored poem. Presumably, this peculiar reality is why both Shakespeare and his collection have been so intriguing for so long: here we have an author and his work defying the binary categories in which we are used to thinking. We are witnessing, then, a new model of authorship, one that recent scholarship is only now learning to formulate. Among recent critics, Richard Helgerson most succinctly articulates this new model, in an evident attempt to reconcile recent historical theories of social construction with past theories of intentionality, saying of Shakespeare, "He helped make the world that made him" (*Forms*, 215). While recognizing Shakespeare's historical complexity in straddling the divide of early modern authorship – between manuscript and print culture, coterie poet and national poet, Donne and Spenser – we have attended to the second part of the opposition, because what seems missing in recent criticism is the kind of close intertextual work that demonstrates Shakespeare's interest in the Spenserian project.

At least since Charles Gildon and more famously Edmund Malone, critics have tried to capture the special relation that the Sonnets have to the plays, for better or for worse. As we have seen, Shakespeare himself *represented* his own sense of that relation. The Sonnets are surely not theatre, but for that they need not apologize. Yet neither are they the Elizabethan or Jacobean lyric as usual – as testified to by so much criticism on their "dramatic" quality, or on their intimate connection with the inwardness of such plays as *Hamlet*. What is unusual in the Sonnets is Shakespeare's own self-consciousness about precisely this character for his historic composition. The Sonnets are poems not merely *by* a practicing man of the theatre but also *about* a theatrical man who tries to write them. In this, they may well find their final distinction from so much other great English Renaissance poetry. Shakespeare's book of sonnets is historically the dumb presager of his national eloquence.

CHAPTER 8

"Deep-brain'd sonnets" and "tragic shows": Shakespeare's late Ovidian art in A Lover's Complaint

In *A Lover's Complaint*, Shakespeare offers his most concentrated fiction about the relation between poetry and theatre. Among Shakespeare's poems – and even among his plays – his third and last narrative poem is valuable for its lucid narration of a story directly about the cultural function and social interchange between "deep-brain'd sonnets" (209) and "tragic shows" (308). Since recent scholarship concludes that Shakespeare composed this poem in the first decade of the seventeenth century, it joins its companion piece in the famed 1609 quarto in calling into question the dominant models regarding the presence of the poems within a predominantly theatrical career (see chapter 1). By recalling what recent editors of Shakespeare's poems emphasize, that Shakespeare was working on *A Lover's Complaint* at the time that he was composing such "mature" plays as *Hamlet*, *Measure for Measure*, *All's Well*, and *Cymbeline* – that indeed he was redeploying the very discourse from the plays – we might come to find his fiction about the professional relation between poetry and theatre late in his career of considerable value.[1]

As with the Sonnets, admittedly here we do not know what Shakespeare's intentions were. We do not know why he composed this poem or whether he authorized its publication. In other words, *A Lover's Complaint* is another work situated on the borderline between manuscript and print. While some readers will be more comfortable operating on the manuscript side of the border, in this chapter (as in the last) we will acknowledge the question but attend to what does appear in print. Precisely because of the question over the poem as a work of the print poet, we might find the direct representation of poetry and theatre here all the more noteworthy.[2]

---

[1] On *A Lover's Complaint* and the plays, see Kerrigan, ed., *The Sonnets*, 393–94; Roe, ed., *Poems*, 70–72; Burrow, ed., *Sonnets and Poems*, 139–40; Underwood, *Prolegomena*, 117–69. On the special link with *Hamlet*, see Craik, "*A Lover's Complaint*," 439, 444–46.

[2] Shakespeare's predecessors in the complaint form (see Kerrigan, *Motives*) do not include a sustained discourse of poetry and theatre. Daniel's *Rosamond* includes a discourse of "show" (173, 279, 280, 300,

THE FICTION OF SONNET AND SHOW

Briefly, the fiction in *A Lover's Complaint* tells of a male narrator hearing and seeing a "fickle maid full pale" (5). She reaches into her "maund" or basket (36), pulls out "folded schedules" and "many a ring of posied gold and bone" (43, 45), "[T]ear[s]" the "papers," and "break[s] . . . rings a-twain" (6), throwing both sets of artifacts into "a river . . . / Upon whose weeping margent she was set" (38–39). The narrator then sees a "reverend man" (57), once "Of court, of city" (59) but now a cowherd "graz[ing] . . . his cattle nigh" (57), draw near "this afflicted fancy" (61) to inquire "the grounds and motives of her woe" (63). The country maid tells the cowherd a story that takes us through the final words of the poem. In her story, the maid narrates how a young man with the sophistication of a courtier seduces her with an exquisite physical beauty and a compelling internal character that are served by two modes of literary art: the "deep-brain'd sonnets" that the maid receives from the young man; and the "tragic shows" that he performs to win her sympathy. At the core of her story, the maid quotes the young man's own rhetoric of courtship (177–280), including his haunting tale about seducing a nun (232–66), in what constitutes one of Shakespeare's most spectacular versifications of a dangerous sexual theatre.

The story about sonnets and shows – situated in "the familiar Shakespearean territory of sexual betrayal" (Roe, ed., *Poems*, 73) – is even more complex. As part of his seductive performance, the young courtier tells the maid that the sonnets he has given her are compositions he has received from girls he has seduced previously (204–10), leading most critics to assume that these compositions are the ones the maid throws in the river (e.g., J. Kerrigan, *Motives*, 46). Yet Colin Burrow rightly complicates this assumption: "they are a little less transparent than that" ("Life," 28). Burrow goes on to emphasize that "[S]eeing these objects does not give access to the emotions behind a love affair in material form . . . [i]n Shakespeare's poems objects do not reveal emotions; they encrypt them intriguingly, and start his readers on a quest for mind. An object is held up as something which offers a point of access to an experience, but the experience which it signifies, and whatever those mysterious 'deep-brained sonnets' actually relate, is withheld from us" (28).

If Burrow rightly emphasizes the closed contents of the "sonnets," he simultaneously opens Shakespeare's own text to the possibility that the

398, 623, 657, 692), with a vague theatrical ring (173, 278–80, 300, 657), but such discourse is detached from the commercial theatre (see Kerrigan, *Motives*). By contrast, Daniel includes an important and sustained discourse of poetry: "Thames had Swannes as well as ever Po" (728).

young courtier might well have composed the "papers" himself. Certainly, the reader is invited to make this inference up to the moment of his bold declaration to the maid (218–24), but perhaps even afterwards, given the youth's notorious falsehood. In short, we are not certain just who has composed the "papers" or "sonnets," or whether these different words represent even the same documents, and it is reasonable to see that the ambiguity of both their form and their authorship might be part of the representation. The ambiguity extends to the gender of the author(s), which could include both men and women. Is it possible that the country maid is even tearing up documents she has herself composed, furious that the young man has sent as his own the very documents she once sent to him? In short, *A Lover's Complaint*'s representation of the first half of the literary compound, the sonnets, is itself of "double voice" (3) – and on two counts: both double-authored and double-gendered. However we construe the literary economy here, men and women are implicated in both the writing and the reading of the paper forms.

We may extend this principle to the second half of the literary compound, "shows." The maid describes the youth as a tragic playwright when she accuses him of performing "a plenitude of subtle matter," which, "Applied to cautels [deceits], all strange forms receives,"

> Of burning blushes, or of weeping water,
> Or sounding paleness; and he takes and leaves,
> In either's aptness as it best deceives,
> To blush at speeches rank, to weep at woes,
> Or to turn white and sound at tragic shows.
> (*A Lover's Complaint*, 302–08)

To "turn white and sound at tragic shows" evidently means to stage a dangerously chaste theatre empty of artistic and moral integrity. As we shall see, this is not the only theatrical discourse in the poem but rather part of a larger network from the place of the stage. If in a simple reading Shakespeare genders the author of the sonnets female, in an equally simple reading he genders the author of tragedy male. While readers might feel inclined to sympathize with the maid, and thereby to blame the youth for his theatricality, John Kerrigan has encouraged us to press the verity of the maid herself: "Shakespeare indicates that the 'context' of the maid's 'utterance' [the opening echo that the narrator hears resounding through the hills] pre-emptively endangers what is said. The received landscape of complaint (realm of Spenser, William Browne) takes a 'voyce' and makes it 'doble'" (*Motives*, 44). While Kerrigan warns that we "should resist the prompting of 'doble' either wholly to credit what she says or to judge her account mendacious" (44), he nonetheless opens the maid to further scrutiny. For instance, she is the one to unleash theatre into the discourse of the poem as a site of sexual falsehood, prompting us to wonder how she knows about this particular domain. Like the dyer's hand in Shakespeare's famous sonnet on the theatre (111), perhaps her nature is subdued to what it works in.

In short, in *A Lover's Complaint* both poetry and theatre are potentially double-voiced and double-gendered. As the phrases for these twin forms of production suggest – "deep-brain'd sonnets" and "tragic shows" – Shakespeare presents the forms authored and gendered as themselves in opposition, even in conflict. The genre of Petrarchan poetry in which men and women are complicit is fundamentally a subjective, mental, and internal art ("deep-brain'd"), while the Senecan tragic genre in which men and women are also complicit is fundamentally a material, performative, and external one ("show").[3] Despite the poem's phrases for the two arts, however, we can extend the principle of doubleness to their status in the narrative. Since we are not privy to the contents of the "deep-brain'd sonnets," as Burrow observes, they appear paradoxically as *materialized texts*; similarly, the "tragic shows," for all their superficiality, penetrate the brain deeply, as the narrative reveals.

CRITICAL CONTEXTS

The workings and implications of the opposing doubleness of content, form, gender, and authorship for poetry and theatre require some patience to sort out, but that shall be our goal in this final chapter. Surprisingly, critics have neglected the topic. They have, however, touched its perimeters. Most comment on the presence of "deep-brain'd sonnets" in a collection of verse titled *Shake-speares Sonnets* (as does Burrow), prompting fruitful detail about the connections between the Sonnets and *A Lover's Complaint* (see Bell "That which"; Laws, "Generic Complexities")· both poems present narratives of sexual infidelity that feature three erotically related principals in a tragic triangle, consisting of two men and a woman. By contrast, while most critics discuss the theatre through comparisons with the plays, and occasionally identify the young man as an "actor," only Kerrigan has

---

[3] Critics discussing "Shakespeare's Petrarchism" (Braden), tend to neglect *A Lover's Complaint*. On the European development of Petrarchan authorship, including in England, see Kennedy, *Authorizing Petrarch*. On Seneca in the plays, see Miola, *Tragedy*; Helms, *Seneca*. On complaint, Seneca, and Renaissance tragedy in *A Lover's Complaint*, see J. Kerrigan, *Motives*, 55–59.

probed more deeply.[4] Discussing the commonplace intertextuality with Spenser's complaints, both *The Ruines of Time* (which opens in similar terms) and Spenser's contributions to Jan Ver der Noot's *Theatre for Wordlings*, Kerrigan observes: "Like Spenser's Rome . . . [the maid] inhabits a 'theatre for worldlings'" (*Motives*, 42), to the extent that "early readers, attuned to the theatricality of the [complaint] genre, might have thought in terms of a well-known playwright writing for the paper-stage" (43). Later, Kerrigan notes "the impact of the larger [complaint] genre upon drama" – for instance, *The Mirror for Magistrates* upon "Renaissance tragedy" – even raising the question "about the stage worthiness of grief": "complaint is problematic because stagey before it is staged" (55–56). What is left to do is to locate theatre, along with poetry, *in the discourse of the poem itself* and to speculate more fully what it might mean for *this* "well-known playwright" to be "writing for th[is particular] . . . paper-stage."[5]

SHAKESPEAREAN AUTHORSHIP: OVID AND MARLOWE

We may contextualize Shakespeare's double-voiced fiction in terms of the new figure of the Ovidian poet-playwright. One way to read Shakespeare's fiction is as a self-conscious narrative about the arts of poetry and theatre in his own Ovidian career.[6] Even more directly than in his two early experiments in narrative poetry, in this late one Shakespeare makes his fiction about the incompatibility of the sexes and the deadly nature of desire pertain to his writing career.

Moreover, as in *Venus* and *Lucrece*, in *A Lover's Complaint* Shakespeare presents Ovidianism as distinctly Marlovian. Although recent scholarship and criticism neglect Marlowe's presence in the poem, we know too much

---

[4] On the young man as an actor, see Rollins, ed., *Variorum: Poems*, 588–89; Underwood, *Prolegomena*, 83; Rees, "Sidney," 159; Craik, "*A Lover's Complaint*," 442.

[5] The songs and shows are not quite of the same representational economy, but they are close: the sonnets are material artifacts, but the shows tend be more metaphorical, a term for the young courtier's deception. Nonetheless, J. Kerrigan and Burrow allow us to see how *A Lover's Complaint* complicates the distinction, to see that this is exactly how Shakespeare's mind represents the two forms at this point in his career. Cf. Craik: Shakespeare "raises questions we can call theatrical since they concern performativity and audience" ("*A Lover's Complaint*," 443).

[6] Unlike modern editions of *Venus* and *Lucrece*, those of *A Lover's Complaint* contain little annotation on Ovid: Duncan-Jones and Burrow record no intertextuality, while Kerrigan mentions Ovid only once (*The Sonnets*, 400). Among critics, Rees, Kay, and Sharon-Zisser do not mention Ovid; among those who do, see Rollins, ed., *Variorum: Poems*, 589; Underwood, *Prolegomena*, 2, 3–9, 15–16, 47, 50, 55–56, 59; Roe, ed., *Poems*, 64, 66n1; J. Kerrigan, *Motives*, 55–57, 67; Craik, "*A Lover's Complaint*," 438.

about Shakespeare's ongoing struggle with Marlowe's ghost to follow suit.[7] Critics can observe that "Thomas Whythorne and George Gascoigne both wrote poems of courtship and seduction to numerous Elizabethan women" (Bell, "That which," 463), but we might also recall that this mode is virtually Marlowe's signature, especially in his poetry, from *Ovid's Elegies* to "The Passionate Shepherd" to *Hero and Leander*. The country maid's voice at times sounds Marlovian, recalling the narrator's voice in *Hero and Leander*: "For when we rage, advice is often seen / By blunting us to make our wits more keen" (160–61). More particularly, the young courtier's seduction of "a nun, / Or sister sanctified, of holiest note" (232–33), echoes Leander's elaborate seduction of "Venus' nun" in Marlowe's Ovidian narrative (1. 45); indeed, the stories are remarkably similar in outline. But it is the young courtier himself, an Ovidian figure of desire deploying both poetry and theatre, who most compellingly conjures up the perturbed spirit of Christopher Marlowe, his Ovidian career, and what it serves: a counter-Virgilian nationhood – that is, a nonpatriotic form of nationalism that subverts royal power with *libertas* (*Amores*, 3. 15. 9; *Ovid's Elegies*, 3. 14. 9).

If we wonder how Shakespeare's portrait of a heterosexual male bent on female seduction could conjure up a self-avowed writer of homoeroticism, we might recall that Kerrigan traces the complaint in the early modern period to a "common language" (one that we are historicizing in terms of Marlowe), and he speaks of "the sexual ambivalence in *A Lover's Complaint*," citing "the youth's face, a bower for Venus, his voice 'maiden tongu'd'" (Kerrigan, ed., *The Sonnets*, 20–21). Moreover, the young courtier is not merely androgynous; he attracts both men and women: "he did in the general bosom reign / Of young, of old, and sexes both enchanted" (127–28). If this figure's artistic forms are both double-voiced, so is their author.

By attending to the conjunction of poetry and theatre in *A Lover's Complaint*, we can see Shakespeare plotting his characters' aesthetic and subjective struggle for identity amid a love affair in Marlowe's terms, drawn along an Ovidian path of amorous poetry and tragedic theatre. While acknowledging Shakespeare's representation of doubleness in the agent of authorship for both literary forms, we can nonetheless discern a critique of literary production in which both men and woman are complicit in an economy not merely of cultural shame but also of artistic sham.

---

[7] Editions that provide no annotation on Marlowe include J. Kerrigan, Roe, Duncan-Jones, and Burrow. The considerable annotation collected in Rollins' *Variorum: Poems* includes only one reference to Marlowe, by Theobald in 1929 (601). Like editors, critics more often mention Sidney and Daniel (e.g., Rees; Bell; Laws).

THE VIRGILIAN PATH RE-TAKEN: SPENSERIAN AUTHORSHIP

As we should expect, Shakespeare once more plots his Ovidian narrative about Marlovian poetry and theatre in a Virgilian landscape. Amid hills and riverbanks, cattle graze and two conventional pastoral figures preside, the country maid and the cowherd.[8] A third figure, the male narrator, has entered the pastoral domain, evidently for retreat, while the fourth figure, the seductive young man, appears to have made a sojourn to the pastoral world at some point in the past, but hardly for retreat. Yet each of these "pastoral" figures can also be connected to the "court" or "city." Shakespeare makes this principle of dual cultural affiliation explicit in the figure of the "reverend man," who

> graz'd his cattle nigh,
> Sometime a blusterer that the ruffle knew
> Of court, of city, and had let go by
> The swiftest hours, observed as they flew.
> (*A Lover's Complaint*, 57–60)

Kerrigan notes how rare the reverend man's life-pattern is in Elizabethan literature, comparing it to the career of old Melibee in Book 6 of *The Faerie Queene* (cantos 9–12), since both pastoral figures have engaged in what Isabel G. MacCaffrey calls the "formula of out-and-back," which begins in the country, moves to the court, and comes home again.[9]

The life-pattern of the Spenserian character is applicable to the poet who pens it. As we have seen in previous chapters, Spenser was famous among his contemporaries for being a shepherd who began his literary career by writing pastoral and then moving on to epic. While the three-part life-pattern of the reverend man may be rare for Elizabethans, the figure of the shepherd-king, present in a narrative evoking the generic grid of pastoral and epic, is among the most dominant fictions of the period, from Spenser's *Shepheardes Calender*, *Faerie Queene*, and *Colin Clouts Comes Home Againe*, to Sidney's *Arcadia*, Marlowe's *Tamburlaine*, and Shakespeare's *As You Like It*.[10] While various writers use the Virgilian fiction for complex and diverse reasons,

---

[8] In *Variorum: Poems*, Rollins reports that "An anonymous reviewer in *Fraser's Magazine* (Oct., 1855, p. 411) characterized the poem as 'one of the most successful pastorals in the English language'" (586; see 593, 594). Late twentieth-century commentators follow suit: see Underwood, *Prolegomena*, 61; J. Kerrigan, ed., *The Sonnets*, 403–04, *Motives*, 13–14, 21, 46; Roe, ed., *Poems*, 264; Rees "Sidney," 165; Sharon-Zisser "Similes," 206–09; Laws, "Generic Complexities," 81, 86–89.

[9] J. Kerrigan, ed., *The Sonnets*, 402. Quoted in MacCaffrey *Spenser's Allegory*, 366, who emphasizes that "Spenser evidently attached important meanings to this pattern, for it occurs at least four times in his poetry."

[10] In *The Shepheardes Calender*, Colin Clout may well be the first important figure to leave the pastoral world for the "walled townes" (*August*, 157–62) and then to return to the country in lamentation

including to process their middle-class obsession with social mobility, they also process its literary form, a self-reflexive fiction about an author's literary career, especially one structured on a maturational, developmental model.[11]

Thus, just as we may label Shakespeare's Ovidian conjunction of poetry and theatre Marlovian, so we may label his Virgilian conjunction of pastoral and epic Spenserian. In 1790, Malone was the first to observe of Shakespeare that "in this beautiful poem . . . he perhaps meant to break a lance with Spenser. It appears to me to have more of the simplicity and pathetick tenderness of the elder poet, in his smaller pieces, than any other poem of that time" (Rollins, ed., *Variorum: Poems*, 586; see 590, 591, 592, 594, 601). The judgment has held steady for over 200 years: "Spenser [is] . . . a poet to whom *A Lover's Complaint* is more deeply indebted than to any other" (Burrow, ed., *Sonnets and Poems*, 708; see 140, 695, 699, 707).[12] While the opening of *A Lover's Complaint* has long been understood to imitate the opening of *The Ruines of Time* – and more recently of *Prothalamion* – we might take Kerrigan's cue to see the reverend man (in particular) not simply as indebted to Spenser's Melibee but as a fictionalized type of Spenserian figure – an anticipation, if you will, of Milton's "sage and serious poet Spenser . . . a better teacher than Scotus or Aquinas" (*Aereopagitica*, 728–29). Kerrigan is on the verge of voicing this idea: "Shakespeare clearly enjoys . . . the 'reverend' man's Spenserian trappings" – adding, "somewhat arch even in 1609" (*Motives*, 66). Indeed, the reverend man voices one of the recurrent beliefs of *The Faerie Queene*: that articulation of a problem can bring consolation, especially through counseling. Thus, Prince Arthur counsels Una in Book 1: "wofull Ladie let me you intrete, / For to unfold the anguish of your hart: / Mishaps are maistred by advice discrete, / And counsell mittigates the greatest smart" (7. 40).

Yet part of Shakespeare's enjoyment of the reverend man likely derives from his shading of the portrait into parody. The word "blusterer" arouses immediate suspicion; the *Oxford English Dictionary* cites Shakespeare's usage as its first example for its first definition: "One who utters loud empty boasts or menaces; a loud or violent inflated talker, a braggart." That last

---

over sexual betrayal. The biographical pattern pertains not merely to Spenser but also to Shakespeare (see Rollins, ed., *Variorum: Poems*, 587).

[11] Critics also neglect Virgil; the only commentary comes from Underwood, who traces Shakespeare's use of the female complaint through Ovid's *Heroides* to Dido in the *Aeneid* (*Prolegomena*, xiv, 3–4). Cf. Rees "Sidney," 161.

[12] Following Malone, modern critics routinely find Spenser. See Underwood, *Prolegomena*, 39–42; Kerrigan, ed., *The Sonnets*, 15, 390–92; Rees, "Sidney," 157; Roe, ed., *Poems*, 61–65; Duncan-Jones, ed., *Sonnets*, 436, 441; J. Kerrigan, *Motives*, 21, 30, 32–34, 41–42, 53; Jackson, "Echoes"; D. Kay, *Shakespeare*, 145, 147–49; Laws "Generic Complexities," 88.

word takes us where we need to go: to Spenser's great figure of bluster in *The Faerie Queene*: Braggadocchio. It is as if Shakespeare conjoins Braggadocchio with the gentle shepherd Melibee, the foster-father of Pastorella and future father-in-law of Calidore, Knight of Courtesy, in order to parody Spenserian pastoral retreat, wisdom, and authority. If so, the reverend man recalls Archimago, the magician in disguise as a hermit who uses his smooth tongue to bring the Redcrosse Knight and Una home to his hermitage in the opening canto of *The Faerie Queene* – with unholy consequences. Not surprisingly, Shakespeare's reverend man even conceals the sexuality that Florimell discovers in the old fisher in Book 3, canto 8 – an impotent old man who, like Archimago, derives from a figure in Ariosto. Indeed, not merely has Shakespeare's old cowherd been "Sometime a blusterer," but he moves a little too "fastly" to the maid, wishing to "know" only "in brief" the "origin of her woe," while his mode of operation is itself tinged with erotic desire: "So slides he down upon his grained bat, / And comely distant sits he by her side, / When he again desires her, being sat, / Her grievance with his hearing to divide" (64–66). That last word is ominous, and is a favorite of Spenser's, recalling Archimago's pleasure at seeing Redcrosse and Una "divided into double parts" (1. 2. 9). Apparently, Shakespeare turns Spenser against himself, conflating several of his figures of virtue and vice into an ambiguous old man who blurs the boundary between caring wisdom and sexual hypocrisy.[13]

Like the other two narrative poems, *A Lover's Complaint* is not an allegory about an artistic confrontation between Spenser and Marlowe over the question of female chastity, but Shakespeare does appear to evoke precisely such a confrontation. Thus he tells a fiction in which Spenserian and Marlovian figures function in oppositional relationship with the country maid. The Marlovian figure of the young courtier uses Ovidian poetry and theatre to take female chastity away, while the Spenserian figure of the reverend man uses his Virgilian life pattern of pastoral and epic counsel to bring (more than) solace to her suffering. By recognizing Shakespeare's penning of such a fiction during the first decade of the seventeenth century, we can revise the received wisdom that Shakespeare passed beyond Spenser back in 1593–94 (Paglia, *Sexual Personae*, 194).

In the 1609 quarto, Shakespeare treats the Spenserian/Virgilian characters with the unsettling doubleness of an arch-magus. Usually, critics identify the maid as a figure from the country, citing her hat, "a platted hive of straw"

---

[13] Editors usually gloss the reverend man's "grained bat" with the "handsome bat" of the false Ape in *Mother Hubberds Tale* (217; see Duncan-Jones, ed., *Sonnets*, 436). On the reverend man as "the incestuous, non-erectional desire of a feminized Father," see Sharon-Zisser, "Similies," 208.

(8). Editors, however, suggest that even though such a hat was worn in the country, it was also worn by women from the court, including Queen Elizabeth (Duncan-Jones, ed., *Sonnets*, 432). Like the reverend man, the maid could either be a country girl (who has even perhaps sojourned to the court) or a court girl (who has retreated to the country). The identity of the narrator is even more enigmatic: while his voice and poetic art mark him as courtly, he appears first as a visitor to the pastoral world. Thus he has performed a telescoped version of the pattern outlined for the reverend man: he has left the city for the country. Finally, we may extend this Virgilian narrative pattern to the young man, who, as we have said, appears to join the narrator in being a courtier who has made a visit to the pastoral world. In short, we may plot all of the fictional principals moving along a Virgilian path.

In trying to determine what Shakespeare might be up to here, we need to recall that Marlowe's ghost was still in competition with Spenser's over the writing of the nation, his art grounded in a "counter-nationhood." In *A Lover's Complaint*, Shakespeare removes the action from the obvious site of nationhood, the court and city, but he does follow Spenser and Marlowe in linking the pastoral domain with the political one. The maid is not a figure for Rome, as Spenser's complaining female is in *The Ruines of Rome*, or Verlame, as in *The Ruines of Time*, but nonetheless Shakespeare's "woman is a city (176)" (D. Kay, *Shakespeare*, 145), as the woman herself laments: "And long upon these terms I held my city, / Till thus he gan besiege me" (176–77). Long ago, J. M. Robertson observed that *A Lover's Complaint* "employs no Greek Mythus (like *Venus and Adonis*), no Roman Tale (like *Lucrece*)" (Rollins, ed., *Variorum: Poems*, 600). Unlike both earlier narrative poems, too, *A Lover's Complaint* contains no concrete reference to a "queen" or in other ways evokes Elizabeth (cf. "monarch" at line 41). Nonetheless, the straw hat preserved in the historical record just happens to have been worn by Shakespeare's former monarch, and readers have occasionally identified the maid with his recently deceased queen (Rollins, ed., *Variorum: Poems*, 592, 602).

Moreover, as an "Elizabethan minor epic" composed around the time of the queen's death in 1603, *A Lover's Complaint* contains other epic topoi: the canon imagery describing the maid's "levell'd eyes" (22); the young man's chivalric excellence in riding his horse (106–12; cf. *Fairie Queene*, I. i. 1); and the young man's reference to the female as an androgynous warrior (like Britomart, a well-known Elizabeth figure) who escapes the "scars of battle" with her "flight, / And makes her absence valiant" (244–45). Yet, as to be expected in an Ovidian minor epic, Virgilian "arms" are eroticized through verbal play, as voiced by the duplicitous rider of chivalric romance himself: "'Love's arms are peace, 'gainst rule, 'gainst sense, 'gainst shame'" (271). Such details are sustained enough to suggest an Ovidian form of nationhood.[14] In the clear opposition between the young man who has seduced the maid with "sonnets" and "shows" and the old man who has left the epic world of the court for the pastoral world of the country, Shakespeare appears to represent a struggle between Marlowe's counternationalism – the writer's narcissistic service of his own art – and Spenser's royal nationhood in communal service to the Virgilian state. Intriguingly, in the middle of this dispute over the body politic is the body of female chastity itself.

From this more detailed review of the fiction, *A Lover's Complaint* can be seen to present a complexly nuanced fiction in which Marlovian and Spenserian characters write and read Ovidian poems and perform Ovidian dramatic roles along the Virgilian path of court and country, epic and pastoral, in a competition between two forms of nationhood: Ovidian liberty and Virgilian monarchy. While *A Lover's Complaint* may not be either an allegory of art or a biography of the artist, it does represent a literary collision important to early modern England and a professional dilemma at the heart of Shakespeare's own professional career.

ART OF CRAFT

Indeed, *A Lover's Complaint* tells a disturbing, tragic story of a male and a female who enter a cultural economy in which poetry and theatre conjoin to "daff" the era's most treasured ideal: the "white stole of chastity." In the maid's haunting narration:

> "For lo his passion, but an art of craft,
> Even there resolv'd my reason into tears,
> There my white stole of chastity I daff'd,
> Shook off my sober guards and civil fears;
> Appear to him as he to me appears,
> All melting, though our drops this diff'rence bore:
> His poison'd me, and mine did him restore."
>   (*A Lover's Complaint*, 295–301)

Through the young man's performance of "passion," his "art of craft," the young maid "melt[s]" into sympathy for and with the suffering youth. The

---

[14] Muir observes, "The largest group of images . . . is taken from war, and these express the battle between the sexes" ("'Complaint,'" 164).

moment of sympathy reduces the maid's physical frame to "tears," shakes off her protective rational armor – "sober guards and civil fears" – creates the psychological "Appear[ance]" of mutuality, and leads swiftly to a moment of undressing, the final consequence of which is an exchange of (coital) "drops" – an exchange that, as Sonnet 129 more famously laments, swiftly separates the sexes, in all their "diff'rence": "His poison'd me, and mine did him restore." As if in parody of Cordelia with "holy water" in her "heavenly eyes" (*King Lear*, 4. 3. 30), the maid has become a martyr to the male cause. In this astonishing depiction of the loss of female virginity, Shakespeare apprises himself, and certainly his reader, of what is finally at stake in the use and abuse of the twin arts he himself produces – especially in his role as the heir of Spenser and Marlowe. Not surprisingly, then, the "passion" that is an art of craft has both poetic and theatrical associations, as Burrow's gloss indicates; "emotion; but also 'A poem, literary composition, or passage marked by deep or strong emotion; a passionate speech or outburst' (*OED*, 6d), with potentially a theatrical edge to it, as when in *Dream*, 5. 1. 310 Theseus says of Flute playing Thisbe, 'Here she comes, and her passion ends the play'" (Burrow, ed., *Sonnets and Poems*, 715).

That *A Lover's Complaint* is about the discourse of poetry and theatre is clear from the outset, where poetry appears in the opening stanza, in more ways than one:

> From off a hill whose concave womb reworded
> A plaintful story from a sist'ring vale,
> My spirits t' attend this double voice accorded,
> And down I laid to list the sad-tun'd tale,
> Ere long espied a fickle maid full pale
> Tearing of papers, breaking rings a-twain,
> Storming her world with sorrow's wind and rain.
> *(A Lover's Complaint, 1–7)*

Not merely does the maid tear "papers" that likely include "deep-brain'd sonnets," and not merely does the narrator lie down to hear her "sad tun'd tale," but also the landscape in which these literary events occur is humanized as a type of poet – a female poet. Thus a "hill" (or displaced *mons veneris*) bears a "concave womb" that *rewords* a "plaintful story" from the "sist'ring vale." Like Lavinia in Virgil's imperial epic, the *Aeneid*, or Shakespeare's own Ovidian tragedy *Titus Andronicus*, the female is identified with the land. She sings her sad-tuned tale, and the hills echo it harmoniously, making the tempest of her private grief available to a listening audience. As Kerrigan and others note, echo is an ancient trope of poetic fame, and whether the author of the tale wishes it or not, we are witnessing here a process of poetic succession and thus of poetic immortality, the precise import of which we cannot sort out here at the beginning (we shall return to it at the end). What we can say now is that the opening stanza invites us to read into the gender mythos a literary representation about the author and his (or her) art.[15]

While listening to the maid's tale, the narrator also sees her tearing "papers," breaking "rings," and throwing them into the river, in a concerted effort to consign them to oblivion:

> Of folded schedules had she many a one,
> Which she perus'd, sigh'd, tore, and gave the flood,
> Crack'd many a ring of posied gold and bone,
> Bidding them find their sepulchers in mud.
>   (*A Lover's Complaint*, 43–46)

Here we see more fully a process of literary reception: from initial reading, to subjective or internal response, to physical violence of the papers' material form, to their final burial in the watery earth. While Burrow is right to emphasize the closed contents of the papers – indeed, they are "seal'd to curious secrecy" (49) – we are nonetheless privy to their effect on the intended reader: "in top of rage the lines she rents, / Big discontent so breaking their contents" (55–56). Whatever the specific "contents" of these documents, they produce a Senecan "rage" in the female who inherits them. Recalling Lucrece with the Trojan painting of Sinon in the 1594 narrative poem, the maid here seeks revenge on the author by attacking his artifact. This time the artifact is poetry itself.

OF TIME AND THE RIVER

To grasp this representation more fully, we might glance briefly at one story that resembles Shakespeare's: Ariosto's story of Father Time, his literary plaques, and the river Lethe in the *Orlando Furioso*. In canto 35, Ariosto narrates how St. John helps Astolpho recover Orlando's lost wits on the moon, pausing to insert his most famous verse treatise on the art of poetry and its *telos*. The two travelers see an old man filling his lap with a "precious load of plaques" and throwing them "in the stream, named Lethe" (11), yet "Out of a hundred thousand thus obscured / Beneath the silt, scarce one, he saw, endured" (12). Suddenly, the travelers see a "flock of

---

[15] Cf. Kerrigan, *Motives*, 43; D. Kay, *Shakespeare*, 148; Sharon-Zisser, "Similies," 196.

vultures" and other birds of prey swoop down and bear away "These shining tokens of renown" (13); however, "when such birds attempt to soar on
high, / They lack the stamina to bear the weight, / And of the names they
choose, howe'er they try, / Oblivion in Lethe is their fate" (14). Ariosto
contrasts these birds with "Two silver swans" that "can sing the praises
of the great: / . . . in their mouths fame is secure" (14: 7–8). Accordingly,
the travelers witness the swans bearing certain plaques to "a noble temple
crowned . . . / Sacred it is to immortality," and presided over by a "fair
nymph": "These plaques the nymph so consecrates and tends / That their
renown will shine for evermore / In poetry and legendary lore" (35. 15–16).
Soon St. John interprets the allegorical sight to the wondering knight: the
old man is Father Time; the river, Lethe; the plaques the man seeks to
throw into the river and the birds of preys' futile effort to recover them, the
temporal process of poetic oblivion; the swans who succeed in carrying the
plaques to the temple of the nymph, the great poets who can render their
poems immortal in the Temple of Lady Fame.[16]

   We need not determine whether Shakespeare knew this story or had
it in mind in order to see its significance for the opening action of *A
Lover's Complaint*: like Father Time with the plaques in the River Lethe,
the maid is reversing the process of poetic fame by burying the documents
in the "sepulchers of mud." In an astonishing way, the *telos* of these "deep-
brain'd sonnets" *reverses* the fiction of fame so renowned in Shakespeare's
Sonnets themselves. The subjectivity of the author dooms his documents
unwittingly, precisely because he has misused them. Only as the story
unfolds do we understand what has compelled the maid to become involved
in this complex process of literary entombment.[17] If, as critics believe,
Shakespeare's river is the Thames, the great English symbol of poetic fame,
we may witness here more than simple imitation of the opening of Spenser's
Prothalamion (see Jackson, "Echoes"); we may find instead a concerted
critique of Spenser's (pastoral) claims to poetic immortality.[18] Here, then, we
can discover Shakespeare's historic revision of the Spenserian erotic project:
whereas the New Poet had foregrounded the masculine representation of
virgin consciousness, turning this fascination into a new genre, the betrothal

---

[16] On this episode, see Cheney, *Flight*, 123–24, 276n17.

[17] As such, the maid appears to reverse the project of Renaissance humanism itself, as excavated by
Greene in *The Light of Troy*: "The Renaissance . . . chose to open a polemic against the Dark Ages.
The ubiquitous imagery of disinterment, resurrection, and renascence needed a death and burial to
justify itself" (3). See also 30–31, 92–93, and esp. 220–41: "At the core of humanism lies this instinct
to reach out into chaos, oblivion, mystery, the alien, the subterranean, the dead, even the demonic,
to reach out and in the act of reaching out already to be reviving and restoring" (235).

[18] On the river in *A Lover's Complaint* as the Thames, see D. Kay, *Shakespeare*, 149. On *Prothalamion*,
see Cheney, *Flight*, 225–45; Cheney and Prescott, "Teaching."

poem (Cheney and Prescott, "Teaching"), Shakespeare takes us into the "territory of sexual betrayal," representing the feminine consciousness of betrayed virginity.

Shakespeare's Ovidian critique of pastoral in general – and of Spenserian pastoral in particular – is evident in his use of the "maund" or basket holding the "deep-brain'd sonnets." In the opening to *Prothalamion*, Spenser presents himself leaving "Princes Court" in a state of "discontent" after "long fruitlesse stay" (6–7) and walking down to the Thames, where he espies a vision: "A Flocke of Nymphes" with "greenish locks" gather "flowers," each to fill "a little wicker basket," in order to "decke their Bridegromes posies" (20–34). Usually, editors gloss the baskets with Ovid's *Fasti* – either 4. 435 on the baskets Proserpina's girls use for gathering flowers before her abduction or *Fasti* 5. 217–18 on the similar baskets the Hours use for flower-gathering.[19] No doubt Shakespeare's basket has these Ovidian baskets as its intertexts, but for a basket literally associated with the art of poetry and the genre of pastoral we probably need to recall the most famous basket of all: that which Virgil twines in the concluding lines of his *Eclogues*: "These strains, Muses divine, it will be enough for your poet to have sung, while he sits idle and twines a basket of slender hibiscus. These ye shall make of highest worth in Gallus' eyes" (10. 70–72). Effectively, Shakespeare's country maid empties out the baskets of Virgil, Ovid, and Spenser, discarding their pastoral contents in the (Ariostan) river of oblivion.

CRAFT OF WILL

As in Ariosto, so in Shakespeare an old man appears, but Shakespeare's interest is not in the discarded documents so much as in the maid herself, whose "suffering ecstasy" the reverend man seeks to "assuage," for "'Tis promis'd in the charity of age" (69–70). The reverend man convinces the maid to tell him her story, and it is here that we learn of the young man's use of theatre, as she herself narrates:

> Small show of man was yet upon his chin,
> His phoenix down began but to appear
> Like unshorn velvet on that termless skin,
> Whose bare outbragg'd the web it seem'd to wear;
> Yet showed his visage by that cost more dear,
> And nice affections wavering stood in doubt
> If best were as it was, or best without.
>
> (*A Lover's Complaint*, 92–98)

---

[19] McCabe cites *Fasti* 4. 435 (ed., 730); Brooks-Davies, *Fasti* 5. 217–18 (ed., 392).

From the outset, the maid theatricalizes the youth's body in terms of the actor's falsifying costume.[20] Introducing a subtle strand of stage discourse that she will consolidate later in the phrase "tragic shows," she imagines the emergence of manliness on the youth's face as itself a "Small show of man," his budding beard a "web" that he has put on as a kind of "visage" – or mask – simply to "wear" for the sake of appearance (see Roe, ed., *Poems*, 269). Yet it is precisely such a "show" that affects the maid, since he appears "by that cost more dear" – the word "cost," as J. W. Mackail long ago observed, picking up the costume imagery (see J. Kerrigan, ed., *The Sonnets*, 405), punning on the French word "*coste, côte* = 'coat'" (Roe, ed., *Poems*, 269). Significantly, the young man's physiognomial theatre of the chin affects his audience's "nice affections," creating "wavering" and "doubt" whether "his *visage* was better with its *cost* . . . or better without" (Kerrigan, ed., *The Sonnets*, 406).

The young man's physiognomial theatre is particularly effective, though, because it extends to a more internalized, materialized locale within his body:

> So on the tip of his subduing tongue
> All kind of arguments and question deep,
> All replication prompt and reason strong,
> For his advantage still did wake and sleep.
> To make the weeper laugh, the laugher weep,
> He had the dialect and different skill,
> Catching all passions in his craft of will.
>
> (*A Lover's Complaint*, 120–26)

Craft of will: the phrase is indeed a catching one. According to John Roe, it is "a dense phrase meaning 'shrewd application of appetite'" (*Poems*, 271). Supplying more detail, Kerrigan observes,

Craft simultaneously suggests the young man's accomplishment in general (as in "the shoemaker's *craft*") and his "skilful exercise" of this ("the shoe was a work of *craft*"). As so often in Shakespeare, *will* operates across a range of senses from "purpose, powerful expression of volition" on the one hand to "desire" in the sense of "affective emotion, lust" on the other. Enriched still further by its collocation with the ambiguous phrase *Catching all passions, craft of will* compromises several shades of significance, from "cunning lust" to the "crafting of language into persuasion" and "verbal power" or "discourse, the articulation of volition." (Kerrigan, ed., *The Sonnets*, 408–09)

---

[20] See Muir, "'Complaint'": "clothing imagery" expresses the "underlying theme . . . the difficulty of distinguishing between appearance and reality" ("*A Lover's Complaint*," 164).

The maid's phrase *craft of will* is a perfect one for describing the young man's use of both poetry and theatre to seduce her. It anticipates the word "craft" in "an art of craft" (already discussed). *Art of craft, craft of will*: these phrases echo throughout the maid's story, drawing attention to the young man's use of a deceptive art that both originates in the will and targets it:

> What with his art in youth and youth in art,
> Threw my affections in his charmed power,
> Reserv'd the stalk and gave him all my flower.
> *(A Lover's Complaint,* 145–47)

The word "charmed" derives from *carmen,* meaning *song,* and during the period magic and witchcraft are indeed a recurrent metaphor – not simply a cultural practice – for the literary arts (see Cheney and Klemp, "Spenser's Dance"). As the "flower" reference further suggests, the young man's magic art does double duty as a form of pastoral gardening – an idea soon amplified:

> For further I could say this man's untrue,
> And knew the patterns of his foul beguiling,
> Heard where his plants in others' orchards grew,
> Saw how deceits were gilded in his smiling,
> Knew vows were ever brokers to defiling,
> Thought characters and words merely but art,
> And bastards of his foul adulterate heart.
> *(A Lover's Complaint,* 169–75)

The conceit of the orchard as the female womb is conventional, but it may glance at the climactic moment in Marlowe's Ovidian narrative poem: "Leander now, like Theban Hercules, / Entered the orchard of th' Hesperides, / Whose fruit none rightly can describe but he / That pulls or shakes it from the golden tree" (2. 297–300). Spenser had foregrounded virgin consciousness, while here Marlowe poignantly maps the violent consensual loss of female virginity, yet Shakespeare overgoes both by charting the masculine betrayal of the female. His young man's gardening skills turn out to be prodigious, and what this stanza carefully traces is a process of reception for his "art" – a process that moves ever inward toward the fruit of subjective revelation: she "Heard . . . Saw . . . Knew . . . Thought." And what she finally realizes is indeed haunting: that "characters and words" are "merely but art," the ultimate breakers of (marital) faith, the illegitimate children of his "foul adulterate heart."

Among readers, George Steevens was the first to catch the authorial significance of "craft for will" (Rollins, ed., *Variorum: Poems,* 345), but more recently Ilona Bell has discovered Will Shakespeare making a "punning allusion to [his] . . . own 'craft of will'" (465). This idea encourages us to see Shakespeare's portrait of the maid – a female who, on the one hand, has lost her chastity through Marlovian subjection to Ovidian poetry and theatre, and, on the other, is receiving an ambiguously reverend courtesy from a Spenserian pastoral-epicist – as a kind of authorial stamp grimly afflicted with a literary crisis. Such an authorial portrait is available today through Wendy Wall's superb work on Elizabethan authors, from Gascoigne and Spenser to Daniel and Shakespeare himself, all of whom precisely use the genre of the female complaint to "cross-dress" their authorial voices, literally "taking on the voice of a fallen woman" (*Imprint*, 260): "The female respondent becomes one of the doubles that the writer uses . . . to introduce his own authority through masquerade. The fallen woman's critique becomes a central part of the architecture of poetic authority, as it establishes an acceptable idiom through which the new poet can be presented and formally contained" (260).[21] Wall briefly suggests that in *A Lover's Complaint* "Petrarchan poet and female auditor are associated and disassociated as complaining publishers. And again this complaint adds a layer of voices to the sonnet book that renders the work more plural and multivocal" (259).

THE COMPOSITOR'S EYE

To this line of thought, we can add a corresponding discourse about the theatre, as the cross-dressed "Petrarchan poet" finds him/herself subjected to a penetrating androgynous theatrical show. Interestingly enough, the primary textual crux of *A Lover's Complaint* occurs over just this discourse, as the compositor for the 1609 quarto repeated one of Shakespeare's theatrical terms; in her cross-dressed voice, the maid repeats the young courtier's dramatic voice to the reverend man:

> But, O my sweet, what labor is't to leave
> The thing we have not, mast'ring what not strives,
> *Playing* the place which did no form receive,
> *Playing* patient sports in unconstrained gyves?
> (*A Lover's Complaint*, 239–42; emphasis added)

---

[21] Wall also relates this authorial strategy to the Virgilian idea of a literary career, mapped onto the transition from a manuscript to a print culture (*Imprint*, 230). D. Kay says of the maid's straw hat and river-site complaint: "As the Globe's wooden structure took shape, with 'upon her head a platted hive of straw' (8), there could have been no better place in England than the 'weeping margent' of the Thames from which to contemplate the broad shapes of history and meditate on the relationship between the gilded monuments of princes and the powerful rhymes of poets" (*Shakespeare*, 149).

In that repetition of "Playing" in the two initial line positions, all editors see a compositorial slip. Back in the eighteenth century, Malone observed, "the compositor's eye after he had printed the former line, I suppose glanced again upon it, and caught the first word of it instead of the first word of the line [242] he was then composing" (Rollins, ed., *Variorum: Poems*, 357). Yet we might pause here a bit longer than conventional bibliography has done, to discern how the poem's most famous textual crux fixes and elongates the theatrical discourse during an extremely intense poetic moment, as if the compositor himself were caught in an authorial craft of will. Shakespeare's original readers would no doubt have read – and most likely breezed through – the doubleness of "Playing." Significantly, as Malone also noted, Shakespeare's theatrical trope imitates Spenser's versification of theatre in *The Faerie Queene*: "Playing their sportes, that joyd her to behold" (1. 10. 31; see also 5. 1. 6; quoted in Rollins, ed., *Variorum: Poems*, 358). The *playing* here is "double" – not just textually but intertextually – and it presents the compositor's slip as a testament to the Craft of Will.

THE THEOLOGY OF EPIC THEATRE

At the end of the poem, the theatrical discourse intensifies. In fact, each of the last four stanzas contains a theatrical term or image. In addition to "tragic shows" in the fourth to last stanza, in the third to last we see a fusion of tragedy and epic, theatre and poetry:

> That not a heart which in his level came
> Could scape the hail of his all-hurting aim,
> Showing fair nature is both kind and tame;
> And veil'd in them did win whom he would maim.
> Against the thing he sought he would exclaim:
> When he most burnt in heart-wish'd luxury,
> He preach'd pure maid, and prais'd cold chastity.
> (*A Lover's Complaint*, 309–15)

The presence of theatrical imagery in this stanza is important, because the maid lucidly articulates what readers find so intriguing and original about the young man's theatre of seduction: "Against the thing he sought he would exclaim."[22] In an image that picks up the confessional or theological

---

[22] Roe calls the young man's strategy "the most interesting thing in the entire poem" (Roe, ed., *Poems*, 69): "firstly, he presents himself as a sinner in need of redemption: secondly, he presents himself as emotionally untouched and therefore chaste, a male virgin, no less; and lastly he presents *her* as a redeemer – not only of himself but of all those wounded hearts who have suffered through him" (70; Roe's emphasis). See D. Kay, *Shakespeare*, 148.

profession from the figure of the "reverend man," the young man *preaches* "pure maid" and praises "cold chastity." In his theologically epic theatre of the hunting marksman, the young man successfully "level[s]" against every "heart" coming within military sight of his "all-hurting aim," successfully staging a "show" in which "a good disposition ('fair nature') is generous and acquiescent" (Roe, ed., *Poems*, 281). As Roe points out, the word "veil'd" means "disguised," while the phrase "in them" refers back to the "strange forms" of line 303 that the young man adopts as his disguises (282). Not merely does the youth preach the purity of maidenhood and praise chastity in this "tragic show," but as an actor "veil'd" in his costume he cross-dresses himself by speaking "like a chaste or virginal young girl" (282). Finally, then, the youth's theatre manages to hold a mirror up to the maid's natural character, creating perfect sympathy between feminine subject and masculine object, their androgynous discourse being the tragic point of identification.

The next or penultimate stanza continues the theatrical imagery of disguise and costume but moves it more formally into the theological domain:

> Thus merely with the garment of a Grace
> The naked and concealed fiend he cover'd,
> That th' unexperient gave the tempter place,
> Which like a cherubin above them hover'd.
> Who, young and simple, would not be so lover'd?
> Ay me, I fell, and yet do question make
> What I should do again for such a sake.
>
> (*A Lover's Complaint*, 316–22)

Playing the role of actor on the stage of sexual seduction, the young man *covers* the "naked and concealed fiend" with the "garment of a Grace." In this Ovidian theatre, he uses the costume of character to metamorphose from demon to angel. The metaphysical metaphors confuse the boundaries of the Christian cosmos (as in Shakespeare's Marlovian Sonnet 144), so that in the mind of the "unexperient" the "tempter" appears a "cherubin." As the earlier floral imagery anticipates, the maid's simple utterance "I fell" transplants the local loss of virginity into the re-productive site of the Edenic Fall.[23]

---

[23] Cf. Underwood, *Prolegomena*, 101: "The hovering 'cherubin' finally reminds one of *Doctor Faustus*"; see 102 on "Marlovian resemblances." On the Reformation context of *A Lover's Complaint*, see Kerrigan, *Motives*, 39–41.

The word "Grace" appears several times earlier – six to be precise (79, 114, 119 [twice], 261, 285). In its first appearance, the word pertains to female body space, meaning maiden virginity or the concave womb itself: "I attended / A youthful suit – it was to gain my grace" (78–79). Despite neglect in modern editions, the word "suit" is exquisite; in the context of the poem's theatrical discourse, are we not invited to read the word doubly: not merely as "the request of a youthful suitor" (Duncan-Jones, ed., *Sonnets*, 436) but also as *the performance of a youthful suitor*, as the theatrical ring in "attended" would seem to confirm? For a young woman to attend a "youthful suit" is thus to audit a theatre of young masculinity; at center stage is a concept that, for Spenser as for Shakespeare, is not merely sexual but theological, as the last word of this stanza, "deified," makes plain: "gain my grace" (see, e.g., Spenser, *Hymne of Beautie*, 27, 277). As in Sonnet 146 famously, Shakespeare economizes the high stakes of salvation with business "terms divine" (11). The young man's theatre is a "Small show of man" oufitted in "youthful suit," economized to purchase the white stole of chastity. As the maid laments, she "attended" this Satanic theatre of dis-grace "too early," even though she would "do [so] again for such a sake."

In the second, third, and fourth uses of *grace*, all of which appear in the same stanza, Shakespeare again dresses the word in theatrical guise, in a remarkable interlacing with the theological:

> But quickly on this side the verdict went:
> His real habitude gave life and grace
> To appertainings and to ornament,
> Accomplish'd in himself, not in his case;
> All aids, themselves made fairer by their place,
> [Came] for additions, yet their purpos'd trim
> Piec'd not his grace but were all grac'd by him.
>   (*A Lover's Complaint*, 113–19)

While the word *grace* and its cognates appear three times in seven lines, six other terms pertain to clothing, costume, and thus theatrical disguise, as modern annotation confirms. Katherine Duncan-Jones glosses "case" as "container, outward clothing," and "trim" as "adornment, trappings" (Duncan-Jones, ed., *Sonnets*, 439), while Roe glosses "real habitude" as "regal bearing" and "appertainings" as "appurtenances (trimmings, costume)" (Roe, ed., *Poems*, 270). Kerrigan catches "Piec'd" as "patched, mended" (Kerrigan, ed., *The Sonnets*, 407). Editors do not gloss "ornament," because it so obviously contributes to this dressing of the young man in outward garb. Among these terms, however, "habitude" is the most engaging, because it means both inward "character or disposition" (Duncan-Jones, ed., *Sonnets*, 439) and outward habit or attire. The drift is clear when we recall that such a remarkable portrait of a young man results from the "verdict" of those beholding him. In the young man's theatre, the audience is to judge his character – both his inward and outward person – in order to become complicit in his role as a contradictory figure of grace: "Piec'ed not his grace but were all grac'd by him."[24]

The fifth use of *grace* also includes an intriguing theatrical linkage: "'My parts had pow'r to charm a sacred [nun], / Who disciplin'd, ay, dieted in grace, / Believ'd her eyes'" (260–62). Editors usually miss the pun on "parts," glossing it merely as both "limbs, parts of the body" and "accomplishments, good qualities" (Kerrigan, ed., *The Sonnets*, 418), but Duncan-Jones prepares us to see a theatrical pun: "talents, attractions" (Duncan-Jones, ed., *Sonnets*, 448). One of the youth's "talents" *is* his "attraction": his ability to perform a "part," to put his body parts and his accomplishments to play on the maid's interiority, working here as a form of magic, with "pow're to charm" even "a sacred nun." This second young woman is not merely institutionally protected by the sanctity of the holy cloister, but she is morally trained ("disciplin'd") and physiologically regulated ("dieted") in the order of divine "grace." Here the work of Michael C. Schoenfeldt on the early modern regime of self-regulation amplifies the absolute danger of the young man's power to seduce both the nun and the maid (*Bodies*). For, unlike Spenser in the Castle of Alma in Book 2 of *The Faerie Queene*, or Shakespeare himself in Sonnet 94 ("They that have pow'r to hurt"), in *A Lover's Complaint* only men have access to self-regulation, and they use it to imperil the "physiology and inwardness" of their tragic victims – those women who have regulated themselves successfully, whether in the cloister or in the country.[25]

The youth's inset story, of a nun who believed in God's grace but then haplessly sold it for the sexual grace of a young courtier, is among the most stunning parts of the poem. Like *Hero and Leander*, the story calls into question the entire project of Christian humanism, including that in Spenser's Legend of Chastity, the dream of which is to fulfill the "generall end" of The *Faerie Queene*: "to fashion a gentleman or noble

---

[24] On the theatre and the "livery guilds" in ways that inform *A Lover's Complaint*, see Stallybrass, "Worn."

[25] As Kerrigan adds, the wording here "was often applied to those who had, sometimes fiercely, mortified the flesh" (Kerrigan, ed., *The Sonnets*, 419).

person in vertuous and gentle discipline" (*Letter to Ralegh*). Specifically, Shakespeare's young man appears to be modeled not only on the Marlovian author but on Spenser's Paridell in Book 3, who similarly specializes in the Ovidian art of love, as the famous imitation of the spilt wine at *Faerie Queene*, 3. 9. 30 – from *Amores*, 2. 5. 17–18 and *Heroides* 17. 75–90 – makes patently clear (see Hamilton, ed., *The Fairie Queene*, 388; Maclean and Prescott, eds., *Spenser's Poetry*, 354). A descendent of Paris of Troy fame, Paridell woos the ominously named Hellenore, who is no nun:

> when apart (if ever her apart)
> He found, then his false engins fast he plyde,
> And all the sleights unbosomd in his hart;
> He sighed, he sobd, he swownd, he perdy dyde,
> And cast himselfe onground her fast besyde:
> Tho when againe he him bethought to live,
> He wept, and wayld, and false laments belyde,
> Saying, but if she Mercie would him give
> That he mote algates dye, yet did his death forgive.
> (*Faerie Queene*, 3. 10. 7)

Paridell's theatrical strategy of seduction does not merely anticipate that of Shakespeare's young man; so does the literary art of Spenser's "learned lover" (*Fairie Queene*, 3. 10. 6): "And otherwhiles with . . . / . . . pleasing toyes he would her entertaine, / Now singing sweetly, to surprise her sprights, / Now making layes of love and lovers paine, / Bransles, Ballads, virelayes, and verses vaine" (3. 10. 8). If here Paridell functions as a dangerous Ovidian (and Petrarchan) poet of courtly love, earlier he functions as a false Virgilian epic poet when he narrates the story of the fall of Troy to Britomart (3. 9. 33–37) – not just as Aeneas did in Virgil's *Aeneid* but more importantly as Ovid attenuated Virgilian epic in the *Metamorphoses*. Spenser overgoes both classical epicists by having his learned lover contain the epic story in five nine-line stanzas. Just as Spenser makes Paridell falsify his own Virgilian and Ovidian art – "Fashioning worlds of fancies evermore / In her fraile wit" (3. 9. 52) – so Shakespeare makes his young man falsify his own Ovidian art of poetry and theatre.

The young man's story also recalls that of Tarquin in *The Rape of Lucrece*, when Shakespeare writes that "hot burning will" has the power to *freeze* "conscience" (247). In the case of the nun, sexual love for the young courtier blinds her to God's grace: "Religious love put out religion's eye" (250). Deftly, Shakespeare suggests how sexual desire evaporates Christian faith. This is a haunting idea, and must have been especially so to readers during the Reformation. In the context of Spenser's poetry of grace, the haunting acquires a literary force: Christian grace is subject to (Marlovian) poetry and theatre; human art is more powerful than the grace of God.[26]

Among Shakespeare's seven uses of the word *grace*, the last is the only one not cohabiting with theatricality; it does, however, occur at a climactic point in the maid's narration, when the youth breaks into tears, the very moment when speech gives way to emotion, staged in terms of chivalric epic: "This said, his wat'ry eyes he did dismount, / Whose sights till then were levell'd on my face . . . / o how the channel to the stream gave grace!" (281–85). His tears of grace prove to be the final seduction in the maid's fall, leading to the crucial stanza declaring his "passion" to be "but an art of craft."

If *A Lover's Complaint* begins with poetry, it ends with theatre:

> O, that infected moisture of his eye,
> O, that false fire which in his cheek so glowed,
> O, that forc'd thunder from his heart did fly,
> O, that sad breath his spungy lungs bestowed,
> O, all that borrowed motion seeming owed,
> Would yet again betray the fore-betray'd,
> And new pervert a reconciled maid!
>
> (*A Lover's Complaint*, 323–29)

Roe glosses "borrowed motion" in line 5 above as "imitated or feigned show of feeling," but adds, "A 'motion' was a puppet-show or mime, as in WT 4. 3. 96–7" (Roe, ed., *Poems*, 282). The reference to *The Winter's Tale* points to a neglected link between *A Lover's Complaint* and Shakespeare's late plays: the young man joins one of Shakespeare's greatest poet-playwright figures, Autolycus, who reports that his art is able to "compass . . . a motion of the Prodigal Son." As we shall see further in the Epilogue, the trickster joins a whole host of Shakespearean dramatic characters in putting poetry and theatre to use, whether like Edgar for benevolent purposes or like Iago for that of pure malevolence. Rhetorically, the theatrical phrase "borrowed motion" occurs as the center of the poem's final stanza, functioning as both the summarizing idea for the incredible initial anaphora of lines 1–4 – the "succession of disjointed exclamations" that becomes a "collective rhetoric which betrays the maid even as she re-invokes it in her attempt at self-purgation" (Duncan-Jones, ed., *Sonnets*, 452) – and

---

[26] For a recent book-length study of Spenser's "biblical poetics," see Kaske.

the closing idea in lines 6–7 that haunt's the poem's final utterance: the youth's theatre is so *real* that the maid would entertain it again if she could.

Perhaps critical attention to the word "reconciled" has interfered with our interest in the theatrical form of the poem's conclusion. Critics rightly understand the theological and doctrinal significance of the larger utterance (Kerrigan, ed., *The Sonnets*, 425). Kerrigan nicely compares the structural frame with that of both Daniel's *Complaint of Rosamond* and Spenser's *Ruines of Time*, wherein (especially in the latter) "the poet's reaction provides a measure for our own," noting that "Shakespeare, characteristically, unsettles our sense of the ending by omitting both the *maid's* departure and the poet's re-emergence" (425; Kerrigan's emphasis). Kerrigan's final comment leads us to our own "dramatic" conclusion: "In *A Lovers Complaint*, the opening cannot close the text; line 5 remains intractable; and the heroine grows beyond the conventions which enclose her, developing an intense and human inconsistency which might be called *dramatic*. If the poem starts in the territory of Spenser and Daniel, it ends, like the problem plays, with the incorrigibility of passion" (425; emphasis added). Let us take Kerrigan – and Shakespeare – at his word.

In their terms, *A Lover's Complaint* literally migrates from the "territory" of Spenserian poetry to the dramatic landscape of Shakespeare's own problem plays, from the poetic "papers" of the opening stanza to the "borrowed motion" of the last: effectively, from "deep-brained sonnets" to "tragic shows." What is especially disturbing – or heroic – about the conclusion to *A Lover's Complaint* is the way it uses poetry to challenge one of the dominant projects of Shakespeare's plays – from *Titus Andronicus* to *The Tempest*: we become fully human only through compassion for the other. ". . . if you now behold them," Ariel says to Prospero of the inhabitants shipwrecked on the island, "your affections / Would become tender"; and Prospero agrees: "The rarer action is / In virtue than in vengeance" (5. 1. 18–19, 27–28). Perhaps the fickle maid knows about Shakespearean poetry and theatre because she has become not merely their greatest auditor but also their purest author.

THE SISTERING VALE

The ending of *A Lover's Complaint* remains the most baffling denouement in the canon. We are baffled because Shakespeare does not complete the narrative with which he began. We know that both the narrator and the reverend man have listened to the maid's story, and we know that the reverend man has wanted to hear the story in order to offer "charity." We expect some narrative resolution, but we do not receive it.[27]

Yet critics remain divided over just how to interpret this baffling event. Kerrigan argues that "Shakespeare refuses to disentangle self-justification . . . from the intractable problem of honesty": "To be true to her experience (seeking spiritual 'reconciliation'), the 'fickle maid' must recoil into a rapt subjectivity which excludes us . . . In place of articulate 'example', Shakespeare writes towards perplexity" (*Motives*, 50). By contrast, Shirley Sharon-Zisser believes that Shakespeare writes toward fulfillment, even (feminine) "orgasm," as the maid voices her complaint against the young man – and to the reverend man – in order to experience the "*jouissance*" of psychological "transference" – a process that "transforms the poem as a whole from 'complaint' to an epithalamium" ("Similies," 218–19).

While acknowledging the difficulty here, we might observe how effectively Shakespeare's narrative technique manages to transfer the landscape of the poem to the mindscape of the reader: it is we who read the story and are left with it; it is not just the maid who is left in a state of "rapt subjectivity" – and it does not exclude us. We, too, have overheard the Shakespearean maid's story about the abuse of poetry and theatre as active agents in the losing of chastity. The author makes her story available to us; it has applicability to our experience. Indeed, of all the works in the Shakespeare canon, *A Lover's Complaint* is singular for its power to perform cultural work, today as well as yesterday: in living through the maid's tragic choice – to daft her white stole of chastity in order to grace masculine charisma – male and female reader alike discover the strongest grounds and motives to protect their own chastity.

For his part, Shakespeare's combined engagement with the works of Spenser and Marlowe in a narrative poem late in his career helps us to redraw our profile of the world's most famed man of the theatre. In *A Lover's Complaint*, Shakespeare's simultaneous rivalry with Spenser and Marlowe as late as 1609, together with his exceptional intertwining of a discourse of theatre with a discourse of poetry, compels us to see Shakespeare as more than a Marlovian man of the theatre or simply an immature rival of Spenser. Within just a few years of his retirement, he is working vigorously to reconcile the Virgilian poetry of Spenser with the Ovidian poetry and theatre of Marlowe, and to fictionalize a culture besieged by these twin

---

[27] As Kerrigan reminds us, the complaint tradition sets up the expectation that we will receive a gifted lesson for having endured so much woe. Yet no such gift is forthcoming (*Motives*, 50). Lukas Erne reminds me that the baffling denouement is "mirrored . . . in the ending of *The Taming of the Shrew*, which has an induction but does not have a frame" (personal communication, 9 May 2003).

literary powers. It is as if our greatest English poet-playwright were making one final plea for court and country to use both "sonnet" and "show" with care. Above all, he appears to be making that plea to himself.

Through the criticism of Kerrigan and Duncan-Jones in particular, readers today have come to see Shakespeare's 1609 volume of sonnet sequence and narrative poem as part of a larger literary practice, best known through volumes by Daniel and Spenser. What criticism has not registered, however, are two follow-up points. The first is that both Daniel and Spenser published their volumes as distinct points along the continuum of their "laureate" careers. Daniel understood *Delia* and *Rosamond* as preparation for his higher flight to national epic, while Spenser understood *Amoretti* and *Epithalamion* as a regenerative bridge between pastoral and epic.[28] Second, Shakespeare may have followed Daniel and Spenser in understanding his 1609 volume to be more than simply an isolated publication gotten up during yet another closing of the theatres; it, too, could be an announcement for a distinct phase of a career – a late version of the kind of announcements he had made in his prose dedications to *Venus* and *Lucrece* – as when (most famously) he promises Southampton that after his "idle houres" spent in writing *Venus* he will go on to pen "some graver labour" (*Riverside*, 1799).[29] Unlike both Daniel and Spenser, however, Shakespeare did not bequeath an epic in verse, or, like Jonson, an (unfulfilled) plan to write one.[30] Nonetheless, like Marlowe in *Hero and Leander* and *Lucan's First Book*, Shakespeare did bequeath an "Ovidian" pre-figuration for such a national art – one that subsequent ages have been content to locate elsewhere in his canon.

Yet *A Lover's Complaint* is important in the Shakespeare canon because it maps out a sad, complex model of national literary production. In this model, Marlowe's Ovidian, counter-national art "takes" chastity away and "leaves" the victim to complain like a lover, while Spenser's national art hypocritically fails to provide the advertised counsel and consolation. Shakespeare's own art, a formal fusion of the two, becomes complicit in the shame and sham of psychic female "reconciliation." To read through *A Lover's Complaint* is to witness the failure of Elizabethan masculine literature's greatest art to achieve its intended cultural goal: the theological protection of the "concave womb" within the "sist'ring vale."

---

[28] On Daniel's volume in his laureate career, see his dedicatory poem to Mary Sidney prefacing his *Works* (chapter 2). On Spenser's 1595 marriage volume, see Cheney, *Flight*, 149–94.

[29] Critics follow Heminge and Condel in speculating that Shakespeare had plans for an edition of his plays: Wells, "Foreword," v; Duncan-Jones, *Ungentle*, 264; Erne, *Literary Dramatist*, 109–13. We might further speculate that such an edition would have included the poems, like Jonson's *Works*.

[30] On Jonson's plan to write "an epic poem entitled *Herologia*, of the worthies of his country," see "Conversations with William Drummond" (*Ben Jonson: Poems*, ed. Parfitt, 461).

And yet, as often in Shakespearean tragedy, perhaps we find ourselves wondering at the marvel created – wondering whether the river with which the poem opens is not simply Ariosto's Lethe but Spenser's Thames, English literature's great river not of oblivion but of immortality: "Sweete Themmes runne softly, till I end my Song" (*Prothalamion*, 18). As the sustained praise for *A Lover's Complaint* between Malone and Kerrigan suggests, within the poet's opaque fiction of artistic failure, we may witness a supreme art of unperverted reconciliation.

Epilogue: Ariel and Autolycus: Shakespeare's counter-laureate authorship

The year 1623 saw two quite different testaments to the life and work of William Shakespeare. Seven years after the author's death, the First Folio presents "Mr. William Shakespeare" as a man of the theatre who produced "Comedies, Histories, & Tragedies" (*Riverside*, 91). In that same book, however, Leonard Digges refers to the "Stratford monument" at Holy Trinity Church (*Shakspere Allusion-Book*, 1: 318), where the author alternatively appears as a wise philosophical poet in the great European tradition.[1] By looking briefly at these two posthumous testaments, we may bring the present book to its own conclusion.

The least discussed of the testaments, the Stratford monument, exhibits two features worth observing here: the bust of the author and the inscription beneath it (Figure 7). This particular kind of monument, writes Katherine Duncan-Jones, was "designed to commemorate a talented individual, not the head of a family," since it sculpts a "'scholar's type' half-length front-facing effigy" (*Ungentle*, 272). The bust shows a likeness of Shakespeare holding a quill in his right hand as a writing implement, while his left rests comfortably upon a sheet of paper spread open on a cushion. In other words, the bust remembers Shakespeare as an author, not as an actor.[2] Even so, the bust of the author does retain some residue of the theatrical man; not simply does he wear the costume of a scholar's gown, he also performs the dramatic role of poet, "for his mouth is open to declaim his just-composed verses" (Schoenbaum, *Life*, 254).[3] Effectively, the bust portrays William Shakespeare as a poet-playwright figure, the immortal author of his last performance.

---

[1] We do not know when the monument was built, but Schoenbaum is representative: "It had been installed by 1623" (*Life*, 256).

[2] Cf. Honan: "in the parish church he was to be fixed in effigy not as an actor, but as a poet" (*A Life*, 292).

[3] Schoenbaum adds that it is "possible that [Gheerart] Janssen [the Southwark sculptor], working as he did on Bankside, benefited from the suggestions of Shakespeare's former colleagues in the King's Men" (*Life*, 254).

Figure 7. Shakespeare monument with bust and inscription (inscription appears beneath) at Holy Trinity Church, Stratford-upon-Avon.

The inscription beneath the bust divides in two, the first part in Latin, the second a six-line verse in English couplets:

IUDICIO PYLUM, GENIO SOCRATEM, ARTE MARONEM:
TERRA TEGIT, POPULUS MAERET, OLYMPUS HABET.[4]

> Stay Passenger, why goest thou by so fast?
> Read if thou canst, whom envious Death hath plast
> Within this monument Shakspeare: with whom
> Quick nature died: whose name doth deck this tomb
> Far more than cost: sith all that he hath writ
> Leaves living art, but page to serve his wit.
>
> (reprinted in Duncan-Jones, *Ungentle*, 272)

In the English poem, "Death" is not simply "envious" but miraculously generous, since he has given "Shakspeare" *life* "Within this monument." Still, there is loss, for "Quick nature" herself has "died"; the ambiguous phrasing equates the "name" of Nature with that of Shakespeare, and thus rather skillfully represents theatrical cross-dressing. The name itself is invaluable, more so than the materials making up the monument, for all subsequent writing is the "page" to the "wit" of "all that he hath writ." Duncan-Jones finds the pun on the word *page* "slightly lumbering" (*Ungentle*, 272), but it does create an authorial typology, with "Shakspeare" typologically prefiguring "living art."[5] Moreover, the pun transacts a sly typology between poetry and theatre: the "page" of the printed poem transposes into the mini-drama of a servant-messenger or page working for the author. One wonders, then, whether the inscription glances not merely at the Sonnets but at Ariel's relation with Prospero in *The Tempest*, the play printed first in Heminge and Condell's folio edition.

On the monument, the Latin lines preceding the English poem script an authorial process of a (rather socialized) apotheosis: the earth covers the body of the dead man; above ground, the "people" mourn him; and finally Olympus holds his spirit immortally. In this formulation, "Shakspeare" arises from the sullen earth, receives applause from the populace, and enters a pagan pantheon, where he performs the divine judgment of Nestor, the philosophy of Socrates, and the literary skill of Virgil. He possesses the

---

[4] "'The earth covers, the people mourn, Olympus holds [a man who was] a Pylius [= Nestor] in judgement, a Socrates in wisdom, a Virgil in literary skill'" (reprinted in Duncan-Jones, *Ungentle*, 272). Duncan-Jones speculates that Shakespeare's son-in-law, John Hall, may have composed both sets of verses (272).

[5] Hall's comparison between masonic mortality and poetic immortality further suggests that he was thinking of the Sonnets, perhaps Sonnet 55.

kind of practical judgment exhibited by Homer's Nestor, not simply in military matters at Troy (the *Iliad*) but more precisely at Pylos in affairs of the family (the *Odyssey*). Yet Shakespeare complements such social judgment with the deep philosophical wisdom rehearsed by Plato's Socrates – a wisdom, we may assume, about the supreme value of the spirit. Finally, Shakespeare suits his judgment and wisdom to the kind of technical skill so well versed by Rome's great national poet, Virgil: "Arte Maronem." Shakespeare, not Spenser (the Stratford monument seems to cry out from rural Warwickshire) is the authentic Virgil of England: the wise and just national poet. Since long ago George Steevens speculated (tantalizingly) that the scribe originally wrote "Sophoclem," not "Socratem" (*Shakspere Allusion-Book*, 1: 267), we might wonder whether the Stratford monument originally presented its distinguished citizen as an English poet-playwright in the Greco-Roman tradition.

Be that as it may, the First Folio ends up presenting its own version of this compound literary identity despite its theatrical agenda. While Heminge and Condell clearly portray Shakespeare as a man of the theatre – specified by Jonson in his memorial poem as a playwright surpassing Greek and Roman tragedians and comedians – the three-part generic structure of *Mr. William Shakespeares Comedies, Histories, & Tragedies* imitates a Virgilian textual model, "consciously followed," adds Margaret Tudeau-Clayton, "by Spenser amongst others" (*Jonson*, 4). The book accommodates the Roman poetic progression of pastoral, georgic, and epic to an English dramatic progression, from the lower genre of comedy, to the middle genre of history, to the higher genre of tragedy.[6] During the sixteenth century, Tudeau-Clayton reminds us, schoolboys like Shakespeare encountered Virgil in a three-part educational sequence that moved them through the three poetic genres, the *Eclogues* first, the *Georgics* second, and the *Aeneid* last: this "career [was] assiduously followed by Spenser . . . and echoed in the first folio organization of the Shakespearean corpus" (54).

In differing ways, then, the First Folio and the Stratford monument together immortalize Shakespeare as a national poet and playwright. Whereas the First Folio uses a Virgilian, Spenserian poetic model to present "Shakespeare" primarily as a playwright, the monument presents him primarily as a poet performing the role of author. Although different, the two posthumous testaments take cues posed in Shakespeare's own poems and plays, the forms of which often dramatically traverse

---

[6] Tudeau-Clayton, *Jonson*, cites Bullman on the histories as occupying the position of Shakespeare's georgics.

Spenser's Virgilian landscape. Nowhere is the conjunction of poetry and theatre more intense than in the plays from the last phase of Shakespeare's professional career. For this phase, the *Oxford Shakespeare* lists six works:

> *The Winter's Tale*
> *Cymbeline, King of Britain*
> *The Tempest*
> *Cardenio*
> *All Is True* (*Henry VIII*)
> *The Two Noble Kinsmen.*

The first three plays are traditionally grouped with *Pericles* as "romances" or "tragicomedies," while both *Kinsmen* and (probably) the lost *Cardenio* qualify as well (both written with John Fletcher), with *Henry VIII* the lone history. Yet even this national narrative of the late queen's father exhibits the musical masque form characteristic of the Jacobean romances: "*Hoboys. Enter King and others as Maskers, habited like shepherds*" (1. 4. s.d. after line 63). Together, the six plays complete what we know of Shakespeare's combination of the three dramatic forms advertised on the Folio title page. Yet of the four phases of plays we have examined, this is perhaps the least stable; one of the six plays is lost and two of the others are collaborations, leaving only three thought to be fully by Shakespeare. Nonetheless, the salient feature emerging is how constant the author is in composing these forms throughout his career. He is also constant in writing theatre through with poetry, and in continuing his national dialogue with the Virgilian Spenser and the Ovidian Marlowe.

Cymbeline, *The Winter's Tale*, and *The Tempest* all require detailed analysis, but even the others inspire comment. Poet-playwright figures in this phase include Jachimo, Posthumous, and to an extent Imogen in *Cymbeline*; Autolycus in *The Winter's Tale*; and Prospero and Ariel in *The Tempest* (who are parodied in Stephano and Caliban). Not surprisingly, books and performance often come into close alignment, including syntactically, as when Posthumous awakens from his sleep to behold both a theatrical dream of the pagan deities and a book lying on his chest: "What fairies haunt this ground? A book? O rare one, / Be not, as is our fangled world, a garment / Nobler than it covers" (5. 4. 133–35).

Moreover, Shakespeare's three major romances are all known to be cut along Ovidian/Virgilian axes. The Virgilian landscape of pastoral country and epic court is played out most obviously in *The Winter's Tale* but recurs in the court and country scenes of *Cymbeline* and in the contrast between

Prospero's island and his original home, the court of Milan.[7] These plays continue to refer to Virgil's *Aeneid*, and not merely *The Tempest* with its famous discussion of "wido Dido" (2.1.77).[8] In *Cymbeline*, Imogen tells Pisano,

> True honest men being heard, like false Aeneas,
> Were in his time thought false; and Sinon's weeping
> Did scandal many a holy tear, took pity
> From most true wretchedness.   (3.4.58–61)

In *The Winter's Tale*, Florizel is among Shakespeare's most important representations of the shepherd-king figure, while perhaps more surprisingly even the masking shepherd Henry VIII qualifies; in *Cymbeline*, Belarius and Arviragus are displaced versions, as are Stephano and Caliban. A play like *Kinsmen* does not simply put Chaucer on the stage; it puts on that part of Chaucer understood by Spenser to be an epic, "The Knight's Tale," which Spenser imitates in *The Faerie Queene* when he completes "The Squire's Tale."[9]

The Spenserian dynamic of the late romances has become a commonplace of criticism.[10] Periodically, we encounter priceless echoes: "I'll bring a bevy, / A hundred black-ey'd maids that love as I do," the Wooer in *Kinsmen* tells the Jailer (4.1.71–72), conjuring up (and playfully discoloring) Colin Clout's Dance of the Graces in the Legend of Courtesy: "A hundred naked maidens lilly white" (6.10.11).[11]

Yet the late plays are even more noteworthy for their staging of Ovid: *The Tempest*, for Prospero's great rehearsal of Ovid's Medea in his farewell to magic (5.1.33–57); *The Winter's Tale*, for Paulina's re-deployment of Pygmalion's statue (5.3); and *Cymbeline*, for its re-enactment of the *Metamorphoses* itself as a stage prop, with "the leaf's . . . turn'd down / Where

---

[7] Bruster's analysis (see *Quoting Shakespeare*) of the Jailer's Daughter as a figure of the country (ch. 5), in opposition to the noble figures of Palamon, Arcite, and Theseus, suggests that *Kinsmen* is about the historic cultural shift from an ideology of court to one of country, represented in the professional transition from the drama of Shakespeare to that of Fletcher, the collaborating authors who simultaneously evoke the relation between pastoral and epic.

[8] For details on Virgil, see, e.g., D. Hamilton, *Virgil*; Bono, *Transvaluation*; Tudeau-Clayton, *Jonson*; James, *Shakespeare's Troy*.

[9] Cheney, "Spenser's Completion," "'Novells.'"

[10] On Spenser in *The Winter's Tale*, see Alpers, *What is Pastoral?*, 204, 221. For a recent view of how Spenser underpins the late plays, see Palfrey, *Late Shakespeare*, 14, 36–37, 109, 113–14; O'Connell, "Experiment," 221. For a specific moment in *The Tempest*, see D. C. Kay, "Source."

[11] On this unusual numerical iconography, see Cheney, "Spenser's Dance." The *Riverside* assigns this scene to Fletcher, but the work on the Jailer's Daughter by Bruster, *Quoting Shakespeare* (in particular) complicates this authorial scenario.

Philomele gave up" (2. 245–46).[12] This last phrasing intimates a complex intertextual scene, complete with an early seventeenth-century glance back not simply to Shakespeare's first printed play, *Titus Andronicus*, which also puts the *Metamorphoses* on stage, but to that other 1594 book, *The Rape of Lucrece*: "Our Tarquin thus / Did softly press the rushes ere he waken'd / The chastity he wounded" (2. 2. 12–14). Perhaps for this reason, the play ends with a speech containing the word we have emphasized in the conclusion to Shakespeare's second minor epic: "*Publish* we this peace / To all our subjects" (5. 5. 478–79; emphasis added).

Shakespeare's Ovidianism is occasionally evocative of Marlowe, with *The Tempest* long understood to be a response to *Doctor Faustus* (and Jonson's *Alchemist*).[13] Less conspicuously, in this late play we witness a displaced shepherd who would be king, calling up "The Passionate Shepherd to His love": "Wilt thou go with me?" Caliban asks Stephano and Trinculo (2. 2. 172).[14] Yet perhaps it is in the Iago-like Wolsey from *Henry VIII* in whom the Marlovian overreacher most returns with a vengeance:

> I can see his pride / Peep through each part of him . . .
> If not from hell, the devil is a niggard,
> Or has given all before, and he begins
> A new hell in himself.
> (1. 1. 68–72; cf. *Faustus* A text 2. 1. 123–25)

Yet Shakespeare's intertextuality is more complex than this, for the Lord Chamberlain calls Wolsey "This bold bad man" (2. 2. 43). The phrase quotes Spenser's description of the black magician Archimago: "A bold bad man, that dar'd to call by name / Great Gorgon" (*Fairie Queene*, 1. 1. 37). Spenser's description of Archimago here reads like a portrait of a Marlovian and Faustian overreacher – and Shakespeare's use of the Spenserian phrase to portray the Marlovian Wolsey suggests he read Archimago just this way.[15]

Yet it is in *The Winter's Tale* that Shakespeare stages perhaps one of his most splendid authorial figures: Autolycus. This engaging figure routinely sings erotic songs and acts out parts in dramas of his own device. The first time we see him he is singing an erotic song, "When daffadils begin to

---

[12] For details, see Bate, *Ovid*, ch. 6: "In the last plays, as Shakespeare tried out a more mythic mode of composition, Ovid returned to the surface of the drama" (215).

[13] See, e.g., Mebane, *Magic*.

[14] Cf. Shapiro, *Rival*: "in the Faustian moments of *Macbeth* or *The Tempest* we find no verbal recollections, or parodies, of Marlowe's play" (96).

[15] See Cheney, *Profession*, 300n16. The English Online database identifies Spenser as the first to use the phrase, and Shakespeare the second, with an intriguing afterlife in centuries following, starting with Massinger.

appear," which he tells us "Are summer songs for me and my aunts, / While we lie tumbling in the hay" (4. 3. 1–12). Immediately following, however, Autolycus tricks the Old Shepherd's son, the Clown, by playing the part of one who has been robbed by a "servant of the Prince" (87) – a figure at court who has "compass'd a motion of the Prodigal Son" (96–97) – as we have seen, staged a puppet show – and who has now taken Autolycus' clothes and dressed him in his own "garments" (of course, this figure is Autolycus himself). While Autolycus routinely combines such theatrical trickery with erotic singing, Shakespeare situates this Ovidian generic activity in a locale that is distinctly Virgilian: first, the pastoral landscape of Bohemia; and later, the courtly kingdom of Sicilia. Quite literally, the Ovidian Autolycus sings songs and puts on plays along the Virgilian path of pastoral and epic. He is at once an Ovidian poet-playwright and a Virgilian shepherd-courtier.

As a professional thief, Autolycus begins the play committed to his own will power, as he tries to rob the simple Bohemian shepherds of their money, as he himself confesses to the audience at the outset: "My traffic is sheets . . . With die and drab I purchas'd this comparison, and my revenue is the silly cheet" (4. 3. 23–28). Yet, as the strange and wondrous action of the play unfolds, Autolycus finds himself mysteriously swept along by events he no longer can control, until he is forced to admit: "I have done good . . . against my will" (5. 2. 124). Of self-conscious literary origin – "litter'd under Mercury" (4. 3. 25) – this superlative trickster, who often quite literally steals the show in performance, looks conspicuously like a careful parody of his witty creator. Specifically, both Shakespeare and Autolycus, during their respective careers of creation and crime, enact a fundamentally sixteenth-century form of authorship, not seen since the closing of the theatres in antiquity, and only then in intermittent form: the sustained combination of poetry and drama within a single career.

Such a representation raises the question of agency – especially authorial agency. Unlike that other famous clown caught in an epic world of royalty and nobility, Spenser's Colin Clout, Autolycus does not retreat to the pastoral space of Mount Acidale to pipe alone his serene, ephemeral vision of mysterious grace. In fact, what seems required to gambol with Autolycus is precisely an interpretive model of authorship that allows for both intentionality and social forces.[16]

As the case of Autolycus intimates, the late plays self-consciously foreground the theatre, and not simply because of the dramatic Jacobean flair

---

[16] For a similar view of Autolycus, see Pitcher, "Some Call Him Autolycus." On the central importance of Mercury in the poetics of Spenser, see Brooks-Davies, *Mercurean Monarch*. These comments appear in slightly different form in my introduction to *European Literary Careers*.

for masques and machines. According to Harold C. Goddard, "one of the supreme spiritual utterances of England's supreme poet, and, by that fact, of England," emerges in Posthumous' self-consciously theatrical speech opening Act 5, where we witness "the all-importance of the soul and its power to conquer death," much as in Sonnet 146, "which comes as close as anything he ever wrote to being a personal religious creed" (*Meaning*, 2: 259–60):

> Let me make men know
> More valor in me than my habits show.
> Gods, put the strength o' th' Leonati in me!
> To shame the guise o' th' world, I will begin
> The fashion: less without and more within.
> (*Cymbeline*, 5. 1. 29–33)

Yet here we can historicize the religious and political origin of such a creed, Queen Elizabeth's Protestant policy (especially important to Catholics), which required, says Peter Lake, only "outward . . . behavior," not "inward conviction":

This . . . opened up a gap between the inward and the outward, the real inner convictions of a person and his or her outward behavior, a space which . . . could be exploited for all sorts of dissimulation and pretence by the faithless and the unscrupulous. Here, rather than in some nebulous practice called 'Renaissance self-fashioning,' may be a major source of the contemporary dissimulation and the *de facto* atheism of the Machiavel. ("Religious Identities," 64)

As Posthumous makes clear, however, one did not have to be a Machiavel to tap into the terms of Elizabeth's chief religious policy.

Moreover, in these late plays there are intimations that something besides a pure theatre of outward behavior and inner conviction is afoot. In the duet sung by Guiderius and Arviragus over the apparently dead body of Imogen, we find "quite possibly the most resonant lyric lines Shakespeare ever composed" (H. Smith, intro. to *Cymbeline, Riverside*, 1568):

> Fear no more the heat o' th' sun,
> Nor the furious winter's rages,
> Thou thy worldly task hast done,
> Home art gone, and ta'en thy wages.
> Golden lads and girls all must,
> As chimney-sweepers, come to dust.
> (*Cymbeline*, 4. 2. 258–63)

Supplying more detail, Goddard pieces together an informed narrative that some today would recognize as infused with too much Romantic sentiment: "From *The Comedy of Errors* to *Antony and Cleopatra*, the story is one of the gradual subjection of the theatrical to the poetical" (*Meaning*, 2: 203). If Goddard has not quite got the "story" right, he at least sets its terms with characteristic eloquence and insight.

Goddard is correct about the arch-theatricality in *The Comedy of Errors*, but something more complex organizes Shakespeare's late dramatic art than the purifying of theatre through poesis. Goddard himself brings us to a momentous event with *The Tempest*: "When it is he [Ariel] who whispers the hint in Prospero's ear and Prospero obeys *him*, the wonder of a spiritual miracle occurs. Music replaces magic; Ariel's songs achieve what is beyond the scope of Prospero's wand" (*Meaning*, 2: 284; Goddard's emphasis). *Ariel's songs, Prospero's wand*: this is an important dynamic. Nearly unanimously, critics associate Prospero's wand with the art of theatre, and much in the play encourages this identification, as revealed famously in his "Our revels now are ended" speech, with its technical reference to "actors" and the Globe Theatre (4. 1. 148, 152). Yet, as Goddard reminds us, Prospero typically lets Ariel perform the magic for him: "The higher the nature of the miracle sought, the more Prospero seems to entrust its execution to Ariel's improvisation" (*Meaning*, 2: 282). To Prospero's playwright, Ariel functions as lead actor.[17] Yet not merely does the sprite conjure up theatrical shows, as in the grim banquet of the harpies (3. 3) or the wedding masque of Juno and Ceres (4. 1); Ariel repeatedly turns to lyric song to perform his miracles, sounding some of the most profoundly childlike poetry in English:

> Full fadom five thy father lies,
>   Of his bones are coral made:
> Those are pearls that were his eyes:
>   Nothing of him that doth fade,
> But doth suffer a sea-change
> Into something rich and strange
> Sea-nymphs hourly ring his knell:
>   *Burthen [within]*. Ding-dong.
> Hark how I hear them – ding-dong bell.
>   (*The Tempest*, 1. 2. 397–405)

The crystalline presence of Ariel's six recorded songs constitutes a virtual poetics, and requires acute detail to articulate. In "Full fadom five," for instance, he performs a lyric of life beyond death, the imagination's power to pluck immortality from the black beyond. As the auditor of the song,

---

[17] Recent critics continue to recoil from the "colonialist *Tempest*," as does Bruster, *Quoting Shakespeare*, in "the Playhouse in *The Tempest*" (ch. 4 title), which argues for a "'theatrical' *Tempest*" (see 119–120). Cf. Burnett, who turns from "colonialist paradigms" (125) to the "spatial chorography" of the Jacobean "fairground" ("*Monsters*," 126).

Ferdinand, puts it, "The ditty does remember my drown'd father. / This is no mortal business, nor no sound / That the earth owes. I hear it now above me" (1. 2. 406–08). Certainly, technical developments and tastes in Jacobean culture, especially on display at the Blackfriars Theatre, encouraged Shakespeare to intensify his commitment to the performance of lyric song. Yet this commitment, here at the close of his career, does not suddenly appear, but is, as Goddard knew, the apex of his achievement.

In 1995, Alvin B. Kernan summed up a long-standing critical tradition about the authorial temperament producing this achievement: "Shakespeare was not an autobiographical poet, not at least in any simple, direct sense. Anything but. He remains, in fact, the most anonymous of our great writers – we seem always to glimpse only the back of his head just as he slips around the corner" (*King's Playwright*, 179). In the present book, we have attempted to bring the back of the authorial head into focus – to get the author to pause, turn around, and show his face, before he slips around the next corner.[18] The Shakespeare we have tried to glimpse indeed resembles the picture engraved by William Marshall in John Benson's 1640 edition of the *Poems*: as seen at the outset, he is the supreme theatrical author who dramatically holds the leaves of the laureate poet (see Figure 2 above).

If we look around the literary scene during Shakespeare's career, we see a rather large group of laureate-like authors, from Sidney, Spenser, and Daniel to Drayton, Chapman, and Jonson, all of whom are making loud claims for the national value of literary art to England. In the vanguard was England's New Poet himself, Renaissance England's "first laureate" (Helgerson, *Laureates*, 100), whose legacy extended beyond the age of Jonson to that of Milton. Caught up in the power was Marlowe, who, amid his thundering threat, could not extricate his art from the spell of the laureates, and so produced what we have termed a counter-national art. Shakespeare inherits the opposition between Marlowe and Spenser, but he stands above it, precisely to bridge it. He uses the received authorial frame of self-promotion to invent a frame of self-effacement.[19]

---

[18] In "Personal Shakespeare," W. Kerrigan identifies "three clues" to "the personality of the author" (175): "a deep attunement to acting, a fascination with improbable couples, and an uneasy vulnerability to a peculiarly sexual or genital form of misogyny" (185). The last two traits clearly group under gender; to augment Kerrigan's first trait, we could well address a deep attunement to *poesis* (for support, see Schalkwyk, *Performance*, on "the imaginary space of theatrical and poetic production" [49]). Kerrigan sees *Antony and Cleopatra* as "a tragedy in which acting and improbable love triumph over sexual disillusionment, which turned out to be the same thing as staging a counterepic that absorbs and subordinates the imperial drives of his age" (190). Missing in Kerrigan's account are the authors who most helped Shakespeare accomplish this feat: Ovid, Spenser, and Marlowe.

[19] For a similar view of Shakespeare, see Bednarz, *Poets' War*, 257–64.

Rather than asserting his voice as a national author, Shakespeare chooses to *displace* his voice, and nowhere more eloquently than in the poem many consider "Shakespeare's best poem" (Everett, "Golden Bough," 13). "The Phoenix and Turtle" is well known to have origins in Chaucer's *Parlement of Foules*, and indeed Spenser's Old Poet may be the primary model for Shakespeare's authorial self-effacement. In Book 3 of *The House of Fame*, the definitive Chaucerian moment occurs: "Frend," asks Aeolus of Chaucer himself, "what is thy name? / Artow come hider to han fame?" / "Nay, for soothe, frend," says the poet, "I came nought hyder, graunt mercy, / For no such cause, by my hed!" (1871–75).[20] Like Spenser, Shakespeare engaged with Chaucer in intriguingly measurable ways, from *Love's Labor's Lost* to *Troilus and Cressida* to *Two Noble Kinsmen*.[21] Unlike Spenser, however, Shakespeare never claims to participate in the process Spenser calls "traduction" (*Fairie Queene*, 4. 3. 13), a Pythagorean principle of metempsychosis through which Chaucer's "spirit . . . survive[s]" in him (4. 2. 34). Milton told Dryden that he considered Spenser his great original, while Blake said the same of Milton, but Shakespeare stands outside this authorial genealogy of English poetry, linking the fourteenth through the nineteenth centuries.[22] While both Shakespeare and Spenser in particular may in the end "revive" the "labours lost" of Chaucer's "sacred happie spirit" (*Fairie Queene*, 4. 2. 34), they represent radically different ways of positioning the author's cultural authority.

We know well enough what to call Spenser's laureate authorship, but we seem to have trouble characterizing Shakespeare's. We might call it a *counter-laureate authorship*, because it has the clear national ambitions of the Spenserian laureate without its dominant strategy of artistic self-crowning.[23] Throughout this book, we have seen how the man from Stratford joins print culture in presenting a dramatic author with pen in hand. We have accounted for the presence of both poems and plays in his professional career by recalling the sixteenth-century poet-playwright around Europe, as well as in England, principally in the Ovidian Marlowe, in dialogue

---

[20] Thanks to Robert R. Edwards for this reference (personal communication, 5 April 2003). On Chaucer as "a poet of indirection," see Edwards, "Dreamwork."

[21] The two most authoritative studies are by Talbot Donaldson, *The Swan*, and Thompson, *Shakespeare's Chaucer*.

[22] As we have seen, Meres re-routes Pythagorean metempsychosis to Shakespeare's relation with a classical author, Ovid.

[23] See Hattaway, "History Play": in the history plays, Shakespeare responds to Homeric, Virgilian, and finally Spenserian epic. Whereas Spenser in *October* announces the poet's need to turn from pastoral to epic to celebrate national fame, "Shakespeare implicitly asserts that if a poet is to address the ancient topics of heroism and return to the depiction of knights fighting for fame and honour, it is necessary to eschew the pieties of romance epic that emerge in *The Faerie Queene*" (10).

with the Virgilian Spenser. In Shakespeare's hands, intertextuality becomes a premier technique and principle of authorship itself.

We have concentrated on the poems, and tried to see them as a corpus in its own right that complements the larger body of plays. No doubt Shakespeare's poems form part of a generational project, initially centered around Sir Philip Sidney and finally championed most decisively by Spenser and then by Jonson, to create a patriotic body of English literature that can rival the vernaculars of Europe, especially Italy and France.[24] For the most part, however, the poems of Shakespeare, unlike many of his plays, seem to challenge and even to explode this very project. In *Venus*, *Lucrece*, the Sonnets, and *A Lover's Complaint* (as in *The Passionate Pilgrim*), desire is in grave trouble, and even in "The Phoenix and Turtle" the married chastity of the avian principals ends up *dead*. For reasons to which we are not privy, for Shakespeare the penning of poetry seems to have been a fundamentally somber affair; in terms of narrative shape, there is no romantic comedy, and little chance among the living to survive. Desire *is* death, even though occasionally this turns into something of a laughing matter, as it does with Venus, whose body is a deer park for a grazing dear, or with Will's mistress, whose eyes are nothing like the sun. Yet, despite the humor, and the sadness, Shakespeare's poems decisively enter the authorial list, in what constitutes one of the most impressive early modern typological competitions with English and European poetry on record, from Virgil and Ovid to Spenser and Marlowe. Perhaps what makes Shakespeare's poems challenging as a body is their unusual combination of absolute literariness with disconcerting "scandal" – the key term surfacing in modern commentary on the Sonnets in particular (e.g., de Grazia, "Scandal").

The poems are not the plays, and lack their very range of sentiment and mode, but the poems' existence precisely calls into question our dominant view of Shakespeare as the working dramatist. In the end, he bequeathed to posterity England's most extraordinary literary canon, spread across the dramatic genres of comedy, history, tragedy, and romance and the poetic genres of minor epic, sonnet sequence, philosophical hymn, and complaint. As such, we need to extend a favored conclusion from the past century: "only once in the history of Western drama, not in fifth-century Athens but in late sixteenth- and early seventeenth-century England, has a playwright given living warrant to the proposition," articulated by Socrates in Plato's *Symposium*, that the genius of comedy coheres with the genius of

[24] See Hyland on this important context for Shakespeare's poems (*Introduction to Shakespeare's Poems*, 47).

tragedy (Danson, "The Comedies," 239). In this book, we have tried to give living warrant to a slightly different proposition: not merely that comedy and tragedy are possible to conjoin in a single career, but that these twin dramatic forms are possible to combine with an array of poetic forms. Shakespeare's world-class standing derives from his achievement not only in tragedy and comedy but also in sonnet and lyric. Without question, he is the first European author to produce sustained and enduring masterpieces in both poetry and theatre, for both the nascent printing press and the new commercial theatre.

While Shakespeare's sonnets are the high watermark for achievement in the European Petrarchan form, and "The Phoenix and Turtle" perhaps the most perfect poem in any language, *Venus*, *Lucrece*, and *A Lover's Complaint* constitute his most sustained print practice in a single poetic form, from the early 1590s through the first decade of the seventeenth century. Shakespeare, we might conclude, may have turned to "narrative poetry" so recurrently because he discovered in this form an absolute fusion of theatre to poetry.

We have tried to account for the erasure of this fusion in the principal story our culture has told about the literary corpus of this beloved author. What we have not yet reported here is the curious way in which this erasure occurred palpably to the monumental body of "Shakspeare" himself. Not long after 1623 the quill held by the poet in Holy Trinity Church quite naturally disappeared (and would continue to do so over the centuries), so that when Sir William Dugdale arrived in 1634 to make the first known sketch of the monument, the author virtually disappeared, including his paper and writing cushion, leaving in his place "a commodity dealer" (Price, "Function of Imagery," 168), a Falstaff-like holder of an actual sack. Subsequently, Wenceslaus Hollar used the Dugdale drawing for his influential engraving, published in the 1656 (and later the 1730) edition of Sir William Dugdale's *Antiquities of Warwickshire* (Figure 8), which made its way into Rowe's 1709 edition of Shakespeare. Without being able to see the pen, Diana Price speculates, Dugdale "may have simply missed the paper" (172), and thus easily distorted the cushion into a rather lumpy bag, effectively metamorphosing the great Virgilian poet into a simple "sackholder." Significantly, she adds, in 1748–49 a "monument beautification project" removed the impersonating commodity dealer and returned "the literary effigy" (174) – not too far in advance of Edmund Malone's pioneering restoration of the poems alongside the plays in his monumental editions (especially 1790).

At the same time – and in contradistinction to recent scholarship (de Grazia, *Verbatim*; Alexander, "Province of Pirates") – we might wish to say

Figure 8. Wenceslaus Hollar's 1656 engraving, published in the 1656 (and later the 1730) edition of Sir William Dugdale's *Antiquities of Warwickshire*.

that for all his achievement Malone ends up *institutionalizing a problem*, which prevails today: caught up in the cultural process of authenticating "Shakespeare" as an author, Malone ends up falsifying the historical record by printing the poems as merely a "Supplement" to the plays. Despite both the textual and the pictorial beautification projects, at the beginning of the twenty-first century we have not fully restored Shakespeare's poems to their rightful position beside his plays. Accordingly, we may wish to reverse the practice exhibited between Malone and the *Riverside Shakespeare*, alternatively placing the poems, not at the back, but at the front, fully printing Shakespeare in his original stature as national poet-playwright.

Authoring a nonpareil corpus of poems and plays, Shakespeare goes on to perform a leading role in the founding of a new English and European author. Presumably, the closing of the English theatres in 1642 created a challenge to the life of this author, but what seems safe to say is that from Milton and Dryden, to Shelley, Byron, and Goethe, to Yeats, Eliot, and Auden, no author could ignore the authority of the Shakespearean poet-playwright. In fact, it may be important to look at the plays of these fundamentally gifted poets in terms of the anxiety of Shakespearean "dramatic" influence. At the same time, we might wish to emphasize how unique the late sixteenth and early seventeenth centuries are in the English tradition, because at no time in England's history did the author as a poet-playwright flourish as intensively and extensively as it did then. For the most part, the leading authors of the English Augustan age, the Romantic period, and the Victorian era were all poets or novelists, not dramatists (major exceptions include Dryden, Shelley, and Byron), while even in the twentieth century the plays of Yeats, Eliot, and Auden had less influence than had their poetry – an influence that continues to be heard today (in Derek Walcott, for instance, or Sam Shepard). A fuller study of this fascinating evolution remains to be written, but scholars in early modern studies may wish to re-define at least one segment of the traditional story about the Renaissance as an age of rebirth, as well as Shakespeare's seminal place in the story. After such well-documented cultural events as the discovery and recovery of classical texts, the invention of the printing press, the transition from a feudal to a capitalist society, the return to a purified Church, the building of the new commercial theatres, the advent of modern science, and the discovery and colonization of the Americas, we may wish to include as a notable literary event the emergence of the author as a poet-playwright.

When Ariel comes to sing his last song, he does not simply draw on an ancient trope of the poet as an imitative artist, employed famously by Jonson, who would succeed Spenser and Marlowe as Shakespeare's greatest rival: "to draw forth out of the best, and choicest flowers, with the bee, and turn all into honey" (*Discoveries*, 3057–81, in *Ben Jonson*, ed., Parfitt). Nor does Ariel only locate the naturalist *telos* of Shakespeare's art of spiritual immanence. The page of Prospero releases the art of poetry into the theatre:

> Where the bee sucks, there suck I,
> In a cowslip's bell I lie;
> There I couch when owls do cry.
> On the bat's back I do fly
> After summer merrily.
> Merrily, merrily shall I live now,
> Under the blossom that hangs on the bough.
>
> (*The Tempest*, 5. 1. 88–94)

Works cited

Abrams, Rick, and Don Foster. "Abrams and Foster on 'A Funeral Elegy.'" *Shaksper: The Global Electronic Shakespeare Conference.* 12 June 2002. www.shaksper.net/archives/2002/1484.html.

Adams, Joseph Quincy, ed. *The Passionate Pilgrim.* New York: Scribner's, 1939.

Aeschylus. *Aeschylus I: Oresteia: Agamemnon, The Libation Bearers, The Eumenides.* Trans. Richmond Lattimore. The Complete Greek Tragedies. Ed. David Grene and Richmond Lattimore. Chicago: University of Chicago Press, 1953.

Alexander, Catherine M. S. "Province of Pirates: The Editing and Publication of Shakespeare's Poems in the Eighteenth Century." *Reading Readings: Essays on Shakespeare Editing in the Eighteenth Century.* Ed. Joanna Gondris. Madison: Fairleigh Dickinson University Press; London: Associated University Presses, 1998. 345–64.

Allen, Don Cameron. "On *Venus and Adonis.*" *Elizabethan and Jacobean Studies Presented to F. P. Wilson on His Seventieth Birthday.* Ed. H. Davis and H. Gardner. Oxford: Clarendon, 1959. 100–11.

Allen, Michael J. B. "The Chase: The Development of a Renaissance Theme." *Comparative Literature* 20 (1968): 301–12.

Alpers, Paul. *What is Pastoral?* Chicago: University of Chicago Press, 1996.

Andrews, Michael Cameron. "Music's 'Silver Sound': A Note on *Romeo and Juliet.*" *Notes and Queries* 36 (1989): 322–23.

Ariosto, Ludovico. *Orlando Furioso (The Frenzy of Orlando): A Romantic Epic by Ludovico Ariosto.* Trans. Barbara Reynolds. 2 vols. Harmondsworth: Penguin, 1975.

Aristotle. *The Basic Works of Aristotle.* Ed. Richard McKeon. New York: Random House, 1941.

Asquith, Clare. "A Phoenix for Palm Sunday." *Times Literary Supplement,* 13 April 2001: 14–15.

Augustine, St. *"Confessions" and "Enchiridion."* Trans. Albert C. Outler. The Library of Christian Classics. Philadelphia: Westminster Press, 1965.

Augustine: Concerning the City of God against the Pagans. Trans. Henry Bettenson. 1972; Harmondsworth: Penguin, 1984.

Axton, Marie. "Miraculous Succession: 'The Phoenix and the Turtle' (1601)." *The Queen's Two Bodies: Drama and the Elizabethan Succession.* London: Royal Historical Society, 1977. 116–30.

Baines, Barbara J. "Effacing Rape in Early Modern Representation." *ELH* 65 (1998): 69–98.

Baker, David. "Cavalier Shakespeare: The 1640 *Poems* of John Benson." *Studies in Philology* 95 (1998): 152–73.

Barkan, Leonard. *The Gods Made Flesh: Metamorphosis and the Pursuit of Paganism.* New Haven: Yale University Press, 1986.

Barnfield, Richard. *The Complete Poems: Richard Barnfield.* Ed. George Klawitter. Selinsgrove, PA: Susquehanna University Press; London: Associated University Presses, 1990.

Barroll, J. Leeds. *Politics, Plague, and Shakespeare's Theater: The Stuart Years.* Ithaca: Cornell University Press, 1991.

Bate, Jonathan, *Shakespearean Constitutions: Politics, Theatre, Criticism 1730–1830.* Oxford: Clarendon, 1989.

    Shakespeare and Ovid. Oxford: Clarendon, 1993.

    The Genius of Shakespeare. London: Macmillan-Picador, 1997.

Bate, Jonathan, ed. *Titus Andronicus.* By William Shakespeare. Arden Shakespeare. 3rd Series. London: Thomas Nelson, 1995.

Bates, Ronald. "Shakespeare's 'The Phoenix and Turtle.'" *Shakespeare Quarterly* 6 (1955): 19–30.

Baumlin, Tita French. "The Birth of the Bard: *Venus and Adonis* and Poetic Apotheosis." *Papers on Language and Literature* 26 (1990): 191–211.

Bednarz, James P. "Imitations of Spenser in *A Midsummer Night's Dream.*" *Renaissance Drama* 14 (1983): 79–102.

    "Alençon." *Spenser Encyclopedia.* (1990). 14–15.

    Shakespeare and the Poets' War. New York: Columbia University Press, 2001.

Bell, Ilona. "'That which thou hast done': Shakespeare's Sonnets and *A Lover's Complaint.*" Schiffer, ed. *Shakespeare's Sonnets: Critical Essays.* 455–74.

Belsey, Catherine. "Love as Trompe-L'oeil: Taxonomies of Desire in *Venus and Adonis* (1995)." Kolin, ed. *"Venus and Adonis": Critical Essays.* 261–85.

    "Tarquin Dispossessed: Expropriation and Consent in *The Rape of Lucrece.*" *Shakespeare Quarterly* 52 (2001): 315–25.

Benson, John, ed. *Poems: Written By Wil. Shake-speare. Gent.* London, 1640.

Berger, Harry, Jr. *Imaginary Audition: Shakespeare on Stage and Page.* Berkeley: University of California Press, 1989.

    "Actaeon at the Hinder Gate: The Stag Party in Spenser's Gardens of Adonis." Finucci and Schwartz, eds. *Desire in the Renaissance*: *Psychoanalysis and Literature.* 91–119.

Bernard, John. "'To Constancie Confin'de': The Poetics of Shakespeare's Sonnets." *PMLA* 94 (1979): 77–90.

Berry, Edward. "Twentieth-Century Shakespeare Criticism: The Histories." S. Wells, ed. *Cambridge Companion to Shakespeare Studies.* 249–56.

    Shakespeare and the Hunt: A Cultural and Social Study. Cambridge: Cambridge University Press, 2001.

Berry, Philippa. "Woman, Language, and History in *The Rape of Lucrece.*" *Shakespeare Survey* 44 (1992): 33–39.

Bliss, Lee. "'Don Quixote' in England: The Case for 'The Knight of the Burning Pestle.'" *Viator* 18 (1987): 361–80.

Blissett, William. "Lucan's Caesar and the Elizabethan Villain." *Studies in Philology* 53 (1956): 553–75.

Bloom, Harold. *The Anxiety of Influence: A Theory of Poetry*. 2nd edn. New York: Oxford University Press, 1997.

Shakespeare: The Invention of the Human. New York: Riverhead-Penguin Putnam, 1998.

Genius: A Mosaic of One Hundred Exemplary Creative Minds. New York: Warner, 2002.

Bono, Barbara J. *Literary Transvaluation: From Vergilian Epic to Shakespearean Tragicomedy*. Berkeley: University of California Press, 1984.

Booth, Stephen, ed. *Shakespeare's Sonnets*. New Haven: Yale University Press, 1977.

Bradbrook, M. C. "*The Phoenix and the Turtle*." *Shakespeare Quarterly* 6 (1955): 356–58.

Shakespeare and Elizabethan Poetry. London: Chatto and Windus, 1961.

"Beasts and Gods: Greene's *Groats-Worth of Witte* and the Social Purpose of *Venus and Adonis*." *Shakespeare Survey* 15 (1962): 62–72.

"Shakespeare's Recollections of Marlowe." *Shakespeare's Styles: Essays in Honour of Kenneth Muir*. Ed. Philip Edwards, Inga-Stina Ewbank, and G. K. Hunter. Cambridge: Cambridge University Press, 1980. 199–204.

Braden, Gordon. *Renaissance Tragedy and the Senecan Tradition: Anger's Privilege*. New Haven: Yale University Press, 1985.

"Shakespeare's Petrarchism." Schiffer, ed. *Shakespeare's Sonnets: Critical Essays*. 163–84.

"Ovid, Petrarch, and Shakespeare's Sonnets." A. B. Taylor, ed. *Shakespeare's Ovid: The "Metamorphoses" in the Plays and Poems*. 96–112.

Braudy, Leo. *The Frenzy of Renown: Fame and Its History*. New York: Oxford University Press, 1986.

Breitenberg, Mark. *Anxious Masculinity in Early Modern England*. Cambridge: Cambridge University Press, 1996.

Bristol, Michael. *Big Time Shakespeare*. New York: Routledge, 1996.

Bromley, Laura G. "Lucrece's Recreation." *Shakespeare Quarterly* 34 (1983): 200–11.

Brooks, Cleanth. *The Well Wrought Urn: Studies in the Structure of Poetry*. London: Methuen, 1971.

Brooks-Davies, Douglas. *The Mercurian Monarch: Magical Politics from Spenser to Pope*. Manchester: Manchester University Press, 1983.

Brooks-Davies, Douglas, ed. *Edmund Spenser: Selected Shorter Poems*. London: Longman, 1995.

Brown, Carleton, ed. *Poems by Sir John Salusbury and Robert Chester*. Early English Text Studies. London: K. Paul, Trench, Trübner, 1914.

Brown, Georgia. "Breaking the Canon: Marlowe's Challenge to the Literary Status Quo in *Hero and Leander*." White, ed. *Marlowe, History, and Sexuality: New Critical Essays on Christopher Marlowe*. 59–75.

Brown, James Neil. "'A Calendar, A Calendar! Look in the Almanac.'" *Notes and Queries* 27 (1980): 162–65.

Bruster, Douglas. *Quoting Shakespeare: Form and Culture in Early Modern Drama.* Lincoln: University of Nebraska Press, 2000.

Bullman, George. "Shakespeare's Georgic Histories." *Shakespeare Survey* 38 (1985): 37–47.

Burckhardt, Jacob. *The Civilization of the Renaissance in Italy.* 2 vols. 1929; New York: Harper, 1975.

Burnett, Mark Thornton. *Constructing "Monsters" in Shakespearean Drama and Early Modern Culture.* Basingstoke: Palgrave Macmillan, 2002.

Burnett, Mark Thornton, ed. *Christopher Marlowe: The Complete Plays.* Everyman Library. London: Dent; Rutland, VT: Tuttle, 1999.

Burrow, Colin. *Epic Romance: Homer to Milton.* Oxford: Clarendon, 1993.

"Life and Work in Shakespeare's Poems." Chatterton Lecture on Poetry. *Proceedings of the British Academy* 97 (1998): 15–50.

"The Sixteenth Century." Kinney, ed. *Cambridge Companion to English Literature, 1500–1600.* 11–28.

"*Lucrece*: The Politics of Reading." Paper presented at the Shakespeare's Narrative Poems Conference. University of London, London, England. July 2001.

Burrow, Colin, ed. *William Shakespeare: The Complete Sonnets and Poems.* Oxford World's Classics. Oxford: Oxford University Press, 2002.

Bush, Douglas. "Notes on Shakespeare's Classical Mythology." *Philological Quarterly* 6 (1927): 301.

Mythology and the Renaissance Tradition in English Poetry. New York: Norton, 1963.

"*Venus and Adonis* and Mythology (1932)." Kolin, ed. *"Venus and Adonis": Critical Essays.* 91–102.

Buxton, John. "Two Dead Birds: A Note on *The Phoenix and Turtle.*" *English Renaissance Studies Presented to Dame Helen Gardner in Honour of Her Seventieth Birthday.* Ed. John Carey. Oxford: Clarendon, 1980. 44–55.

Cain, Thomas H. "Spenser and the Renaissance Orpheus." *University of Toronto Quarterly* 41 (1971): 24–47.

Praise in "The Faerie Queene." Lincoln: University of Nebraska Press, 1978.

Callimachus. *Callimachus: "Hymns" and "Epigrams"; Lycophron; Aratus.* Trans. G. R. Mair. Loeb Classical Library. Cambridge, MA: Harvard University Press; London: Heinemann, 1955.

Cannan, Paul D. "Early Shakespeare Criticism, Charles Gildon, and the Making of Shakespeare the Playwright-Poet." *Modern Philology.* Forthcoming.

Cartelli, Thomas. *Marlowe, Shakespeare, and the Economy of Theatrical Experience.* Philadelphia: University Pennsylvania Press, 1991.

Cascardi, Anthony J., ed. *The Cambridge Companion to Cervantes.* Cambridge: Cambridge University Press, 2002.

Cervantes Saavedra, Miguel de. *Don Quixote of La Mancha.* Trans. Walter Starkie. New American Library. 1957; New York: Signet, 1964.

Charney, Maurice. "Jessica's Turquoise Ring and Abigail's Poisoned Porridge: Shakespeare and Marlowe as Rivals and Imitators." *Renaissance Drama* 10 (1979): 33–44.

Chaucer, Geoffrey. *Chaucer's Major Poetry.* Ed. Albert C. Baugh. New York: Meredith, 1963.

Cheney, Patrick. "Alcestis and the 'Passion for Immortality': Milton's *Sonnet XXIII* and Plato's *Symposium.*" *Milton Studies* 18 (1983): 63–76.

"Spenser's Dance of the Graces and Tasso's Dance of the Sylvan Nymphs." *English Language Notes* 22 (1984): 5–9.

"Spenser's Completion of *The Squire's Tale*: Love, Magic, and Heroic Action in the Legend of Cambell and Triamond." *Journal of Medieval and Renaissance Studies* 15 (1985): 135–55.

Spenser's Famous Flight: A Renaissance Idea of a Literary Career. Toronto: University of Toronto Press, 1993.

Marlowe's Counterfeit Profession: Ovid, Spenser, Counter-Nationhood. Toronto: University of Toronto Press, 1997.

"'O, let my books be . . . dumb presagers': Poetry and Theater in Shakespeare's Sonnets." *Shakespeare Quarterly* 52 (2001): 222–54.

"Recent Studies in Marlowe (1987–1998)." *English Literary Renaissance* 31 (2001): 288–328.

"Shakespeare's Sonnet 106, Spenser's National Epic, and Counter-Petrarchism." *English Literary Renaissance* 31 (2001): 331–64.

"Spenser's Pastorals: *The Shepheardes Calender* and *Colin Clouts Come Home Againe.*" *The Cambridge Companion to Spenser.* Ed. Andrew Hadfield. Cambridge: Cambridge University Press, 2001. 79–105.

"'Novells of his devise': Chaucerian and Virgilian Career Paths in Spenser's *Februarie* Eclogue." Cheney and de Armas, eds. *European Literary Careers: The Author from Antiquity to the Renaissance.* 231–67.

"Dido to Daphne: Early Modern Death in Spenser's Shorter Poems." *Spenser Studies* 18 (2003): 143–63.

"Biographical Representations: Marlowe's Life of the Author." *New Directions in Biographies of Marlowe, Shakespeare, and Jonson.* Ed. Ronnie Mulryne and Takashi Kozuka. Forthcoming.

Cheney, Patrick, ed. *The Cambridge Companion to Christopher Marlowe.* Cambridge: Cambridge University Press, 2004.

Cheney, Patrick, and Paul J. Klemp. "Spenser's Dance of the Graces and the Ptolemaic Universe." *Studia Neophilologica* 56 (1984): 27–33.

Cheney, Patrick, and Frederick A. de Armas, eds. *European Literary Careers: The Author from Antiquity to the Renaissance.* Toronto: University of Toronto Press, 2002.

Cheney, Patrick, and Anne Lake Prescott. "Teaching Spenser's Marriage Poetry: *Amoretti, Epithalamion, Prothalamion.*" Cheney and Prescott, eds. *Approaches to Teaching Shorter Elizabethan Poetry.* 226–38.

Cheney, Patrick, and Anne Lake Prescott, eds. *Approaches to Teaching Shorter Elizabethan Poetry.* New York: Modern Language Association, 2000.

Cinthio, Giovambattista Giraldi. *Discorsidi*. Venice, 1554.

Cohen, Walter. *Drama of a Nation: Public Theater in Renaissance England and Spain*. Ithaca: Cornell University Press, 1985.

Collinson, Patrick. "The Monarchical Republic of Queen Elizabeth I." *Bulletin of the John Ryland's Library* 69 (1987): 394–424.

Cook, Carol. "The Fatal Cleopatra." *Shakespearean Tragedy and Gender*. Ed. Shirley Nelson Garner and Madelon Sprengnether. Bloomington: Indiana University Press, 1996. 241–67.

Coolidge, John S. "Great Things and Small: The Virgilian Progression." *Comparative Literature* 17 (1965): 1–23.

Cousins, A. D. *Shakespeare's Sonnets and Narrative Poems*. Harlow: Longman, 2000.

Cousins, A. D., ed. *Certaine Learned and Elegant Workes (1633) By Fulke Greville: A Facsimile Reproduction*. Delmar, NY: Scholars' Facsimiles and Reprints, 1990.

Coyle, Martin. "*King Lear* and *The Faerie Queene*." *Notes and Queries* 31 (1984): 205–07.

Craik, Katharine A. "Shakespeare's *A Lover's Complaint* and Early Modern Criminal Confession." *Shakespeare Quarterly* 53 (2002): 437–59.

Crewe, Jonathan. "Shakespeare's Figure of Lucrece: Writing Rape." *Trials of Authorship: Anterior Forms and Poetic Reconstruction from Wyatt to Shakespeare*. Berkeley: University of California Press, 1990. 140–63.

Crewe, Jonathan, ed. *William Shakespeare: The Narrative Poems*. The Pelican Shakespeare. New York: Penguin, 1999.

Cruttwell, Patrick. *The Shakespearean Moment and Its Place in the Poetry of the 17th Century*. New York: Random House, 1960.

Cummings, R. M., ed. *Spenser: The Critical Heritage*. New York: Barnes & Noble, 1971.

Cunningham, J. V. "'Essence' and the '*Phoenix and Turtle*.'" *ELH* 19 (1952): 256–76.

Currie, H. MacL. "Ovid and the Roman Stage." *Aufstieg und Niedergang der römischen Welt* 31 (1981): 2701–42.

Daniel, Samuel. *The Works of Samuel Daniel, Newly Augmented*. London, 1602. *Delia. Elizabethan Sonnets*. Ed. Maurice Evans; rev. Roy J. Booth. Everyman Library. London: Dent; Rutland, VT: Tuttle, 1994. 58–80.

Danson, Lawrence. "Twentieth-Century Shakespeare Criticism: The Comedies." S. Wells, ed. *Cambridge Companion to Shakespeare Studies*. 231–39.

Dante Alighieri. *The Divine Comedy*. Trans. Allen Mandelbaum. Everyman Library. New York: Knopf, 1995.

Davies, H. Neville. "The Phoenix and Turtle: Requiem and Rite." *Review of English Studies* 46 (1995): 525–30.

Davis, John T. "*Fictus Adulter*": Poet as Actor in the "*Amores*." Amsterdam: J. C. Gieben, 1989.

De Armas, Frederick A. "Cervantes and the Italian Renaissance." Cascardi, ed. *Cambridge Companion to Cervantes*. 32–57.

"Cervantes and the Virgilian Wheel: The Portrayal of a Literary Career." Cheney and de Armas, eds. *European Literary Careers: The Author from Antiquity to the Renaissance.* 268–85.

De Grazia, Margreta. "The Motive for Interiority: Shakespeare's Sonnets and *Hamlet.*" *Style* 23 (1989): 430–44.

Shakespeare Verbatim: The Reproduction of Authenticity and the 1790 Apparatus. Oxford: Clarendon, 1991.

"The Scandal of Shakespeare's Sonnets." *Shakespeare Survey* 46 (1994): 35–49.

De Grazia, Margreta, and Peter Stallybrass. "The Materiality of the Shakespearean Text." *Shakespeare Quarterly* 44 (1993): 255–83.

De Grazia, Margreta, Maureen Quilligan, and Peter Stallybrass, eds. *Subject and Object in Renaissance Culture.* Cambridge: Cambridge University Press, 1996.

De Grazia, Margreta, and Stanley Wells, eds. *The Cambridge Companion to Shakespeare.* Cambridge: Cambridge University Press, 2001.

Del Rio, Martini Antonii, ed. *L. Annaei Senecae Cordubensis Poetae Gravissimi Tragoedias Dicem.* Antwerp, 1576.

DeNeef, A. Leigh. "The Poetics of Orpheus: The Text and a Study of *Orpheus His Journey to Hell* (1595)." *Studies in Philology* 89 (1992): 20–70.

De Vroom, Thersia. "Mediating Myth: The Art of Marlowe's *Hero and Leander.*" *CLA Journal* 37 (1994): 425–42.

Dobson, Michael. *The Making of the National Poet: Shakespeare, Adaptation, and Authorship, 1660–1769.* Oxford: Clarendon, 1992.

Doebler, John. "The Many Faces of Love: Shakespeare's *Venus and Adonis.*" *Shakespeare Studies* 16 (1983): 33–43.

Dollimore, Jonathan. *Radical Tragedy: Religion, Ideology and Power in the Drama of Shakespeare and His Contemporaries.* Chicago, University Chicago Press, 1984.

"Desire is Death." De Grazia, Quilligan, and Stallybrass, eds. *Subject and Object in Renaissance Culture.* 369–86.

Dolven, Jeffrey. "Spenser's Troubled Theaters." *English Literary Renaissance* 29 (1999): 179–200.

Donaldson, E. Talbot. *The Swan at the Well: Shakespeare Reading Chaucer.* New Haven: Yale University Press, 1985.

Donaldson, Ian. *The Rapes of Lucretia: A Myth and Its Transformations.* Oxford: Clarendon, 1982.

Donne, John. *The Poems of John Donne.* Ed. Herbert J. C. Grierson. 2 vols. Oxford: Clarendon, 1912.

Dowden, Edward, ed. *"The Passionate Pilgrim."* London, 1883.

Dronke, Peter. *Poetic Individuality in the Middle Ages: New Departures in Poetry 1000–1150.* 2nd edn. London: Westfield Publications in Medieval Studies, 1986.

Dubrow, Heather. "A Mirror for Complaints: Shakespeare's *Lucrece* and Generic Tradition." *Renaissance Genres: Essays on Theory, History, and Interpretation.* Ed. Barbara Kiefer Lewalski. Cambridge, MA: Harvard University Press, 1986. 399–417.

"The Rape of Clio: Attitudes of History in Shakespeare's *Lucrece*." *English Literary Renaissance* 16 (1986): 425–41.

Captive Victors: Shakespeare's Narrative Poems and Sonnets. Ithaca: Cornell University Press, 1987.

"'Incertainties now crown themselves assur'd': The Politics of Plotting Shakespeare's Sonnets." Schiffer, ed. *Shakespeare's Sonnets: Critical Eassays*. 113–34.

Shakespeare and Domestic Loss: Forms of Deprivation, Mourning, and Recuperation. Cambridge: Cambridge University Press, 1999.

"Lyric Forms." Kinney, ed. *Cambridge Companion to English Literature 1500–1600*. 178–99.

"'These so differing twins': The Interplay of Narrative and Lyric in Shakespeare's Narrative Poems." Paper presented at the Shakespeare's Narrative Poems Conference. University of London, London, England. July 2001.

Duncan-Jones, Katherine. "Was the 1609 *Shake-speares Sonnets* Really Unauthorized?" *Review of English Studies* 34 (1983): 151–71.

"Much Ado With Red and White: The Earliest Readers of Shakespeare's *Venus and Adonis*." *Review of English Studies* 44 (1993): 479–501.

"What are Shakespeare's Sonnets Called?" *Essays in Criticism* 47 (1997): 1–12.

Ungentle Shakespeare: Scenes from His Life. The Arden Shakespeare. 3rd Series. London: Thomson Learning, 2001.

Duncan-Jones, Katherine, ed. *Shakespeare's Sonnets*. Arden Shakespeare. 3rd ser. London: Thomas Nelson, 1997.

Durling, Robert M., ed. *Petrarch's Lyric Poems: The "Rime sparse" and Other Lyrics*. Cambridge, MA: Harvard University Press, 1976.

Dutton, Richard. *Licensing, Censorship and Authorship in Early Modern England: Buggeswords*. Basingstoke: Palgrave, 2000.

Dzelzainis, Martin. "Shakespeare and Political Thought." Kastan, ed. *A Companion to Shakespeare*. 100–16.

Easterling, P. E., and E. J. Kinney, eds. *Cambridge History of Classical Literature*. 9 vols. Paperback edition. 1982–85; Cambridge: Cambridge University Press, 1989.

Edwards, Robert R. "Ricardian Dreamwork: Chaucer, Cupid, and Loyal Lovers." *Critical Essays on Chaucer's "Legend of Good Women."* Ed. Carolyn Collette. London: Boydell & Brewer, forthcoming.

Edwards, Robert R., ed. *John Lydgate: "Troy Book": Selections*. Kalamazoo, MI: TEAMS, 1998.

El-Gabalawy, Saad. "The Ethical Question of *Lucrece*: A Case of Rape." *Mosaic* 12 (1979): 75–85.

Eliot, T. S. *Elizabethan Dramatists*. London: Faber and Faber, 1963.

Elizabeth I. *Elizabeth I: Collected Works*. Ed. Leah S. Marcus, Janel Mueller, and Mary Beth Rose. Chicago: University of Chicago Press, 2000.

Elliott, John R., Jr., ed. *The Prince of Poets: Essays on Edmund Spenser*. New York: New York University Press, 1968.

Ellrodt, Robert. "An Anatomy of 'The Phoenix and the Turtle.'" *Shakespeare Survey* 15 (1962): 99–110.

"Shakespeare the Non-Dramatic Poet." S. Wells, ed. *Cambridge Companion to Shakespeare Studies*. 35–48.

Empson, William. "*The Phoenix and the Turtle*." *Essays in Criticism* 16 (1966): 147–53.

Some Versions of Pastoral. 1935; New York: New Directions, 1974.

"The Narrative Poems." *Essays in Shakespeare*. Ed. David B. Pirie. Cambridge: Cambridge University Press, 1986. 1–28.

Engle, Lars. "Afloat in Thick Deeps: Shakespeare's Sonnets on Certainty." *PMLA* 104 (1989): 832–43.

"'I am that I am': Shakespeare's Sonnets and the Economy of Shame." Schiffer, ed. *Shakespeare's Sonnets: Critical Essays*. 185–98.

Enterline, Lynn. "Embodied Voices: Petrarch Reading (Himself Reading) Ovid." Finucci and Schwartz, eds. *Desire in the Renaissance: Psychoanalysis and Literature*. 120–45.

The Rhetoric of the Body: From Ovid to Shakespeare. Cambridge: Cambridge University Press, 2000.

Eriksen, Roy T. "'Un certo amoroso martire': Shakespeare's 'The Phoenix and the Turtle' and Giordano Bruno's *De gli eroici furori*." *Spenser Studies* 2 (1981): 193–215.

"Marlowe's Petrarch: *In Morte di Madonna Laura*." *Cahiers Elisabethains* 29 (1986): 13–25.

Erne, Lukas. "Shakespeare's 'Ever-Fixed Mark': Theological Implications in Sonnet 116." *English Studies* 81 (2000): 293–304.

Beyond "The Spanish Tragedy": A Study of the Works of Thomas Kyd. Manchester: Manchester University Press, 2001.

Shakespeare as Literary Dramatist. Cambridge: Cambridge University Press, 2003.

Evans, G. Blakemore, ed. *The Sonnets*. Cambridge: Cambridge University Press, 1996.

Everett, Barbara. "Set upon a Golden Bough to Sing: Shakespeare's Debt to Sidney in 'The Phoenix and Turtle.'" *Times Literary Supplement*, 16 February 2001: 13–15.

Faas, Ekbert, *Shakespeare's Poetics* Cambridge: Cambridge University Press, 1996.

Farrell, Joseph. *Virgil's "Georgics" and the Traditions of Ancient Epic: The Art of Allusion in Literary History*. New York: Oxford University Press, 1991.

"Greek Lives and Roman Careers in the Classical *Vita* Tradition." Cheney and de Armas, eds. *European Literary Careers: The Author from Antiquity to the Renaissance*. 24–46.

Feeney, Denis C. *The Gods in Epic: Poets and Critics of the Classical Tradition*. Oxford: Clarendon, 1991.

Ferry, Anne. *The "Inward" Language: Sonnets of Wyatt, Sidney, Shakespeare, Donne*. Chicago: University of Chicago Press, 1983.

Fienberg, Nona. "Thematics of Value in *Venus and Adonis* (1989)." Kolin, ed. *"Venus and Adonis": Critical Essays*. 247–58.

Fineman, Joel. *Shakespeare's Perjured Eye: The Invention of Poetic Subjectivity in the Sonnets*. Berkeley: University of California Press, 1986.

"Shakespeare's Will: The Temporality of Rape." *Representations* 20 (1987): 25–76.

Finnis, John, and Patrick Martin. "Another turn for the Turtle: Shakespeare's Intercession for *Love's Martyr*." *Times Literary Supplement*, 18 April 2003: 12–14.

Finucci, Valerie, and Regina Schwartz, eds. *Desire in the Renaissance: Psychoanalysis and Literature*. Princeton: Princeton University Press, 1994.

Fletcher, Angus. *The Prophetic Moment: An Essay on Spenser*. Chicago: University of Chicago Press, 1971.

Foucault, Michel. *The Foucault Reader*. Ed. Paul Rabinow. New York: Pantheon Books, 1984.

Fowler, Alastair. *Kinds of Literature: An Introduction to the Theory of Genres and Modes*. Cambridge, MA: Harvard University Press, 1982.

Fraser, Russell A., and Norman Rabkin, eds. *Drama of the English Renaissance*. 2 vols. Upper Saddle River, NJ: Prentice-Hall, 1976.

Freeman, Arthur, and Paul Grinke. "Four New Shakespeare Quartos?" *Times Literary Supplement*, 5 April 2003: 17–18.

Freinkel, Lisa. "The Name of the Rose: Christian Figurality and Shakespeare's Sonnets." Schiffer, ed. *Shakespeare's Sonnets: Critical Essays*. 241–61.

Reading Shakespeare's Will: The Theology of Figure from Augustine to the Sonnets. New York: Columbia University Press, 2002.

French, Tita. "A 'badge of fame': Shakespeare's Rhetorical Lucrece." *Explorations In Renaissance Culture* 10 (1984): 97–106.

Froes, Joao. "Shakespeare's Venus and the Venus of Classical Mythology." Kolin, ed. *"Venus and Adonis": Critical Essays*. 301–07.

Frye, Northrop. *Anatomy of Criticism: Four Essays*. Princeton: Princeton University Press, 1957.

"How True a Twain." *Fables of Identity: Studies in Poetic Mythology*. New York: Harcourt-Harbinger, 1963. 88–106.

Frye, Roland Mushat. "Shakespeare's Composition of *Lucrece*: New Evidence." *Shakespeare Quarterly* 16 (1965): 289–96.

Fuller, David, ed. *Tamburlaine the Great Parts 1 and 2*. Oxford: Clarendon, 1998. Vol. 5 in *The Complete Works of Christopher Marlowe*. Ed. Roma Gill. 5 vols. Oxford: Clarendon, 1987–98.

Fumerton, Patricia. *Cultural Aesthetics: Renaissance Literature and the Practice of Social Ornament*. Chicago: University of Chicago Press, 1991.

Ganim, John M. *Chaucerian Theatricality*. Princeton: Princeton University Press, 1990.

Garber, Marjorie. "Marlovian Vision/Shakespearean Revision." *Research Opportunities in Renaissance Drama* 22 (1979): 3–9.

Garrod, H. W. "The Nightingale in Poetry." *The Profession of Poetry and Other Lectures*. Oxford: Clarendon, 1929. 131–59.

The Geneva Bible: A Facsimile Edition. Ed. Lloyd E. Berry. Madison: University of Wisconsin Press, 1969.

Goddard, Harold C. *The Meaning of Shakespeare.* 2 vols. 1951; Chicago: University of Chicago P-Phoenix, 1960.

Golding, Arthur, trans. *"Metamorphoses." Shakespeare's Ovid.* Ed. W. H. D. Rouse. New York: Norton, 1966.

Gosson, Stephen. *The Schoole of Abuse.* London, 1579.

Gower, John. *Ovid's Festivalls, or Roman Calender.* Cambridge, 1640.

Grady, Hugh. *The Modernist Shakespeare: Critical Texts in a Material World.* Oxford: Clarendon, 1991.

Grantley, Darryll. "'What meanes this shew?': Theatricalism, Camp, and Subversion in *Doctor Faustus* and *The Jew of Malta." Christopher Marlowe and English Renaissance Culture.* Ed. Darryll Grantley and Peter Roberts. Aldershot: Scolar Press, 1996. 224–38.

Gratwick, A. S. "The Origins of Roman Drama." Easterling and Kenney, eds. *Cambridge History of Classical Literature.* 2. 1: 77–93.

Green, John. *A Refutation of the Apology for Actors.* London, 1615.

Greenblatt, Stephen. *Sir Walter Ralegh: The Renaissance Man and His Roles.* New Haven: Yale University Press, 1973.

  Renaissance Self-Fashioning: From More to Shakespeare. Chicago: University of Chicago Press, 1980.

  Shakespearean Negotiations: The Circulation of Social Energy in Renaissance England. Berkeley: University of California Press, 1988.

  Hamlet in Purgatory. Princeton: Princeton University Press, 2001.

Greene, Thomas M. *The Light in Troy: Imitation and Discovery in Renaissance Poetry.* New Haven: Yale University Press, 1982.

  "Pitiful Thrivers: Failed Husbandry in the Sonnets." Parker and Hartman, eds. *Shakespeare and the Question of Theory.* 230–44.

Greenfield, Sayre N. "Allegorical Impulses and Critical Ends: Shakespeare's and Spenser's Venus and Adonis." *Criticism* 36 (1994): 475–98.

Griffin, Robert J. "'These Contraries Such Unity Do Hold': Patterned Imagery in Shakespeare's Narrative Poems." *Studies in English Literature 1500–1900* 4 (1964): 43–55.

Grosart, Alexander B., ed. *Robert Chester's Love's Martyr, or Rosalins Complaint (1601), with its Supplement, "Diverse Poeticall Essaies" on the Turtle and Phoenix by Shakspere, Ben Jonson, George Chapman, John Marston.* New Shakspere Society Series 8, No. 2. London, 1878.

Gross, Kenneth. *The Dream of the Moving Statue.* Ithaca: Cornell University Press, 1992.

  "The Postures of Allegory." *Edmund Spenser: Essays on Culture and Allegory.* Ed. Jennifer Klein Morrison and Matthew Greenfield. Aldershot, Hants, Eng.: Ashgate, 2000. 167–79.

  Shakespeare's Noise. Chicago: University of Chicago Press, 2001.

Gurr, Andrew. "Shakespeare's First Poem: Sonnet 145." *Essays in Criticism* 21 (1971): 221–26.

Hadfield, Andrew. *Shakespeare and Renaissance Political Culture*. Arden Shakespeare. 3rd Series. New York: Thomson Learning, 2003.

Halpern, Richard. "'Pining Their Maws': Female Readers and the Erotic Ontology of the Text in Shakespeare's *Venus and Adonis*." Kolin, ed. *"Venus and Adonis": Critical Essays*. 377–88.

Shakespeare among the Moderns. Ithaca: Cornell University Press, 1997.

Hamilton, A. C. "Venus and Adonis." *Studies in English Literature 1500–1900* 1 (1961): 1–15.

Hamilton, A. C., ed. *The Faerie Queene*. New York: Longman, 1977.

Hamilton, Donna B. *Virgil and "The Tempest": The Politics of Imitation*. Columbus: Ohio State University Press, 1990.

Hammond, Gerald. *The Reader and Shakespeare's Young Man Sonnets*. London: Macmillan, 1981.

Handley, E. W. "The Earliest Comic Drama." Easterling and Kenney, eds. *Cambridge History of Classical Literature*. 1. 2: 110–15.

Hardie, Philip. *The Epic Successors of Virgil: A Study in the Dynamics of a Tradition*. Cambridge: Cambridge University Press, 1993.

Ovid's Poetics of Illusion. Cambridge: Cambridge University Press, 2002.

Hardie, Philip, ed. *The Cambridge Companion to Ovid*. Cambridge: Cambridge University Press, 2002.

Harrison, Stephen. "Ovid and Genre: Evolutions of an Elegist." Hardie, ed. *Cambridge Companion to Ovid*. 79–94.

Harrison, Thomas P. "*Love's Martyr* by Robert Chester: A New Interpretation." *University of Texas Studies in Literature* 30 (1951): 66–85.

Hattaway, Michael. "The Shakespearean History Play." *The Cambridge Companion to Shakespeare's History Plays*. Ed. Michael Hattaway. Cambridge: Cambridge University Press, 2002. 3–24.

Helgerson, Richard. *Self-Crowned Laureates: Spenser, Jonson, Milton, and the Literary System*. Berkeley: University of California Press, 1983.

Forms of Nationhood: The Elizabethan Writing of England. Chicago: University of Chicago Press, 1992.

Adulterous Alliances: Home, State, and History in Early Modern European Drama and Painting. Chicago: University of Chicago Press, 2000.

Helms, Lorraine. *Seneca by Candlelight and Other Stories of Renaissance Drama*. Philadelphia: University of Pennsylvania Press, 1997.

Henderson, Diane E. *Passion Made Public: Elizabethan Lyric, Gender, and Performance*. Urbana: University of Illinois Press, 1995.

Hendricks, Margo. "'A word, sweet Lucrece': Confession, Feminism, and *The Rape of Lucrece*." *A Feminist Companion to Shakespeare*. Ed. Dympna Callaghan. Oxford: Blackwell, 2001.

Hensius, Daniel, ed. *L. Annaei Senecae Et Aliorum Tragoediae Serio Emendatae*. [No place of publication]. 1611.

Herman, Peter C. "What's the Use? Or, The Problematic of Economy in Shakespeare's Procreation Sonnets." Schiffer, ed. *Shakespeare's Sonnets: Critical Essays*. 263–83.

Hernadi, Paul. *Beyond Genre: New Directions in Literary Classification.* Ithaca: Cornell University Press, 1972.

Hexter, Ralph. "Sidonian Dido." *Innovations of Antiquity.* Ed. Ralph Hexter and Daniel Selden. New York: Routledge, 1992. 332–84.

Heywood, Thomas. *Apology for Actors.* London, 1612.

Hieatt, A. Kent. "The Genesis of Shakespeare's *Sonnets*: Spenser's *Ruines of Rome: by Bellay.*" *PMLA* 98 (1983): 800–14.

"Shakespeare, William." *Spenser Encyclopedia.* (1990). 641–43.

Hieatt, A. K., T. G. Bishop, and E. A. Nicholson. "Shakespeare's Rare Words: *A Lover's Complaint, Cymbeline,* and *Sonnets.*" *Notes and Queries* 34 (1987): 219–24.

Hieatt, Charles W. "Dating *King John*: The Implications of the Influence of Edmund Spenser's *Ruins of Rome* on Shakespeare's Text." *Notes and Queries* 35 (1988): 458–63.

Hieatt, Charles W., Kent Hieatt, and Anne Lake Prescott. "When Did Shakespeare Write Sonnets 1609?" *Studies in Philology* 88 (1991): 69–109.

Hillman, Richard. "Gower's Lucrece: A New Old Source for the *Rape of Lucrece.*" *Chaucer Review* 24 (1990): 263–70.

Hinds, Stephen. *The Metamorphosis of Persephone: Ovid and the Self-Conscious Muse.* Cambridge: Cambridge University Press, 1987.

Hobday, C. H. "Shakespeare's Venus and Adonis Sonnets." *Shakespeare Survey* 26 (1973): 103–09.

Holland, Norman N., Sidney Homan, and Bernard J. Paris, eds. *Shakespeare's Personality.* Berkeley: University of California Press, 1989.

Honan, Park. *Shakespeare: A Life.* Oxford: Oxford University Press, 1999.

Honigmann, E. A. J. *Shakespeare: The "Lost Years."* 2nd edn. Manchester: Manchester University Press, 1998.

Hope, A. D. "*Tamburlaine*: The Argument of Arms." *Christopher Marlowe.* Ed. Harold Bloom. New York: Chelsea House, 1986. 45–54.

Hubler, Edward. *The Sense of Shakespeare's Sonnets.* New York: Hill and Wang, 1962.

Hubler, Edward, ed. *Shakespeare's Songs and Poems.* New York: McGraw Hill, 1959.

Hughes, Ted. *Shakespeare and the Goddess of Complete Being.* New York: Farrar Straus Giroux, 1992.

Hulse, Clark. *Metamorphic Verse: The Elizabethan Minor Epic.* Princeton: Princeton University Press, 1981.

"Tudor Aesthetics." Kinney, ed. *Cambridge Companion to English Literature, 1500–1600.* 29–63.

Hume, Anthea. "*Love's Martyr,* 'The Phoenix and the Turtle,' and the Aftermath of the Essex Rebellion." *Review of English Studies* 40 (1989): 48–71.

Hunter, G. K. "The Dramatic Technique of Shakespeare's Sonnets." *Essays in Criticism* 3 (1953): 152–64.

Hyland, Peter. *An Introduction to Shakespeare's Poems.* Basingstoke: Palgrave Macmillan, 2003.

Hynes, Sam. "The Rape of Tarquin." *Shakespeare Quarterly* 10 (1959): 451–53.

Jackson, M. P. "Echoes of Spenser's *Prothalamion* as Evidence against an Early Date for Shakespeare's *A Lover's Complaint.*" *Notes and Queries* 37 (1990): 180–82.

James, Heather. *Shakespeare's Troy: Drama, Politics, and the Translation of Empire.* Cambridge: Cambridge University Press, 1997.

Jed, Stephanie H. *Chaste Thinking: The Rape of Lucretia and the Birth of Humanism.* Bloomington: Indiana University Press, 1989.

Johnson, W. R. "The Problem of the Counter-Classical Sensibility and its Critics." *California Studies in Classical Antiquity* 3 (1970): 123–51.

Jones, Emrys. *The Origins of Shakespeare.* Oxford: Clarendon, 1977.

Jonson, Ben. *Works of Ben Jonson.* London, 1616.

    Ben Jonson. Ed. C. H. Herford and Percy and Evelyn Simpson. 11 vols. Oxford: Clarendon, 1925–52.

    Ben Jonson: The Complete Poems. Ed. George Parfitt. 1975; Harmondsworth: Penguin, 1988.

Kahn, Coppélia. "The Rape in Shakespeare's *Lucrece.*" *Shakespeare Studies* 9 (1976): 45–72.

    "Self and Eros in *Venus and Adonis* (1976)." Kolin, ed. *"Venus and Adonis": Critical Essays.* 181–202.

Kaske, Carol V. *Spenser and Biblical Poetics.* Cornell: Cornell University Press, 1999.

Kastan, David Scott. *Shakespeare and the Book.* Cambridge: Cambridge University Press, 2001.

Kastan, David Scott, ed. *A Companion to Shakespeare.* Oxford: Blackwell, 1999.

Kay, D. C. "A Spenserian Source for Shakespeare's Claribel?" *Notes and Queries* 31 (1984): 217.

Kay, Dennis. "William Shakespeare." *Sixteenth-Century British Nondramatic Writers.* Ed. David A. Richardson. *Dictionary of Literary Biography.* 172. Detroit: Gale Research, 1996. 217–37.

    William Shakespeare: Sonnets and Poems. New York: Twayne, 1998.

Keach, William. *Elizabethan Erotic Narratives: Irony and Pathos in the Ovidian Poetry of Shakespeare, Marlowe and Their Contemporaries.* New Brunswick: Rutgers University Press, 1977.

Kennedy, William J. *Authorizing Petrarch.* Cornell: Cornell University Press, 1994.

    "Versions of a Career: Petrarch and His Renaissance Commentators." Cheney and de Armas, eds. *European Literary Careers: The Author from Antiquity to the Renaissance.* 146–64.

Kenney, E. J. "Nequitiae Poeta." *Ovidiana.* Ed. Niculae I. Herescu. Paris: Les Belles Lettres, 1958. 201–09.

    "Ovid." Easterling and Kenney, eds. *Cambridge History of Classical Literature.* 2. 3: 124–61.

Kermode, Frank. *Shakespeare's Language.* London: Allen Lane-Penguin, 2000.

Kernan, Alvin. *Shakespeare, the King's Playwright: Theater in the Stuart Court, 1603–1613.* New Haven: Yale University Press, 1995.

Kerrigan, John. *Motives of Woe: Shakespeare and "Female Complaint."* Oxford: Clarendon, 1991.

"Shakespeare's Poems." De Grazia and Wells, eds. *Cambridge Companion to Shakespeare*. 65–81.

Kerrigan, John, ed. *"The Sonnets" and "A Lover's Complaint."* 1986; New York: Penguin, 1995.

Kerrigan, William. "The Personal Shakespeare: Thee Clues." Holland, Homan, and Paris, eds. *Shakespeare's Personality*. 175–90.

Kerrigan, William, and Gordon Braden. *The Idea of the Renaissance*. Baltimore: Johns Hopkins University Press, 1989.

Kiernan, Pauline. *"Venus and Adonis* and Ovidian Indecorous Wit." A. B. Taylor, ed. *Shakespeare's Ovid: The "Metamorphoses" in the Plays and Poems*. 81–95.

Kinney, Arthur F., ed., *The Cambridge Companion to English Literature 1500–1600*. Cambridge: Cambridge University Press, 2000.

Kinney, Clare R. "Feigning Female Faining: Spenser, Lodge, Shakespeare, and Rosalind." *Modern Philology* 95 (1998): 291–315.

Klause, John. "'The Phoenix and Turtle' in Its Time." *In the Company of Shakespeare*. Ed. Thomas Moisan and Douglas Bruster. Madison, NJ: Fairleigh Dickinson University Press; London: Associated University Presses, 2002. 206–30.

Knapp, Jeffrey. *Shakespeare's Tribe: Church, Nation and Theater in Renaissance England*. Chicago: University of Chicago Press, 2002.

Knight, G. Wilson. *The Mutual Flame: On Shakespeare's "Sonnets" and "The Phoenix and the Turtle."* London: Methuen, 1962.

Kocher, Paul H. "A Marlowe Sonnet." *Philological Quarterly* 24 (1945): 39–45.

Kolin, Philip C., ed. *"Venus and Adonis": Critical Essays*. New York: Garland, 1997.

Kramer, Jerome A., and Judith Kaminsky. "'These Contraries Such Unity Do Hold': Structure in *The Rape of Lucrece*." *Mosaic* 10 (1977): 143–55.

Krier, Theresa M. *Birth Passages: Maternity and Nostalgia, Antiquity to Shakespeare*. Ithaca: Cornell University Press, 2001.

Lake, Peter. "Religious Identities in Shakespeare's England." Kastan, ed. *A Companion to Shakespeare*. 57–84.

Lanham, Richard A. "The Ovidian Shakespeare: *Venus and Adonis* and *Lucrece*." *The Motives of Eloquence: Literary Rhetoric in the Renaissance*. New Haven: Yale University Press, 1976. 82–110.

"The Politics of *Lucrece*." *Hebrew University Studies in Literature* 8 (1980): 66–76.

Laws, Jennifer. "The Generic Complexities of *A Lover's Complaint* and its Relationship to the Sonnets in Shakespeare's 1609 Volume." *Journal of the Australasian Universities Modern Language Association* 89 (1998): 79–97.

Lee, Sidney. "Introduction to Shakespeare's *Venus and Adonis*." Kolin, ed. *"Venus and Adonis": Critical Essays*. 89–102.

Lee, Sidney, ed. *The Passionate Pilgrim*. Oxford: Clarendon, 1905.

Leech, Clifford. "Venus and Her Nun: Portraits of Women in Love by Shakespeare and Marlowe." *Studies in English Literature 1500–1900* 5 (1965): 247–68.

Leishman, J. B. *Themes and Variations in Shakespeare's Sonnets*. New York: Harper and Row, 1963.

Levin, Harry. "Critical Approaches to Shakespeare from 1660–1904." S. Wells, ed. *Cambridge Companion to Shakespeare Studies*. 213–29.

Levin, Richard. "Another Possible Clue to the Identity of the Rival Poet." *Shakespeare Quarterly* 36 (1985): 213–14.

Lewis, C. S. *English Literature in the Sixteenth Century Excluding Drama*. 1954; London: Oxford University Press, 1973.

Lodge, Thomas. *The Complete Works of Thomas Lodge*. New York: Russell & Russell, 1963.

Longman Shakespeare. The Complete Works of William Shakespeare. Ed. David Bevington. New York: Longman, 1997.

Love, Harold. *Scribal Publications in Seventeenth-Century England*. Oxford: Clarendon, 1993.

Low, Anthony. "*Hamlet* and the Ghost of Purgatory: Intimations of Killing the Father." *English Literary Renaissance* 29 (1999): 22–43.

Lucan. *Lucan: "Pharsalia."* Trans. Jane Wilson Joyce. Ithaca: Cornell University Press, 1993.

Lyne, Raphael. *Ovid's Changing Worlds: English "Metamorphoses," 1567–1632*. Oxford: Oxford University Press, 2001.

MacCaffrey, Isabel G. *Spenser's Allegory: The Anatomy of Imagination*. Princeton: Princeton University Press, 1976.

Macfie, Pamela. "Ovid's Poetry of Allusion, *All Ovid's Elegies*, and Marlowe's *Hero and Leander*." Paper presented at the Fifth International Marlowe Conference. University of Cambridge, Cambridge, England. July 2003.

MacLean, Gerald M. "The Debate over Lucan's *Pharsalia*." *Time's Witness: Historical Representation in English Poetry, 1603–1660*. Madison: University of Wisconsin Press, 1990. 26–44.

Maclean, Hugh. "*Complaints*." *Spenser Encyclopedia* (1990). 177–81.

Maclean, Hugh, and Anne Lake Prescott, eds. *Edmund Spenser's Poetry: Authoritative Texts and Criticism*. 3rd edn. New York: Norton, 1993.

Maguire, Laurie E. *Shakespearean Suspect Texts: The "Bad" Quartos and Their Contexts*. Cambridge: Cambridge University Press, 1996.

Majors, G. W. "Shakespeare's First Brutus: His Role in *Lucrece*." *Modern Language Quarterly* 35 (1974): 339–51.

Malago, Rossella. "Shakespeare and Tasso." Ph.D. diss. Pennsylvania State University. University Park, PA. 2001.

Mallette, Richard. "Rosalind." *Spenser Encyclopedia*. (1990). 622–23.

Malone, Edmund, ed. *Plays and Poems of William Shakespeare*. London, 1790.

Marcus, Leah S. *Puzzling Shakespeare: Local Reading and Its Discontents*. Berkeley: University of California Press, 1988.

Marotti, Arthur F. "Shakespeare's Sonnets as Literary Property." *Soliciting Interpretation: Literary Theory and Seventeenth-Century English Poetry*. Ed. Elizabeth D. Harvey and Katharine Eisaman Maus. Chicago: University of Chicago Press, 1990. 143–73.

Manuscript, Print, and the English Renaissance Lyric. Ithaca: Cornell University Press, 1995.

Martin, Christopher. *Policy in Love: Lyric and Public in Ovid, Petrarch, and Shakespeare*. Pittsburgh: Duquesne University Press, 1994.

Martindale, Charles. *Redeeming the Text: Latin Poetry and the Hermeneutics of Reception*. Cambridge: Cambridge University Press, 1993.

Martindale, Charles, and Michelle Martindale. *Shakespeare and the Uses of Antiquity: An Introductory Essay*. London: Routledge, 1990.

Massinger, Philip. *The Roman Actor*. Intro. Martin Butler. London: Nick Hern Books, 2002.

Masten, Jeffrey. "Playwrighting: Authorship and Collaboration." *A New History of Early English Drama*. Ed. John D. Cox and David Scott Kastan. New York: Columbia University Press, 1997. 357–82.

Textual Intercourse: Collaboration, Authorship, and Sexualities in Renaissance Drama. Cambridge: Cambridge University Press, 1997.

Matchett, William H. *"The Phoenix and the Turtle": Shakespeare's Poem and Chester's "Loues Martyr."* London: Mouton, 1965.

Maus, Katharine Eisaman. "Taking Tropes Seriously: Language and Violence in Shakespeare's *Rape of Lucrece*." *Shakespeare Quarterly* 37 (1986): 66–82.

McCabe, Richard A. *Incest, Drama, and Nature's Law, 1550–1700*. Cambridge: Cambridge University Press, 1993.

McCabe, Richard A., ed. *Edmund Spenser: The Shorter Poems*. Harmondsworth: Penguin, 1999.

McCoy, Richard C. *The Rites of Knighthood: The Literature and Politics of Elizabethan Chivalry*. Berkeley: University of California Press, 1989.

"Love's Martyrs: Shakespeare's 'Phoenix and Turtle' and the Sacrificial Sonnets." *Religion and Culture in Renaissance England*. Ed. Claire McEachern and Debora Shuger. Cambridge: Cambridge University Press, 1997. 188–208.

McDonald, Russ. *The Bedford Companion to Shakespeare: An Introduction with Documents*. 2nd edn. Boston: Bedford-St. Martin's, 2001.

McKendrick, Melveena. "Writings for the Stage." Cascardi, ed. *Cambridge Companion to Cervantes*. 131–59.

McKerrow, Ronald B., ed. *The Works of Thomas Nashe*. Rev. F. P. Wilson. 5 vols. Oxford: Blackwell, 1958.

Mebane, John S. *Renaissance Magic and the Return of the Golden Age*. Lincoln: University of Nebraska Press, 1989.

Melchiori, Giorgio, *Shakespeare's Dramatic Meditations: An Experiment in Criticism*. Oxford: Oxford University Press, 1976.

Merrix, Robert P. "'Lo, In This Hollow Cradle Take Thy Rest': Sexual Conflict and Resolution in *Venus and Adonis*." Kolin, ed. *"Venus and Adonis": Critical Essays*. 341–58.

Miller, Jane M. "Some Versions of Pygmalion." *Ovid Renewed: Ovidian Influences on Literature and Art from the Middle Ages to the Twentieth Century*. Ed. Charles Martindale. Cambridge: Cambridge University Press, 1988. 205–14.

Miller, Naomi J. "Playing 'the mother's part': Shakespeare's Sonnets and Early Modern Codes of Maternity." Schiffer, ed., *Shakespeare's Sonnets: Critical Essays*. 347–68.

Miola, Robert S. *Shakespeare's Rome*. Cambridge: Cambridge University Press, 1983.

Shakespeare and Classical Tragedy: The Influence of Seneca. Oxford: Clarendon, 1992.

Shakespeare's Reading. Oxford: Oxford University Press, 2000.

Milton, John. *John Milton: Complete Poems and Major Prose*. Ed. Merritt Y. Hughes. Indianapolis: Odyssey, 1957.

Monsarrat, G. D. "*A Funeral Elegy*: Ford, W. S., and Shakespeare." *Review of English Studies* 53 (2002): 186–203.

Montrose, Louis. "The Elizabethan Subject and the Spenserian Text." *Literary Theory/Renaissance Texts*. Ed. Patricia Parker and David Quint. Baltimore: Johns Hopkins University Press, 1986. 303–40.

"Spenser's Domestic Domain: Poetry, Property, and the Early Modern Subject." De Grazia, Quilligan, and Stallybrass, eds. *Subject and Object in Renaissance Culture*. 83–130.

Morgan, Paul. "'Our Will Shakespeare' and Lope de Vega: An Unrecorded Contemporary Document." *Shakespeare Survey* 16 (1963): 118–20.

Mortimer, Anthony. *Variable Passions: A Reading of Shakespeare's "Venus and Adonis."* New York: AMS, 2000.

Muir, Kenneth. "*A Lover's Complaint*: A Reconsideration." *Shakespeare 1564–1964*. Ed. Edward Bloom. Providence: Brown University Press, 1964. 154–66.

"*Venus and Adonis*: Comedy or Tragedy?" *Tennessee Studies in Literature* 2 (1964): 1–13.

"Twentieth-Century Shakespeare Criticism: The Tragedies." S. Wells, ed. *Cambridge Companion to Shakespeare Studies*. 241–48.

Mullaney, Steven. *The Place of the Stage: License, Play, and Power in Renaissance England*. Chicago: University of Chicago Press, 1988.

Murphy, Patrick M. "Wriothesley's Resistance: Wardship Practices, and Ovidian Narratives in Shakespeare's *Venus and Adonis*." Kolin, ed. *"Venus and Adonis": Critical Essays*. 323–40.

Nass, Barry. "The Law and Politics of Treason in Shakespeare's *Lucrece*." *Shakespeare and Hungary*. Ed. Holgar Klein and Péter Dávidházi. Lewiston, NY: Edwin Mellen Press, 1996. 291–311.

Neill, Michael. *Issues of Death: Mortality and Identity in English Renaissance Tragedy*. Oxford: Clarendon, 1997.

Newdigate, Bernard, ed. *"The Phoenix and Turtle": By William Shakespeare, John Marston, George Chapman, Ben Jonson and Others*. Oxford: Shakespeare Head P-Blackwell, 1937.

Newman, Jane O. "'And Let Mild Women to Him Lose Their Mildness': Philomela, Female Violence, and Shakespeare's *The Rape of Lucrece*." *Shakespeare Quarterly* 45 (1994): 304–25.

Nikolaidis, A. G. "Some Observations on Ovid's Lost *Medea*." *Latomus* 44 (1985): 383–87.

Norbrook, David. *Writing the English Republic: Poetry, Rhetoric, and Politics, 1627–1660*. Cambridge: Cambridge University Press, 1999.

Norton Shakespeare: Based on the Oxford Edition. Ed. Stephen Greenblatt, et al. New York: Norton, 1997.

Oakeshott, Walter. "*Love's Martyr.*" *Huntington Library Quarterly* 39 (1975–76): 29–49.

O'Connell, Michael. "The Experiment of Romance." *The Cambridge Companion to Shakespearean Comedy.* Ed. Alexander Leggatt. Cambridge: Cambridge University Press, 2002. 215–29.

Ong, Walter J. "Metaphor and the Twinned Vision: 'The Phoenix and the Turtle.'" *Sewanee Review* 63 (1955): 193–200.

Oram, William A., et al., eds. *The Yale Edition of the Shorter Poems of Edmund Spenser.* New Haven: Yale University Press, 1989.

Orgel, Stephen, "The Renaissance Artist as Plagiarist." *ELH* 48 (1981): 476–95.

"What Is a Text?" *Staging the Renaissance: Reinterpretations of Elizabethan and Jacobean Drama.* Ed. David Scott Kastan and Peter Stallybrass. New York: Routledge, 1991. 83–87.

Impersonations: The Performance of Gender in Shakespeare's England. Cambridge: Cambridge University Press, 1996.

Orgel, Stephen, ed. *Christopher Marlowe: The Complete Poems and Translations.* Harmondsworth: Penguin, 1971.

Oruch, Jack B. "Works, Lost." *Spenser Encyclopedia* (1990). 737–38.

Ovid. *Ovid.* 2nd edn. Trans. Frank Justus Miller; rev. G. P. Goold. Loeb Classical Library. 6 vols. Cambridge, MA: Harvard University Press; London: Heinemann, 1984.

The Oxford Shakespeare. William Shakespeare: The Complete Works: Compact Edition. Ed. Stanley Wells and Gary Taylor. Oxford: Clarendon, 1988.

Paglia, Camille. *Sexual Personae: Art and Decadence from Nefertiti to Emily Dickenson.* New Haven: Yale University Press, 1990.

Palfrey, Simon. *Late Shakespeare: A New World of Words.* Oxford: Clarendon, 1997.

Parker, Patricia. *Shakespeare from the Margins: Language, Culture, Context.* Chicago: University of Chicago Press, 1996.

Parker, Patricia, and Geoffrey Hartman, eds. *Shakespeare and the Question of Theory.* New York: Methuen, 1985.

Patterson, Annabel. *Shakespeare and the Popular Voice.* Oxford: Blackwell, 1989.

Reading Between the Lines. Madison: University of Wisconsin Press, 1993.

Pearcy, Lee T. *The Mediated Muse: English Translations of Ovid 1560–1700.* Hamden, CT: Archon, 1984.

Pequigney, Joseph. *Such is My Love: A Study of Shakespeare's Sonnets.* Chicago: University of Chicago Press, 1985.

"Sonnets 71–74: Texts and Contexts." Schiffer, ed. *Shakespeare's Sonnets: Critical Essays.* 285–304.

Pendry, E. D., and J. C. Maxwell, eds. *Christopher Marlowe: Complete Plays and Poems.* London: J. M. Dent, 1976.

Pitcher, John. "Some Call Him Autolycus." *In Arden: Editing Shakespeare: Essays in Honour of Richard Proudfoot.* Ed. Ann Thompson and Gordon McMullan. 3rd Arden Series. London: Arden Shakespeare, 2003. 252–68.

Platt, Michael. *Rome and Romans According to Shakespeare*. Lanham, MD: University Press of America, 1983.

Plato. *The Collected Dialogues of Plato*. Ed. Edith Hamilton and Huntington Cairns. Princeton: Princeton University Press, 1961.

Pliny. *Natural History*. Trans. H. Rackham. Loeb Classical Library. 10 vols. Cambridge, MA: Harvard University Press; London: Heinemann, 1940.

Pope, Alexander, ed. *The Works of Mr. William Shakespeare*. London, 1725.

Prescott, Anne Lake, and A. Kent Hieatt. "Forum." *PMLA* 98 (1985): 200–02.

Price, Diana. "Reconsidering Shakespeare's Monument." *Review of English Studies* 48 (1997): 168–82.

Price, Hereward T. "Function of Imagery in *Venus and Adonis* (1945)." Kolin, ed. *"Venus and Adonis": Critical Essays*. 107–22.

Prince, F. T., ed. *The Poems*. By William Shakespeare. The Arden Shakespeare. 2nd edn. London: Methuen, 1960.

Putney, Rufus. "Venus *Agonistes* (1953)." Kolin, ed. *"Venus and Adonis": Critical Essays*. 123–40.

Quarles, John, ed. *The Rape of Lucrece, Committed by Tarquin the Sixt; And The remarkable judgments that befel him for it. By The incomparable Master of our English Poetry, Will: Shakespeare Gent*. London, 1655.

Quint, David. *Epic and Empire: Politics and Generic Form from Virgil to Milton*. Princeton: Princeton University Press, 1993.

"The Anatomy of Epic in Book 2 of *The Faerie Queene*." *The Spenser Review* 34 (2003): 28–45.

Quintilian. *The "Institutio Oratoria" of Quintilian*. Trans. H. E. Butler. Loeb Classical Library. 4 vols. Cambridge, MA: Harvard University Press; London: Heinemann, 1969.

Rambuss, Richard. *Spenser's Secret Career*. Cambridge: Cambridge University Press, 1993.

Rees, Joan. "Sidney and *A Lover's Complaint*." *Review of English Studies* 42 (1991): 157–67.

Reese, M. M., ed. *Elizabethan Verse Romances*. London: Routledge & Kegan Paul, 1968.

Richards, I. A. *Poetries: Their Media and Ends*. Ed. Trevor Eaton. The Netherlands: Mouton, 1974.

Riggs, David. "Marlowe's Quarrel with God." White, ed. *Marlowe, History, and Sexuality: New Critical Essays on Christopher Marlowe*. 15–37.

Righter, Anne. *Shakespeare and the Idea of the Play*. London: Chatto & Windus, 1964.

Ringler, William A., Jr., ed. *The Poems of Sir Philip Sidney*. Oxford: Clarendon, 1962.

The Riverside Shakespeare. Ed. G. Blakemore Evans, et al. 2nd edition. Boston: Houghton, 1997.

Roberts, Josephine A., ed. *The Poems of Lady Mary Wroth*. Baton Rouge: Louisiana State University Press, 1983.

Roberts, Sasha. *Reading Shakespeare's Poems in Early Modern England*. Basingstoke: Palgrave Macmillan, 2003.

Roe, John. "Ovid 'Renascent' in *Venus and Adonis* and *Hero and Leander.*" A. B. Taylor, ed. *Shakespeare's Ovid: The "Metamorphoses" in the Plays and Poems.* 31–46.

Roe, John, ed. *The Poems. By William Shakespeare.* New Cambridge Shakespeare. Cambridge: Cambridge University Press, 1992.

Rollins, Hyder Edward, ed. *A New Variorum Shakespeare: The Poems.* Philadelphia: J. B. Lippincott, 1938.

A New Variorum Edition of Shakespeare: The Sonnets. 2 vols. Philadelphia: J. B. Lippincott, 1944.

"*The Passionate Pilgrim.*" New York: Scribner's, 1940.

Rollins, Hyder E, and Hershel Baker, eds. *The Renaissance in England: Non-Dramatic Prose and Verse of the Sixteenth Century.* Lexington, MA: Heath, 1954.

Rosenmeyer, Thomas G. *The Green Cabinet: Theocritus and the European Pastoral Lyric.* Berkeley: University of California Press, 1969.

Sagaser, Elizabeth Harris. "Shakespeare's Sweet Leaves: Mourning, Pleasure, and the Triumph of Thought in the Renaissance Love Lyric." *ELH* 61 (1994): 1–26.

Sandys, George, trans. *Ovid's Metamorphosis Englished.* London, 1626.

Sannazaro, Jacopo. "*Arcadia*" and "*Piscatorial Eclogues.*" Trans. Ralph Nash. Detroit: Wayne State University Press, 1966.

Schalkwyk, David. "'She never told her love': Embodiment, Textuality, and Silence in Shakespeare's Sonnets and Plays." *Shakespeare Quarterly* 45 (1994): 381–407.

"What May Words Do? The Performative of Praise in Shakespeare's Sonnets." *Shakespeare Quarterly* 49 (1998): 251–68.

Speech and Performance in Shakespeare's Sonnets and Plays. Cambridge: Cambridge University Press, 2002.

Schiffer, James. "Shakespeare's *Venus and Adonis*: A Lacanian Tragicomedy of Desire." Kolin, ed. "*Venus and Adonis*": *Critical Essays.* 359–76.

Schiffer, James, ed. *Shakespeare's Sonnets: Critical Essays.* New York: Garland, 1999.

Schmidgall, Gary. *Shakespeare and the Poet's Life.* Lexington: University Press of Kentucky, 1990.

Schoenbaum, S. *William Shakespeare: A Documentary Life.* New York: Oxford University Press-Scolar Press, 1975.

Schoenfeldt, Michael C. *Bodies and Selves in Early Modern England: Physiology and Interiority in Spenser, Shakespeare, Herbert and Milton.* Cambridge: Cambridge University Press, 1999.

"Making Shakespeare's *Sonnets* Matter in the Classroom." Cheney and Prescott, eds. *Approaches to Teaching Shorter Elizabethan Poetry.* 239–44.

Schwartz, Murray M. "Shakespeare through Contemporary Psychoanalysis." *Representing Shakespeare: New Psychoanalytic Essays.* Ed. Murray M. Schwartz and Coppélia Kahn. Baltimore: Johns Hopkins University Press, 1980. 21–32.

Segal, Charles. *Orpheus: The Myth of the Poet.* Baltimore: Johns Hopkins University Press, 1989.

Seneca. *Thyestes: Lucius Annaeus Seneca.* Trans. Jasper Heywood. Ed. Joseph Daalder. London: Ernest Benn; New York: Norton, 1982.

Seneca the Elder. *The Elder Seneca: Declamations.* Trans. Michael Winterbottom. Loeb Classical Library. Cambridge, MA: Harvard University Press; London: Heinemann, 1974.

The Shakspere Allusion-Book: A Collection of Allusions to Shakspere from 1591 to 1700. Ed. C. M. Ingleby, L. Toulmin Smith, and F. J. Furnivall; rev. edn. John Munro; preface Edmund Chambers. 2 vols. 1909; Freeport, NY: Books for Libraries Press, 1970.

Shapiro, James. "'Metre meete to furnish Lucans style': Reconsidering Marlowe's *Lucan*." *"A Poet and a Filthy Play-Maker": New Essays on Christopher Marlowe.* Ed. Kenneth Friedenreich, Roma Gill, and Constance B. Kuriyama. New York: AMS, 1988. 315–25.

  Rival Playwrights: Marlowe, Jonson, Shakespeare. New York: Columbia University Press, 1991.

Sharon-Zisser, Shirley, "Similes hollow'd with Sighs: The Transferential Erotics of the Similaic Copula in Shakespeare's *A Lover's Comlaint*." *Exemplaria* 11 (1999): 195–220.

Sharrock, Alison. *Seduction and Repetition in Ovid's "Ars Amatoria."* Oxford: Clarendon, 1994.

Sherburne, Edward, trans. *Medea: A Tragedie.* London, 1648.

Smith, Bruce R. *Homosexual Desire in Shakespeare's England: A Cultural Poetics.* Chicago: University of Chicago Press, 1991.

  "I, You, He, She, and We: On the Sexual Politics of Shakespeare's Sonnets." Schiffer, ed. *Shakespeare's Sonnets: Critical Essays.* 411–29.

Smith, G. Gregory, ed. *Elizabethan Critical Essays.* 2 vols. London: Oxford University Press, 1904.

Smith, Hallett. *Elizabethan Poetry: A Study in Conventions, Meaning, and Expression.* Cambridge, MA: Harvard University Press, 1952.

  The Tension of the Lyre: Poetry in Shakespeare's Sonnets. San Marino: Huntington Library, 1981.

Spenser, Edmund. *The Poetical Works of Edmund Spenser.* Ed. J. C. Smith and Ernest De Sélincourt. 3 vols. Oxford: Clarendon, 1909–10.

Spenser Encyclopedia. Gen. ed. A. C. Hamilton. Toronto: University of Toronto Press, 1990.

Sprengnether, Madelon. "The Boy Actor and Femininity in *Antony and Cleopatra*." Holland, Homan, and Paris, eds. *Shakespeare's Personality.* 191–205.

Stallybrass, Peter. "Editing as Cultural Formation: The Sexing of Shakespeare's Sonnets." *The Uses of Literary History.* Ed. Marshall Brown. Durham: Duke University Press, 1995. 129–41.

  "Worn Worlds: Clothes and Identity on the Renaissance Stage." De Grazia, Quilligan, and Stallybrass, eds. *Subject and Object in Renaissance Culture.* 289–320.

Stanivukovic, Goran V. "'Kissing the Boar': Queer Adonis and Critical Practice." *Straight With a Twist: Queer Theory and the Subject of Heterosexuality.* Ed. Calvin Thomas. Chicago: University of Illinois Press, 2000. 87–108.

Stanivukovic, Goran V., ed. *Ovid and the Renaissance Body.* Toronto: University of Toronto Press, 2001.

Stapleton, M. L. *Harmful Eloquence: Ovid's "Amores" from Antiquity to Shakespeare.* Ann Arbor: University of Michigan Press, 1996.

"Venus as *Praeceptor*: The *Ars Amatoria* in *Venus and Adonis*." Kolin, ed., *"Venus and Adonis": Critical Essays.* 309–21.

Streitberger, W. R. "Ideal Conduct in *Venus and Adonis* (1975)." Kolin, ed. *"Venus and Adonis": Critical Essays.* 171–79.

Stubbes, Phillip. *The Anatomie of Abuses.* London, 1583.

Sullivan, Garrett. "'Be this sweet Helen's knell, and now forget her': Forgetting, Memory, and Identity in *All's Well That Ends Well*." *Shakespeare Quarterly* 50 (1999): 51–69.

Sutphen, Joyce. "'A dateless lively heat': Storing Loss in the Sonnets." Schiffer, ed. *Shakespeare's Sonnets: Critical Essays.* 199–217.

Suzuki, Mihoko. *Metamorphoses of Helen: Authority and Difference in Homer, Virgil, Spenser, and Shakespeare.* Ithaca: Cornell University Press, 1989.

Swinburne, Algernon Charles. *Studies in Prose and Poetry.* London: Chatto & Windus, 1907.

Tarrant, R. J. "Senecan Drama and Its Antecedents." *Harvard Studies in Classical Philology* 82 (1978): 213–63.

Taylor, A. B., ed. *Shakespeare's Ovid: The "Metamorphoses" in the Plays and Poems.* Cambridge: Cambridge University Press, 2000.

Taylor, Gary. "Some Manuscripts of Shakespeare's Sonnets." *Bulletin of the John Rylands University Library* 68 (1986): 210–46.

Reinventing Shakespeare: A Cultural History from the Restoration to the Present. London: Vintage, 1991.

Taylor, Michael. *Shakespeare Criticism in the Twentieth Century.* Oxford: Oxford University Press, 2001.

Thiébaux, Marcelle. "The Mouth of the Boar as a Symbol in Medieval Literature." *Romance Philology* 22 (1968): 281–99.

Thomas, Max W. "Eschewing Credit: Heywood, Shakespeare, and Plagiarism before Copyright." *New Literary History* 31 (2000): 277–93.

Thompson, Ann. *Shakespeare's Chaucer: A Study in Literary Origins.* Liverpool: Liverpool University Press, 1978.

Thomson, Peter. *Shakespeare's Professional Career.* 1992; Cambridge: Cambridge University Press-Canto, 1994.

Tipton, Alzada. "The Transformation of the Earl of Essex: Post-Execution Ballads and 'The Phoenix and the Turtle.'" *Studies in Philology* 99 (2002): 57–80.

Tobin, J. J. M. "Spenserian Parallels." *Essays in Criticism* 29 (1979): 264–69.

"Malbecco, Yet Again." *Notes and Queries* 23 (1985): 478–79.

Tolbert, James M. "The Argument of Shakespeare's *Lucrece*: Its Sources and Authorship." *Texas Studies in English* 29 (1950): 77–90.

Traub, Valerie. "Sex without Issue: Sodomy, Reproduction, and Signification in Shakespeare's Sonnets." Schiffer, ed., *Shakespeare's Sonnets: Critical Essays.* 431–52.

Tudeau-Clayton, Margaret. *Jonson, Shakespeare and Early Modern Virgil.* Cambridge: Cambridge University Press, 1998.

Tydeman, Thomas, ed. *Two Tudor Tragedies: "Gorboduc"... "The Spanish Tragedy."* Harmondsworth: Penguin, 1992.

Tylus, Jane. "Spenser, Virgil, and the Politics of Poetic Labor." *ELH* 55 (1988): 53–78.

Underwood, Richard Allan. *Shakespeare's "The Phoenix and Turtle": A Survey of Scholarship*. Salzburg: Institute for English Language and Literature, University of Salzburg, 1974.

Shakespeare on Love: The Poems and the Plays. Prolegomena to a Variorum Edition of "A Lover's Complaint." Salzburg: Institute for English and American Language and Literature, University of Salzburg, 1985.

Valbuena, Olga L. "'The dyer's hand': The Reproduction of Coercion and Blot in Shakespeare's Sonnets." Schiffer, ed. *Shakespeare's Sonnets: Critical Essays.* 325–45.

Vendler, Helen Hennessy, ed. *The Art of Shakespeare's Sonnets*. Cambridge, MA: Harvard University Press, 1997.

Vickers, Brian. *"Counterfeiting" Shakespeare: Evidence, Authorship, and John Ford's "Funerall elegye."* Cambridge: Cambridge University Press, 2002.

Shakespeare as Co-Author: A Historical Study of Five Collaborative Plays. Oxford: Oxford University Press, 2002.

Vickers, Brian, ed. *Shakespeare: The Critical Heritage*. 6 vols. London: Routledge & Kegal Paul, 1974–1981.

Vickers, Nancy J. "Diana Described: Scattered Woman and Scattered Rhyme." *Critical Inquiry* 8 (1981–82): 265–79.

"'This Heraldry in Lucrece's Face.'" *Poetics Today* 6 (1985): 349–62.

"'The blazon of sweet beauty's best': Shakespeare's *Lucrece*." Parker and Hartman, eds. *Shakespeare and the Question of Theory.* 95–115.

Virgil. *Virgil*. Trans. H. Rushton Fairclough. Loeb Classical Library. 2 vols. 1916–18; Cambridge, MA: Harvard University Press; London: Heinemann, 1934–35.

Wall, Wendy. *The Imprint of Gender: Authorship and Publication in the English Renaissance*. Ithaca: Cornell University Press, 1993.

Walley, Harold R. "*The Rape of Lucrece* and Shakespearian Tragedy." *PMLA* 76 (1961): 480–87.

Watson, Donald G. "The Contraries of *Venus and Adonis*." *Studies in Philology* 75 (1978): 32–63.

Watson, Robert N. *The Rest is Silence: Death as Annihilation in the English Renaissance*. Berkeley: University of California Press, 1994.

Weimann, Robert. *Author's Pen and Actor's Voice: Playing and Writing in Shakespeare's Theatre*. Ed. Helen Higbee and William West. Cambridge: Cambridge University Press, 2000.

Wells, Marion A. "'To find a face where all distress is stell'd': Enargeia, Ekphrasis, and Mourning in *The Rape of Lucrece* and the *Aeneid*." *Comparative Literature* 54 (2002): 97–126.

Wells, Stanley, "Foreword." *The Shakespeare First Folio*. Ed. Anthony James West. Oxford: Oxford University Press, 2001. v.

Shakespeare: A Life in Drama. New York: Norton, 1995.

Wells, Stanley, ed. *The Cambridge Companion to Shakespeare Studies*. Cambridge: Cambridge University Press, 1986.

Wheeler, Stephen. *A Discourse of Wonders: Audience and Performance in Ovid's "Metamorphoses."* Philadelphia: University of Pennsylvania Press, 1999.

"Lucan's Reception of Ovid's *Metamorphoses*." *Arethusa* 35 (2002): 361–80.

White, Paul Whitfield, ed. *Marlowe, History, and Sexuality: New Critical Essays on Christopher Marlowe*. New York: AMS, 1998.

Wilbur, Richard, and Alfred Harbage, eds. *William Shakespeare: The Narrative Poems and Poems of Doubtful Authenticity*. The Pelican Shakespeare. 1966; Harmondsworth: Penguin, 1974.

Willbern, David. *Poetic Will: Shakespeare and the Play of Language*. Philadelphia: University of Pennsylvania Press, 1997.

Williams, Gordon. "The Coming of Age of Shakespeare's Adonis." *Modern Language Review* 78 (1983): 769–76.

Willoughby, Edwin. *A Printer of Shakespeare: The Books and Times of William Jaggard*. London: P. Allan, 1934.

Wilson, John Dover, ed. *"The Sonnets." The Works of Shakespeare*. Cambridge: Cambridge University Press, 1967.

Winnington-Ingram, R. P. "The Origins of Tragedy." Easterling and Kenney, eds. *Cambridge History of Classical Literature*. 1. 2: 1–6.

Wright, George T. "The Silent Speech of Shakespeare's Sonnets (1998)." Schiffer, ed. *Shakespeare's Sonnets: Critical Essays*. 135–58.

Yachnin, Paul. *Stage-Wrights: Shakespeare, Jonson, Middleton, and the Making of Theatrical Value*. Philadelphia: University of Pennsylvania Press, 1997.

Yoch, James J. "The Eye of Venus: Shakespeare's Erotic Landscape." *Studies in English Literature 1500–1900* 20 (1980): 59–71.

Ziegler, Georgianna. "My Lady's Chamber: Female Space, Female Chastity in Shakespeare." *Textual Practice* 4 (1990): 73–90.

Index